W9-ATB-984

Borderless Behavior Analytics

Who's Inside? What're They Doing?

Second Edition

Saryu Nayyar

CEO, Gurucul Solutions, LLC

Contributors:

Jerry Archer – CSO, Major Financial Services Company
Devin Bhatt – CISO, U.S. Federal Agency
Nilesh Dherange – CTO, Gurucul
Gary Eppinger – CISO, Carnival Cruises
Gary Harbison – CISO, Monsanto
Leslie K. Lambert – CISO at Large
Jairo Orea – CISO, Kimberly-Clark
Robert Rodriguez – CEO, SINET
Jim Routh – CSO, Aetna
William Scandrett – CISO, Allina Health
Joe Sullivan – CSO at Large
Teri Takai – CIO at Large

Senior Contributing Editor – Patrick S. Barry

BORDERLESS BEHAVIOR ANALYTICS
Who's Inside? What're They Doing?
Second Edition

Copyright © 2018 by Saryu Nayyar.

All rights reserved. Printed in the United States of America. No part of this book may be used or reproduced in any manner whatsoever without written permission, except in the case of brief quotations embodied in critical articles and reviews.

For more information contact:
Gurucul Solutions, LLC
www.gurucul.com

Publisher: Ankur Chadda
Managing Editor, Second Edition: Leslie K. Lambert
Managing Editor, First Edition: Tom Clare
Graphics: Raghunath Sontakke
Cover Design: 99 QUEEN

ISBN: 13: 978-1986763332

"There are only two kinds of companies.
Those that were hacked
and those that don't yet know they were hacked."

Popular Cybersecurity Credo

"The world has changed.
Security and data will be something
that goes on for hundreds of years in the future.
We are at the beginning of that stage."

Tim Armstrong – CEO, AOL

BORDERLESS BEHAVIOR ANALYTICS
Who's Inside? What're They Doing?
Second Edition

CONTENTS

ACKNOWLEDGMENTS

Vishal Salvi, Renee Guttmann-Stark,
Craig Cooper, Tom Clare,
Ankur Chadda, Craig Kensek

Special Acknowledgment
from the Publisher and Managing Editor

We would like to recognize Patrick S. Barry's invaluable contribution to the development of both the first and second edition of this book. He has been the driving force for many aspects of this project. His marathon of dedication to excellence and this book is deeply appreciated.

Foreword

Digital transformation (DT) means different things to different people. Its purpose is all about providing ideal connectivity, where an organization's different systems are seamlessly integrated, delivering the most optimal user experience possible. To achieve this objective requires building the right ecosystem with numerous processes and process optimization. This all means greater opportunity, yet amplified challenges at the same time.

Looking at DT from an IT perspective, as a large IT service provider, my company, Infosys, has numerous digital transformation programs focused on the transition of legacy applications into what organizations need to modernize and facilitate the demands of a state-of-the-art ecosystem. These initiatives often employ new technologies empowered with strong machine learning, AI models, integrating with open source solutions, APIs and more. Yet there's another consideration that must be taken into account to ensure a successful digital transformation: It must all be safe and protected.

Concerns from a CISO's perspective relate to the perpetual challenge of delivering the assurance of data integrity and confidentiality to their stakeholders. This represents a significant conundrum due to the broad array of complex technologies involved. The popular analogy for security experts is that we're mid-flight on an aircraft, where we must fix all problems onboard, maybe even change the wings, while we're flying! To a traditional security practitioner it may seem an impossible task, yet to the forward-looking CISO, this is their new normal.

Amplifying that challenge, a number of the resources CISOs require have not yet been fully developed. As well, the role of CIO is rapidly changing. All the books they've read relating to controlling technology and infrastructure approach obsolescence. The old rules are going away. For our profession to successfully embrace the future challenges posed by DT, we must have more agile and adaptable cybersecurity programs. This means being able to make leapfrog changes, and not be shackled by methodologies of the past, where we otherwise remain two or three cycles behind in technology innovation.

The adaptable agility required today for emerging cybersecurity programs exists in the realm of borderless behavior analytics. This class of security analytics addresses an increasingly porous security perimeter challenged by the expanding use of IoT, mobility, BYOD and the onslaught of widespread cloud adoption. Except for unique circumstances and requirements, the standalone monolithic on-premises environment has become a footnote in tech history. On-premises environments, while they remain important for many organizations for the foreseeable future, represent a fractional and a continuously diminishing element of the larger DT landscape.

How do borderless behavior analytics contend with this extreme complexity?

Building solutions, systems and processes that ensure optimal data integrity and confidentiality for information stakeholders, plus providing holistic monitoring of behavior, are acknowledged as keys to success. With those capabilities, we can analyze behavior across all aspects of the work humans do; by adding entity activity, this further enables us to identify and predict good or bad behavior. This entails a comprehensive mapping of hybrid environments, the identities within them, and building algorithms that quickly and reliably identify any outliers, to deliver effective attribution of true positives for risk-based security alerts. As well, there's a need to continually improve these capabilities as criminal threat tactics evolve.

Driven by mature machine learning, and drawing context from big data across an environment's data silos, the power of user and entity behavior analytics (UEBA) delivers the capability for that one hop to quick attribution, which in the past had been fundamentally impossible in a complex IT environment. To identify who that one person, that one identity, associated with a particular malicious act, is crucial. Because of that, I believe there's great promise for UEBA in the future. It all depends on how models mature and in turn reliably identify and predict the evolving range of bad behaviors with accuracy and rapid attribution.

Security leaders must make their own assessments to support the future planning required for a successful DT initiative, and decide on the three or four areas where they'll bet big as far as their long-term security strategy is concerned. In the past, SIEM (security information and event management) solutions were one of those big bets, which in the long term failed to continue delivering the enduring value many experts thought they would. When it comes to technology, the CISO's journey will always be an evolutionary one. From the advanced security analytics focus, this book, now in its second edition, represents one of the important new entries in the CIO and CISO's library, to assist in that journey, to realize the promise of digital transformation.

Vishal Salvi
CISO, Infosys

Vishal Salvi is Chief Information Security Officer and SVP at Infosys. Vishal has more than 24 years of industry experience in IT service delivery and cybersecurity with positions at Crompton Greaves, Development Credit Bank, Global Trust Bank, Standard Chartered Bank, HDFC Bank and PwC. He performed leadership roles in cybersecurity at these organizations for over 18 years, with his previous role serving as a partner in cybersecurity practice at  PwC. Vishal has extensive management and domain experience in driving the information and cybersecurity programs in all key aspects A well-known leader in information security industry within India as well as globally, Vishal has rich experience delivering large scale, mission critical projects on time and under budget.

Introduction

With the advent of ubiquitous mobility and ever-expanding cloud adoption, humanity has crossed the threshold into a brave new world, yet not everyone knows that nor understands the implications. Yet the number people lacking that understanding has lessened somewhat through the benefit of the first edition of this book, with over five thousand copies in circulation among today's security community, and with demand still going strong. Indeed, the praise for the book has been gratifying. One example is Dan Lohrmann, of the online magazine *Government Technology*, who gave a rave review for the first edition of the book, stating *"...this is a MUST READ for understanding the next generation of security solutions..."* Providing that kind of needed resource is why we have been determined to provide the second edition of this book with expanded insights.

This passage into a new reality of security requirements simultaneously represents profoundly exciting possibilities, delivering empowered productivity and enhanced cost savings, and, at the same time, ushers in sobering trends in risk management. Those who understand this transition stand in position to take advantage of the possibilities, as well as to protect themselves against the perilous developments inherent in the journey. We have, in effect, left the comparatively safe confines of a modern suburban world and now find ourselves in something of a Wild West frontier, replete with the legendary gold rush where fortunes can be made overnight, or livelihoods may be destroyed by misguided actions based on uninformed perceptions and weak strategic decisions.

With the rapid and widespread adoption of mobile devices, along with the IoT (Internet of Things) becoming integrated into the most intimate niches of our lives – from bio wristbands that count our steps and monitor our heart rate, to applications on our mobile phones that budget our calorie intake, and keep us up-to-date with the inventory in our refrigerator – the massive amount of human data has ballooned to staggering proportions. Experts forecast this digital exhaust will reach 44 zettabytes by 2020. ABI Research estimates the global wireless connectivity market (excluding cellular), will exceed 10 billion integrated circuit (IC) shipments annually by 2021. This ocean of data, and data delivery nodes, is not only growing rapidly to gargantuan proportions, but the unique and complex segments in which data resides is expanding and evolving, as well. Now in business, the same rapid and widespread explosion of digital exhaust generated by both mobility and cloud adoption inside the enterprise has reached beyond the capabilities of human analysis. The security perimeter has been blurred and for most intents and purposes, simply faded away.

Organizations are seismically impacted by this paradigm shift of cloud and mobility as they strive to adjust to the manner in which their employees and customers use and manage technology. The infusion of bring your own device (BYOD), high-speed internet connectivity and the use of cloud-based applications are continually redefining enterprise networks, not through proactive planning and change management, but in an ad hoc reactive manner. The use profile is 24/7, global, instantaneous, and rich in consumer-driven IT. Everyone is accessing everything on the internet, all the time, and in a staggering volume of activity. At the same time, however, there persists a comparatively low awareness of the risks associated with access and activity, plus their importance, among the general population of today's employees. This reality courts disaster, enabling more emerging undefined gray areas of risk than declarative defenses can ever address. A new awareness of access and activity risks is urgently needed and one from a risk-based solution perspective which holistically quantifies risk as quickly as possible.

Gone are the days when attacks on a system such as internet worms, email spam and opportunistic hacks were the prevalent security issues of the day – which have been addressed through the layering of defense-in-depth technologies such as firewalls, antivirus software and spam filtering mechanisms. Intellectual property and regulated information no longer resides only behind firewalls; this singular control point of protection has disappeared. Instead, there's a much more complex hybrid IT security challenge of on-premises environments being connected to a host of cloud applications, all being accessed via an expanding array of mobile devices.

An enduring popular quote among security pundits is, "There are only two kinds of companies. Those that have been hacked and those that don't know they've been hacked." Now, however, attacks against any business are likely to be stealthier, targeted in a far more sophisticated manner, while always changing and evolving. Nation states and highly skilled individuals, with vast resources and seasoned knowledge of the most effective way to attack companies' vulnerabilities, carry them out. They move quietly within organizations, sometimes for years, rather than months, moving laterally throughout the computing environment, steadily acquiring everything they need for their malicious assaults.

At the root of modern threats is the compromise and misuse of identity which gives the attacker access to the keys of the kingdom. Identity is the critical access mechanism, a threat plane unacknowledged by far too many organizations. With identity-based access, attackers easily bypass declarative defenses based on static rules, signatures and patterns. Traditional defenses identify known bads (red) and safe profiles (green). Yet with identity as a primary risk, attention must now be focused on the vast gray areas between the red and the green. This is why a new form of risk management, which includes precise risk scoring, extracting context from big data, moving from detective, through predictive, to prescriptive, has become so essential.

With most traditional security solutions focused on prevention, and detection, the impact of these emerging influences on older security systems is profound. Firewall, security information and event management (SIEM), intrusion detection systems (IDS), intrusion protection systems (IPS), data loss prevention (DLP), vulnerability assessment, sandboxing – were all primarily designed to look for, to detect, the known, often from the outside. While this has been effective for preventing and detecting a specific class of external attacks, these techniques rarely expose the malicious insider because they're moving through the environment exploiting approved access. The majority of organizations' access privileges are far too over-provisioned. Industry experts observe that most Fortune 500 companies have 50% or more of their privileged access occurring outside sanctioned account lists and vaults as hidden unknowns. In one specific real-world use case, Gurucul's direct solution delivery experience observed a large enterprise where they discovered over 70% of their privileged access had been unknown, hence ineffectively controlled, or uncontrolled, including application privileges representing serious and unrecognized risks to the organization.

More concerning, insider attacks are on the rise. According to Verizon's *2017 Data Breach Investigations Report (DBIR)*, a 46% rise in insider threat occurred over the last year, where network intrusions have involved employee identity and weak credentials. In addition, existing traditional identity management solutions are not designed to address this kind of challenge. They don't take into account how access is used. Unfortunately, these solutions have been eclipsed in their standalone ability to manage identity and access effectively. The scale of unmanaged access often represents millions of entitlements that an organization must contend with. An influence which has contributed to this troubling trend has been Sarbanes-Oxley requirements, resulting in the unsound practice of rubber-stamping broad swaths of account access certifications and the practice of access cloning. As a result, excess access has become institutionalized, a default, yet risky, organizational process.

Years of investment in traditional security approaches have not improved the outcomes. The CyberEdge Group's *2017 Cyberthreat Defense Report* states that 79.3% of organizations were breached in the 12 months before the survey, a distinct rise over the preceding year. This represents a disquieting and rising upward trend. Yet with the factors described above, what are security teams trying to detect? Known bads? Or unknown unknowns?

Meanwhile, *CSO* magazine observes organizations are unable to keep pace with the dramatic rise in cybercrime and are a refocusing their defenses from PCs and laptops to smartphones, mobile devices and billions of under-protected IoT devices. This has prompted estimates of spending for security in the range of one trillion dollars between 2017 and 2021. Organizations find they don't have all the tools they need to assure the security of their environments. What's required is an ability to tighten the identity access plane that modern attackers are leveraging through phishing and other forms of social attacks. The discovery gap of unknown privileged access entitlements must be closed with the awareness gap of how access entitlements are being utilized for an effective identity and access management program. As well, an integral part of the risk management strategy should include an ability to provide visibility into all instances of access entitlement, to monitor what access is being provided, how it is being used, and to have the capability to assess those instances with timely and reliable risk-based scoring.

Security leaders should assume attackers are inside their networks and that they must be detected and shut down. The most effective way to detect them and to find high risk is through their behavior. What we need to be looking for, and *seeing*, in the future, is the unknown, most often from the inside. The question is: what is their behavior and what is the relative risk of that behavior? Yet within a growing sea of digital exhaust, the scope of the challenge now lies well beyond manual human capabilities. Without a precise prescriptive behavior analytic solution, driven by advanced machine learning and drawing from big data for context – identifying inside threats in near real-time – the ability to identify and stop these attacks, only with human capacity, becomes simply impossible.

Now, in the wake of the 2017 Equifax mega breach – and following close behind, revelations of the troubling Security Exchange Commission (SEC) breach, where they were warned repeatedly about weaknesses in their security – the stakes have reached a critical magnitude. The need to identify unknown threats and risky behaviors is growing within the circles of forward-looking security leaders. This approach represents the only effective and realistic path to analyze the surface area of identity for access risk, while detecting behavioral anomalies from advanced machine learning baselining. We call this solution approach Borderless Behavior Analytics.

In this second edition of our book, we have added to the assembled thought leaders who are from a range of different industries – from financial services, healthcare, transportation, agricultural biotechnology, manufacturing, cutting-edge social media, government, hospitality and more. They have witnessed the changes in this landscape and have delivered solutions to address it. We share their experience, and their lessons learned, so that others following similar paths might benefit, and possibly avoid wrong turns. We also draw from industry analysts, leveraging as well, the deep bench of seasoned expertise at Gurucul, to share insights into how data access and use are changing, to offer a resource that might help assure the success of your organization's future.

By reading this book you're joining a journey of discovery which defines the evolving future of cybersecurity and the robust challenges of addressing access and activity risks. We hope to help make your journey a productive one.

Saryu Nayyar
CEO, Gurucul

Impact of Cloud and Mobility
for Identity

The Evolution of Urgency for Change

So how did we get here? How did we arrive at this kaleidoscopic world of security challenges?

About ten years ago, the traditional chief information security officer's strategy for companies was to have a hard outside shell and a soft inside, something like an exoskeleton. This paradigm was established in the 70's and 80's. During that era, many mainframe set-ups maintained their data centers in central locations and built their security to protect these monoliths of data.

With the advent of technology developments in business that delivered more convenience and productivity, security teams were compelled to move to more of a distributed and open security policy. Business demanded that. Over the last seven years, with the widespread use of the multifunctional mobile smartphones in business and companies experiencing the expanded BYOD (bring your own device) demand, the relevance and value of these original traditional security perspectives and strategies were coming to an end. Concurrently, the advent of cloud adoption had been expanding. A paradigm shift for security of this evolving technology was at hand.

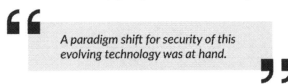

A paradigm shift for security of this evolving technology was at hand.

Cloud adoption first began as a shadow IT activity, beyond an IT organization's supervision. The trend started with small pockets of users using different software solutions that were easy to set up, and often free, to share files, instant text, post professional profiles, and more, (Box, Dropbox, Skype, LinkedIn, etc.) for their perceived advantages. These were completely outside IT's visibility. This usage took root across business units where employees resolved challenges which IT was unable to address in a timely, responsive manner, by accessing easily available cloud-based applications. Unsanctioned employee-driven IT had established itself in the business setting and this raised security concerns. While these solutions delivered enhanced productivity and flexibility, they did not focus on availability, scalability or security concerns. Then, a number of companies began to offer tools to provide visibility into what applications were being used within an organization's environment.

This ease of use and heightened efficiencies, however, led to expanded offerings and utilization of cloud applications. Organizations also witnessed groups within the corporate structure adopt top-down applications like Salesforce, with its sales force automation capabilities, to meet their business goals. This trend represented a growing migration for enterprise applications. As organizations would adopt a software as a service (SaaS) solution from the internet, the pattern of corporate adoption would expand — both within an organization and across the marketplace — eventually manifesting into the wide array of public and private cloud applications we see today. Migration of corporate information had moved outside the firewall, again without IT's official sanction. These popular cloud business applications included Zoho for enterprise business applications, as well as DocuSign for secure document signature management, and others, all delivering robust productivity within their specialized niches. The kaleidoscopic world of security challenges was well on its way.

Salesforce.com became acknowledged as the first widely adopted cloud business application. Their SaaS solutions originally offered portal access for different customers. Over time, they expanded and productized their solution to the point where it became a standard for sales organizations within a broad range of companies. More cloud solutions proliferated, offering new modes of productivity enhancement and other advantages. And as cloud gained in popularity, more and more data moved outside the perimeter.

In the recent past, organizations' adoptions of more comprehensive cloud solutions, such as Amazon Web Services, Rackspace, Azure, Office 365, Google Apps, and other cloud solutions, have subsequently become standards. Business was dictating to IT: "We're going in this direction." This wholesale migration began about six to eight years ago as business applications like this came into more widespread availability. At that point, with broad sets of data residing in the cloud, the question for security leaders was: "Is it secure?" Demands for assurance of security in this newly evolving IT hybrid environment moved to the forefront, and rightfully so. Today, trends reveal the growing preponderance of specialized cloud adoptions in larger companies, where 82% of enterprises larger than 1000 employees have a multi-cloud strategy, with 71% hybrid cloud (*RightScale 2016 State of the Cloud Report*), all trending up from the previous year.

One of the advantages that cloud solutions provided was that they did not have legacy application and infrastructure to integrate into their solutions and the majority designed environments with security built in from the beginning.

An early driver for establishing policies for security and the protection of privacy was the Security Breach Statute – California Senate Bill 1386 (SB-1386, July 2003). This was the first piece of major legislation mandating that if a company lost any customer information, and it was not encrypted, then the company was required to report it to the customer. The statute also stipulated that *"...any business that violates, proposes to violate, or has violated this title may be enjoined."* So any enterprise representing themselves as being responsible for handling or managing sensitive customer information would be subject to a mandate requiring that customer information must be protected in a secure and standardized manner. Transparent and timely disclosure of any serious change in security status was a strict requirement. To do otherwise would be a risk for any business with paralyzing and costly legal sanctions.

The appearance of the chief information security officer (CISO) title on IT org charts, and the accompanying official roles and responsibilities, evolved in the early 2000's. The CISO's job was to protect a company's revenue producing business and the constituent sensitive pieces of data which support that objective. Yet with all a given organization's important data in the cloud, and with business applications on mobile phones, tablets, etc., being used 24/7 from everywhere, the burning question for security leaders had become: "How am I going to manage the risk with all these devices and applications — both on and off the cloud?" Data was no longer behind the firewall. That single security control point was gone. The border was gone. The data was no longer safe inside the fortress, because there was no fortress. The data resided in multiple locations outside the enterprise.

> **"** *The data was no longer safe inside the fortress, because there was no fortress.* **"**

Since the complexity of this usage trend was often initiated by business leaders in organizations outside the chief information officer's (CIO's) sphere of responsibility, some CISOs found their mandate at cross-purposes, generally taking a reflexive 'Dr. No' position on these productivity enhancing innovations. Earlier, instead of threat hunting, the traditional security tools from five to fifteen years ago involved the process that would entail placing a constraint, but only if a potential threat was understood. Of course, if an organization shut everyone out, there would be no threat, but without access, the business operations would cease. Yet the challenge remained that "we don't know what's coming at us next" concern. Nevertheless, successful CISO's generally recognized the importance and value adopting a consultant and partner-like role with the rest of the business, and helping them understand what best practices were required to assure effective security in their rapidly evolving hybrid IT environments. That meant CISOs needed to raise their game and take responsibility for all the new complexities an enterprise was taking on, or considering to take on.

This brave new evolving and complex networking world has represented a serious challenge for businesses. At first, organizations provided limited transparency. Then, to comply with government mandates, security teams had to know if data had been breached. They needed to identify what tools they possessed to assess the magnitude and direction of a breach. Yet traditional firewalls and other security applications were all designed to detect breaches coming from outside of the network and via known attack vectors. They were weak at detecting threats emanating from the inside. Security information and event management (SIEM) solutions had delivered value for over a decade of centralized visibility, mainly for compliance and operations, yet only recently provided selected threat hunting capabilities. Intrusion detection systems and intrusion protection systems (IDS/IPS), as well as data loss prevention (DLP), were designed more for awareness, than protection, resulting in event and alert input into SIEMs for more context to lower the noise factor. These tools, however, could not address the persistent risk of malicious insiders, which security experts recognized was on the rise and showing no signs of abatement.

Several years of escalating breaches were delivering an alarming quantity of alerts, creating fatigue among security staffers, with far too many futile false positives. Declarative defenses were not managing the challenge. New attack trends could not be fingerprinted when they were analyzed, because many attack signatures were unique due to massive polymorphism. There was a surge of cybercrime beyond the scope of signatures, patterns and rules in declarative defenses. The complete breakdown of the perimeter had become manifest. This sobering observation ushered in the realization among CISOs that they no longer had effective controls to address the urgent evolving challenge. They recognized that a serious systemic threat to their organization's livelihood was at hand.

> *This sobering observation ushered in the realization among CISOs that they no longer had effective controls to address the urgent evolving challenge.*

Accentuating that realization of pandemic exposure, numerous events occurred between 2009 and 2012 that served to heighten security leaders' concerns, which included Operation Aurora and Stuxnet. Launched by a group affiliated with the People's Liberation Army of China, Aurora involved a series of cyber-attacks conducted against a host of American companies, including Google, Adobe Systems, Juniper Networks, Rackspace, Symantec, Northrop Grumman, Morgan Stanley and Dow Chemical. The objective was penetrating security and gaining access to the crown jewels of these high tech, security and defense contractor companies. Stuxnet was a targeted worm virus, alleged to have been developed by Israeli and U.S. groups. It was used to paralyze Iran's nuclear program by targeting Siemens computer systems which controlled Iran's nuclear centrifuges, of which one fifth were ruined. This event demonstrated that even physical assets could be compromised or destroyed (by changing the speed of the centrifuges) through cyber-attacks. The Stuxnet breach methodology also included leveraging four zero-day attacks, where just one zero-day exploit itself is highly valued. On a wider scale, a swarm of other zero-based events proliferated in the cyber world and continued to rise in frequency. A new alarming era of exposure had arrived.

Organizations saw that a new awareness and paradigm were required — a new way to look at, assess and strengthen the security of a business's crown jewels, their data. Sarbanes-Oxley certification requirements were in place. Earlier attitudes treated compliance reporting as an afterthought. Now, a number of larger organizations approached this requirement in a similar way service providers had with service level agreements (SLAs), a serious requirement of due diligence, giving this reporting a much higher priority. Conversely, some organizations sought to circumvent the meticulous requirements, and falsified their certifications. Meanwhile, enterprises recognized that intellectual property (IP) theft was on the rise from insiders. Cases included groups of employees and contractors at high tech companies, sometimes disgruntled, who moved to other companies taking their work with them, feeling unfounded entitled ownership of the intellectual property, despite employee contracts to the contrary. The complexity of exposure and risk for enterprises both outside and inside the organizational framework continued to unfold and amplify.

More recently (between 2012 and 2015), an evolutionary development of SIEM took place representing a functional amplification of the solution set, fortifying SOC's (security operations centers) capabilities with enhanced solution features such as the 'single pane of glass' concept, providing a centralized view of all system events and alerts. This further enabled forensic security capabilities that delivered insight into the pattern of an attack and how it happened. This meant SOCs could generate and manage their own threat intelligence. During this period, solutions like FireEye's advanced persistent threat (APT) detection appliances and sand boxes became more common. At this stage of security evolution, organizations were developing their own security intelligence, taking ownership of understanding the steps in the cyber kill chain (1-7) and developing a deeper awareness of how attack methods evolved. During this time, however, the declarative statement method to assess cybersecurity maturity was being challenged for the increasingly constrained value it delivered to security.

To respond successfully to this challenge, businesses needed to initiate a new perspective on the focus of identity, access and entitlements. Everyone should have their own ID, everyone

> **What was crucially different now, however, was the amplified view of the value of identity and access.**

should have their own set of permissions and credentials for the systems and applications they interface with. Otherwise, traceability would not exist. What was crucially different now, however, was the amplified view of the value of identity and access. Before, like compliance reporting, these elements were secondary in security priority. Now, they were becoming elevated to a crucial strategic role. How business and security viewed the role of identity and access in an organization defined how successful an organization's security strategy would be.

Yet, there was now too much data in the SIEM, and it was doubling every year. Any serious prospect of managing security analysis solely by human means was quickly becoming futile. Around this time, the misuse and compromise of identity emerged as a serious threat plane. Mismanaged with outdated legacy policies and rules, identity became an easy attack plane to compromise over-privileged accounts. Effective identity management was impaired. While its access enabling function remained important, its ability to actually see what identities were doing in the environment was piecemeal at best. Vast gray areas of activity anomalies remained unknown, and they were growing. Behavior was a blind spot. The behavior of activist insiders like Edward Snowden, and disgruntled employees, elevated the profile and visibility of the insider threat, highlighting the potential for severe negative impact on organizations. The perimeter was officially gone. A reliable new approach in security, capable of evolving with the changing environment was needed. This entailed effective behavior visibility and monitoring.

Identity and access are core components of a classification process to achieve the best method to define normal and abnormal user and entity behaviors. If a threat actor wanted to steal data from a network, they would need access to that data. The threat plane is comprised of identities and their associated credentials. That's the basis of access and the direct route to anything in an organization's network. With the evolving challenges, and sobering lessons learned with from recent high profile data breaches, the importance of identity and access was now better understood and perceived much more strategically by forward-looking security leaders. Security teams needed to know who was in their environment, what they had access to, and what they were doing there.

> The threat plane is comprised of identities and their associated credentials. That's the basis of access and the direct route to anything in an organization's network.

These undefined activities represented gray areas of unknown risk. Addressing this challenge requires a comprehensive, accurate and timely measurement of the risks that lurk in the uncharted gray areas. Within that requirement is a recognition that visibility of privileged access accounts and entitlements risk is at the forefront of concerns, because a majority of privileged access within an organization is simply unknown at the entitlement level and within applications. This risk-based assessment capability has undergone various phases of evolution, based on need, while harnessing state-of-the-art technology capable of developing and delivering next generation security monitoring.

The first generation of information security professionals was generally comprised of forensic investigators who could discover and define the kill chain. They thrived on solving the mystery of how a threat actor broke into their system, from where and what method was used, and then closing the security hole. Over time, however, as environment complexity and the number of endpoints grew, it became too cumbersome, time-consuming, and expensive, to do a deep security dive. In addition, this approach did not improve security teams' abilities to stop these attacks.

During this time, an industry-wide awareness of this challenge grew. By 2008, the Center for Internet Security (CIS) and the SANS Institute had been participating in a public-private partnership with the NSA. This ultimately expanded to a wider consortium, which included international participation to examine the problem more holistically. An important outcome of this initiative was refining a list of security controls (*CIS Critical Controls*) that were most effective in preventing known attacks. These controls were widely adopted and continue to be periodically revised, encouraging shared continuous diagnostic investigation. A new proactive security framework had begun to evolve, promoting a structure for constructive security. Prescriptive advice began to show up in the role of security, along with fundamentals of security hygiene and best practices. Recognizing the need to target identity and implement behavior monitoring had begun during this phase of security evolution. This requirement, however, would also need to address more complex environments, demanding the application of new perspectives.

A new risk challenge emerged — 'dwell time' — the average time between intruder infection and detection. It was far too lengthy, by industry estimates, with the average often exceeding 200 days, and currently estimated at 206 days. Attackers were spending months inside an environment undiscovered. SOC team effectiveness declined markedly, and became a major concern, even as new versions of SIEM were unable to improve the detection rate. Using a compromised identity, malicious attackers would move unimpeded, laterally, inside an environment. A risk-based solution was required to comprehensively address the myriad of challenges plaguing security teams dealing with account compromise and misuse, plus unknown anomalies based on access and activity in their hybrid environments. The era of user and entity behavior analytics (UEBA) and identity analytics (IdA)* security solutions had arrived, and none too soon.

Filling the gap of SIEMs, UEBA delivered identity-based behavior analysis of access and activity for new data sources including SIEMs, directories and applications with insight beyond what technical experts had previously been able to view with log access files. As well, IdA helped close the discovery gap of unknown access risks, with a special emphasis on the vast threat plane of privileged access. Now the prospect of preventing data exfiltration, detecting insider threats, as well as compromise and misuse of identity through phishing and social attacks, had become a realistic goal. These

---

* While IdA, as standalone class of solution, has been available for years from select UEBA vendors, Gartner Research coined the term in early 2016, identifying it as an essential component of advanced security analytics.

solutions delivered a new effective method to leverage and monitor an identity to establish what's normal and what's not. Finally, security analysts could answer, "What access risk does this user have? What activity risks does this user have?" and "What is the context of these risks?" This provided granular insight into how an identity's access and activity behavior was different from what their peer groups were doing, in all the different variables of: who, where, when, how, what action, and how these actions correlated with baseline definitions of established normal behavior.

The essential component of a successful and best-of-breed UEBA and IdA solution model involves machine learning. Drawing from big data for context, across all environments, machine learning delivers the mechanism to enable a broad range of issues to be managed, to find the red herrings, to discover what's going on and what's different or out of the ordinary. Advanced machine learning is designed to recognize that just because a behavior is different, it doesn't mean it's bad, and it eliminates potential red herrings from consideration.

> *...machine learning is designed to recognize that just because a behavior is different, it doesn't mean it's bad...*

Ultimately, a mature UEBA-IdA solution would furnish businesses with a centralized easy-to-use single view that encompasses all the users and entities in the hybrid environment. UEBA then provides holistic monitoring of access and activity where various levels of users and solutions leverage prescriptive risk scores to reduce access risks and detect unknown anomalies. While SOC teams will likely leverage risk scores within a UI, bidirectional API integration with solutions enables risk scores to drive automated risk responses. Forward-looking organizations finally have a cost-effective, efficient and reliable approach to address the urgent security priorities in their global environments, 24/7.

In this brave new world, there are, of course, early adopters who have traveled the road of integrating UEBA and IdA solutions and faced the challenges they represent. Each organization and industry segment has their own influences, challenges and requirements. In this book, we are proud to present to you CISO, CSO and CIO leaders from a range of business sectors who share their own insights and experiences on the UEBA and IdA journey through Borderless Behavior Analytics, facing the challenges of today's new evolving hybrid IT environments. They also discuss their strategies, goals and objectives of next-generation-facing UEBA and IdA solution requirements.

While the introduction and this chapter position UEBA and IdA via machine learning from the context of big data as an answer to cybersecurity challenges, the journey in the forthcoming interviews is rich with wisdom and experience beyond any possibly perceived promotional partiality.

Our first expert, Gary Eppinger has served in a broad range of industries, and arrived at a setting he calls a 'hyper-hybrid environment'. The challenges he has faced are unique, and his perspectives on the solutions required to address those challenges draw from his extensive security experience in a number of different vertical markets, from finance, manufacturing, retail, health care and more.

BORDERLESS EXPERT INSIGHTS

Gary Eppinger, CISO *
Carnival Corporation

Global VP, Chief Information Security and Privacy Officer for Carnival Corporation, Gary Eppinger conceives, implements, and leads technology solutions that protect corporate assets, increase organizational capability, and advance productivity for Fortune 100 companies. He is recognized globally as a highly valued resource with an exceptional ability to build and develop IT teams that deliver critical business objectives in companies within transformation. Ranked 24th in ExecRank's "Top Security Executive Rankings," Gary is an active speaker on IT and cybersecurity. He also assists numerous companies serving as a valued board advisor.

A member of Gurucul's Board of Advisers, Gary has provided valuable guidance in the company's evolution through the complex path of challenges facing the company's emergence in the field of UEBA security. He shares some of his seasoned in-depth insights into the challenges of hybrid cloud security and behavior analytics' place in it.

Overview

Eppinger begins with his observations on how data access is changing today's environments. He provides insights on the symptoms that reveal security defenses are a problem today, and then discusses the business vulnerabilities of a compromise leading to a breach. The critical drivers around the importance of insider threats are examined, as he notes the growing concerns about privilege misuse. Drawing from his unique Carnival Corporation experience, Eppinger shares insights on the impact on security defenses with a constant flow of insiders and customers traveling on ships, to land locations, or in combination. This systemic view incorporates environments around the world, across different on-premises locations, in the cloud and on the sea, and includes the profound impact on this exceptional hybrid environment's security requirements. The new role of identity-based access and activity risks, and how they tie together, are explored along with the key solution components required to address the needs of constantly changing security conditions. This topic also expands into the handling of the vast and growing scale of data for security analysis. Eppinger shares his perspectives on machine learning and predictive security analytics adoption in the environment and within his industry vertical. Finally, he provides his distinctive perspectives of security evolution through the wide range of vertical markets he has worked in which has shaped his approach to work in one of the most complex hybrid environments imaginable, something he calls the 'hyper-hybrid environment'.

---

* The views and opinions expressed by Gary Eppinger in this book are his own, and do not necessarily reflect those of Carnival Corporation, or any of his previous employers.

How data access is changing today's environments

Carnival Corporation's strategy for managing data has changed over the last few years. Originally, we were primarily a corporate holding company. Each of our ten brands was a standalone cruise company which we ran independently. They competed for customers internally, as well as with external competitors. Carnival just happened to acquire them and put them under the same umbrella.

Separate siloed views of data. This meant from a data perspective that corporate and customer data, the fuel of the company, was separated and isolated from each particular brand. For example, the information on customers for Carnival Cruises, AIDA, and for Princess, were all stored and accessed independently. When Gary Eppinger cruised on ships from all three lines, we were only capable of seeing that information associated with him separately, in each silo of data, with no correlation whatsoever.

Phased migration to a centralized view. We have worked to concatenate and bring that critical data together in phases, and over the last three years we have acquired more of the consolidated views of our customer data. This means if I am a customer of all three of those brands, corporate Carnival can now see all this in a single repository. As well as that, we market to customers differently because we can now correlate and use this information effectively and have insight into the preferences a customer has established on any ship and cruise line. More consolidated cruise brand views are in the works.

> **We have worked to concatenate and bring that critical data together in phases...**

Centralized identity value. An example of the advantage this new visibility provides is if I sailed on Carnival fifty times, Carnival has a great deal of value data and information on me as a cruiser. When I go with Princess and Costa one time, I may look like a new customer to them, with no history. Now we can add visibility into these fifty Carnival cruises. They now know what food I like, they know if I'm a spa person, the types of spas I prefer, and the types of rooms that might make sense for me. So my identity represents great value information that can be leveraged to make my vacation a great experience.

New capabilities in risk management. As we bring that data together, it also gives us more of a capability to detect a higher level of risk to the information. As the data becomes concatenated into a single place, we know more effectively if it's compromised, a higher risk, or not protected properly. When it was spread between ten different brands, and two hundred different locations, it was much harder to get to and monitor properly. Now that it is coming together, it also raises the bar of what we have to do to protect that information.

The symptoms revealing security defenses are a problem today

No longer is it an environment where a CISO might have fifteen branches and a fixed number of connections, along with access and users connecting into their environment. That was manageable then. Today, however, there are millions of customers, millions of entry points, millions of devices connecting into our environments all over the world. That's millions of connection points we're responsible for. Now it's no longer possible to rely only on the entry point into our network, into our environment, to provide security assurance.

> " Today... there are millions of customers, millions of entry points, millions of devices connecting into our environments all over the world. "

Moving security closer to the data. Generally the closer you can put your controls to the data, the better you are. If you think about the traditional approach CISOs took for the last twenty plus years, we originally built the walls as far as we could from the data, just at the network layer, and then this model was no longer viable. In response, the focus moved to the application layer and data was controlled at the ERP (enterprise resource planning) level with multiple applications together. Finally, the objective became to move the security focus to the database level.

Maintaining the right controls on data. Today, it's a multi-tiered approach where you need to have appropriate controls across all the different channels and/or layers to make sense. Yet at the same time, it includes sustaining the objective of maintaining controls much more closely to that data, no matter where the data resides, as well as how that data flows and where it flows to. Some of these controls need to go along with the data as it moves to its destination, because data does not reside within the servers of an isolated DMZ all the time. It's continuously being leveraged, moved and adapted from system to system. In addition, you need to think about your controls based on location or point of time.

Technology evolution and new security perspectives. With technology and data use patterns continually evolving and changing, the old strategies of manual security monitoring have become unrealistic. This clearly indicates that an era of information security has passed and that the new age will require entirely new perspectives and solutions on how to achieve the same original goal of twenty years ago: to protect the information.

> " This clearly indicates that an era of information security has passed and that the new age will require entirely new perspectives and solutions... to protect the information. "

Security driving business value

Carnival protects a great deal of critical information — from credit cards, passports, driver's licenses, to health records, and more. This, of course, includes massive amounts of critical information for a huge number of customers who sail with us every day. Millions of customers entrust us with that information because it's essential for us to be able to deliver a high quality vacation for them. We take this responsibility very seriously. The prospect of damaging that trust represents a threat to our brand reputation. Without our brand reputation, customers' loyalty erodes and people simply choose other vacation destinations.

A range of security concerns. Anything that could damage our reputation is, of course, a serious matter, but data exfiltration, customer hacking, or customer information threats are all top priority critical concerns for us. We also think about safety and security at the highest level of importance to the company and to our employees. From our perspective, in an industry which services so many customers traveling through the world, our focus includes anything that involves the physical safety, or the perceived safety of an individual. Anything that might harm a customer, or one of our employees, is a foremost concern and priority. Therefore, any issue that could create a question over whether someone might somehow be physically harmed is paramount. This is all part of our DNA. It's part of what makes us successful and differentiates Carnival.

The focus on financial protections. Following very closely, of course, is the mandate to protect against any kind of financial threat. Here, the range of risk, which could translate into financial threat, is varied and wide. The theft of money itself, the theft of IP, the misuse of assets that incurs financial damage, and brand damage, are all part of this perspective. This expands to include other concerns as well, such as protection of onboard medical records and more.

A broader set of requirements than most enterprises. In addition, any issue concerning the proper running of our ships and the systems that control them are also our concern. This includes the medical centers, navigations systems for the ships, the computerized operations that run system safety checks and all those unseen processes that are taken for granted by the public. These remain our sacred trust to ensure their integrity is assured. The scope of security responsibilities for us is much broader than traditional land-based corporations. It's what I call a 'hyper-hybrid environment'. Within this complex world, the core essence of our information security mandate is: protect your people, your information and the finances.

Facing the prospect of insider threats

Businesses run on the concept of entrusting their employees to do the right thing with their access to the environment, access to the data, and access to their customer's data. It's been said many times: employees are our biggest assets and are our biggest risk exposure — so insider threat is a big deal to us. Of course, it is often the case that an outside threat first appears as an insider threat to a security analyst because of a compromised identity. However, either way, these people may be using the data inappropriately, not for its

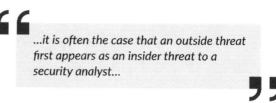

...it is often the case that an outside threat first appears as an insider threat to a security analyst...

intended use, nor to the benefit of the company or our customers, and quite possibly to the advantage of our competitors.

A range of risk from breaches. The serious damage from insider threats can impact any and all of the areas of business vulnerability. These include brand reputation, customer trust, along with liability, loss of position in the market against competition, or fines, and the list goes on from there. While protecting the financial well-being of Carnival is a top concern for us, along with the well-being of our customers and our employees, the potential of an insider breach remains an equally important security mandate.

Growing concerns about privilege misuse and compromise

Privilege misuse is an issue that scares me relentlessly. This is especially the case with employees who have the higher privileged accounts and capabilities. As my colleagues in the UK say, it's "The Keys of the Kingdom" — and that's the last place you want the bad guys to be able to get to. From there, with the right HPA (high privileged access), and without the right safeguards in place, they can exploit your environment with impunity.

...it's "The Keys of the Kingdom" – and that's the last place you want the bad guys to be able to get to.

A fundamental security requirement. Understanding where those accounts and entitlements are, how to maintain them, how to restrict these privileges, and how to limit the risk and exposure, is critical for every company, no matter what their size. These proficiencies must be fundamental capabilities from the security perspective. In addition, as we expand our utility of predictive security analytics and machine learning, enhancing and empowering these objectives for our HPA accounts, security is at the center of our priorities to achieve.

The hyper-hybrid security environment: A constant flow of insiders and customers on ships, land locations, or in combination

The security of our hyper-hybrid environments must be adaptable to these different changes of user behavior based on location, on high volume, or based on need. We're in the process of implementing a long-term strategy to enhance our identity capabilities to be able to meet these new demands; it's a high priority.

A single view of identity is needed. Our employees and customers are included in this planning where their identities must be managed at a much higher level, enabling a holistic unified visibility of the individual. It's a highly complex challenge, especially with our customers. As a model, consider the type of individual who has one or two banking accounts, a car loan, and credit cards. They have multiple financial companies that they deal with every day, all with different identities. All must be managed separately. That's very complicated, even for individual accountability. So how do you do this across multiple companies within a corporation? Resolving this challenge is our objective.

The complex journey to achieve a single view of identity. While we may have the same customer on our different lines, we do not yet have the singular centralized view of them, and this is where the industry is going. From the Carnival corporate perspective, with our ten different companies, we are working through phases to achieve that goal, starting with the first two consolidated brands clustered and migrated into a single view. It's important to understand where it all began as well. We've made decisive strides away from the time when cruisers sailed with all ten different companies, and would have ten different identities, which had ten different configurations, forcing Carnival to interface with you as a single person in ten different ways. Our ultimate path forward will be a single path, a single way of managing this as a single identity across all environments. The magnitude of all this information, originally residing in ten separate silos of different architectures and levels of maturity, is a considerable factor of the challenge.

The impact on hybrid environment security: Systems around the world, on-premises, in the cloud and on the sea

One of the things we talk about as we look at our security model, and strategy, is the level of maturity in our security capabilities, now and in the future. In doing so, we try to maintain as realistic a perspective as possible when we talk about what solutions we need in place to assure security in the future. We also know once we get there, because of the rapid evolution of technology and the cloud, that it will probably no longer be completely adequate.

A realistic view of phased progress. With this understanding of constant evolution in technology, we don't need to take a solution to what some might consider an ultimate world-class level. We do need take it to a level of reliable functionality. With that perspective, we maintain the strategy of continuous development and improvement, not adopt some monolithic

> *...we maintain the strategy of continuous development and improvement, not adopt some monolithic solution that might be outdated as soon as it is finally implemented.*

solution that might be outdated as soon as it is finally implemented. For security, solutions must be light and flexible, capable of evolving in the same way, to integrate and grow with the various phases, and with all the complex variables. This is where user and entity behavior analytics (UEBA) and identity analytics (IdA) represents the potential for productive growth with us at Carnival.

Integrating analytics and machine learning through phases in the environment. Of utmost importance, we have focused on the level of complexity required to move a global organization, which has data and information, as well as processes on-premises, off-premises, at sea, in the cloud, and across ten different brands. These were originally at different maturity levels, along with the varied applications, systems and infrastructure. From the start, we've dealt with a massive level of complexity. The goal we maintain is to drive the unified maturity of all our brands, to that same level, no matter where the data resides. This is especially true now that we have so many different places we have to be monitoring to assess risk and assure security. As we consolidate our views of the different businesses, machine learning is part of that integration process, which provides a strengthening of defenses at each phase by identifying risks and unknown threats.

Robust machine learning required for comprehensive security. It boils down to that old adage; we are as strong as our weakest link. If we're strong within the on-premises, and the cloud protection is weak, then we're collectively weak. If we're strong within the on-premises, at corporate offices, but weaker on the ship, then we're all weak. How do you identify that weakest link? As we view the challenges holistically and consistently across all of our stationary environments, as well as the constantly moving elements of our global environment, this is the focus of our strategy. Because of this wide-scaled environment, with increasingly high data volume to analyze, we needed big data and behavior analytics to find those weak links.

> *Because of this wide-scaled environment, with increasingly high data volume to analyze, we needed big data and behavior analytics to find those weak links.*

Adjustments required to assure security in hyper-hybrid environments

It was a challenge for me to adapt at first. As a traditional professional who believed in risk management, and in the security principles that developed over so many years in the space, experience in the evolving complexities of the hybrid world has shown me a new reality. This is not an uncommon realization for CISOs to experience today.

A new normal of viewing security. I now have the perspective of, "It's not *if* I get compromised, it's *when* I get compromised." More importantly, upon reaching that recognition the priority then quickly becomes, "How do I determine exactly when it happens so I can react in the most efficient way to bring the environment back into compliance and ultimately stability?" These priority concerns center on resiliency. Keep in mind, you still need all of the preventive controls discussed earlier, but you also need the balanced detective and responsive controls in place as well.

Strategies for strong recovery following a breach. Because of this new perspective on today's security realities, we've changed our paradigm. We're no longer saying "if." By implementing a prescribed selection, along with a number of controls and declarative defenses, we know certain security events are managed. Yet, now we're also saying that when it happens, how do we know it happened and what was the magnitude? That's critical to know the extent of the compromise and the proper remedial steps required to prevent further attacks of this nature. This also leads directly to how we react to that breach as it is happening and bringing the system back into compliance and a maintainable state as quickly as possible.

The new role of identity and access: How they tie together

Identity and access have been around since the beginning of network security. However, that essential commissioning capability companies have had in the past must migrate to a higher level, delivering security assurance and enduring value. CISOs begin with the perspective that they want to assure their employees, contractors, partners, customers, and vendors, have the right access at the right time. This includes no more access than is required, with access ending when it is no longer needed. This is a fundamental business objective and absolutely important. But if you think about an employee — or a customer — along with their lifecycle of access requirements, they have changed. The access control objective hasn't changed. What has changed is our ability to assure the right access at the right time, at the right location, based on legitimate need.

Perpetually fluctuating user access. Specifically from the employee perspective, an example of the challenge is we have a range of accountants with Carnival Corporation. One may be working on one of our ships, and their use profile and requirements might be distinctly different from an accountant who is working in our corporate office. Then we might have an accountant who is traveling from the corporate office, or to Asia, or is onboard one of our ships. Their access life cycle might be very different, as well, and may change periodically, based on their legitimate work role requirements. The challenge becomes how we make sure they have the right access at the right time. Of course, behind all of that is the need to assure the right person has gained that access.

Risks with limited visibility into a wide range of users and access requests. The variables of these circumstances are accelerating or deaccelerating perpetually based on the needs at a particular moment. That's where serious risks occur. If you don't know who your users, your employees, and your customers are, then you have no chance of ensuring you're giving the right access at the right time. Multiply that user environment by the amount of employees, partners and customers, and the magnitude of complexity and risk reaches staggering proportions. It's this next layer of identity that determines the importance of solid solutions for access and identity that are essential to the success of security.

> If you don't know who your users, your employees, and your customers are, then you have no chance of ensuring you're giving the right access at the right time.

Key solution components required for constantly changing security conditions

Elements we have initiated include identity lifecycle management tools with the ability to integrate the identity in the cloud, versus on-premises, versus any one of our environments. The other initiative we are integrating is machine learning analytics capabilities and tools. We have also flattened our network from an active directory perspective. We originally had many active directories and then integrated them into one, flattening the network down to a single tree. This makes it possible for us to have complete individual visibility.

A challenging orchestration of solution elements. We're also working on embedding role-based security principles into our strategy from an identity perspective. However, the challenges continue as we investigate how we integrate the entire application layer. Incorporating application security and application capabilities into our roles, and into our identity manager, are key objectives for us. Those are some of the solution elements we are leveraging to give us a heightened level of capability so we can connect them gaining optimal visibility and controls. Without machine learning, none of this would be possible.

Handling the overwhelming scale of entitlements for identity management and security

Dealing with the huge scale of big data is the ten million dollar question for us. There's an evolving challenge with scale we've seen building over the last several years. Traditionally, we try to develop our solutions from a people, process and technology perspective. The days of just throwing people at a challenge to solve the problem are over, especially for companies with our size and complexity.

The staggering scale of big data. When organizations continue to adopt cloud solutions to improve their business flexibility and amplify productivity, they generate huge amounts of data to sift through – the digital exhaust of big data. From the complexity, size and demand perspectives, it's dramatically more complicated. We need to process increasingly larger amounts of data that must be adjudicated quickly in order to be able to get answers and to insure we're providing the right visibility for access as needed. This requirement can no longer be guaranteed through manual processes. That puts the organization's welfare at risk.

> " *This requirement can no longer be guaranteed through manual processes. That puts the organization's welfare at risk.* "

Traditional approach does not scale for complexity. Running security analysis, threat hunting and manual efforts on growing amounts of data in the traditional way becomes exponentially difficult. Add to that an identity perspective and there is simply no realistic way enterprises can scale internally to these demands. There needs to be a drastic game changer. It's something where you must leverage the cloud, big data, and machine learning with predictive security analytics solutions that include UEBA and IdA models and use cases.

The equalizing impact of UEBA and IdA. With a balanced approach of people, process and technology, woven together, we're driving to address the scalability problem that is growing faster than we ever imagined. We see all three of these elements coming together with cloud based providers that help us from the perspective of scalability. That's where solutions like UEBA, integrated with IdA, can help level the playing field for customers like us. UEBA and IdA combined is easily capable of running on this kind of a scale, with productive and actionable risk-scored results.

> " *...we're driving to address the scalability problem... That's where solutions like UEBA, integrated with IdA, can help level the playing field for customers like us.* "

People, process and technology benefit from UEBA and IdA. By using this solution, technology organizations leverage the computational capabilities of machine learning drawing from big data for context. This helps in terms of scaling, addressing security and identity challenges. From the perspectives of analytics processing, the systems are running more efficiently with fewer false positives. From the people perspective, the highly qualified security analysts are being freed from time-consuming manual investigations and able to focus on higher business critical tasks supporting the evolving needs of the security group. UEBA and IdA change and adapt the business process in a measurable way, integrating and optimizing a combination of people, process and technology.

How past behavior is predictive of potential future anomalies

When monitored effectively, some past behaviors provide a great indication for predicting future security issues. Timely, accurate data and context are the key. Yet because of the vast amount of data in today's environments, it can't be processed effectively without the robust reinforcement of machine learning. With that enhancement supporting the analytics, we have much more data that can be processed properly to deliver the all-important context which enables us to understand more of those future predictable scenarios with anomalies that arise. These anomalies will be undetected without the analysis of large amounts of data made possible by machine learning.

Increasing quality of results over time. The potential to uncover those anomalies through user behavior analytics will increase over time. First, the bigger anomalies and some of the obvious ones will surface. But as the learning process refines, and the baselines become more comprehensive, that number will double and triple six months or a year from now. Five years from now this number will be increased by a factor of five hundred. As we and the machine learning solution continually learn, we connect more of the dots. We continue to improve the evidence, and with it our ability to accurately predict at an increasingly specific level.

Identity management in a silo. We must assure the issue of identity is properly addressed. Too often, identity management from a security standpoint is in its own siloed IT framework, separate from security. A result has been that many times in the past organizations would perform certifications in separate systems. They would be unsuccessful in identifying anomalies, as they would possess an extremely limited visibility of the access risk plane.

Un-siloed identity is critical for useful analytics. When you flatten out the environment and examine this entire big behemoth of access data, then you can recognize the need to focus on identity, and then from there run identity analytics on the data. This will

> *This is often access that was in fact there, sometimes for many years, but because of the siloed segmentation, it was invisible.*

give identity access management teams a much richer context, where they can pick out the excess access and access outliers which otherwise go unnoticed. This is often access that was in fact there, sometimes for many years, but because of the siloed segmentation and human effort, it was invisible.

Machine learning adoption in the environment and industry verticals

It's interesting how some security people used to look at analytics very narrowly where they would have to come up with a rule or a query. This is great if they know exactly what they're looking for. However, this reliance solely on rules and queries limits security assurance and misses the critical issue of the unknown unknowns. Security analysts can't possibly think of all the ways an attacker might try to get into their environment. While they may try to think from their attacker's perspective, they can't reproduce every scenario. They have to be right every time, while the attackers only need to be right once. That's why user and entity behavior analytics and identity analytics are critical in today's environments.

Big data and machine learning lowers false positives. We're comparatively early into the adoption of machine learning. We're learning from some of the initial successes. First, we needed to confirm how well the solution characterizes normal behavior and then see how well we could detect abnormal behavior. The more we learn, the better we understand the wider capability of leveraging user behavior analytics to take us to the next level and understand how much of the detection would be false positives. We're improving on filtering the false positives as we get deeper context from our peer group baselines and mining the big data more effectively.

> *We're improving on filtering the false positives as we get deeper context from our peer group baselines and mining the big data more effectively.*

Analytics and machine learning models of other verticals. If you examine some of the early adopter industries, such as banking, their models show us the immediacy of what we'd like to have in our environment. For example, my credit card gets used in three different locations all within two minutes and my cell phone goes off. This is the kind of analytics capabilities we're working to achieve for security controls that match the quality of that particular customer process. These other vertical solution capabilities are continually evolving. Today, there are probably fifty different scenarios which are triggers for the banking space that they didn't have two years ago. We intend to achieve the same kind of growth potential in our predictive security analytics solution within our own unique vertical.

Adoption trends for machine learning within the cruise line vertical

From a cruise line perspective, we're beginning to see early adoptions. The industry is recognizing how the unique challenges of their hyper-hybrid environments require unique solutions. With complex environments along with the element of ships constantly in movement around the world, hosting a range of technologies and users – some of it going through satellites — advanced security analytics is a solution that fits with their needs, goals and security objectives.

Visibility delivered with each integration phase. Specifically with Carnival, we're still in the early design and implementation of bringing all of our systems together into this integrated environment. We see huge upsides for us. We're now able to do things that previously would have taken us weeks, if not months to accomplish, or we couldn't do at all in the past.

Perspectives of security evolution through a range of verticals

After working over twenty-five years in a range of verticals, primarily with a security focus, my career path brought me to Carnival. Originally beginning as a programmer analyst for the Federal Reserve Bank of Cleveland, my work involved disaster recovery of systems, including old mainframe security systems, before moving into IT security. Positions in steel manufacturing, and healthcare with Blue Cross Family followed. After working in healthcare insurance, my work in the field led to medical imaging products manufacturing for GE HealthCare, where my responsibilities included building and managing a global security team. During that time, my portfolio broadened as the quality leader for the corporation responsible for Six Sigma across the global organization. Finally, just before joining Carnival, I held the CISO position at SuperValu, a large distribution and retail conglomerate grocery store chain.

Carnival hosts an array of businesses in one model. My position at Carnival is unique in that the organization contains a multitude of businesses that I worked within through the years, as well as a few new ones. Carnival is many things. It is like a corporation with a collection of small floating cities. It is a conglomerate of a huge supply chain organization, a transportation/people moving business, a hotel, restaurant and entertainment services enterprise, and a retail store chain that sells product all over the world. We have the largest collection of casinos afloat and a dedicated casino vertical. Carnival also has a medical services component. All of our ships have medical clinic centers, which carries a security perspective for the protection and control required for the clinics and their healthcare records.

> *Carnival is many things. It is like a corporation with a collection of small floating cities.*

A global operation with thousands of customers. Carnival has the traditional physical environment, with the corporate offices needing to protect IP. In addition, our security model must include some of our ships with over 4,000 customers and 1,000 plus crew. That translates into over 120,000 employees, of which 70% are on the ship at any given day, across the world, versus traditional corporate offices with locations that don't move. Add to that our responsibility for over one hundred ships around the world, all with moving data centers, which also need to be able to run off satellites when far off shore. It's a new layer of complexity of how to deliver IT services specifically to the customer as well as to the employees who run the ship.

Witnessing the road of security evolution with big data and machine learning. As I have witnessed the trends in the security industry evolve from the traditional on-premises to the hybrid cloud, and on to what I call Carnival Corporation's hyper-hybrid environment, I have come to recognize and appreciate the continuous state of evolution and development required to keep pace with the challenges, the new threat planes and development in technology. For the foreseeable future, predictive security analytics and machine learning driven by big data will be part of that evolution.

CONCLUSIONS & TAKEAWAYS:
Recognizing the urgency for change in security

Gary Eppinger's *hyper-hybrid environment* is a unique model of security challenge, contending with the complexities of environments on-premises, in the cloud, at sea, and in constant motion. Any one of the separate business verticals within Carnival Corporation's multifaceted umbrella environment would represent a full slate of demanding responsibilities for many enterprise CISOs. As Eppinger improves his security environment, and concatenates his company's ten brands into one view, along with developing the required security solutions to wrap around his hyper-hybrid environment, he observes the importance of maintaining flexibility with growth, and phased solution evolution. This contrasts with some monolithic solution approaches that entail 'rip and replace' which are often outdated upon completion of implementation.

Balancing people, process and technology, Eppinger calls out the objective of achieving reliable functionality over perfection with each phase. Perfection is virtually impossible to achieve since technology is perpetually evolving. This phased strategy includes the integration of risk-based predictive security analytics and capitalizing on the short-term benefits, while refining the long-term goals and increasing the critical mass of quality over time. Eppinger's objectives include bringing unique and separate siloed environments under one centralized management approach. His strategy also includes moving security closer to the data itself, with the right controls.

At the core of this strategy is the holistic need for centralized identity, which optimizes the capabilities of risk management through robust identity analytics. None of this would be possible without the implementation of machine learning to leverage the burgeoning scale of big data in today's evolving hybrid environments.

The devil, of course, is always in the details. To achieve their security goals, security leaders must constantly update their understanding of a broad range of factors, including the importance of emerging trends in the misuse and the compromise of identity to keep in pace with their responsibilities for Borderless Behavior Analytics. This will be explored in the next chapter. For some high tech executives, however, an understanding of security risks should not be taken for granted. We'll see this in the following *Borderless Breach Flashcard*. These one-page case studies featured at the end of each expert interview section highlight the wide range of breach scenarios that security leaders face in protecting their evolving environments today.

BORDERLESS BREACH FLASHCARD	
High-Tech CEOs in the Crosshairs	
CATEGORY	Social media password theft, account breach, by foreign powers.
WHO	**The target:** Various C-level leaders in tech companies, along with other social media customers.
WHAT	Prominent high-tech executives had their Twitter, and other social media accounts, breached. On a wider scale, many more customers were impacted.
WHEN	2016
WHERE	USA.
WHY	Economic greed, market control.
HOW	A Saudi-based group of hackers sent a Tweet which read: *"Hey, it's OurMine Team we are just testing your security, please send us a message."* Many people responded, including Mark Zuckerberg, founder and CEO of Facebook, Evan Williams, co-founder of Twitter, and Mikkel Svane, CEO of Zendesk, a software tech support firm. Ryan Holmes, CEO of Hootsuite, a social media security management company was included. Hootsuite's IT team confirmed the hackers used Foursquare, an 'app authing' application, to get information to help gain access to the social media accounts. For Holmes, the Foursquare account had been unused for years. Dormant accounts are a prime avenue to access users' accounts in private and corporate use. With Zuckerberg, hackers took advantage of a weak password, unchanged for years: *dadada*. Over 32 million Twitter hacked logins were put on sale on the Dark Web.
HOW BAD?	Individual damage was minor. The image of high-tech-leaders being susceptible to cyber-attacks like these underline the casual attitude some execs adopt toward the importance of security in technology. Social media phishing is a main threat plane for malicious attacks. The damage could have been much worse.
HOW COULD IT BE AVOIDED?	Whether in personal or business accounts, ignoring unverified social media messaging is a key best practice. Using two-factor authentication on Twitter and closing unused dormant accounts are also best practices. If the tech leaders' companies had a UEBA-IdA solution, this might have been averted. Visibility into unusual account access, including social media from locations or devices outside normal patterns, could have raised risk alerts, facilitating timely SOC response. The execs could have avoided the embarrassment of ignoring basic online security rules.

The Compromise and Misuse
of Identity

Recognizing a new reality in security

Is the problem of compromise and misuse of identity really that bad? How can we really know for sure?

Verizon's 2016 Data Breach Digest – Scenarios from the Field, shares a credential theft case study in this area of concern. A law enforcement agency came to a company while investigating malicious activity that had a connection with the company in question. The company was informed that a number of its externally facing IP addresses were associated with the criminal activity under investigation. The law enforcement team provided the company with a list of the suspected IP addresses associated with the company that they had found during the investigation. In response, the company engaged the Verizon RISK team as part of their incident response (IR) escalation process.

Examination of forensic evidence in the suspected compromised systems included numerous web servers, domain controllers, along with administrator and end user systems. Analysis revealed the systems were riddled with an array of malware variants. The scale of compromise far exceeded the list originally identified in the investigation. Continued examination of network log data uncovered that several other systems had been communicating with an external malicious IP address as well. The more the investigation progressed, the more bad news came to light.

The forensic investigation revealed that the initial compromise occurred on one of the victim's web servers several months earlier than indicated by the law enforcement investigators. Using a web shell, the threat actors had gone undetected for several months during which they had broad access of the network. This compromise was not the ultimate objective. Malware capable of dumping passwords, stealing credentials and performing exfiltration of data were all uploaded via the web shell. The ultimate goal of the malware: to penetrate deeper into the network using malware specifically designed to leverage existing credentials.

> "The ultimate goal of the malware: to penetrate deeper into the network using malware specifically designed to leverage existing credentials."

The threat actors successfully compromised numerous administrator accounts using password dumping, password cracking and keylogging. The scope of the credential theft was even greater than originally thought. A deleted spreadsheet containing more than 100 usernames and passwords associated with a particular high privileged access administrator was subsequently discovered. This set of compromised credentials led to access for gaining even more credentials and ultimately provided the threat actors with access to numerous network locations, including several domain controllers. Given the amount of time the adversary had dwelled in the environment, the volume of data at risk was severely critical.

As a standalone story, it's sobering. But unfortunately this kind of event is not a rarity. Citing the Verizon *2016 Data Breach Investigations Report* (DBIR), the new upward trend is Web application attacks for the financial services sector. Here the attack kill chain involves credentials compromised to obtain more access credentials to log back into the financial services websites to commit financial fraud for these stolen accounts. This trend ranked at 82%, whereas it was only 31% the previous year.

The compromise and misuse of identity expands beyond employees to business partners and even customers. The kill chain starts with the compromise of employees to get the account data. Quoting the DBIR in relation to this trend: *"These breaches, uncovered through the forensic analysis performed on several C2* (command and control) *servers, tell the tale of phished customer > C2 > Drop Keylogger > Export captured data > Use stolen credentials."* Given this significant increase in threat activity, prudent banking and financial customers are investing heavily in new identity-based defenses to stop this trend.

Given this new perspective, a better question to ask at the beginning of this section might be, "Do I have the right tools and solutions in place for visibility of compromise and misuse of identity, and am I prepared if it's really that bad?"

Answering this question requires acknowledging that identity is the easiest doorway into your network. It's also the quickest pathway to the enterprise's kingdom of valuable

> *...identity is the easiest doorway into your network... the quickest pathway to the enterprise's kingdom of value assets.*

assets. An identity consists of the user or entity, their accounts and entitlements. Gaining access to these is the root cause of most data breaches and theft. Recognizing this, and having solutions in place to manage this comprehensively is key to establishing detection early in the kill chain with advanced security analytics for identity compromise and misuse.

Part of the challenge facing organizations today lies in the functional gap that often exists between IAM (identity and access management) and security teams. While security is focused on malware detection, finding threats, and delivering responses, IAM teams are focused on providing access, often in excess. They are too often working at cross-purposes regarding critical elements of the same access risk and threat plane. Herein lies the dilemma. For success to occur, IT and SOCs must agree that the compromise and misuse of identity are at the core of modern threats and they need to collaborate effectively. Identity is an access risk and threat plane that must have its surface area reduced and then monitored for compromise and abuse.

Identity consists of users, or their accounts, access entitlements and activity, both on-premises and in the cloud. Identity issues include excess access, access outliers, orphan and dormant accounts, as well as, unknown privileged access risks. Security teams especially must have a high awareness and detailed understanding of the concept of identity as a threat plane and its prioritization. On the IT side, awareness of how group and role proliferation are part of the problem is needed. Unfortunately, IAM has had been increasingly constrained by inflexible and inefficient manual processes for compliance with legacy rules to define roles. If identity is core to modern threats, how do we deal with flexible access to data?

Who can forget the 2013 Target nightmare? Unfortunately, too many forget exactly *how* it happened. Partner credentials were the doorway for this data breach. Identity is the new attack vector for everyone. Protecting identity is also the key to the future in the cloud/mobility world. If that isn't concerning enough, organizations must look beyond employees to partners and customers. Plus, more than just data, 'safety' is now

part of the game for everyone. CISOs need to know how important identity and access are for their business partners in relation to their own organization's security and safety.

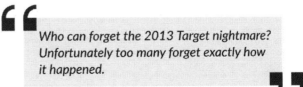

> *Who can forget the 2013 Target nightmare? Unfortunately too many forget exactly how it happened.*

While account compromise and misuse remain a concern for all organizations, it's all a matter of prioritization and focus. Our expert contributor Jerry Archer, CSO of a prominent financial services enterprise, draws from a vast range of first-hand experience in information security since its earliest days. He shares his seasoned insights on the evolution of security with a special focus on the financial market vertical, along with the outcomes of employing big data machine learning for user and entity behavior analytics (UEBA) and identity analytics (IdA) in that space.

BORDERLESS EXPERT INSIGHTS

Jerry Archer, CISO*
Major Financial Services Company

As CSO of a major financial services enterprise, Jerry Archer's responsibilities include securing and protecting all of the organization's systems and offerings, and for security initiatives across the company. He has more than 30 years of experience at other leading companies and government agencies, including Intuit, Visa, and the CIA. He is a founder and board member of the Cloud Security Alliance; a fellow at the Ponemon Institute; a member of the Advisory Board for George Mason University International Cyber Center; President, Security Adviser Alliance; serves on the Security Innovation Network (SINET) Showcase steering committee; and is a member of numerous industry and corporate advisory boards. Archer was also named the 2011 North American Information Security Executive of the Year by Information Security Executive® (ISE).

As a member of Gurucul's Executive Advisory Board, Archer has provided critical guidance for the company's strategic growth and evolution in the UEBA-IdA field of machine learning and big data. He draws from his firsthand and seasoned insights into the inception of the first generation of security strategies, where he has continued to work through evolving developments in cybersecurity and machine learning for predictive security analytics.

Overview

In this chapter, Archer begins by observing the dynamic between CIO and CISO objectives of productivity versus security and discusses the symptoms of inadequate security defenses. Part of his insight includes the recognition that security data volume exceeds manual processing capabilities. Archer provides insights on the requirements for detecting account compromise and misuse and he also observes aspects of risk in maintaining a status quo security strategy. While the importance of monitoring the endpoint remains constant, impacting factors of traditional security perspective versus those in hybrid environments are reviewed. Archer then explores the importance of insider threats, the drivers of this threat, and the need for establishing a single identity for users in both on-premises and in the cloud. This includes requirements for coordinated security measures against insider threat and privileged access abuse. Leveraging analytics to improve the identity access side of security is a key to success in this objective. Archer observes factors influencing UEBA and IdA adoption as a supplement to security strategy. He then discusses early and long-term objectives for

* The views and opinions expressed by Jerry Archer in this book are his own, and do not necessarily reflect those of his current, or any of his previous employers.

UEBA implementation, as well as the benefits of UEBA. Archer concludes with insights into the growth and evolution of security strategies he has observed during his decades in the field.

Productivity versus security: The dynamic between CIO and CISO priorities

There will always be a natural tension between the CISO and the CIO. This dynamic is determined by the fact that the CIO is driven to provide more and better services at lower costs, while a CISO's job is to protect everything, the data, environment, transactions, and to maintain the assurance of confidentiality, integrity availability and safety. Every one of those attributes is potentially contrary to what the CIO wants to do, at least in the fundamental technical sense.

The partnership of common goals. While there is this natural tension between the two, it is in their common interest to cooperate and collaborate with an eye on the organization's goals, objectives and needs, as well as facilitate safe productivity and profitability. It is important to recognize that the CISO of the future must understand much more about what's in the cloud and how they can take advantage of this world of empowering possibilities. As the cloud creates issues around security, the cloud also provides solutions. Security provided through the cloud is an important element in the IT mix.

Big data's place in today's security. A great deal of the work performed today in security revolves around big data. Security teams now use the cloud for security purposes to do analytical work that could in no realistic way be performed if the cloud was unavailable to do it. This advantage is both from a cost, as well as a human resource bandwidth perspective. The evolution of security solutions — as is exemplified by new versions of SIEMs (security incident and event management solutions) — is now becoming heavily based on big data. This is where mature UEBA vendors like Gurucul help to support both the CIO's and CISO's goals. Gurucul in essence is a big data analytical engine that leverages the low cost and productivity enhancing capabilities in the cloud and hybrid environments. This represents a real boon to the security community. For a CIO and CISO, it represents the best of both of their worlds.

Symptoms of inadequate security defenses

There have been two factors in today's environments that revealed defenses could not keep up with the rising trends of security threats. One has been the rapid mutation of malware. If you look at the number of new malware instances occurring yearly, there's a new variant of malware being created every 200 milliseconds. These attack scenarios which cyber criminals have been using continue to evolve so quickly that it's virtually impossible for anything signature-based to contend with them. Organizations must be right every single time as a defender, but the perpetrator only has to be right once to succeed. As a result, a number of organizations are moving to a solution which is not searching for predefined specifics, but looking for actors doing something nefarious.

> *...a number of organizations are moving to a solution which is not searching for predefined specifics, but looking for actors doing something nefarious.*

Evolving requirements for security monitoring. The second problem was that most malware today comes into the environment and it doesn't even have a payload. SOCs don't know what its intent is until someone downloads the payload into a piece of malware to execute a command directed at stealing credentials, penetrating sensitive data, injecting ransomware, and so forth. Ultimately, the only way to effectively defend the environment is to monitor behavior with an ability to alert security teams if there's something wrong with the system or the end user.

Overwhelming majority of threats at the endpoint. Monitoring behavior effectively in the environment represents a complex challenge. For example, many companies employ network activity analysis solutions which are used extensively to look for advanced threats on the network along with malware and bad actors throughout the network environment. A closer investigation of the problem, however, indicates that probably 60% of the threat problem exists at the endpoint.

Rapid threat change through the human interface. While CISOs have been very effective defending their networks at the front end, with their interfaces to the internet, the hackers — logically — have moved to the endpoint, the weakest point, which is where humans are. The human interface into the environment is by far the one being attacked the most today. Looking at it from this perspective, signatures can't accomplish the task, because the threat model changes so rapidly.

Solutions detecting abnormal behavior. In response to this challenge, a growing number of organizations are adopting a behavior analytics system to detect what is normal and abnormal behavior in the environment, then to have the ability to flag the abnormal behavior and take action on it as needed. As a number of CISOs have witnessed the steady progression of the attack scenarios and strategies, their logical response with UEBA adoption has been a natural evolution of defending against those attacks.

Transformation realities: Security data volume exceeds manual processing capabilities

In 2012, as part of the response to the new challenges in defense, security architects targeted analytical work around Web log files, which became a significant initiative. Yet it was quickly discovered that in order to produce anything resembling useful data output, a Hadoop environment was necessary to perform the data analysis. At that time, security experts were already seeing the impact of digital exhaust which necessitated a form of outsourced services to do analytical work around big data.

> *At that time, security experts were already seeing the impact of digital exhaust which necessitated a form of outsourced services to do analytical work around big data.*

Scalability for crunching today's security data. Machine learning is different from artificial intelligence (AI). Machine learning looks at routine and being able to describe incidences that occur, so the machine can understand them in a useful way for analytical purposes and then flag the legitimate behavior anomalies. Machine learning is well on the path to performing that functionality with robust results. Security analytics are not yet close to AI, however, where SOCs can look for completely unforeseen kinds of anomalies. That will come over time.

False positive reduction via machine learning. The ability to crunch the numbers and deliver tangible results through machine learning is already here. It can be done today with negligible constraints. What the security community sees coming out of its analytical work is quite solid, with machine learning computational capabilities for the scale of data needed with the coverage required in a growing number of use cases. What machine learning is achieving today is very good and getting better, delivering fewer false positives. The key is getting rid of the false positives in a measurable way, and machine learning is getting increasingly better at that.

Experienced insights into behavior analytics requirements. Organizations that have arrived at this milestone in security for understanding the need and the importance of big data are very likely to be in a stronger position to see the advantages of a mature UEBA solution to supplement the security strategy for their environment. In addition, as each environment is unique, the challenge becomes defining the custom requirements for any enterprise considering a UEBA solution's function, fit and breadth of use cases.

Requirements for detecting account compromise and misuse

Most environments contain sensitive, customer or corporate information. It's extremely important to be able to detect misuse, misuse of credentials, and misuse of accounts — any activity that correlates with trying to get at sensitive data. Most companies today have an intensive focus in terms of the use, as well as application and storage of sensitive information. It's a high priority to be able to detect account compromise and misuse.

Visibility on the weakest point. To be successful at that requirement, however, demands that security analysts must have effective visibility to monitor the endpoint.

That's now the weakest point and the target that most hackers are attacking. It remains of the utmost importance to protect that information at the endpoint. If that is not achieved, a business's viability is at risk. This mandate is not just about protecting the information. It also includes maintaining secure systems from both a regulatory perspective, and a customer trust perspective.

> *...security analysts must have effective visibility to monitor the endpoint.*

Vulnerabilities in the status quo security

In most companies, the vast majority of the workforce performs the same routine task every day. They access the same data and generally the same amount of data. Their behavior, day-to-day, month-to-month, and year-to-year, is fundamentally the same.

Past behavior defining normal context. The concept of past behavior being a predictor of future behavior holds a great deal of truth. As a result, it's easy to look at that behavior, and it quickly becomes apparent when someone is doing something different. That immediately becomes a flag since an employee's behavior is typically routine.

Challenges with depth and focus of visibility. As soon as an intruder gains access to someone's credentials, they start exploring the environment, yet in a manner unlike the valid credential owner. Utilizing a user behavior analytics solution which identifies such anomalous behavior, it in turn generates alerts for analysts to investigate. The challenge also relates to the depth and focus of visibility and monitoring within the environment.

Closer monitoring capability of the endpoint required. Network activity and analysis solutions work well on the network backbones and major trunks, but are not as effective down toward the endpoints and in the last links. There are simply too many of them. While monitoring traffic on the backbone remains constant, at the first level on the network, someone could still explore the environment. Visibility at the endpoint is essential.

Invisible attackers persist without the right solution. As long as an attacker remains on the device, as long as they stay with what's available to that person through their credentials, and unless we have something on the endpoint to monitor, we can't even see the breach and observe nefarious activity happening.

Impacting the endpoint: Traditional security perspectives versus the complexity of hybrid environments

The cloud presents an entirely new set of problems for any organization's security team. One is the ability to gain visibility into the cloud, which is for the most part opaque. Cloud providers, particularly in the public cloud space — will not allow customers to look at detailed nuanced behavior within their environment. They provide some visibility. However, it will be by necessity limited visibility.

Enduring endpoint criticality in cloud expansion. It's difficult to get into the environment in a way that was done in traditional on-premises environments, where organizations owned the infrastructure. So the ability now to use some sort of a behavior analysis on the endpoint is much more important. The next element of this challenge is the fact that we now have cloud providers communicating on our behalf to other cloud providers, and then to other cloud providers, and so on. As a result, organizations will continually struggle to effectively manage the communication between elements in their environments. And, in many cases, that will be managed by cloud providers themselves.

Shifting workload models change security strategies. As the challenge factors progress, CISOs must find ways to look at security that doesn't involve placing devices in-line, in communications streams, between cloud providers, or between environments, because they will evolve, they will move. Essentially, workloads will become fungible and facilitate the ability to arbitrage between cloud providers, particularly as containers evolve. As a result, there will be a seismic shift in security, away from the perimeter-based models.

> *...there will be a seismic shift in security, away from the perimeter-based models.*

Evolving cloud security frameworks. Different kinds of solutions we'll call IPS or firewalls will be involved in this next generation of cloud security options. However, they will be virtual. They'll be more microscopic in nature and operate more like a microservice. An application will have its own firewall, its own IPS system. Endpoints will need to be more protective of themselves. Tools will have to be developed for the endpoint and security teams will monitor that endpoint, regardless of where it's being driven from.

Data origins uncertain in the future. As the cloud evolves, in the future, you won't even know where the data is coming from. It can come from any place, from any provider. That's a pressing problem to solve for data governance and integrity.

Impacting the traditional perimeter: Emerging factors of hybrid access

The perimeter is, of course, quickly disappearing. Even today most organizations simply cannot draw a perimeter around an entire environment because of the adoption of some form of cloud

> *The reality is that the perimeter will shrink to one individual, one application, or one small set of applications.*

solution. CISOs create what we call boundaries and within them are various systems, but those systems have broad access and broad capabilities. So in reality, these boundaries are more of an abstraction, something like a conceptual drawing. They're not real. The reality is that the perimeter will shrink to one individual, one application, or one small set of applications.

New challenges define tomorrow's solutions. Solutions like containers, microservices and built-in security, will become more the norm than what we have today, which is trying to place a lot of appliances in line to cope with the challenge. Until those become widely available, the current state-of-the-art security solution for today's environments must include some form of a mature monitoring and a behavior analytics solution to assure 24/7 global visibility at the granular level of the endpoint.

The importance of insider threats

Breaches due to insiders represent a significant percentage and are not going away. The insider threat problem is one of those situations where, as the defenses continue to improve, one of the key areas attackers will target is the insider because they have knowledge and they have access. Account compromise is the goal for these attackers. Ultimately many security leaders expect the insider threat will become the biggest threat. Today, it's probably less so, because the avenues to get into an environment are still relatively easy enough, so that attackers don't need to go and recruit insiders.

Trends moving to the insider threat. Over time the threat will evolve. As the perimeters are tightened and additional security policies are applied to people who access from the outside, we'll see trends moving more toward the inside with the insider threat problem. What a majority of security teams look for now is not so much an individual going bad, or rogue, but instead they consider an individual starts acting badly because they have a piece of malware on their VDI (virtual desktop infrastructure) or their laptop. It's not really the legitimate insider; it's someone pretending to be one.

Monitoring for indicators of intrusion. The focus in effect becomes more on the technical perspective. This may entail looking for indicators of the intruder impersonating a real person versus the real person going bad. It could be an account compromise or hijacking in an environment which is a common path outsiders will use where they pretend to be a legitimate user.

Breach without system compromise. One of the most notable breaches was at E-Trade, a few years ago. Attackers had a Trojan that targeted high volume traders, and they simply put trades into the path of that stream. The hackers had first located the high volume traders

> *It cost E-Trade over ten million dollars in losses without a single E-Trade system being compromised.*

using E-Trade. They then put a Trojan on the target workstations and they were simply injecting trades into the trade system that the legitimate users were performing. It cost E-Trade over ten million dollars in losses without a single E-Trade system being compromised.

Drivers for insider threat

There are two facets of the insider threat problem. If you look at the true insider threat where you have a rogue employee, it's typically due to the fact that a person is unhappy at work. They also believe they have something of value they can sell. There's a certain level of emotion. It could be desperation. It could be anger. That emotion drives people to feel they need or deserve something which does not belong to them, and it compels them to take that asset of value. The public and all security leaders are quite familiar with these scenarios.

Rogue employees versus irrational behavior. In most cases — and this brings us to the second facet of the insider threat problem — CISOs find it's someone doing something that's basically stupid. You can't stop stupid. You can't always eliminate stupid through training. Stupid exists in every company. Rogue employees are a minor problem when you stack them up against stupid. Stupid will find a way around just about anything. Remember Hanlon's razor: "Never attribute to malice that which is adequately explained by stupidity."

> " Remember Hanlon's razor: "Never attribute to malice that which is adequately explained by stupidity. "

Severe consequences of irrational actions. The bluntness in the choice of the word describing this behavior is intentional. Because the severe consequences which result from this kind of anomalous behavior was originally initiated by good intentions and unintentional actions, some security leaders might place this vulnerability factor at a lower level of priority in their considerations. To do so would be to place their environment and their organization's welfare in jeopardy. Stupid behavior within the secure environment is real and a grave risk to any enterprise. It's only a question of magnitude. Take for example, in 2006, the head of AOL Research released a compressed text file on one of its websites containing 20 million search keywords used by more than 650,000 subscribers. While the file was intended for research purposes, it was mistakenly posted publicly. Customer confidence and trust in AOL were impacted as a result.

Priorities for establishing a single identity for users on-premises and in the cloud

A first priority for security leaders is establishing the segregation of duties and access appropriate to roles. This includes partitioning employees' access from information they don't need to do their job. Those measures are important today, and they'll be equally important in the future — perhaps more so. Being able to create a stringent identity around somebody and what they can do, and what they have access to, will become essential security hygiene.

> *Being able to create a stringent identity around somebody and what they can do, and what they have access to, will become essential security hygiene.*

Challenges of effective monitoring and segregation of duties. Successful segregation and partitioning represents something of a parent-child problem. How can I get the security information required by going through various paths? What options exist to achieve the visibility required? On some level, security analysts must be able to look at the endpoint to determine what applications and data content the endpoint is accessing. In the process of achieving this kind of monitoring, it's critical to make sure the entire segregation of duties model has not been subverted, or to fail granting appropriate access.

Security measures against insider threat and privileged access abuse

One of the biggest problems is if organizations have an insider who goes rogue with privileged access. That's basically the Holy Grail cybercriminals seek. Generally, enforcement of many policies and numerous processes that don't involve machine learning identity analytics is the primary model for management. They relate more to the segregation of duties, the segregation of accounts, a strong auditing of accounts, and similar procedures to make sure an insider with elevated privileges can't act out in some malicious way.

> *One of the biggest problems is if organizations have an insider who goes rogue with privileged access.*

Machine learning's critical role monitoring privileged access. A solution like Gurucul definitely comes into play in terms of detecting or alerting when a privileged user is doing something strange, or outside the range of 'normal'. There are several security approaches today, in addition to Gurucul, which also look at what this individual is doing, including strong audit trails, not using the same IDs, or specialized accounts that don't have internet access — all of those types of measures that seriously tighten down the controls on privileged users. Assuring complete discovery of all privileged access entitlements is also critical, and very few PAM (privileged access management) solutions can manage the complete inventory of an organization's instances of privileged access entitlements. A small selection of mature UEBA vendors like Gurucul also offer identity analytics (IdA), drawing from big data and empowered by machine learning, to address this discovery gap.

Deep monitoring capabilities. UEBA and IdA — and more specifically solutions with the maturity of Gurucul — provide the needed tools that deliver the capability of seeing into the network to the endpoint. Moreover, doing this delivers a granularity of monitoring into who has access to what. UEBA and IdA don't replace existing capabilities, they supplement them. Without them, there would be a serious gap in the security model. As the industry is continually making improvements to security solutions, Gurucul is there as well, advancing its machine learning models and use cases.

> *UEBA and IdA don't replace existing capabilities, they supplement them. Without them, there would be a serious gap in the security model.*

Leveraging analytics to improve the identity access side of security

Regular monitoring of access log files has become essential. This can be leveraged to not only see who has access to what, but also to see who is accessing the data. One of the functions traditional identity management tools don't really perform is looking at activity: who's accessing the data. On a deeper level security analysts are able to get insight into: What are their access entitlements? Have they looked at the data? Do they have access entitlements they don't need? Those kinds of details security teams can now see with an identity analytics tool that could not be seen efficiently with the typical identity management tools, which would require a much more labor-intensive effort. Many critical nuances around identity management are becoming available which have not been seen before.

Precise access controls. This solution set also solves much of the parent-child problem. This means that, because an IT department gives someone access, to system A, the system A path gave the user access to data in system B, which the security team did not want them to have. The problem is obviously much more complex than the A and B scenario, but it articulates the general idea. This has been one of the most difficult problems to solve in identity management, which is giving someone direct access to data unintentionally when they shouldn't have had it. Organizations usually find out about the consequences only when something bad happens.

Policies for managing excess access. As it relates to excessive access, contrary to companies in other verticals, financial services focuses heavily on access appropriate for role without excessive access. This means if someone transfers, this person only gets the access associated with the profile associated with the job. If they wanted anything other than the assigned profile access, it would be an exception, which would require approval, and have a time limit on it.

Zero baseline access policy. Essentially every time someone transfers to a new position, their access is brought to a zero baseline. All of their access is eliminated and IT then gives them back only what they need. Financial services companies probably suffer less of the excess access issue than other industries.

Quarterly certifications ensure zero baseline adherence. Excessive access is generally identified during certification processes. It's difficult for someone to accumulate access, because every manager is required to attest to the fact that every one of his employee's access is appropriate to their role. Financial services companies must demonstrate zero-baselining for all access.

Factors influencing UEBA adoption as a security supplement

Financial organizations have leveraged a number of security controls, through network activity and analysis, automated threat forensics, and dynamic malware protection against advanced cyber threats into the network, and into their email streams. From there, moving to a UEBA environment fills an important gap in the security strategy. For many organizations, it is simply a next logical step in the buildout of a resilient defense model.

> *...moving to a UEBA environment, fills an important gap in the security strategy. For many organizations, it is simply a next logical step in the buildout of a resilient defense model.*

Cloud's rapid evolution and forward-thinking adoption. Added to the gap UEBA filled, is the fact that the world of cloud and technology is evolving at such a rapid pace that UEBA is important to have in place. Some security leaders see user and entity behavior analytics adoption not just part of a recognition of addressing a new reality and security requirement. It has actually become something of a goal for them to achieve because of the value they can extract from it on a daily basis.

Early and long-term objectives for UEBA implementation

One of the primary uses of UEBA is to characterize normal behavior. Then security teams can detect abnormal behavior and understand how much of the detection would be false positives. The next step is to refine processes to gain richer and deeper context from user baseline profiles to reduce false positives.

Simple evolution of the tool utility. A UEBA-IdA solution adoption starts off simply, by reducing excess access, dormant and orphaned accounts, and unknown privileged access risks, with IdA, thereby drastically reducing the surface area of the access risk plane. From there, a natural evolution is using the tool to look at segregation of duties, access appropriate to role, and to limit access to data users shouldn't have. This facilitates optimal UEBA monitoring for anomalous behavior, which follows. In addition, identity analytics can evolve to become an adjunct to identity management for automated risk response.

Broader applications of UEBA. An important focus CISOs are also looking at now is much more in terms of a broad-brush view of identity access and the behavior of an identity in terms of meeting true holistic security needs and supporting compliance requirements. That entire area of access certification, access appropriate to role, segregation of duties, risk associated with access to systems, all of these requirements are now elements of the whole process of which UEBA-IdA is becoming a critical part.

The benefits of a UEBA solution: A first-hand view

The primary benefit most enterprises experience is that UEBA reveals abnormal behaviors which were invisible to security analysts in the past. It empowers a SOC team to say, "This person is doing something abnormal and we have to go find out why."

This translates into the ability to discover things going wrong in the environment which had not been possible to see before. It delivers a critical visibility into those kinds of issues.

> *...UEBA ...empowers a SOC team to say, "This person is doing something abnormal and we have to find out why."*

Discovering solution advantages. There are the two big benefits CISOs traditionally see at a comparatively early state of the solution adoption. The first is expected — the ability to see abnormal behavior in the environment — and the second is being able to use UEBA-IdA for a risk-based approach for identity and access management. In addition, the capability of being able to use the solution as a strong tool for identity and access management is a key utility which becomes more apparent as the use of the tool matures.

UEBA and the value of a self-audit solution

The self-audit is a solution that uses a singular user identity view across all environments and applications where UEBA analyzes all activities of that end user in an organization and generates a regular report. It can be sent as a periodic email statement, usually weekly, with customizable levels of abstraction. It's something like a credit card statement, which says, "This is what we see in terms of your risk-scored access and activity on your account."

Virtually no false positives. Employees review the report regularly to see if there's anything off balance. If they see something's wrong, they report it. This results in virtually no false positives and allows the end users, or employees, to become deputized into the security solution. Organizations as large as 60,000 employees have successfully adopted this kind of self-audit solution.

Evolution of security strategies

My experience over the last 30 years suggests that security strategies are ever-changing and that tools and technologies drive this change at an increasing rate. Adaptation to that change is necessary and essential to maintain an adequate defense. While a CISO must deal with the problems at hand, he must also keep an eye to the future to surf the wave and not be drowned by it.

Change targeted on future requirements. Recognizing the need to adopt productive change in a timely manner, striving to stay ahead of the curve, to understand what's happening in environments in the present, and to anticipate what will be happening two to three years from now, are key mandates for CISOs. To do so successfully, means to stay current with trends and to listen to the right people who understand the deeper details of technology. With this perspective — as opposed to implementing any seismic or comprehensive replacement of systems — it appears that at times a layered or phased approach to security solution evolution is the most sensible strategy.

Flexibility needed in security solution evolution. This concept speaks to the recognition that as the hybrid cloud evolves, organizations have a requirement to evolve with them. Having the flexibility to execute on that strategy can be better achieved if the environment has the capability to evolve. Adopting a wholesale institutional infrastructure changeout rarely has the capability for that kind of flexibility. Security solutions that are able to be part of that evolution, that have the compatibility to work with an

> *Security solutions that are able to be part of that evolution... have the best chance of success in helping an organization... with reliable security.*

array of best-of-breed solutions, have the best chance of success in helping an organization move to the next level of dynamic productivity coupled with reliable security.

Priorities for security in the hybrid environment

Looking at any organization's strategies and tactics for security is, in effect, a snapshot in time. Years ago, strategies were focused on the perimeter. With the rapid expansion of the internet, and then the hybrid cloud, strategies changed again and evolved.

Currently, the idea behind a resilient defense model is important. It centers on developing strategies to live with an active breach, because those are the realities of the future. Being able to establish defensive models with various perimeters of isolation, so organizations can continue to function, is at the very heart of this objective. Best practices centered on that top priority is what industry experts see moving forward.

The importance of metrics. One related area organizations are increasing their focus on includes metrics. Boards are now more interested in cybersecurity. They need to see measurable specifics. Being able to effectively communicate with management and the board of directors is important. Resiliency after a breach and metrics are probably the biggest areas of focus security experts see today.

Resilient defense and UEBA securing the environment

One key to building a successful security program is resilient defense. This consists of protecting against inbound threats, but also implementing equal amounts of measures to deter unauthorized outbound activity. So even if an intruder can get into the environment, and they can get access to data, it is difficult for them to exit with it. User and entity behavior analytics is one way to support that objective. This is part of an implementation of an array of different systems and tools to stop people from exfiltrating the data.

A critical focus on outbound. The idea is to focus as much on outbound as you do on inbound. The reality is that a hacker will get into an environment if they're determined enough. Getting into the environment represents an infinite number of paths. But once someone succeeds, and once they steal something, they then need to exfiltrate it. On the security side, security analysts know what the target data looks like, where it's located and that the hacker wants to exit with it.

The advantage of knowing the attacker's target. The key is to know what they want and what they're going to try to steal. Then they have a payload they must carry on their way out of the intranet. This slows them down. This also means that the activity, whatever they touch, generates telltales and digital exhaust. It creates evidence. When they're carrying a payload, they're clearly less agile on the outbound side as they were on the inbound. It's easier to detect and that's to the SOC's advantage. As a result, security teams can be well-prepared for exfiltration prevention capability. It's an easier job to defend against the outbound side than the inbound side.

> *When they're carrying a payload they're clearly not as agile on the outbound side as they were on the inbound. It's easier to detect...*

Deep monitoring of all priority points. A major element of that ease of defense has to do with UEBA, which facilitates monitoring with the highest priority for the exact points that CISOs know are sensitive and represent the primary targets attackers want to penetrate. Every aspect of activity and access interacting with these priority points can be monitored, empowered by machine learning, and leveraging big data for context.

Not all environments benefit from the same strategy. It's important to observe that different organizations have different environment architecture configurations and resources that must be protected. In a financial institution, the attackers' targets are straightforward, financially based, and easier to prepare for since security teams know what they're after. However, it's much more challenging for an organization like an engineering company, for example. It's hard to characterize what their intellectual property looks like. It's harder for companies that have this very difficult challenge to tag sensitive data effectively, since by its nature, it's more complex and it is generally not as well structured. It doesn't have any real telltales to it. It's harder to discern. Having a mature UEBA solution would be a critical part of any large engineering company's portfolio to help address these kinds of challenges for defending their environments.

Anticipated long-term utilities of UEBA and IdA

As hybrid cloud challenges and attackers' sophistication evolve, there is an evolution of security into more of a microservice type function where user and entity behavior analytics risk scores and analytic response codes would provide something like a holistic security wrapper that goes around an end user which is continuously updated. The possibilities expand from there.

UEBA and IdA evolving with the environment. One can envision all kinds of things UEBA-IdA could do for an organization. I would expect it to evolve as the environment evolved to perform many other functions such as risk-based intrusion protection, intrusion detection, and more. With IdA's ability close the awareness gap between access provided and activity, and to fill the discovery gap in identifying unknown risks in privileged access entitlements, a full holistic view of identity and access in the environment is now possible.

CONCLUSIONS & TAKEAWAYS:
Optimizing new realities in security

Jerry Archer's tenure in security at the early development of the internet provides him with a seasoned, holistic and nuanced perspective on the ever-changing nature of requirements needed to ensure an organization's security. His observations of the various symptoms of inadequate security defenses, including that a new variant of malware is being created every 200 milliseconds, might be alarming for new professionals in the security field. This acknowledgement also includes his observation of rising threats on the endpoint, where 60% of the risk resides. Solutions to address these and others in emerging hybrid environments can no longer be managed with manual security solutions. This challenge is complicated by the evolution of hybrid cloud access and the plethora of devices, a majority of them mobile, which malicious actors take advantage of. Security data volume exceeds manual processing capabilities as anomalous behavior continues to rise. The overwhelming scale of false positives can only be reduced through machine learning and mature behavior analytics. These must also incorporate the holistic use of identity analytics to reduce access risk. This solution set delivers comprehensive visibility and monitoring of both physical and hybrid environments.

With this new paradigm of security solutions in place, detecting account compromise and misuse becomes a realistic objective. This is an important requirement, since the emerging factors of hybrid access are continuing to grow and evolve, with no sign of abatement. At the core of this requirement is addressing a new risk trend, the insider threat. Leveraged as a user, or entity account with entitlements, or through partner access, identity compromise and misuse is the root cause of most data theft and breaches. Whether actual insiders within an organization, or attackers posing as insiders with compromised identity, the risk associated with this trend can be a systemic threat for organizations. This underlines the urgent need for a single identity risk profile for users both on-premises and in the cloud.

The problem of excess access, access outliers, and orphan or dormant accounts is widespread among enterprises. The gap between IAM and security teams, however, is a challenge as these groups in some organizations are working at cross-purposes. Archer observes the benefits of cooperative strategic partnerships with CIOs and CISOs. Archer endorses a security strategy of resilient defense, making it as difficult as possible for attackers to exit with the data they seek once they have gained access to the environment. Like Eppinger, Archer observes that the phased approach to implementing complex changes in the environment has proven be both cost-effective and strengthens the assurance that the solution is delivered in sync with the original solution requirements.

The next chapter will examine more closely insider threats, account compromise and data exfiltration. These lie at the core of a security team's responsibilities: to protect the data. Heeding the signs of sobering consequences of the potential for security breaches, however, is not a forgone conclusion. In the following *Borderless Breach Flashcard*, one healthcare organization suffered three security breaches over the course of a few years. While one might be understandable from a physical security standpoint with a missing laptop, the second remains under investigation, and the final breach could most likely have been avoided with the right advanced security analytics solutions in place.

BORDERLESS BREACH FLASHCARD	
An Inside Job	
CATEGORY	Insider, former employee exfiltrates key patient information.
WHO	**The target:** Sutter Health, California, regional healthcare provider.
WHAT	A former employee gains access to sensitive billing information on 2,582 patients and emails it to his private account. Patients' social security and driver license information were compromised.
WHEN	2013
WHERE	Northern California.
WHY	Potential economic gain.
HOW	After two serious security breaches, a third breach occurred. The pattern began with a high-profile breach two years earlier, with the data for over four million patients stolen from a lost laptop. A multi-billion dollar class action lawsuit resulted. Later, an unrelated police arrest revealed a cache of stolen patient data, forcing Sutter Health to notify 4,500 patients of a possible compromise. Finally, due to reports of a former employee's alleged illegal activities, Sutter Health's IT team discovered the employee had sent sensitive billing information to his private email. The individual had originally worked in Sutter Physician Services, with billing for Sutter Health's physician medical foundations. Multiple instances of patient data compromise were confirmed.
HOW BAD?	Sutter Health offered free credit monitoring services to all patients impacted. The actual monetary damage in this case is comparatively, low due to the minimal volume. The brand damage, however, is inestimable. Sutter Health already had a reputation for faulty security. Customer trust erodes as a result. With Accenture forecasting cyber-attacks will cost hospitals over $305 billion in the next five years, where one in 13 patients will have data compromised by a hack, Sutter Health must take notice. Operating 24 hospitals, 27 ambulatory care facilities, home healthcare and hospice services in Northern California, with a network of over 5,000 physicians, Sutter Health must consider itself a primary target of enterprising hackers and future attacks.
HOW COULD IT BE AVOIDED?	First with C-level awareness, as a government mandate on standardized electronic records thrust healthcare into the digital age, leaving security strategies behind other businesses'. With a UEBA solution in place, the emailing of sensitive billing records to a private email address would have likely triggered an immediate alert, followed by remedial action.

3

Insider Threats, Account Compromise and Data Exfiltration

The enduring challenge of the insider threat

Is steady incremental improvement of security systems a standard operating procedure for organizations?

In 2008, the Carnegie Mellon University (CMU) Software Engineering Institute CERT (Community Emergency Response Team) Program, along with the U.S. Secret Service, analyzed 150 insider cybercrimes across U.S. critical infrastructure sectors (*The 'Big Picture' of Insider IT Sabotage Across U.S. Critical Infrastructures*). Additional research by CERT involved more detailed group modeling and analysis of 30 cases from the 150 total cases of insider IT sabotage in the report. The researchers made a number of observations, one of which has an enduring criticality as it relates to Borderless Behavior Analytics. That was that the lack of physical and electronic access controls facilitated these attacks. More concerning, 93% of the malicious insiders in the cases studied exploited inadequate access controls. Of these, 75% of these insiders created or used access paths unknown to management to set up their attack and conceal their identity or actions.

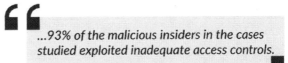

...93% of the malicious insiders in the cases studied exploited inadequate access controls.

In 2012, the CMU CERT program published its fourth edition of the *Common Sense Guide to Mitigating Insider Threats*, outlining nineteen best practices, all of which are aligned with mature security frameworks. With this body of well-established institutional understanding and insight in place from CMU CERT, as well as equivalently important findings from a host of other industry and academic experts providing additional security wisdom, one would hope the security communities in enterprises today had taken notice of the original risks noted above and adopted appropriate incremental measures to address them. Hope, however, is never a plan for success.

One industry observation puts that concern into perspective. Craig Cooper is Gurucul's COO, and former financial industry information security officer. He observed that currently, most Fortune 500 companies have more privileged access risks outside their IAM (identity and access management) and PAM (privileged access management) vaults, than inside. That means more than half of the most prized access entitlements hackers seek to compromise are not even on these organizations' radar screens for access management.

> *...more than half of the most prized access entitlements hackers seek to compromise are not even on these organizations' radar screens for access management.*

That's an unmanaged access risk plane of sobering proportions.

Why has this concerning trend been allowed to occur? Tight budgets and prioritization of security and IT initiatives, limited to what was perceived to be the most urgent and pressing issues, accounts for some of it. In addition, access management and security in the evolving environments of today has not kept pace with the growing challenges. A driver for security since 2003 has been compliance, which resulted in rubber-stamping and user account cloning. This, in turn, created excess access and access outliers. Over time, security leaders at many organizations came to face entitlement levels which often went into millions. Yet managing this mass of data, and to understand it at a detailed level, was futile for humans. Only recently, in 2015, have industry analysts identified the urgent need to see what the risks are at the entitlement level. However, due to the massive amount of entitlements involved, it was not possible without the advent of machine learning. Now, with the right identity analytics solution, it had become possible to clean up these excess and outlier entitlements, where too much access had been given out, resulting in high risk. Effective discovery of access as a risk plane was finally available. Widespread adoption of this solution capability, however, is in the early adopter phase.

Compounding the challenge CISOs face, is the rapid growth of the access risk plane by virtue of cloud adoptions, with BYOD (bring your own device), IoT (the Internet of things)and global access to systems, and the originally employed security strategies designed for traditional on-premises use. Moreover, that term 'traditional' represents a potential CISO mindset gap for today's emerging requirements in assuring comprehensive and holistic security assurance.

As Gary Eppinger observed in the first chapter of this book, it was not an easy transition away from his old school security perspectives and strategies. These were originally built on solid thinking at the time, based on well-established principles. Traditional security tactics, like threat hunting using rules, patterns and signatures, still have a place in SOCs. However, that's the issue. It's only part of the solution, and over the long-term, an increasingly smaller part of the big picture. While using rules, patterns and signatures is an important resource for lowering the signal to noise ratio for known threats, this approach in no way addresses the unknown unknowns. For forward-looking security leaders, that's the elephant in the room.

Detection continues to be popular, but it is limited to what humans know. Today, most organizations only detect what they know about with signatures, patterns and rules. They have hit a wall for prevention. After decades of declarative defenses, the continuously growing volume of big data underscores and defines the requirements for the new frontier of security. Dwell time (the time between compromise and breach detection) remains near 206 days, with some breaches only being discovered when the attackers themselves declare it. The recently revealed 2014 breach at Yahoo with over 500 million accounts compromised — some experts say, the largest in history — is a case in point.

How do you detect what you do not know? Where do you start? How do you ensure you cover all the bases? Limited skilled resources, budgets and time for detection are a constant challenge for security leaders. Those who understand the problem know that just throwing more humans at the security problem will not solve it. Humans are not the solution, because the scale and complexity of the unknowns is far beyond human capability. A force multiplier of these efforts is required. It must facilitate the ability to ingest the big data, to process it accurately, to minimize access risks and detect unknown threats across all environments in an organization's infrastructure. That's where machine learning provides an optimal and cost effective answer to the challenges of insider threats, account compromise and data exfiltration.

Machine learning, with context of big data for UEBA and IdA, finds the unknowns on the identity access risk and threat plane. This puts security teams back in control of protecting their environments with confidence.

> *....the scale and complexity of the unknowns is far beyond human capability. A force multiplier of these efforts is required.*

While some traditional security leaders maintain the status quo, others have forged on into the new frontier of the hybrid environment to discover the broad range of requirements and challenges facing them. Our expert contributor Joe Sullivan, CSO at large, and past CSO of Uber and Facebook, with a vast range of first-hand experience in information security, will share his experience with the growing evolution of behavior analytics, machine learning and big data. He will also highlight the benefits they deliver to Borderless Behavior Analytics.

BORDERLESS EXPERT INSIGHTS

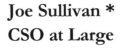

Joe Sullivan *
CSO at Large

Currently a CSO at Large, Joe Sullivan was the Chief Security Officer at Uber where he was responsible for all aspects of safety and security—rider and driver safety, data security, physical security, and investigations. Before joining Uber in early 2015, Sullivan was the CSO at Facebook where he led their information security, product security, investigations, and law enforcement relationship teams for 6 years. Prior to joining Facebook, Sullivan spent 6 years working in a number of security and legal roles at eBay and PayPal, culminating in managing PayPal's North America legal team (and for a time serving as Acting General Counsel of PayPal). Before entering the private sector, Sullivan spent 8 years with the United States Department of Justice. As a prosecutor in the U.S. Attorney's Office for the Northern District of California, he was a founding member of a unit dedicated to full time investigation and prosecution of technology-related crimes, including the technical aspects of the 9/11 investigation. Sullivan was appointed by President Obama in 2016 to serve as a commissioner on the Presidential Commission on Enhancing National Cybersecurity. Sullivan has also volunteered his time with a number of organizations that promote internet safety and security, including the National Cyber Security Alliance, the Action Alliance for Suicide Prevention, and the Bay Area CSO Council. He serves on the External Advisory Committee for the Center for Long-Term Cybersecurity at the University of California at Berkeley. He has also served on the advisory boards of a number of startups, including AirBnB, BlueCava, Gurucul, and RiskIQ.

A member of Gurucul's Executive Advisory Board, Sullivan has provided his insights and stewardship for Gurucul's growth and evolution in developing next generation solutions in the field of UEBA and IdA security disciplines. He shares insights from his broad experience with the challenges and solutions of UEBA and IdA for hybrid cloud security.

Overview

In this segment, Sullivan begins with comparing the CIO and CISO's perspectives, which segues into his insights on the symptoms of today's environments struggling with unknown threats. His discussion observes the need for new approaches to address gaps in traditional non-identity based security solutions. He then explores cloud and mobility's impact on visibility and the security challenges in hybrid network

---

* The views and opinions expressed by Joe Sullivan in this book are his own, and do not necessarily reflect those of any of his previous employers.

environments. This investigation brings a deeper look at the challenge of effectively monitoring and analyzing security data in global organizations in the midst of big data and cloud scalability. Sullivan then cites the challenges with detecting account compromise and misuse, along with observing the patterns of insider threats, privilege misuse and data exfiltration. This brings into focus the critical challenge of confronting the unknown unknowns while addressing attackers' constant innovation. While coping with budgets and limited resources and the impact on CISOs' goals and priorities in security solution adoptions, Sullivan observes the logistical implementation priorities for prospective predictive security analytics customers. He then shares his insights on CIO and CISO preference trends within machine learning solution adoption. He concludes with his forecast of security solution requirements for the next two to five years.

Comparing the CIO and CISO perspectives

The head of security's mission is to manage and reduce risk for the company. The CIO's goal is to enable the business to move fast through technology to mobilize and empower their workforce and optimize their productivity. That's why they're both moving in the direction of the varied cloud solutions. Yet they don't want to create friction for employees in the way that traditional identity management frameworks work. Their approach to security strives to produce as little friction as possible for good employees doing good work. This ideal strikes to the heart of a CIO's sense of balance. They want to be able to satisfy the risk management folks, while optimizing the efficiency and effectiveness for their employees. Any solution that allows employees to go fast is a good solution in their eyes. The CISO, however, needs to keep an eye on the threat factors, wherever they may lie.

CIOs drive solutions into a borderless world. A CISO's focus remains to strive to facilitate the new cloud-driven advantages, while assuring the protections and coverage, and at the same time, to enable optimal productivity of the workforce. Some CISOs will be left behind if they don't embrace solutions like this, since the CIO is already moving to a borderless world and building an approach that will allow all employees to have access to all the data they need. The CISO must align with the program and implement solutions that manage risk in this new environment.

Maintaining an optimal balance is key. The challenge between CIO and CISO priorities can be tricky, of course, especially for the CISO, because they must support the speed and productivity of the programs. However, if there is any breach in the meantime, or the security solution is not in step with where the solutions are going, then it's a problem for the CISO. That's the nature of being a CISO.

Symptoms in today's environments struggling with unknown threats

Most of the existing security defenses have been built for a model of an enterprise technology architecture that no longer exists. If you look at a castle, you can build a moat around it. This has been the basic approach enterprises have taken to securing their technology stack by establishing a moat-like perimeter or layer between the company and the internet.

> *Most of the existing security defenses have been built for a model of an enterprise technology architecture that no longer exists.*

Traditional defense models no longer adequate. Originally, and at the highest level, that model was generally effective if you could work around that barrier and focus your defenses on the perimeter. That's why enterprises have network security, VPNs, and tools that monitor all the identities and traffic that comes from the outside world, to control who is allowed inside the corporate network. The fundamental problem is that modern companies no longer have that architecture.

Business units adopt cloud solutions outside IT's purview. In varying degrees, all enterprises now have a hybrid or effectively borderless architecture. That's the trend in modern companies. The corporate IT department is being left behind as a result. It used to be that security teams would ride on the coattails of the IT team, where the corporate IT's team was responsible for all of an organization's technology. Today, more frequently, the corporate IT team doesn't even know about what technology is being used, as other business units adopt cloud technologies, circumventing their IT department.

New normal: Decentralization and fragmentation of environments. In every context that used to be managed internally — whether it was email, customer relationship management, data storage, computation, customer support, product development — today it's being done in a much more fragmented way, decentralized and outside the original network set of contexts. As a result, you can no longer build a moat, or set up the kind of monitoring around your perimeter in the traditional sense. An unintended consequence of this is that a new set of risks have manifested themselves. This new norm is where security defenses must now be evaluated.

> *....you can no longer build a moat, or set up the kind of monitoring around your perimeter in the traditional sense... a new set of risks have manifested themselves.*

The need for new approaches to address gaps in traditional non-identity-based security solutions

For my colleagues and me, the growing awareness of the borderless side of network security began around 2012. Three years before that we also recognized the need to have an identity-based anomaly detection engine solution. This approach involves seeing how our employees worked and viewing the data they were accessing.

Responsible control of employee access to customer data. At one of my prior companies, our business model involved enabling people with their own choices in how to store and share their information online. That meant a good percentage of our employees needed access to some of this information at certain times to do their job to support the customers. It didn't mean every employee in the company needed access all the time. We also had to articulate to regulators how we oversaw responsible employee access to user access data.

Controlling access for legitimate use only. Everyone in our security group realized a traditional role-based approach to access control would be insufficient. While we recognized some employees would always need to have access to celebrities' accounts to help them manage their pages, that didn't mean the employees should feel entitled to be

> *Everyone in our security group realized a traditional role-based approach to access control would be insufficient.*

voyeuristic in exploring those celebrities' accounts. Therefore, we needed to build a solution to facilitate our monitoring and understanding employees who were authorized to look at these accounts. We also needed to manage access, and control it if a particular instance of access was not for a legitimate purpose.

Recognizing future trends of big data requirements. It was in this context where I began to appreciate that organizations needed more than just the traditional role-based access. Access needed to be tied to specific legitimate uses. We knew of no solution that addressed this challenge at the time. That's when I began working in this area of security. At a prior company, before Uber, we began building a custom solution to support this requirement. And as I researched it more deeply — seeing that every company was storing increasingly more data — I came to realize that the future was in big data. That was when I first spoke with Gurucul. They seemed to be one of the only vendors out there at the time building something similar to

> *...as I researched it more deeply... I came to realize that the future was in big data.*

what we had tried to build on our own.

Aligning customer challenges with behavior analytics solutions. Gurucul was already dealing with customer challenges similar to ours. In one case, they had a customer in a consumer-based environment who wanted to cross-correlate what customer support calls were coming in and what accounts the customer support representatives were opening. The issue of concern was that in opening a customer account, the support reps had access to everything. Since a call could come from anywhere in the country, the reps needed the ability to have global access to anyone's account to service the call. The fact that all those accounts could be looked at was considered a critical risk. Gurucul's customer wanted to cross-correlate what access was being initiated and ensure it was tied to specific customer support responsibilities. Another concern was that this enterprise also had celebrity customers. Gurucul's customer needed to ensure their people were looking at these and any other accounts only for legitimate reasons.

Machine learning use case models with wider applications. This concern and use case models for machine learning behavior analytics extends into other verticals as well, for example, with financial institutions and bank tellers. The leading banks have a majority of the entire population of the country covered. More often than not, most will have celebrity accounts accessible from any bank branch. Yet if an employee is looking at this information just for entertainment, or to misuse this data for malicious intent, then organizations must be able to recognize this quickly and have the monitor, alert and response capabilities in place to effectively stop this kind of behavior quickly.

Cloud and mobility's impact on visibility: Security challenges in hybrid network environments

Cloud and mobility's impact on visibility is profound. Companies are putting an increasing amount of sensitive applications and data in different cloud solutions. This use pattern will only grow and broaden going forward. The challenge of reliable visibility within the hybrid cloud is complex and a top concern of many CISOs.

The need to address the complexities of hybrid environments. In response to cloud and mobility's impact on visibility, organizations must have an identity management framework and anomaly detection system that incorporates all the attributes found in a traditional old network security. It requires the objective for the solution to work just as well, if not better, than those original systems. However, that's where many of the traditional security tools have fallen short. They're just not flexible enough to be able to expand into that more complex hybrid environment.

Account provisioning limitations. Part of the visibility challenge includes provisioning, deep provisioning, as well as activating and deactivating all those accounts. The timing of these procedures is especially critical with the recognition of new employment models in play, as organizations adjust to terms and the conditions of the emerging 'gig economy'. People may now work with a company as contractors or partners, not for years, but instead for weeks or months.

Cloud accounts outside of IT's control or responsibility. Managing the timely and precise activation and deactivation of those accounts is critical and challenging. Moreover, when an employee is terminated, how do organizations ensure the termination successfully includes severance of their access to a myriad of different cloud environments that a company is trying to manage? This wide array of cloud solutions outside of IT's responsibility and involvement complicates the challenge of keeping on top of these accounts and maintaining comprehensive and reliable visibility. Complicating this challenge, a number of cloud environments do not always provide the visibility required. Application program interface (API) standards for the visibility required with cloud applications are still evolving. Many cloud applications don't have an API, so the data needed for visibility is simply not always available, leaving customers lacking the data they need for machine learning models in identity analytics. As a result, many companies struggle with the situation of keeping their cloud solutions managed effectively.

New requirements for security defenses in the hybrid environment

Instead of tracking a network perimeter, SOCs must now track the individual, and build a program tied to the multiple components, the employees, business partners, and the applications. The challenge is that the applications are fragmented all over the place, and employees are fragmented in dispersed locations as well. As a result, security teams need to develop tools aligned with securing those key elements in an insecure world.

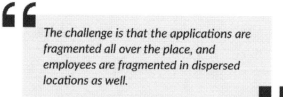

> The challenge is that the applications are fragmented all over the place, and employees are fragmented in dispersed locations as well.

Solutions required to track both employees and applications. An important component of this requirement is fulfilled with a mature UEBA solution that also incorporates comprehensive identity analytics (IdA) across application access and activity for all employees. Both UEBA and IdA employ fuzzy logic as a critical characteristic of machine learning. For IdA, this provides a risk-based approach for identity access management, reducing excess access and access outliers. For UEBA, the objective is to detect compromised identity and suspect activity from behavior anomalies of normal baselines and peering which would remain unknown without this type of security monitoring.

The challenge of effectively monitoring and analyzing security data in global organizations

With security today, it's about anomaly detection and determining if a person should be allowed to cross the bridge and into a particular environment, at a certain time, for a specific purpose. Companies can't hire enough security engineers and analysts to keep an eye on a hundred thousand employees, using twenty thousand

> Companies can't hire enough security engineers... to keep an eye on a hundred thousand employees, using twenty thousand applications, scattered across an array of different public and private clouds.

applications, scattered across an array of different public and private clouds. The bandwidth requirements are staggering. Instead, enterprises must rely on technology, have a good faith foundation of identity, and maintain good tracking of the applications. They require a system that reviews and brings state-of-the-art identity management into this world.

Three-part security program. Identity management systems that service the old networked environments are role-based and blunt. They don't allow for today's flexible workforce where employees are frequently shifting roles and responsibilities. To address this challenge, a three-part security program is required. One part is to secure the applications. The second is to lock down identity. The third involves looking at how the authorized identities are using the

> Identity management systems that service the old networked environments are role-based and blunt. They don't allow for today's flexible workforce where employees are frequently shifting roles and responsibilities.

applications, or behavior analytics.

Growing multi-tiered data expansion and proliferation. The other reality of today's applications is that much more sensitive data is in them. It's being stored in many more places, and accessed by many more employees, for an increasing amount of legitimate reasons. Where one technology expert might say, "Every company is becoming a software company," it now appears the statement "Every company is becoming a data company" represents the next generation's reality. Every company now has sensitive data which may include intellectual property. It also might be where companies are storing more of their customer data and recognizing that half of their employee population may need access to some of this data.

New realities in big data require new strategies in security. As every company becomes a data company, trying to get insights about their customer, using artificial intelligence to perform customer support, and big data machine learning to figure out which customer should get what — there must be different expectations around data storage and security. Traditional identity management systems don't scale in these new environments. In fact, in many cases they suffer from a severe discovery gap in privileged access risks at the entitlement level within applications. This represents a serious and growing access risk plane. To manage the vast scope of analysis required, a new approach must be adopted, one that integrates identity management, with identity analytics from machine learning models analyzing both access and activity data.

Exponential data generation and cloud scalability: Challenges with detecting account compromise and misuse

To enhance protection and response, and to confront the unavoidable rising challenges in today's environments, security teams must adopt advanced machine learning analytics solutions, drawing from the value of big data. Within this funnel, a proven behavior anomaly detection engine can monitor users' behavior and evaluate what unknown risks might exist. To manage identity risk and access entitlements beyond current IAM and PAM capabilities, a next-generation identity analytics solution would reduce access risk. Collectively, they form a funnel of integrated analytics providing risk scoring at each layer that ensure security assurance in today's environments. In the graphic below, data flows down the left side, while analytics and risk scoring flow up on the right side.

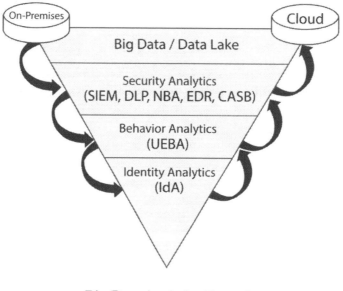

Big Data Analytics Funnel
Figure 3.1

Surfacing anomalous behavior. A scenario of when access and threat analytics would be applied is with a product development team that might have a hundred employees, and all of them work consistently with a particular data set for specific purposes. Then, for some reason, one employee starts interacting with an entirely different set of data. That's the kind of behavior anomaly security teams must surface and then ensure an analyst individually reviews it or compares it to what the employee's project work has been. Another example might be a customer service representative responsible for a particular region who begins interacting with data on customers outside their regional domain. Considering the vast volume of

> *...the more of this qualified anomaly identification that can be performed with technology, and the less the security analysts have to surface for manual review, the better.*

data a security team must contend with, the more of this qualified anomaly identification that can be performed with technology, and the less security analysts have to surface for manual review, the better. This frees up security analysts' time to deal with other priority issues.

Leveraging specialized solutions and qualified expertise. When security teams can leverage the computing power of machine learning with scalability of today's hybrid and cloud solutions, for the increasing amount of constantly expanding big data, they are better able to manage the needles in the haystack. It's no longer realistic for a security leader to just plan for his team to log all the data and mandate his data science team to build a specialized kind of capability, homegrown within the environment. Instead, an experienced CISO will likely rely on outside companies, preferably best-of-breed, with proven expertise in data science and behavior analytics, to build that system for them. These solution partners who provide these security analytics tools should also have acquired a comprehensive understanding of the range of threats and risks across industries.

Quality and breadth of data assures monitoring value. In the world of anomaly detection, it is critical to have incredibly large data sets incorporated into this kind of machine learning. This facilitates predicting and identifying legitimate versus anomalous behavior. Within this data framework, having a rich set of true positives to build out an effective data science approach is required, which a mature UEBA solution provides. In addition, security teams can add and incorporate their organization's own historical data. With this data, individual baselines of all users' past behavior are created and correlated with their team's baseline behavior. This raises the level and quality of good data which is crucial for the information to be effective and actionable. It further empowers a SOC team's ability to detect nefarious anomalies. This quantity and quality of the data is essential to reduce the amount of time it takes to pinpoint what's going on in the environment.

Rich context lowers false positives. The biggest challenge in setting up a security program with the objective of either detecting a compromised insider account, or malicious insider, is that you must go deep into the data to examine the behavior. Too many of the existing systems utilize a security approach that delivers a high volume of false positives. No security leader wants to have a situation where his team takes an employee in a room and starts asking pointed questions without being

> *...you must go deep into the data to examine the behavior. Too many of the existing systems utilize a security approach that delivers a high volume of false positives.*

completely sure of the issue. What's needed, and what a mature UEBA solution provides, is context. Even when there's an alert on something an employee has never done before — or that no one on their team has ever done before — you have a lot of context provided. The result is that an analyst will possess that deeper understanding which provides critically defining additional feedback and insight.

Patterns of insider threats and privilege misuse

When employing an identity-based solution, you're working on detecting two different primary threats. One is where the insider's identity has been compromised. The other involves the insider who has a malicious intent. Yet from most security leaders' perspectives, that almost doesn't matter. Companies traditionally have a high trust of their inside employees. However, when they have worked at detecting a malicious insider, the processes that were implemented and proved the most valuable at detecting them also revealed compromised accounts as well. These attackers aren't just coming through a firewall to find all their target data. They're entering under the guise of a trusted insider.

Double benefit of three-sided security strategy. The three-sided security program referenced earlier — which focuses on strong identity, strong application security, and the identity-based solution that monitors who's using what — is the foundation of this detection capability. Most modern attacks involve some kind of privilege escalation. When attackers gain entry to an enterprise, it involves compromising the identity of an employee and then using their permissions to gain access. This is what so many modern attacks involve: a bad guy using a good person's identity, versus a good person turning into a bad person. Yet they're basically doing the exact same things. This approach to

> *Most modern attacks involve some kind of privilege escalation... This is what so many modern attacks involve, a bad guy using a good person's identity...*

security has a double benefit, when even the outsider threats end up being detected first as an insider threat, where someone who is on the inside is there because valid credentials were being stolen and misused by an outsider.

The criticality of focusing on insider threats. Any good security program must care about both threats. Focusing on insider threats is important because it's been documented extensively that people leave companies and try to take company intellectual property with them. People are bribed, have pressure put on their families, or realize they can monetize internal data or intellectual property. Employees also get disgruntled and want to hurt the company because they feel the company hasn't treated them well. There are many different reasons why someone originally hired as a good employee could ultimately become a risk to the company. It's important to think about threats from both standpoints.

A compromise UEBA could have caught. One perspective related to this type of breach — noted from the *Verizon 2016 Data Breach Digest* — is the story about an employee who actually outsourced his own job to Asia. He would go to the office, give his token to the engineer in Asia, who would then log in using the employee's credential. That person would then do the employee's job. The employee paid the engineer in Asia out of his pocket, at a much cheaper rate, and was getting great yearly performance reviews. This activity went undetected for years before discovery. So in this case the behavior was not intended to steal anything, but the employee decisively compromised the integrity of the company's security solutions, which were set up to protect the data. If a user behavior analytics solution had been in place, it would have detected this compromise much earlier than any of the traditional security solutions that failed for years.

An attacker's first target once inside the environment. Another pattern security experts typically see is when a real outsider gets into the network using a privilege escalation approach cloaked as legitimate insider activity. If an organization allowed a red team to assess and challenge their network's security plan, the team would quickly inform them that one of the first things attackers do when they get inside a company's environment is to search for insiders' usernames and passwords. They also look at org charts and information which specifically tells them who inside the company has the best credentials they should try to leverage for the next step in their attack.

> *...one of the first things attackers do when they get inside a company's environment is to search for insiders' user names and passwords.*

Data exfiltration in hybrid environments versus traditional environments

In the traditional environment, you would have a network TiVo solution (network flight recorder) that allowed security teams to look at all the data passing out of the network. They could tell what data was leaving or what data someone was trying to take out. That network pipe no longer exists. The network perimeter security solutions — whether it was DLP, or advanced firewalls, NetWitness, network TiVo — don't help now with hybrid environments. They can't provide all those logs in a viewable way or in real-time. These outdated security approaches cannot cope with the emerging challenges networks face today.

A new perspective and strategy is required. Beyond this old framework of options and approaches, CISO's must look at new and adjusted solutions to deal with the new kinds of threat planes found in hybrid environments. These adjusted solutions must be much more flexible and robust to address the challenge. A growing majority of security experts feels that the answer lies in a mature predictive security analytics solution with big data.

Confronting the unknown unknowns: Addressing attackers constant innovation

Security teams must leverage other attacker's true positives to help create a probable threat terrain. For example, how do signature-based antiviruses (AV) work? They count on having seen a specific malware attack before. When deploying basic antivirus, it looks for signatures which are a known bad. To a certain extent, every company is on a quest to identify all the known bad patterns or signatures of known attacks. More advanced AV solutions may also rely on heuristic analysis of commands and execution.

Known bad attack signature repositories. The problem is most companies, both large and small, don't have the ability to aggregate all the known bad patterns or signatures of specific malware. That's where collaborating with a qualified and best-of-breed anti-malware solution vendor comes in, along with their repository of known bad signatures, which are constantly being updated. Organizations should choose a solution product that has ingested a large volume of known bads from a wide range of contexts so when that signature of a bad appears in their environment it can be keyed on effectively.

Machine learning keys off known bad patterns. Where UEBA technology has improved, is in defining the specifics of what to alert on as risk-scored anomalous behavior. In the traditional antiviral context, it entailed watching for code, or a known signature, executing in a particular way. The technology is now moving toward identity-based anomaly detection, which is not examining code executing in any particular way, but instead looking at human behavior executing in an anomalous way from known baselines and peer groups. For this aspect in the big data machine learning approach to work there must be patterns of known normal and bad behavior to key off of, learn from, build on, and model against.

Exact attack signatures not required. The good thing in this case is you don't actually have to see the exact attack signature with UEBA. With the traditional antivirus software, the known signature, or precise code, has to operate in a specifically exact profile for it to be flagged. With UEBA and big data machine learning, however, you no longer need that concrete a set of specifics. What is needed is a significant volume of true

> **With UEBA and big data machine learning... you no longer need that concrete a set of specifics.**

positives, big data context, to build on and to learn from. Also, if bad behavior exists when creating a baseline, the use of multiple peer groups will identify the anomalous behavior for the user or entity. This is in contrast to a common misconception about behavior analytics.

Attacker innovation is perpetual. Always keep in mind that innovation is taking place on both sides, on the solution side, as well as with the people trying to get into your environment and breach your data. Originally, phishing emails were so common and typically easy to recognize because their messages were poorly crafted and cast such a broad net. That's changing. Recently emails have become more personalized, where the email might explain that they found the phishing target on a specific industry website which was familiar to the recipient. That familiarity encourages the impression the email is legitimate. These attackers have found ways to automate this whole process, finding the first non-advertised search result to come up when a phishing target name is put in a search engine. That detail adds to the credibility of the email. If it compels the recipient to click the link, their job is done. Mission accomplished. This is all part of the innovation bad actors are performing, and for which security teams must remain constantly on alert. Meanwhile, social engineering continues to get more sophisticated.

Budgets and limited resources: The impact on CISOs' goals and priorities in security solution adoptions

There's currently a talent drought in security. Qualified security analysts are in short supply. According to Forbes.com, as of September 2016, there were over 209,000 unfilled cybersecurity openings in the U.S., and over one million worldwide. Security engineers are paid at a premium, compared to traditional software engineers, and numerous published articles document this fact. Some companies in Silicon Valley pay security engineers up to 20% more than a typical engineer. Indeed, all engineers who meet a high quality bar are hard to find, and the law of supply and demand is in effect.

Bandwidth and headcount cannot handle the challenge. No company can hire and staff up with the number of security engineers they actually want and need to cover the volume of deep

> **Organizations must have alternatives for their comprehensive security coverage through technology.**

investigation required. The digital exhaust of big data is overwhelming. Small companies don't have a shot of getting the highest quality security engineers and their prime skill sets, so the challenge is widespread. Organizations must have alternatives for their comprehensive security coverage through technology.

Logistical priorities for prospective UEBA customers

It's critical for any good UEBA solution to be easy to get up and running. The typical security team lacks the time, energy and technical resources to devote to a bespoke deployment of a new security solution. Therefore the more plug and play the new technology solution is, the better it will be for the adopting company. Having qualified resources from the solution provider to assist with deploying the solution in the customer's security portfolio is critical. Ease of implementation, along with a high degree of accuracy for detection of anomalies, are key components of success.

> *"Ease of implementation, along with a high degree of accuracy... are key components of success."*

Realities of solution requirements tied to custom environments. While having as much plug and play capability as possible, CISOs should also maintain a realistic perspective on this point. Traditionally many customer environments are multilayered and have evolved over time in distinct ways, often homegrown and customized, creating problematic issues, where logging and event data are often incomplete. Also, these environments may have a unique set of variables and technologies, all of which represent complex sets of requirements to interface effectively. While plug and play may appear to be advantageous due to its simplicity, and ease of use, if the logging data produced is inadequate, the solution cannot provide real value in the long run.

The advantage of out-of-the-box UEBA plug-ins for established systems. A key delivery value for experienced and well-established UEBA solution providers is to offer packaged data connectors for the more common and established systems and data sources. This speeds the integration cycle, allowing the UEBA solution vendor to focus on the system components requiring customized data ingestion or API integration. The same holds true for new SaaS applications and silos of access and activity data to provide API access to behavior analytics solutions.

The importance of ease of use. Once the solution has been implemented, the ideal utility model is to deliver both robust capabilities and ease of use with accuracy. This precedent of utilization was established by much of the mobile-based technology which has demonstrated how a range of functions can be performed simply. If you have an application with less buttons or options, but just the important ones to perform the functions needed on a normal daily basis, then the user experience is enhanced and empowered and the security team's efficiency is heightened, delivering better productivity.

CIO and CISO preference trends for machine learning solution adoption

An important perspective to maintain is to recognize the effectiveness of having a large team of analysts performing at the same level. On top of that, there is value in understanding that organizations can use this technology to facilitate their security team's work more efficiently and consistently, raising their productivity and freeing them for more impactful and business-critical work. For example, when you have twenty analysts looking at cases, each person only sees what they alone see; they don't see what the other nineteen analysts see. But if you have a technology that sees what all twenty analysts would have seen, and it's ingesting data from many more different angles and perspectives, then everyone on the team is working at a much higher level of performance. The silos have disappeared. It also frees the security engineers up to perform more intelligent work required to address the evolution of growing threats in the environment. As a result, machine learning raises efficiencies in the organization.

> ....if you have a technology that sees what all twenty analysts would have seen, and it's ingesting data from many more different angles and perspectives, then everyone on the team is working at a much higher level of performance.

UEBA fulfills goals and objectives of the CISO. From a CISO's perspective of productivity goals, and security objectives, the result is to make the employees in the security group more effective with machine learning, where lower priority anomalies are filtered out, leaving only the highly critical cases which require more investigation. Productivity is increased and comprehensive security assurance is empowered. Effectiveness increases measurably on both sides of the equation. At the same time, UEBA can detect anomalies (and more quickly), that a team of analysts may miss entirely.

UEBA optimizing time and efficiency. Instead of looking at a UEBA solution as a method of reducing the staff, the more productive way to see this is that a security team's time is being utilized more effectively. Getting the most out of your analysts is key to a company's ROI on this valuable investment, achieving a great deal more with the same number of people. This is exactly what's needed to face the growing security challenges of expanding digital exhaust evolving in today's hybrid cloud environments.

Security solution requirements in the next two to five years

The CISO's domain will continue in the same direction is has over the last seven years and will eventually result in total fragmentation. Increasingly more employees will be accessing sensitive enterprise data and information from more and more fragmented devices, through fragmented paths. Everyone's going to be on mobile devices, accessing sensitive information over different kinds of network pipes, and it will all be in applications stored in hundreds of different places. That's the path we're on right now, and will continue to be on.

Levels of UEBA solution maturity. As any prospective organization considers adopting a UEBA-IdA solution to face these challenges, they must narrow down the field of qualified vendors as efficiently as possible and understand where a vendor sits within the hierarchy of UEBA-IdA maturity. Generally, UEBA-IdA solution offerings in today's market have three levels of maturity:

- *First generation UEBA* – Tools-based analytics, their functionality primarily focuses on entity link analysis across structured data with the objective of resolving and linking identities and entities. These solutions, however, are limited in capability and ill-suited to deal with the rising fragmentation and complexity in hybrid environments today.

- *Second generation UEBA* – Progressive data integration and early canned use case analytics are in this group. These offer automatically resolved identities and entities using proprietary fuzzy logic and data-matching techniques. The primary use cases offered by both first and second generation UEBA vendors address only forensics and the investigation of threats and risks which have occurred or are continuing. Extensive professional services are usually required to maintain these solutions. Their ability to evolve with hybrid environments is questionable.

- *State-of-the-art UEBA-IdA* – Advanced predictive security analytics for unknown threats and access risks are in this category. This generation of UEBA-IdA innovation delivers predictive packaged analytics which detect and identify insider and advanced threats, plus excess access, access outliers, and orphan or dormant accounts. UEBA solutions in this grouping have exceeded the capabilities of the widely adopted security user monitoring applications like SIEM and DLP and often incorporate identity analytics (IdA). These mature UEBA vendors continue to innovate in the development of their predictive security analytic models, ultimately targeting prescriptive capabilities. The applications will not be reliant on customer-driven analytics or inquiries of the data. These are the best suited solutions for today's evolving network environments.

CONCLUSIONS & TAKEAWAYS:
Facing the realities of the insider threat challenge

Recognizing that enterprises are storing increasingly more data, and that the future is in big data, Joe Sullivan has been at the forefront of evolving security strategies for years. The challenge a majority of CISOs face is that most of the existing security defenses were built for a model of an enterprise technology architecture that no longer exists. This new reality is, in large part, the byproduct of CIOs' well-intentioned goals to make their employees and environments more nimble, productive and efficient, with the adoption of a broad range of cloud solutions and other applications. Sullivan shares two critical observations about this new reality in security: 1) the time has passed for security strategies based mainly on rules and signatures and 2) identity management systems servicing the old networked environments are role-based and blunt, rigid and inflexible.

This hybrid cloud trend empowering organizations opens new gaps in security, creating a host of risks, and a serious threat plane that CISOs must mitigate. As well, some of these cloud solutions are completely outside IT's purview. Sensitive data is being stored globally, in many more places, and being accessed by increasing numbers of employees, partners and customers. Sobering new realities dictate that this is a borderless world, becoming increasingly decentralized and fragmented, where traditional defense models are no longer adequate.

With limited skilled resources, budgets and time for insider threat detection, allocating more humans to security issues will not solve the problem. Sullivan observes the need for new approaches to address the widening gaps in traditional solutions, to control access for legitimate use only. This challenge highlights cloud and mobility's impact on visibility and the growing security challenges in hybrid network environments. At the core of his security strategy is a three-pronged approach to manage employees and applications. One part consists of securing the applications. The second is to lock down identity. The third involves monitoring how the authorized identities use the applications. To meet this challenge, Sullivan recognized early on that risk-based behavior analytics and identity analytics, powered by machine learning, and drawing from big data, were cornerstone requirements to achieve success.

Embedded in this strategy is the capability to reliably identify anomalous behavior which facilitates an automated risk response to attackers' constant innovation. Quality and breadth of data assures monitoring value where rich context lowers false positives. This refined big data helps eliminate blind spots in the environment which represent serious unknowns and translates directly into serious access risks and exposing an unknown threat plane of unwieldy proportions. Building on true positives from big data, through self-learning and self-training machine learning models, behavior and identity analytics continue to evolve with their environments. This generation of predictive security analytics, ultimately ushering in prescriptive capabilities, is a fundamental requirement in security for a future holding accelerated fragmentation, decentralization and attacker innovation.

In the following *Borderless Breach Flashcard*, an employee insider breach threatened to compromise a company's entire proprietary high-tech product line. In the next chapter, the best practices for an effective insider threat program are explored, which also include real-world insights into effective organizational implementation of such a program, as well as, the correlations to Borderless Behavior Analytics.

BORDERLESS BREACH FLASHCARD *Nefarious Retirement Plan*	
CATEGORY	Insider employee exfiltrates key proprietary product data.
WHO	**The target:** DuPont, fourth largest chemical company in the world.
WHAT	A 27-year employee copied and removed tens of thousands of sensitive Cyrel® product information documents for a specialized flexographic printing plate technology with the plans to use them in his new consulting business, after his announced retirement from DuPont.
WHEN	2016
WHERE	New Jersey.
WHY	Economic gain.
HOW	Caught taking photos in a restricted area, and with Anchi Hou's initial refusal to hand over the iPhone he took the pictures with, the company conducted an investigation which included his personal computer. IT investigators discovered over 20,000 DuPont proprietary documents related to their unique Cyrel® flexographic printing technology. These had been originally downloaded from DuPont onto a USB device. This all occurred after the employee announced plans to retire from DuPont.
HOW BAD?	In direct violation of his DuPont confidential information compliance employee agreement, which he reaffirmed during this theft activity, Hou downloaded everything needed to create this proprietary product independently. This included documents outlining the production process for the Cyrel® product, formulations and specifications of chemicals used in the manufacture of the photo-polymeric printing plates, market and customer information, batch sheets, equipment designs, research documents and more. Hou was arrested after authorities learned he was planning to flee the country with his family.
HOW COULD IT BE AVOIDED?	In its legal filing, DuPont described their clearly defined security measures which included data access polices, on-site signage, electronic perimeter controls, security cameras, security guards, some monitoring for suspicious network activity, yet no holistic advanced security analytics solution was noted. With UEBA in place, this breach would have been detected much earlier, based on Hou's plan to retire and the robust nature of his sensitive downloads. It would have quickly raised alerts, especially with numerous documents taken from an electronic secure vault holding the company's most sensitive trade secrets, while all anomalous activities were outside his assigned role and duties.

Insider Threat Programs:
Lessons Learned and Best Practices

CMU-CERT Insider Threat Program Best Practices and their Correlations with Advanced Security Analytics

Insider threat programs are now considered a standard and critical feature of security strategy for a growing number of organizations. Verizon's 2017 *Data Breach Investigation Report* (DBIR) notes that within the insider and privileged misuse category, breach discovery timelines are in the months and years (33/77 and 30/77) as opposed to weeks (6/77). Citing different metrics in the same category not covered in the most recent version, Verizon's 2016 DBIR reported that privileged abuse incidents accounted for more than the other nine categories combined (154/133). The *2016 U.S. State of Cybercrime* report (the CERT [Computer Emergency Readiness Team] division of the CMU SEI [Carnegie Mellon University Software Engineering Institute] in collaboration with *CSO Magazine*) states that 30% of all respondents in their survey indicated insider attacks were more costly and damaging than outside attacks. In reality, every organization needs some

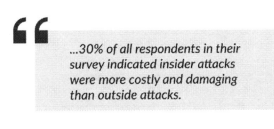

...30% of all respondents in their survey indicated insider attacks were more costly and damaging than outside attacks.

form of an insider threat program. Insider threats are not going away. Far from it. Insider threats manifest themselves in these ways:

- ***Malicious*** – This form of insider threat behavior manifests itself with a distinct intent to break established rules in the organization, violate trust, with a motive to impart harm or damage, or to seek the gain from resources (money, intellectual property, information, etc.) they have no legitimate right to access nor possess.

- **_Negligent_** – When employees feel inconvenienced by security policies or procedures, and use workarounds to bypass security measures seen as a perceived nuisance, their behavior is negligent. While maintaining a general understanding and awareness of their responsibilities, their impulse to choose convenience over prudent security behavior creates a tangible risk within the organization.

- **_Accidental_** – While the general awareness that a potential compromise is 'only one click away', virtually everyone who uses computers has, at one time or another, clicked on a link they should not have. In some cases that click leads to severe consequences. In others, misguided actions can also result in accidental compromise of an organization's sensitive information, for example, by entering an incorrect email address on something being sent out of an organization.

From an organization's perspective, what's at stake from insider threats? Intellectual property (IP) theft, IT sabotage, fraud, and espionage, are prominent objectives of malicious inside attackers or external adversaries leveraging the credentials of the insiders themselves. Damages can extend beyond financial losses to negatively impact an organization's reputation or brand and erode trust in the organization. The significant risk of unintentional compromise, misuse and abuse by insiders themselves only adds to the magnitude of concern for security leaders. The very livelihood of the enterprise can be at stake. Organizations have been crippled and sustained irreparable damage by insider attacks. Without an insider threat program, the security gates for on-premises and cloud environments will always remain ajar.

While stopping insider threats completely is virtually impossible, the goal of an insider threat program is to significantly reduce an organization's exposure to the problem and prevent the most damaging insider attacks. Taking the right approach of planning, development, adoption and integration, are key elements for success for any insider threat program. While cybersecurity is the core focus of this book, a comprehensive insider threat program also consists of initiatives which fall outside of that perspective. Referencing them all at a high

> *Taking the right approach of planning, development, adoption and integration, are key elements for success for any insider threat program.*

level, however, for holistic context, is important to understand their often interrelated characteristics and components corresponding to a program of this nature. The groups within an organization that participate in an insider threat program are: human resources, legal, physical security, business data owners and information technology. Most from this list represent important sources of big data for advanced security analytics (ASA) machine learning models which provide critical context of insiders' activity.

The security industry utilizes an essential body of research as a well-established touchstone for developing insider threat programs, which is a CMU-CERT technical note. Entitled, *Common Sense Guide to Mitigating Insider Threats* (Fifth Edition, December 2016), it has delivered a wealth of wisdom on the topic and provides 20 best practices which have evolved over the years since its original inception in 2001. This initiative has been in close partnership with the Department of Defense, Department of Homeland Security and the U.S. Secret Service. Gurucul has also partnered with CMU for several years, thus it is with a certain pride that we share a distillation of the CMU-CERT insights here. As part of this editing process, we have taken CMU-CERT's invaluable work, and added an organizational framework — a clustering of the different best practices under operational headings — which does not exist in the current report. In addition, we provide an insight into which CMU-CERT best practices have a beneficial correlation with advanced security analytics (consisting of user and entity behavior analytics [UEBA], identity analytics [IdA], privileged access analytics [PAA] and cloud security analytics [CSA]). These will be indicated by an **ASA Note** following the related CMU-CERT best practice.

Our review here represents a high-level snapshot of the documented best practices. It does not replace the value of security experts making themselves more deeply familiar with the entire 175 page CMU-CERT resource. While all the 20 CMU-CERT best practices are summarized below, they do not appear in the exact same order as they do in the most recent report. As noted above, the presentation of the best practices is cataloged more based on a chronological and utilitarian functional flow of the best practices, along with their integration cycles into a host organization. Review of the 2013 version of the CMU-CERT report (with 19 of the 20 best practices) does not follow the same order as is found in the 2016 report. The most recent version of the report cites the evolution of the order of these best practices as being part of their editorial process and goal. Our contribution below, and the titling of the groupings, is one suggested direction to continue that process of evolution.

The groupings of the CMU-CERT insider threat program best practices are:

- Solution planning and development objectives
- Organizational program integration strategies
- Preventative security process policies
- Operational security monitoring objectives

Solution planning and development objectives

- ***Know and protect your critical assets*** – A first step in developing an insider threat program is to implement a systemic plan for tracking and prioritizing the assets (both physical and logical) within the environment. Then, conduct a risk assessment of the protection measures already established for these assets in the environment. Metrics should be in place for the value of each asset and the impact on the organization should it be compromised. Realistic strategies for confronting the challenges of asset identification, along with the importance of establishing a special priority to critical assets must be taken into account. (CMU-CERT ***Practice 1***).

  o **ASA Note:** Adoption of any mature advanced security analytics solution, driven by machine learning and extracting critical context from big data, would include a comprehensive inventorying, ingestion and integration of all data-supporting assets (both physical and logical) within an organization's environment. With that, full and holistic risk-based monitoring would be facilitated for all of these critical assets.

- ***Consider threats from insiders and business partners in enterprise-wide risk assessments*** – Protecting assets against threats from both inside and outside the enterprise must be ensured. This especially includes trusted business partners who may be given insider access to an organization's networks, systems, information, or physical environment. This also includes members of an organization being acquired by a larger enterprise. All members of the main organization should be aware of this concern for understanding risk as a combination of threat, vulnerability and mission impact. A balance of policies, aligned with each organization's requirements (based on size, business sector, etc.) should be adopted. Too many security restrictions can impede the organization's mission, while too few can permit security breaches. Both business processes and technical vulnerabilities (including the emergence of IoT (Internet of Things), mobile devices and BYOD) must be taken into account to ensure the confidentiality, integrity, and availability of the organization's critical information and resources. (CMU-CERT ***Practice 6***).

  > ASA strongly supports this continuous assessment and monitoring capability with its risk-based approach...

  o **ASA Note:** ASA strongly supports this continuous assessment and monitoring capability with its risk-based approach driven by mature machine learning algorithms drawing context from big data. This best practice also echoes the priorities of Gartner's CARTA (continuous adaptive risk and trust assessment) approach for the next-generation of cybersecurity. This involves a policy where ecosystem partners must be continually assessed at the ecosystem level for compatibility and optimal integration within the security array.

- ***Develop a formalized stepped plan for an insider threat program*** – The protective measures required for comprehensive asset protection must be identified. These include (but are not limited to): A formalized and defined program, with a designated insider threat team; Organization-wide participation; Oversight of program compliance and effectiveness; Confidential reporting mechanisms and procedures; Insider threat incident response plan; Communication of insider threat events; Proper alignment with employee rights and civil liberties; Data collection, analysis techniques and practices; Insider threat training and awareness; Prevention, detection and response infrastructure; Insider threat practices for trusted business partners; Insider threat integration with enterprise risk management. Insider threat programs can present a challenge to existing processes within an organization, and understanding probable issues with implementing these protective measures should be part of the process to avoid potential pitfalls. Once the challenges have been accounted for, a governance plan for the insider threat program should be established. (CMU-CERT ***Practice 2***).

  > *…the security analytics capabilities should be machine-learning-driven and draw context from big data for a risk-based approach, which ASA addresses.*

  o **ASA Note:** As mentioned above, the proper data collection and analysis techniques and practices must be assessed, as well as the existence of up-to-date prevention, detection and response infrastructure. If lacking, determining a proper solution choice to fulfill requirements for this aspect of the plan is in order. A POC (proof of concept) is the traditional component of solution adoption, where proper security data collection, analysis techniques, practices and results are vetted. With the state-of-the-art (SOTA) requirements of the EU GDPR (European Union General Data Protection Regulation) being enacted in May 2018, which applies to any organization touching personal data of an EU citizen, the security analytics capabilities should be machine-learning-driven and draw context from big data for a risk-based approach, which ASA addresses.

- ***Structure management and tasks to minimize insider stress and mistake*** – Fostering a work environment minimizing unnecessary stress promotes a workflow that reduces the probability of making mistakes during the course of an employee's workday. High-stress work settings, demanding increased productivity, sometimes requiring rushing tasks and performing multiple functions, increases the likelihood of error as employees perform their work responsibilities. Along with raising the probability of making mistakes in their responsibilities, the circumstances of being overworked can result in unintentional compromise of sensitive information. This can occur through such forms as a susceptibility to unintentional interaction in social engineering, overlooking key security controls, or as simple as communicating before thinking, resulting in inadvertently divulging information. Harried workplace conditions can also create a negative atmosphere in the workforce. Disgruntled workers, who might later become malicious insiders, can be the unintended result of short-sighted and ill-considered management policies. (CMU-CERT *Practice 8*).

- ***Define explicit security agreements for any cloud services, especially access restrictions and monitoring capabilities*** – Cloud services offer easy adoption and rapid provisioning of networks, servers, storage, application and services, delivering ubiquitous convenience, heightened flexibility and productivity, all at a lower cost. At the same time, however, a host of new security challenges for the organization, and opportunities for malicious insiders, arise. A variety of cloud administrator titles, with privileged access, have been identified as having the potential for rogue insider threats.

> *...each organization must be responsible for its own security with any cloud solution adoption and integration.*

Meanwhile, a recent Ponemon Institute study revealed that a majority of cloud service providers believe it is the customer's responsibility to secure the cloud, not theirs. (See *Figure 4.1* below.) As a result, from the early planning stages, before deployment into an organization's environment (whether private, community, public or hybrid cloud), security agreements with any cloud services provider, including clear roles and responsibilities, must be clearly defined. The customer's environment, at the threshold of new cloud adoption, might be on-premises only, or already have other clouds services integrated. All factors add complexity to the organization's security requirements and they must be taken into account accordingly. The same measures an organization employs to protect its data and infrastructure on-premises should extend seamlessly to the cloud service provider. Before adoption, organizations must conduct a thorough end-to-end risk assessment to ultimately ensure appropriate capabilities are in place to ensure the protection of confidentiality, integrity and availability of data at rest, in use, and in motion. As well, they must fully understand who has access to their data and infrastructure, along with what risk mitigation measures are in place. Comprehensive assessment auditing before deployment, and periodic status monitoring after adoption, are required to ensure the integrity and complex configurations of cloud security align with the organization's needs and requirements. A close study of the cloud provider's SLAs (service level agreements) and insurance should be conducted to determine the level of identified risks that are covered. The Cloud Security Alliance has recommended guidelines to review before adoption of a cloud service. The individual organization must assess and implement its own adoption and integration requirements into their security strategy before cloud deployment. This may require qualified expertise from outside the organization. (CMU-CERT *Practice 16*).

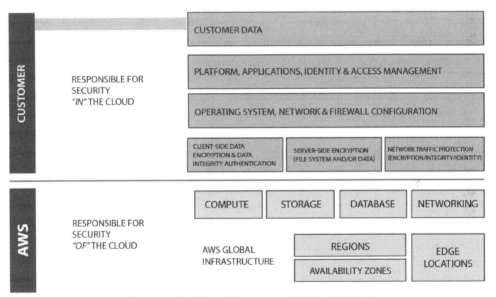

Amazon's Shared Responsibility Model
(Source: http://www.amazon.com)
Figure 4.1

o **ASA Note:** Deducing from the Ponemon Institute study noted above, each organization must be responsible for its own security with any cloud solution adoption and integration. While many cloud solutions offer security capabilities within their solution offerings, the issue of compatibility and configuration across an organization's entire environment, across all its silos of critical data, is the outstanding issue that must be addressed comprehensively. Here, CISOs and hybrid cloud architects should work in partnership to ensure seamless security of the hybrid environment. Choosing a holistic and vendor-agnostic advanced security analytics solution strengthens the prospect of comprehensive security across all cloud solutions and on-premises elements in an enterprise's environment.

Organizational program integration strategies

- ***Incorporate malicious and unintentional insider threat awareness into periodic security training for all employees*** – Maintaining an informed awareness of security policies and procedures within the organization facilitates the prevention of malicious and unintentional threat behavior. Included in this training is an understanding of the severe consequences of insider crimes. As well, it should be understood that no standard profile for a malicious insider exists. They may be low-wage earners to top executives, or range from individuals with minimal to advanced technical abilities, new hires to seasoned veterans, and

  > **"** With self-audit reports in hand, they would have the best contextual perspective of their identity's behavior in the environment... **"**

  their motivations vary. One unifying characteristic, however, is their behavior. Categories exist of telltale behavior for both prospective malicious insiders as well as unintentional erroneous actors. Training should also include understanding the risks of social engineering, of liabilities in business processes and technical vulnerabilities, as well as acceptable use policies, basic password protection and responsibilities for protecting the organization's assets. Participation in training should be organization-wide and involve periodic refreshing, to ensure security awareness remains current and properly focused and also to address the unique characteristics of different groups within an organization. The training should be tied to the organization's mission, values, and critical assets. Training may also include email alerts, newsletters, posters, etc. (CMU-CERT ***Practice 9***).

  - ○ **ASA Note:** As noted above, behavior is the key to identifying malicious activity. User and entity behavior analytics is built on this objective. If an organization has adopted an ASA solution with self-audit capabilities, this would be a component of the training. In it, all employees would understand their partnership in the security process and how the periodic self-audit reports (daily, weekly, monthly, or incident-based, etc.) represent their usage of applications and data in the environment with risk-based scoring. With self-audit reports in hand, they would have the best contextual perspective of their identity's behavior in the environment, and be able to quickly identify any anomalies that could indicate malicious activity.

- *Anticipate and manage negative issues in the work environment* – With clearly communicated workplace policies in place, failure to consistently and properly enforce them can create the perception of injustice and biased enforcement. This may result in a contentious atmosphere leading to disgruntlement within the organization. In addition, organizational changes (layoffs, broken expectation of promotions or raises, mergers, acquisitions, reorganizations, etc.) may also provoke a similar sense of animosity, all of which can lead to the motivation of malicious insiders. Maintaining an attentive perspective on any changes within the organization, or groups within the organization, that might foster individual or collective ill will, is critical. Enacting proactive plans for data protection in advance of impending layoffs is a sensible protective measure. (CMU-CERT *Practice 5*).

  o **ASA Note:** Anomalous Behavior and Watchlists, which includes departing users, should be a standard out-of-the-box UEBA use case offered by any qualified advanced security analytics vendor. Its application here would be an essential element of comprehensive data security for an insider threat program.

- *Develop a comprehensive employee termination procedure* – Severance of an employee requires a number of considered measures to take place to ensure the prospect of insider threat is managed in the most efficient manner possible. Well-defined termination procedures, combined with comprehensive account management practices, ensure former employees no longer have access to the organization's systems. Protection of their rights, as well as the organization's assets and resources, must be kept in proper perspective. At the most fundamental level, failing to delete or block all the accounts associated with a former employee is an invitation to disaster. Retrieval of all their company-issued technology, remote access two-factor authentication tokens, ID badges, payment and credit cards (and closure of associated accounts), etc., should be included in the process. Reaffirming all relevant nondisclosure and IP agreements should be conducted. Special attention should be given to organization resources which are not necessarily directly under IT's management or control, for example SaaS (software as a service) customer relationship management (CRM) services which reside on the cloud. Privileged users, or others, may also have shared account passwords which must be changed immediately. A review of the employee's online actions around the time of termination should be conducted, usually a minimum of 30 days, with 90 days recommended, if the data is available. The review should include email activity that might contain sensitive company data sent either to a personal email address or possibly to a competitor. Cloud activity should also be studied to ensure sensitive data has not been stored on the cloud without authorization. In addition, an organization-wide announcement of an employee's status may be recommended, to ensure all remaining members are informed so the departed colleague cannot access

> *Despite best efforts of closing access to all an employee's accounts, some may remain unknown to IT administrators.*

them under false pretenses. Different departments within an organization may have different procedural requirements for termination of an employee. (CMU-CERT *Practice 20*).

> o **ASA Note:** Despite best efforts of closing access to all an employee's accounts, some may remain unknown to IT administrators. This is especially true with cloud accounts that have been adopted as a shadow IT initiative. This represents a serious unknown threat and risk plane. A comprehensive capability to see all of an identity's accounts and entitlements across the entire environment is essential to ensure holistic security. The UEBA Anomalous Behavior and Watchlists use case should also include terminated users, who represent a class of high-risk users.

Preventative security process policies

- ***Close the doors to unauthorized data exfiltration*** – Understanding how data can be removed from an organization is a first step in establishing protective measures. Organizations must be capable of accounting for a wide range of devices that connect to its systems, as well as physical and wireless connections, which include removable media, internet exit points and services (as well as instant messaging, chat and cloud services), Bluetooth, printers, fax machines, copiers and scanners, along with the prospect of lost or stolen devices. Removable media such as USB drives represent a popular tool for exfiltration, and various security solutions and policies have been created to add controls to this risk. Email and data loss prevention (DLP) are recommended to filter data and enable appropriate actions at this exit point. DLP programs can also support USB exfiltration security requirements as well. Some software and/or product development groups within organizations establish physically separate settings, along with disconnected networks from the internet, to protect source code and related intellectual property. These groups also have highly restricted policies and processes for transferring any data and using any removable media. Procedures for employees using access to SSH, FTP, or SFTP must be closely monitored and strict policies should be in place regarding their use. Trusted business partner access via internet to an organization must also be addressed and demands heightened

> *...privileged access entitlements... (are) a threat plane of unknown and continually expanding proportions...*

scrutiny. Organizations' adoption of SaaS must also be accounted for, since their capability for accessing and storing sensitive data offsite is a fundamental capability. This represents a robust tool for malicious insiders, since cloud service providers commonly expect organizations must be accountable for the main share of security responsibility. (CMU-CERT **Practice 19**).

- o **ASA Note:** This best practice represents a fundamental set of capability requirements for any qualified ASA vendor. A wide collection of use cases within the UEBA, IdA, PAA and CSA disciplines address a range of data exfiltration scenarios for on-premises and in the hybrid cloud. Of critical importance is privileged access analytics, where today, experts cite the majority of organizations' IT groups are not even aware of 50% of the privileged access entitlements in their environments. This is a threat plane of unknown, shifting and continually expanding proportions, and represents serious risk for any organization with no comprehensive solution in place to address it. (See *Chapter 14* for a full overview of advanced security analytics use cases.)

- • ***Clearly document and consistently enforce policies and controls*** – Poorly communicated or enforced policies and/or controls can have a seriously adverse effect within an organization. The reasoning behind a policy's justification, implementation and enforcement must be clearly stated. Special policies for privileged access should also be created. All polices should undergo systematic and periodic review to ensure their goals and objectives remain in sync with the insider threat program's mandate, as well as the organization's requirements. Also, the need to identify any insider who maintains control of data representing a single point of failure must be managed effectively. (CMU-CERT **Practice 3**).

  - o **ASA Note:** If a self-audit program is incorporated within an advanced security analytics strategy, the clear policy documentation of why it is being employed would be addressed here. Including engaged involvement with every member an organization, how such a cooperative program is implemented is critical in laying the groundwork for its top-down and bottom-up organization-wide support and success.

- *Implement strict password and account management policies and practices* – Adherence to strict password policies is one of the most fundamental aspects of cybersecurity. Severe consequences for password violations and misuse must be clearly communicated to the entire organization. The tactics for compromising passwords are legion, stemming from technological innovations, social engineering, or low-tech approaches involving basic on-site physical theft of printed information. Password policies and procedures should ensure that all passwords are strong, and that regular and periodic changing of passwords is a standard practice for all employees at all levels of the organization. Additional precautions with password protected screensavers, and practices for protecting workstation security when an employee steps away from their computer, are also included in these secure procedures. Policies for password sharing with anyone are only allowed under conditions of authorized necessity and close monitoring, never simply for convenience. Periodic account audits are advised along with special attention given to policies for managing terminated employees and contractor accounts. (CMU-CERT *Practice 10*).

  o **ASA Note:** This best practice requirement also a represents a fundamental capability of UEBA and IdA. Supporting use cases include: Dynamic Access Provisioning, Access Governance and Segregation of Duties (SoD) Monitoring, (both IdA) and Step-up Authentication (also known as Adaptive Authentication [UEBA]).

- *Institute stringent access controls and monitoring policies on privileged users* – System administrators and other privileged users have a heightened capability to access and interact with a broad range of sensitive applications, systems, data and other critical resources. As a result, they pose an increased risk to organizations. Because a significant percentage of these privileged users also have a high degree of technical sophistication, specialized strategies for monitoring their access and activity must be implemented with comprehensive oversight for all environments within the organization. Any limitations within these privileged user monitoring strategies and the tools employed to implement them must be clearly understood. Redundancy policies may be required to ensure that no single individual can impact code releases of software, alter systems or other mission-critical initiatives for an organization. Policies and procedures for timely disablement of access for departed privileged users must be adopted, with multi-factor authentication (MFA) in place. Periodic account reviews are advised to prevent privilege creep and to rescind privileges no longer required. (CMU-CERT *Practice 11*).

  o **ASA Note:** Privileged access analytics is specifically designed for the challenges articulated in this best practice. Use cases include: High

Privileged Access Abuse (UEBA), including cloud (CSA); Privileged Access Discovery (IdA), including cloud (CSA). Use cases are organized in three categories: UEBA, IdA and CSA, with PAA use cases overlapping within these groupings.

- *Enforce separation of duties and least privilege* – Often called 'role-based access control', this policy is not to be confused with privileged access entitlement policies. Although related, this entails establishing a separation of duties for all employees engaged in any business activity. This practice involves dividing functions and processes among multiple people to limit the possibility that one person might be able to enact malicious activity without the assistance of others. Numerous organizations use the 'two-person rule' that requires two people to

> " *...the Privileged Access Discovery use case... would likely be a first step to establish with authoritative confidence exactly what privileged access entitlements are already in place within an environment...* "

  be involved for a critical task to be executed. This is a common practice enforcing separation of duties in enterprises, such financial institutions, during important transactions, and with software companies before a code release. The concept of 'least privilege' pertains to allowing employees or contractors access only to resources needed to perform their work responsibilities. Without this measure in place, insiders have compromised strategic products under development and exploited access to financial assets they should not have. This policy procedure must be maintained on an ongoing basis, since employees' movement within an organization may result in the accumulation of unrequired entitlements, and those should be revoked or disabled in a timely manner. Ideally, separation of duties should be designed into the business processes of an organization. (CMU-CERT *Practice 15*).

  o **ASA Note:** This best practice correlates directly with two use cases in IdA: Access Governance and Segregation of Duties (SoD) Monitoring as well as Risk-based Access and Certifications. In addition, the Privileged Access Discovery use case (also in IdA) would likely be a first step to establish with authoritative confidence exactly what privileged access entitlements are already in place within an environment, the majority of which are traditionally unknown to IT groups within organizations.

- *Institutionalize system change controls* – Manipulation of critical production systems by placing malicious code, creating logic bombs, Zero-day exploits, or other means, is a serious threat from nefarious insiders. Implementation of tools for detecting and controlling system changes, and configuration management tools for detecting and controlling changes to source code and other application files should be in place. Ongoing periodic review of configuration baselines against production systems is needed to identify any unauthorized discrepancies. Any proposed application or configuration changes must be submitted by a designated individual to an established change control board to ensure alignment with information security teams, system owners, data owners, users and other stakeholders. Strong baseline documentation of a basic catalog of information providing details including hardware devices, versions of installed software and disk utilization should exist. Measures should be taken to protect the documentation against manipulation with references including cryptographic checksums, interface characterization (such as memory mappings, device options and serial numbers), as well as, recording configuration files. Change logs and backups must also be

> *Controlling the access of individuals who are capable of performing these system change controls is the key to managing their potentially threatening behavior.*

protected. With these solid baselines, any computers implementing configurations will be validated against the baseline version. Some tools with this functionality have automated capabilities to conduct scheduled monitoring of systems to support validation of pending configurations. Any anomalies or discrepancies can then be inspected to determine whether they are benign or malicious. Different systems and their configurations have diverse change requirements, and must be taken into account by organizations. Enforcement of separation of duties, redundant roles and role-based access control should be in place so that no single individual can validate or approve configuration changes. (CMU-CERT *Practice 17*).

> o **ASA Note:** Controlling the access of individuals who are capable of performing these system change controls is the key to managing their potentially threatening behavior. Along with the use cases mentioned above (Access Governance and SoD Monitoring, Risk-based Access and Certifications and Privileged Access Discovery), High Privileged Access Abuse and Anomalous Behavior and Watchlists (both UEBA use cases), would support the requirements of this best practice.

- ***Implement secure backup and recovery processes*** – Maintaining system backups only onsite, or only in one version, creates a highly vulnerable target for insider threats to damage, cripple or destroy an organization's system and data assets. Maintaining multiple copies, and assuring at least one is maintained offsite, with a minimum of organization members having access, is a prudent policy to reduce the potential for malicious insider activity that could otherwise paralyze an organization if critical systems and their only backups are deleted. Backup media with carefully managed encryption keys is advantageous. One recommendation is to create the backed up system on a separate piece of hardware (called a 'bare metal restore'), with no other software or operating system. Safeguards to ensure the backups are properly in the state of readiness required include: performing periodic backup tests, protecting media and content from modification theft and destruction, implementing role-based separation of duties and a two-person rule (to ensure no single person can impact the system) to the backup process and systems. Regular tests and updates of the backup solution should be implemented along with exercises assuring the dedicated personnel are trained and qualified to ensure effective recovery and continuation of operations. In addition, because insiders may be familiar with traditional organizational methods, separate trusted communication paths outside an organization's network may be required to fortify the protection of the backup and the recovery process. (CMU-CERT *Practice 18*).

> o **ASA Note:** Here, the comprehensive controls for access to these secure backup systems, and monitoring of what an employee's activity is, remains critical to ensure. In the preliminary stages, and then ongoing after implementation of the backup system, safeguards include IdA use cases such as: Risk-based Access and Certifications Dynamic Access Provisioning, Role-Access Reconciliation, Role Mining and Intelligent Roles, Access Governance and SoD Monitoring. Once the system is operational, several UEBA use cases would also be employed on an ongoing basis. They include: Step-up Authentication Account Compromise, Hijacking and Sharing, High Privileged Access Abuse, as well as, Insider Threat Detection and Deterrence.

Operational security monitoring objectives

- *Beginning with the hiring process, monitor and respond to suspicious or disruptive behavior* – Even before an employee or partner is granted access to an organization's environment, some form of legally appropriate background check is prudent (with a minimum of a criminal background and credit check). Candidates being considered for positions with a higher level of responsibility and risk should undergo a deeper level of review. Once the candidate becomes a 'trusted' insider, discreet attention to the individual's behavior, once engaged in their work responsibilities, is appropriate. Training of supervisors may be involved to ensure suitable assessment of behavior which includes actions and verbal representations (i.e., threats or boasts of malicious capabilities). Failure to consistently and properly enforce clearly communicated policies can embolden malicious insiders. Notation of concerning behavior may initiate a heightened level of legally vetted monitoring of their activity, both past and present within the environment, to manage potential risk. Caution must be applied to application of monitoring policies to avoid the perception of 'big brother' which can impact morale and productivity. (CMU-CERT *Practice 4*).

> *...the Self-Audit and ID Theft Detection use cases have been deployed into organizations as large as 80,000 identities, with great success.*

- o **ASA Note:** This best practice sits at the foundational purpose of user and entity behavior analytics. Use cases within the UEBA domain that apply to this best practice include, but are not limited to: Account Compromise, Hijacking and Sharing; High Privileged Access Abuse; Data Exfiltration, DLP and IP Protection; Insider Threat Detection and Deterrence; Cyber Fraud Detection and Deterrence. In addition, the Self-Audit and ID Theft Detection use cases have been deployed into organizations as large as 80,000 identities, with great success.

- **Maintain vigilant visibility of social media** – The manner of social media use by members of an organization can be an indicator of nascent concerns related to the employee's potential for nefarious activity. As a medium of sharing personal information, it can also be an avenue of access to these same individuals who may be exploited based on any perceived vulnerabilities. This is especially the case if the employee with the social media account is posting negative remarks about their employer. In addition, communicating via online support forums, to troubleshoot a device or software product, might unintentionally reveal sensitive company information from the employee. Organization polices should clearly define acceptable use of social media and what protections must be given to data of different sensitivity levels. Social engineering and security awareness training can support proper use and insight into the consequences of engaging in problematic social media activity. An organization's monitoring of employees must be conducted with sensitivity to legal and privacy considerations. Some forms of speech may be protected. (CMU-CERT *Practice 7*).

- o **ASA Note:** An organization of any size is susceptible to phishing attacks through social media. After training and security awareness among employees is in place, advanced security analytics is designed to address this area of risk with a set of use cases. They include: Account

Compromise, Hijacking and Sharing; High Privileged Access Abuse; Insider Threat Detection and Deterrence; Anomalous Behavior and Watchlists. As well, Self-Audit and ID Theft Detection has demonstrated a proven benefit to organizations when employees' accounts have been compromised through social media phishing, and the quick discovery of malicious use of their accounts has been proven to deliver high value with virtually no false positives.

- ***Deploy solutions for monitoring employee actions and correlating information from multiple data sources*** – Effective insider threat programs require the capability to holistically collect and analyze data (big data) from across all an organization's environments. Specialized tools are needed to collect, aggregate, correlate and analyze the data from disparate sources with a risk-based approach that focuses on the organization's most critical assets. Activity monitoring can be conducted at the network and host levels. SIEMs (security information and event management) are widely adopted solutions enabling organizations to continuously monitor actions that produce an important source of analytic data an insider threat program must be focused on. SIEMs, however, are sometimes limited to a specific silo within an organization, and horizontal integration with other solutions such as IAM (identity access management) and CASB (cloud access security broker), as well as physical security systems, may be required to ensure seamless monitoring. Since CERT research indicates malicious

  > **The key to an advanced security analytics solution's success... is that it recognizes identity as a threat plane.**

  insiders often conduct malicious activates within 90 days of termination/resignation, timely revocation of all access must be a standard practice. This policy requires established lines of communication between HR and IT to ensure secure environment access integrity. HR should also communicate any instances of employee reprimand or policy violations to the organization's security teams to facilitate or initiate the possibility of enhanced preventive monitoring. Monitoring must be based on a clear understanding of the organization's culture as well as established behavior baseline norms of the individuals and their operational groups. Monitoring programs should be implemented only after creating clear policies and procedures. (CMU-CERT ***Practice 12***).

  - o **ASA Note:** This best practice calls out the requirement for the core value that mature machine learning delivers with a wide range of proven algorithms that draw context from big data. Multiple data sources include: IAM, SIEM, PAM, HR, AD, EDR and many more. The key to an advanced security analytics solution's success, in the context of this best practice, is that it recognizes identity as a threat plane. A solution must have the ability to link accounts associated with an identity and monitor access and activity across all an organization's silos with a risk-based approach that sometimes employs an automated risk response closed-loop deployment.

- ***Establish a baseline of normal behavior for both networks and employees*** – Once an organization has assembled the essential and any corollary data streams associated with its critical assets, the first phase of analytics can be performed. This entails defining normal baselines of activity for networks, peer groups of employees and the employees themselves. This involves establishing traditional work hours as well as access and usage patterns of resources. Deviations from these baselines of normal network or employee behavior represent anomalies that may indicate a security event, and possibly an insider threat. Specialized tools and platform solutions for baselining normal behavior and identifying anomalous behavior are available each with varying degrees of effectiveness. A suitable

  > *The difference between dynamic and static peer groups is that dynamic peer groups are... continually updating the roles and activities of members of a peer group. A static peer group... is more of a fixed snapshot in time...*

  period of time must be allowed to collect comprehensive samplings of data to ensure the normal baselines are accurate and reliable, since variations in activity will likely occur in organizations. Too short a sampling period will possibly miss normal cycles of increased activity, such as sales cycles or database backups. Too long a period increases the likelihood that abnormal and malicious behavior may become part of the baseline. Different data sources will have their unique characteristics which must also be taken into account during this process. (CMU-CERT ***Practice 14***).

  - o **ASA Note:** Establishing a baseline of behavior is one of the fundamental processes of advanced security analytics. One of the keys for this is drawing comprehensive context across all data silos and to establish the baseline behavior with dynamic peer groups, as opposed to static peer groups. The difference between dynamic and static peer groups is that dynamic peer groups are a product of machine learning models that are self-learning and self-training, continually updating the roles and activities of members of a peer group. A static peer group, on the other hand, is more of a fixed snapshot in time of a peer group's activities that gets manually updated on a periodic basis. Having a dynamic peer group for establishing baselines, means the baselines will always be up-to-date. In doing do, it makes risk scoring more accurate and lowers the volume of false positive alerts. Dynamic peer groups can improve outlier accuracy by as much as 8-10x over the use of UEBA solutions that only work with static peer groups.

- ***Monitor and control remote access from all endpoints, including IoT and mobile devices*** – With the advent of the mobile workforce, remote access by insiders has become an increasing concern for security leaders as an emerging platform for malicious insiders. BYOD and IoT innovations enhance telecommuting worker productivity with mobile devices such as personally owned smartphones and tablet computers, and they must be included within insider threat programs due to the risk they represent to an organization's systems and data. Remote attacks by insiders can occur while they are employed, or after termination, leveraging legitimate access granted by the organization. Numerous insiders have admitted that conducting malicious activity is much easier remotely, since they aren't being physically observed. Remote access to critical data, processes or information systems must be provided with great restraint and oversight and include multiple layers of defense to protect against remote attacks. In most cases, remote access to this class of data or systems should only be possible with devices issued and administered by the host organization. An alternative is for an organization to adopt application gateways which facilitates secured terminal services or remote desktop sessions. Legally vetted and careful monitoring practices should be implemented for all devices that interface with the organization at any time. BYOD policies must be weighed carefully, and at a departmental level. Closer logging and frequent auditing of remote transactions may be required in certain cases. (CMU-CERT ***Practice 13***).

  o **ASA Note:** Again, the criteria of monitoring are one of the key concerns for forward-looking security leaders. Having a monitoring capability based on machine learning and extracting context from big data, which crosses the horizontal planes of all silos, and recognizes identity as the new threat plane, is an essential requirement. This capability also includes the endpoints, the wide range of devices global users use from anywhere, 24/7, to gain access to an organization's environment. Security analytics solutions that claim they are machine learning, and rely mostly on signature, rules and queries of known bads, can no longer provide the monitoring capability required for today's fast evolving environments.

Different organizations may have unique requirements for developing a successful insider threat program. These may extend beyond this list, or not require all of the best practices cited above. The CMU-CERT framework, however, provides a well-vetted and fundamental perspective to build from for well-established insider threat programs. Government agencies and private enterprises have employed these with notable success.

Devin Bhatt is a respected security leader who has seen the evolution of the security industry, and insider threat programs, first hand, within both the private and government sector. Currently the CISO and Chief Privacy Officer for an agency within the U.S. Federal Government, he shares his insights related to insider threat programs in the following section.

BORDERLESS EXPERT INSIGHTS
Devin Bhatt, CISO & Chief Privacy Officer*
U.S. Federal Agency

Devin Bhatt is currently the CISO and CPO of a U.S. federal agency. He has an M.S. in Information Assurance from Norwich University and a Federal CIO Certificate from Carnegie Mellon University Heinz College. Bhatt also has multiple security certifications including, CISSP-ISSAP and ISSMP, CCISO, CISM, CISA, CRISC, CGEIT. Awarded the Compass award in 2007 by CSO magazine, he has presented internationally and published articles on topics related to  payment card industry data security standards. Bhatt also volunteers time to promote innovative cybersecurity technology companies through the Security Innovation Network (SINET). He has held executive security positions with a number of companies including WEX Inc. (VP and CISO), ARC (CSO) and Newell Rubbermaid (Corporate Information Security).

Overview

Bhatt begins with noting the importance of information sharing within the security community, along with the challenges of such disclosure and the advantages of cooperative networks, where a community of cybersecurity information sharing is growing. He then explores the fundamental priorities of a CISO, their key mandates, and core concerns. These concerns include a wide array of risk sources, which range from intentional vs. unintentional abuse and misuse. Bhatt states that old strategic perspectives are no longer useful and that continuous evolutionary thinking is required to face the challenges of current and future security defenses. He declares that just compliance with security standards does not ensure security in the face of emerging threats, evolving phishing attacks, ransomware and other malicious tactics. Bhatt comments how new effective security controls are needed which are reactive and targeted security solutions. Noting the perpetual race to stay ahead of the attackers, Bhatt explains how the integration of hybrid cloud security solutions delivers greater value to the security solution array.

Coupled with the emerging influences impacting insider threats, Bhatt notes the importance of data-centric security and controls and the requirement for perpetual due diligence. The scale of big data offering valuable insights for discovering blind spots in security is something Bhatt considers critical. Along with that, identity's critical role in security must be acknowledged by security leaders, along with the imperative to move identity closer to data. He also observes the evolving requirements for identity and access management and the consequences of improper controls for insider access. The

* The views and opinions expressed by Devin Bhatt in this book are his own, and do not necessarily reflect those of his current, or any of his previous employers.

challenges in privileged access security are a critical concern for Bhatt. He advocates reviewing security use cases and abuse cases, as he outlines the need for establishing uniform access controls and policies for privileged access entitlements. He investigates the core criteria for privileged access entitlement policies, as well as risk targets with malicious privileged access intruders. From there, he investigates strategies for managing privileged access as he observes the dangers of the status quo in privileged access management, where a new holistic insight into both access and activity are required.

Fundamental components of an insider threat program are discussed, as the solution development objectives are aligned with organizational program integration strategies. As well, preventative security process policies and operational security monitoring objectives must be in sync for the successful integration of insider threat cybersecurity programs. This is only possible, Bhatt observes, with prudent technical planning and a broader view of engaged organizational commitment in security and responsibility. With the emerging standards and certification requirements, however, compliance and certification must be seen only as a starting point, not an end goal. And incorporating risk-based thinking with compliance adherence is the key to success, along with accounting for the risk of the unknown for abuse cases.

Bhatt observes innovations in security solutions and changing perspectives in organizational culture. Solutions providing heightened context have strong value, with the expanded efficiencies of the self-audit feature in advanced security analytics being a prime example. Considerations of adoption resistance within the organization are discussed, as is the importance of security context and perspective for users to understand which can promote a perspective of shared protection that comes from shared responsibility within the organization. Finally, the CISO's critical role in contributing to organizational policy is a topic close to Bhatt's concerns. Where security mandates are seen in conflict with an enterprise's bottom line, the new kid on the corporate organizational block faces lower prioritization of their mandate, which delivers higher risk to the organization. While he observes that selected business sectors support the CISO agenda, he sees that the status quo in general remains unchanged. Bhatt offers a reality check for future CISOs and their organizations.

The importance of information sharing within the security community

We're all aware of the Darknet, along with the hacker and criminal culture that shares information about innovations in technology, lucrative vulnerabilities, and prime targets. The result is that threat planes and new vulnerabilities are exploited with evolving impunity by growing numbers of criminals. Malicious intrusions thrive, while an ever-expanding list of legitimate enterprises, government agencies and innocent private citizens become victims. Businesses and individual lives are damaged in the process. Unfortunately, this same measure of open information exchange in the targeted victim community does not exist. There are, however, encouraging signs of change.

The challenges of disclosure and advantages cooperative networks. In the past, when I learned of breaches, often through my professional grapevine, I used to reach out to the security leaders in these affected organizations — including credit card companies, and other organizations as well — and I'd request any information possible. I didn't want to be the next victim. Yet it was very difficult. Because of the ongoing investigations, these CISOs could not, and would not, share many details. That's where I began to say, we need some sort of information sharing network of like-minded security practitioners, to help each other out. I had my theories about network security and I wanted to share my knowledge and learn from my peers. Now, organizations like sector-specific Information Sharing and Analysis Centers (ISACs) and SINET (Security Innovation Network) are rising to meet that challenge, bringing together security professionals from the public and private sectors — from across the country and around the globe — to collaborate on sharing their security wisdom, breach case studies, success stories, best practices and technology insights, in workshops and conferences, to raise the awareness of challenges in security. By shedding light on these challenges, the encroaching darkness of malicious actors is confronted with informed insights.

The counterproductive reflex to hide the damage. Instead of sharing information about breaches, on occasion, some organizations do their best to hide it. In some cases, they actively cover up the discovery. The motivations range from concern of customer loyalty erosion, embarrassment, or even ego. Doing so, however, only delays the inevitable, and usually sheds a negative light on the decision makers who chose to conceal the information. One example of this would be a breach at a global technology company and their alleged decision to conceal it. When the public disclosure was finally made, the reputation impact and other brand damage was significant. In contrast, in 2009, Heartland Payment Systems promptly disclosed that they had been breached. Unfortunately, they were wrongly accused that the disclosure was timed to be released so that the largest breach of credit card data in recorded history would be obscured for the greater public, distracted by the Presidential inauguration coverage events in Washington DC. They ultimately had to spend a significant amount of resources to rebuild their

> *Security leaders, and the organizations they serve, help everyone when they are able to share the instances and methods of malicious intrusion.*

reputation and developed their own end-to-end encryption solution. They also created the 'Payment Processor' subgroup under FS-ISAC and shared their lessons learned. Security leaders, and the organizations they serve, help everyone when they are able to share the instances and methods of malicious intrusion.

A widening community of cybersecurity information sharing. More networks of professional information exchange communities have emerged in recent years. FS-ISAC (Financial Services Information Sharing and Analysis Center) and NH-ISAC (National Health) are two excellent examples. Here, security peers share their insights into cybersecurity experiences, best practices, and how effective they have been in facing the challenges of malicious threats, so they can learn from each other. It only makes sense that if the bad guys are sharing information to further their agenda, then the more the good guys can do the right thing, they accelerate the entire cybersecurity profession's agenda more quickly and effectively. Contributing to this book is part of that professional collaborative process. Especially with an entirely new breed of security professionals coming up through the ranks, the faster they can get up to speed on their roles and responsibilities, and gain a holistic understanding of the emerging new world of borderless behavior analytics, the better.

Fundamental priorities of a CISO

In today's constantly changing environments, facing relentless intrusions by malicious intruders, the security leaders' roles and responsibilities are, out of necessity, continuously evolving. Because of that, cybersecurity will remain a hot topic for the foreseeable future, in corporate board agendas, with agencies establishing regulations, and all organizations who store and process sensitive data.

The CISO's key mandate. What exactly does a CISO do? CISOs develop the vision and strategy for the organization-wide information security program and execute on the strategy. The CISO informs senior executives and business units about cyber risks and recommends controls to mitigate the risks. On occasion, especially in the financial sector, some CISOs are responsible for an organization's privacy program. This role requires the implementation of numerous security controls to protect sensitive and confidential information. A CISO's team consists of dedicated security and privacy professionals, who develop policies, perform security assessments, and test security systems. The team also implements a variety of information technology solutions to protect sensitive information.

The CISO's core concerns. The CFO or CIO, or even CEO of an organization often ask their CISOs: "What keeps you up at night? What should we be worried about? What's our biggest threat?" Having been in the field for a long time, I've seen one of the most common things CISOs will always be apprehensive about is protecting the organization's crown jewels from determined and skilled intruders originating from the outside. These can be solitary hackers, organized crime, nation-states or hacktivists who may try to get into your systems and steal important data. Obviously, credit card data has the monetary motivation, but the intellectual property, and any other malicious activity that can harm an organization's reputation, or damage the customer's trust and loyalty to an enterprise, are all critical concerns.

A wide array of risk sources. The focus of what keeps the CISO up at night does not just consist of the traditional external threats — from individual hackers, organized crime, hacktivists, or nation-state-sponsored advanced threats — but also from internal privileged users. In the modern economy, where short-term employee engagements are more common, organizations often have numerous contractors. Add to that, customers, partners, and third party service

> *...major credit card companies were surprised at how many places their sensitive data resided that they did not know about.*

providers, who must all be vetted in order to trust them. In one abuse case from the payment card industry, the exposure came from a completely unexpected source. At one point, when the breaches were being notified to them, major credit card companies were surprised at how many places their sensitive data resided that they did not know about. The exposure came from a third-party contractor, who had in turn engaged with another subcontractor to provide ancillary services. This fourth-party subcontractor was uncertified, got a hold of the credit card data, and the breach occurred from there. These leading credit card companies didn't know these service entities existed within their operational domain, since they were focused on their primary merchants and service providers, assuring they met regulation requirements and were properly certified. For CISOs, it's always the x-factor they haven't thought about that keeps them awake at night.

Intentional vs. unintentional abuse and misuse. Originally, it was mainly the external threats that CISOs commonly focused on. Now security leaders realize that the people within an organization, insiders like employees and contractors, are also a concern. Research shows that many organizations worry about inadvertent activity. These insiders are not malicious, nor trying to do any harm, but take some action by mistake which causes an incident. Breaches occur because of this kind of activity, and that's a significant concern for security leaders. It might be simply getting someone's

email address wrong and sending sensitive data to an unauthorized recipient. That could constitute a breach or incident. Verizon publishes their *Data Breach Investigation Report* (DBIR) annually, with a dedicated focus on these

> *...with the rising critical mass of business processes... and so many different disparate systems... security teams lose reliable visibility into what all is going on within an organization's environment.*

scenarios. These cases require the same level of serious scrutiny, where the same level of damage can occur, as if somebody actually stole the data. Yet at times, with the rising critical mass of business processes, individuals' day-to-day work activities, and so many different disparate systems — with third-party partners, and contractors, and all the elements that touch them, global 24/7 access, including the rising mass of big data — security teams lose reliable visibility into what all is going on within an organization's environment.

Old strategic perspectives no longer useful. I compare and contrast the new normal of ever-increasing complexity with the early days, many years ago, when CISOs' jobs were much easier. Then, all your data was contained in a well-protected data center within your boundaries, on your premises, where you had complete control over it all. If you wanted to, you could go to your data center and perform an audit. You knew you could put as many controls as were deemed necessary, and you knew its reliability and effectiveness. With this sense of physical enclosure, anything inside it was protected and secure. Now, however, the data is going out as a normal workflow process. It no longer resides only on-premises, but somewhere in the cloud as well. There, you don't have full visibility of all the controls, as is the case with any of the well-known clouds. This is why some organizations have been reluctant to adopt those services. Meanwhile, corporate leaders say they need these solutions for the business to increase productivity, speed, cost effectiveness, and flexibility. Yet at the core, the CISOs and CSOs keep looking at the risk these solutions represent, as security remains their biggest concern.

Continuous evolutionary thinking required. Many security leaders are in some phase of coping with migrating from the traditional defenses, which were originally created with the hard physical perimeter idea in mind, to the new normal of cloud environments. With the perimeter becoming porous, a myriad of new sets of access and activity exist in the environment, both on-premises and in the cloud, which has created an entirely different set of variables and risks. What used to be inside versus outside, green versus red, has become thousands of shades of gray. No longer is the wild world just outside. The perimeter has become porous because of so many different factors, like bring your own device (BYOD), the Internet of Things (IoT), mobility, cloud, and 24/7 access which brings activity from anywhere around the world into an organization's environment. All these factors are punching holes in the perimeter so that in reality, it simply no longer can be considered an effective, protective perimeter. That alone may keep countless CISOs up at night.

Challenges of current security defenses

A steadily rising awareness of cybersecurity in the media is the new normal. The frequent national headlines in the political sphere, and elsewhere, now seem to be a daily occurrence. Closer to home, stories about security breaches at well-known retailers, multi-million dollar fraudulent ATM heists, and denial of service attacks on the financial industry, draw heightened attention to cybersecurity. My own sector's adversaries include financially motivated criminals, hacktivists, and even nation-state sponsored units. Employing a tactic commonly known as the advanced persistent threat (APT), they may use sophisticated social engineering attacks on the employees and contractors of both public and private organizations. These attacks too often ultimately compromise an insider's identity credentials.

Emerging threats and evolving security strategies. As the sophistication of cyber-attacks increases, our industry's information security departments, cybersecurity programs, the technical defenses, and the culture itself must evolve — both responsively and proactively

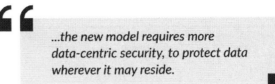

...the new model requires more data-centric security, to protect data wherever it may reside.

— to defend against rising asymmetric cyber threats. Where the old security model focused on network perimeter security to keep the unauthorized people out, the new model requires more data-centric security, to protect data wherever it may reside.

Standards compliance versus ensuring security. For many organizations, the challenge is 'growing' a culture of security, where security is built into everything they do. For example, in the federal space, a large number of employees must be able to work remotely, and there is a clear requirement to balance the needs for mobility, access, and security. Many organizations that recently became victims of cybercrime were compliant with the numerous industry security standards and other regulations. However, compliance does not automatically equal security. Compliance only represents a snapshot in time, and a partial one at that. Ongoing assessments and continuous testing and monitoring are critical. Building a defense-in-depth strategy —

...compliance does not automatically equal security. Compliance only represents a snapshot in time...

which means deploying multiple layers of controls covering people, processes, and technology — is necessary. This is especially the case with insider threat programs.

Phishing attacks, ransomware and effective security controls. Ransomware is increasing. It's simple for malicious actors to take advantage of, often with the root cause originating from phishing attacks. The challenges security teams face is whether they can detect or monitor what's happening. The simplest preemptive control to address this issue is to prevent the files from being encrypted at a mass level which occurs in ransomware scenarios. File integrity monitoring (FIM) software is available, which provides enhanced due diligence capabilities for these kinds of threats, providing an approach to this challenge. In this emerging security response model, if someone tries to change and encrypt all the files on an employee's laptop, or on an organization's server, the security controls should flag it automatically, to enable prevention of this activity from occurring. These capabilities stem from detection systems and prevention systems, and targeting where they can be applied, to control anyone's unauthorized ability to change, delete, or to prevent a user's own legitimate access to the information they own and are fully authorized to use.

Privileged access abuse for convenience. While some threats are malicious and targeted in their intent, other forms of risk manifest themselves with the bypassing or ignoring of strict security policies, sometimes simply for the sake of convenience. While PCI (Payment Card Industry) and numerous security standards require these policies be in place, too often, security teams see logs revealing people sharing generic user ID and passwords, etc. The logs revealed people accessing the environment from different IP addresses and logging on using the same user ID information. Catching this kind of risky activity is only possible after organizations have turned on a database or access monitoring software that identifies this kind of unsanctioned behavior. The activity can't be addressed comprehensively unless the right holistic security analytic solutions are in place to catch all of the access activity in a timely manner, enabling effective remedial responses.

The perpetual race to stay ahead of the attackers. Security leaders recognize that criminals and other malicious actors are becoming increasingly more sophisticated. When cyber criminals see encrypted data in a database, they look for alternative avenues of access. For example, when they can't attack the database anymore, they shift tactics and focus their intrusion on the terminal transfer where the data may be unencrypted, and then exploit that access point to grab the data. Security groups with the responsibility for protecting the data, instead of being behind the curve finding the loophole of the vulnerability after an intrusion, must continually think of the ways their environment could be exploited. The more they can address those risks ahead of time, the stronger their defenses are. Otherwise, they're left trying to detect the nefarious action after the fact, when it's too late.

Hybrid security solution integration for greater value. As security challenges intensify, a broadening trend of security groups adopting more capabilities by integrating supplemental solutions has been observed in the industry. These improved hybrid capabilities are enhancements security experts have been demanding and are becoming more available through a growing number of different technologies. Larger security solution vendors have also recognized this demand. They're continually adding variants of these technologies and incorporating these features to their own solutions. By doing so, current and prospective customers are encouraged to believe a single vendor's solution meets their comprehensive requirements. This is opposed to being forced to integrate an array of point solutions and risk incompatibility with different elements within the security solution array. Certain web application firewalls are one example that has complimented database access management solutions. Vendor agnostic advanced security analytics solutions — leveraging machine-learning-driven UEBA and IdA, and which work with SIEM, CASB, IAM (identity and access management) and DLP, for both on-premises and cloud — is another example of broadening security capabilities integrating with different platforms, for comprehensive security capabilities.

Emerging influences impacting the insider threat

CISOs recognize that the border, or the network perimeter, is becoming continually more porous. The data may reside outside of a company's data center in external cloud environments. The security focus, therefore, must be on the data, not just on the network perimeter. Security controls should be data-centric; it's no longer sufficient to have this focus just at the border level.

> ...security leaders... need to know who has access to what at any given time, as well as, what those users are doing with the data.

When security leaders consider data-centric security, they must also ensure mature identity and access management, logging, and the latest generation of predictive analytical capabilities. They need to know who has access to what at any given time, as well as, what those users are doing with the data.

The challenges of data-centric security and controls. Security leaders require the resources, processes, and technologies to identify where all their data and assets are, and to have the visibility to effectively monitor who's accessing them and how that activity is being conducted. Is it legitimate, normal, or not? The important point is the ability to monitor behavior. Security and compliance teams often face challenges when elevated levels of security controls are required for high transactional production systems. The system administrators are concerned that if the audit logging for all events is turned on, there will be an operational performance degradation, increase in storage space, and cost. This perspective stands clearly in conflict with, and is fundamentally counterproductive to, security objectives. However, educating the system administrators about the risks of not capturing the required data, while addressing the other concerns, will usually be well received.

The requirement for perpetual due diligence. Even when it seems there is no resistance, or groups like system administrators appear to be in compliance, the policy of 'trust, but verify' is essential in security. I recall numerous early payment card industry data security standards-related assessments which were performed by qualified security assessors. In certain instances, when the security team

> ...the policy of 'trust, but verify' is essential in security.

requested confirmation from the system administrators that all the required controls were in place and fully operational, the team received an affirmative answer. Yet performing further due diligence and validation revealed not all the needed security configuration controls were turned on. When asked for an explanation why they weren't, excuses were offered. When one has the technology and capabilities, but chooses not to enable and capture the important log information, then critical forensic investigation and analysis is impossible during any incident response. It would be quite embarrassing, or a career-ending situation, to share the bad news with senior executives and the board of directors that the important log data was never captured. This concerning practice also aids the network intruders, since any record of their activity would not be captured, because the events were never logged. 'Trust, but verify' is a must for security success.

Big data's scale lends invaluable insights. Today, security operations centers (SOCs) and cyber fusion centers are inundated with billions of events from the company network. It's not humanly possible to review every event. That means CISOs must use big data analytical capabilities and machine learning to analyze massive volumes of events quickly. The question security leaders need to answer is: "Can we link the data to produce actionable results?" With so much data volume, how does one meaningfully monitor this effectively and take the right action? Security teams need to perform significant and faster analysis with mature machine learning. These security teams are also seeking to identify all behavior indicators to fortify their monitoring strategy for insider threats. Countless complex questions confront security leaders contending with requirements to provide access to data from anywhere, anytime, and any device. Such demands require full visibility and the collection of all necessary log data.

> The question security leaders need to answer is: "Can we link the data to produce actionable results?"

Security solutions should satisfy requirements comprehensively, instead of being constrained by standalone point solutions.

Discovering blind spots in security. This challenge is exemplified by the following classic incident of industrial espionage and theft of intellectual property. An employee at a manufacturing conglomerate tried to send an email with a huge PowerPoint presentation containing the company's five-year strategic plans. The file contained highly sensitive information about where the enterprise was planning to manufacture certain products overseas in 'low-cost countries'. It listed profitable products and their profit margins. It also included long-term strategic global marketing plans. This file was being sent directly to a competitor. The only reason the activity was discovered was because the employee didn't know about the size limit on attachments that could be sent during normal business hours. This IT policy was in place to prevent delays for normal business users with email services. As a result, the email and attachment was quarantined, to be sent off hours. Yet the file attachment was so large that, even during off hours, it still couldn't be sent. An IT specialist was called in to look at the issue, and upon examining the content, the technician discovered the intended recipient was a competitor. This event raised alarms, and concern among senior executives asking, "How could this happen?" Given this incident was caught by accident, what if the malicious insider had divided the attachment into four or five separate files? It probably wouldn't have been detected, or only detected months later, well after the damage occurred. What if the insider simply printed the entire presentation, took it home, and mailed it to the competitor? This demonstrates the need for having a much broader, holistic security analytics approach in effective insider threat programs.

Commonalities in insider threat programs. While organizations by nature face unique and separate challenges associated with their lines of business, and the factors which differentiate them in the marketplace, a number of common themes prevail. Given data is no longer confined within the corporate data center, data breaches may have significant impact to brand reputation, shareholder value, loss of intellectual property, and other financial losses which can cause irreversible damage. There are likely gaps in appropriate resources, processes and technologies to mitigate these risks. It might be easier to keep unauthorized outsiders away from sensitive data, but very difficult for nefarious insiders, because they are trusted and have access. Instead of relying on declarative defenses, solutions like advanced security analytics, powered by mature machine learning, will help address a growing number of CISO concerns with a risk-based approach.

Integrating emerging advanced security analytics solutions with traditional tools

While tools such as firewalls, intrusion prevention systems, and anti-malware are critical within an environment's array of defenses, they no longer occupy the same prominence of solitary importance they once did. Security teams need the ever-updating signatures list these tools manage as they screen for the plethora of known 'red' issues faced in

> A growing number of security organizations are employing this meshed array of security tools and solutions with proven success.

every environment. However, that's only part of the picture. Without them, the overload of extraneous data can congest and impede security analytics efficiencies. Behavioral analytics, driven by advanced machine learning, and drawing critical context from big data, provides the ability to detect abnormal behavior for which there is no signature. While there may be no previous knowledge (logged as a signature) that a particular behavior is malicious, it is nonetheless clearly atypical and possibly threat activity. This 'gray' behavior diverges from normal behavior established in user profiles and peer group baselines. The anomaly jumps out, whether innocent or malicious, and someone must investigate it. A growing number of security organizations are employing this meshed array of security tools and solutions with proven success.

Applications for insider threat programs. This same security analytic principle can be applied to an assortment of other internal and insider types of threats. This also addresses instances where someone is not being malicious, they are instead inadvertently performing a risky activity, or making a mistake. Without a mature behavior analytics solution in place, the pressing questions for security leaders will always be: "Can we detect and catch the attackers? Can we prevent and deter them or respond in a timely manner?"

> *...the pressing questions for security leaders will always be: "Can we detect and catch the attackers? Can we prevent and deter them or respond in a timely manner?"*

A differentiating value of behavior analytics. The operative answer to the questions plaguing security leaders incorporates the understanding that while attackers may be able to steal an employee's credentials, they cannot steal their behavior. That's the key to everything. While the attacker uses the stolen credentials to get inside the environment, once there, they try to access their target, the organization's crown jewels. In doing so, however, they can't mimic the unique behavior of the original legitimate credential owner. As a result, the intruders trip all sorts of alerts from the behavioral anomalies which are in striking contrast to the normal baseline of behavior. It's something like a bull in a china shop. If someone has illegitimate credentials, yet they don't know the legitimate user's use patterns and habits, the result is the normal baseline of behavior is no longer being exhibited. The intruder's continuing activity only strengthens the anomaly signature and calibrates the risk score more accurately. For example, the legitimate user may have had access to an array of resources, but he never touched them in his normal workflow until now. The new activity reveals the anomaly, and depending on the sensitivity of the data being accessed, a variety of flags can be raised.

Analytics empowered by machine learning. With the rising volume of data that security organizations are responsible for today, it is no longer feasible to throw human resources at the problem. Add to that, experts predict that between 2014 and 2020, the amount of data generated will increase tenfold. A new security paradigm is required. To match the current challenges and manage the vast data growth projections, some kind of robust, scalable and flexible computational capability must be utilized. To date, only machine learning fills that exacting requirement. CISOs simply cannot add another ten, fifty or a hundred SOC analysts on the same project and expect they'll be able to get out in front of the growing challenge. It can no longer be done that way.

Identity's role in security

Because people demand anytime, anywhere, any device access, identity plays a critical role in security and insider threat programs. Organizations must know who the person, machine, or entity is that is accessing information within their secure environment. In support of this objective, some firewall vendors are developing solutions with 'identity aware' policies and rules. They're not just identifying an IP address, but also capturing the user ID, and verifying if it is correct or not. In advanced security analytics, and more specifically identity analytics (IdA), identity plays an integral role in a comprehensive security strategy, throughout an organization's environment, for both on-premises and in the cloud.

The imperative to move identity closer to data. As security leaders acknowledge their perimeter is becoming progressively more porous, essentially non-existent, the next generation of security solution strategy incorporates the objective of moving identity as close to the data as possible. From an equally important perspective, security analytics must also get closer to the identity — human, system or entity — that is accessing the data or the system. In response to customer demand, numerous emerging security solutions target this trend, to enable the

> ...the next generation of security solution strategy incorporates the objective of moving identity as close to the data as possible.

ability to continually update analytics on identity and access to data, to ensure secure anytime, anywhere, access.

Evolving requirements for identity and access management. Security leaders are recognizing a heightened importance for identity and access management as a critical domain within information security. At the same time, however, as a legacy framework, it can no longer provide comprehensive security on its own. Within this domain, the challenge of managing privileged users' access entitlements has grown beyond IAM's capabilities. In response, IAM's requirements have become closely tied to the objectives and capabilities of identity analytics. How identities are created, what access identities have, and the activity identities conduct with their access, is at the core of any insider threat program's viability, and IdA is a critical component fulfilling that need.

Consequences of improper identity controls for insider access. A nightmare breach, that had a widespread impact on the security industry, was with ChoicePoint in 2005. In this abuse case, the attacker was a 'customer', functionally, a trusted insider with privileged access. Using a false identity, the criminals, opened a legitimate business account, paying the initial fees to gain access to personal information. In doing so, they downloaded thousands of credit reports, social security and driver's license numbers. Over 145,000 individuals' personal information was stolen, and from that hundreds of cases of identity theft resulted. After it was finally discovered, record fines ensued, and ChoicePoint was compelled to create the position of Chief Credentialing, Compliance and Privacy Officer. One person was able to fool the system and utilize

> With the right advanced security analytics solution in place, with privileged access analytics capabilities – monitoring identity, access and activity – prevention of abuse cases like these is possible.

their service fraudulently, as a functional 'insider', due to their business customer status. With the right advanced security analytics solution in place, with privileged access analytics capabilities — monitoring identity, access and activity — prevention of abuse cases like these is possible.

Challenges in privileged access security

Privileged access is a critical area of growing risk within enterprises. It has been ineffectively addressed by organizations for years. Even today, too many organizations still depend on single-factor authentication (SFA) for access. More widespread stringent controls and requirements for privileged access must be implemented as multi-factor authentication (MFA) for privileged users, as well as end users, is emerging as a standard requirement. A general awareness-raising initiative, organization-wide, should become established where people at all levels understand that advanced persistent threats (APTs) often focus on exploiting privileged user access.

Use cases versus abuse cases. Security professionals often talk about use cases. Another perspective, with 'abuse cases' in privileged access management, is where security teams must ensure there are no other users, processes, or controls that someone can circumvent. When it comes to the privileged access management side of IAM, many IT professionals do not always realize their inventory process of vaulted privileged access entitlements might be broken. Too often, an administrator grants privileged access entitlements to users that ultimately leads to additional unsanctioned issuance to non-privileged accounts with access

> Too often, an administrator grants privileged access entitlements... that ultimately leads to additional unsanctioned issuance to non-privileged accounts... This can create an unintended threat plane where the risk... rises with each new instance of unknown access entitlement.

entitlements that might be outside the administrator's visibility. This can create an unintended threat plane where the risk of compromise, or abuse, rises with each new instance of unknown access entitlement.

Establishing uniform access controls. If an organization does a good job of defining what the organization's various roles are, and what access the roles require, a solid groundwork for role-based access control is created. As well, privileged policies must be applied controlling access where employees, contractors or partners will not be granted any more access than what their job responsibilities require them to use and when they need to use it.

Elevated positions requiring custom access management. Roles which are a higher level in the organization — such as system administrator or database administrator — and involve elevated responsibilities, require regular access, often remotely, to sensitive data. These requirements set them apart in IT's purview, and management of their accounts demands special attention. How will they be controlled? Should multi-factor authentication be employed? It has been demonstrated that determined and seasoned hackers can steal user IDs and passwords with comparative ease. These concerns heighten the urgency for privileged users, especially in cases where remote access poses tangible risks. This realization brings security and IT leaders' thinking back to the fundamentals: How many people have privileged access entitlements? Do all these people need all of them? Are revised entitlement restriction measures in order?

Policies for privileged access entitlements. Privileged access by default should be granted only to a very limited number of people whose role requires it. Yet industry experts observe a concerning trend: a large percent of privileged access entitlements exist in the organizations. That's a huge concern for IT and security leaders. CIOs and CISOs are now looking at taking a reliable inventory of how many identities are privileged users. When adopting the methodology of a good auditor, surprises may occur. For example, a worst-case scenario cited to me by a colleague, was a case where a company had 500 employees. They also had 500 privileged users. That might be an extreme example, but it highlights the potential for high risk, compromise and malicious abuse.

Core criteria for privileged access entitlement policies. Even if some individuals within the organization insist they need root access, it should be prudently justified. Stringent criteria must be met. A reference point: in 2002, faced with a rising tide of security problems (mostly virus-based) at Microsoft, Bill Gates wrote a seminal memo to the entire organization (the bellwether *Trustworthy Computing* memo). In it, he outlined the criteria that all Microsoft initiatives needed to align with. They were: *security, privacy, reliability,* and business *integrity.* The Trustworthy Computing initiative had an industrywide impact. Because so many viruses and malicious code were being written for Microsoft operating systems, they had to ensure operating systems were not so 'trusting'. The sensibilities behind the memo should also apply to the criteria for justifying and granting privileged access entitlements. Any user must have tightened security enabled around their access entitlements. The organization's privileged access entitlement model cannot allow scenarios where individuals can just take over and take advantage of it, since the stakes for an organization are at the highest level: These people have keys to the crown jewels of an enterprise.

Risk targets with malicious privileged access intruders. The crown jewels of sensitive data are not limited to traditional confidential intellectual property, or financial assets. Logging data is critical as well, and the risk with compromised privileged users is that if a system administrator, or a criminal, deletes the log data, forensic security teams cannot know what actually transpired.

> " *Security leaders must... monitor access and activity holistically, across an organization's entire environment, to analyze the behavior patterns with risk-based assessments and scoring.* "

Privileged users are extremely powerful because of their access. If misused, or abused, massive damage can result. Security leaders must ensure that proper damage control measures are in place. In addition, they should leverage robust advanced security analytics to monitor access and activity holistically, across an organization's entire environment, to analyze the behavior patterns with risk-based assessments and scoring.

Strategies for managing privileged access

Reducing the identity risk and threat plane should be a first step of managing privileged access effectively. With most Fortune 500 companies having more privileged access outside the vault than inside, the problem is acute. Indeed, recent cases have been cited, one in an enterprise where a company reduced their privileged access entitlements by 70% without impacting their business effectiveness, while another company had 83% of their overall access entitlements reduced. Left unchecked, too much unknown excess privileged access in an organization represents an unwieldy and sobering threat plane. Each unknown and unmanaged access and entitlement is a potential risk. The more tight controls organizations have over privileged access entitlements, the more effective their security strategy will be.

Old habits of status quo in privileged access management. Within some organizations, there is a degree of hesitation to reduce access because IT groups don't have the information to know with certainty if an entitlement is being used or not. When faced with the decision to remove access or not, they just let the current entitlements remain unchanged, with the perspective of not wanting to 'break' anything. Other IT groups, however, adopt a 'when it doubt, take it out' policy. Groups taking this approach accept that active users will then call or escalate to regain access. When this method is used, creating a revised inventory of *known* entitlements, with the goal of locking down access, security

> " *The challenge remains, how low can an organization bring their privileged access entitlements to a manageable level, and how reliable is their approach in doing so?* "

groups will still be unable to remove 100% of the risk. The unknown access entitlements remain untouched. The challenge remains, how low can an organization bring their privileged access entitlements to a manageable level, and how reliable is their approach in doing so? Overall a more comprehensive, efficient and effective strategy is required.

Holistic insight into both access and activity. Having the ability to both manage and monitor access is key. Instead of conducting periodic manual access assessment and reduction exercises, a continuous and holistic ability to monitor access and activity is recommended. The most reliable and efficient method is possible through advanced security analytics, using mature machine learning algorithms and drawing from un-siloed big data for critical context. This capability provides security and IT groups with comprehensive access and activity information. With it, for example, they can tell a particular employee has been granted ten accounts. Out of these, only three have been used in the past six months, with the other seven accounts not logged into, dormant and unused. With that level of data visibility, IT can contact the user and inform them their access for the seven dormant accounts will be removed and whenever they need it, they can request temporary access. They don't need to have continuous access for all ten accounts, because they're only using three, based on the activity information that the IT and security teams are seeing. This kind of intelligence is the key to maintaining a comprehensive and up-to-date privileged access management solution and ensures reliable security.

Fundamental components of an insider threat program

Keying off CMU-CERT's technical note, *Common Sense Guide to Mitigating Insider Threats* (Fifth Edition, December 2016), security leaders across all business verticals recognize the best practices this widely-respected evolving program has established through the years on this critical topic. Taking these best practices one step further, from a general list of twenty, and re-grouping them into generally chronological and categorizing them into functional domains, provides an additional tiered context within which to view these recommendations. While covered in detail in the introduction to this chapter, they are distilled here for easy reference. They are:

Solution development objectives
- Know and protect your critical assets
- Consider threats from insiders and business partners in enterprise-wide risk assessments
- Develop a formalized stepped plan for an insider threat program
- Structure management and tasks to minimize insider stress and mistakes
- Define explicit security agreements for any cloud services, especially access restrictions and monitoring capabilities

Organizational program integration strategies

- Incorporate malicious and unintentional insider threat awareness into periodic security training for all employees
- Anticipate and manage negative issues in the work environment
- Develop a comprehensive employee termination procedure

Preventative security process policies

- Close the doors to unauthorized data exfiltration
- Clearly document and consistently enforce policies and controls
- Implement strict password and account management policies and practices
- Institute stringent access controls and monitoring policies on privileged users
- Institutionalize system change controls
- Enforce separation of duties and least privilege
- Implement secure backup and recovery processes

Operational security monitoring objectives

- Beginning with the hiring process, monitor and respond to suspicious or disruptive behavior
- Maintain vigilant visibility of social media
- Deploy solutions for monitoring employee actions and correlating information from multiple data sources
- Establish a baseline of normal behavior for both networks and employees
- Monitor and control remote access from all endpoints, including IoT and mobile devices

Different organizations will very possibly have their own unique requirements for insider threat program success that may extend beyond this list. However, this framework provides a well-vetted and fundamental perspective to build from for well-established insider threat programs.

Recommendations for successful integration of insider threat cybersecurity programs

Cybersecurity naturally represents a major framework of responsibility within insider threat programs. Yet the insider threat challenge is not confined to the realm of information technology, nor cybersecurity and information security alone. It spans the entire organization. As observed in the CMU-CERT best practices for insider threat

> *...the executives in the organization must also agree that this critical threat plane is an area of significant risk, and they must support relevant initiatives through policies, procedures and programs, as well as provide the required resources and budget to assure success.*

programs, this comprehensive approach also includes involving physical security organization, since indicator behavior from the physical plant access perspective can be critical to ensure a holistic picture of the insider's activities. Human resources organizational data should be factored in as well. In addition, the executives in the organization must also agree that this critical threat plane is an area of significant risk, and they must support relevant initiatives through policies, procedures and programs, as well as provide the required resources and budget to ensure success.

Positioning security objectives effectively within organizations. Implementing insider threat programs will not always be easy. In some cases, organization members feel uncomfortable with the change. Attention should be applied to how the program is implemented and promoted. It's not being Big Brother and not about calling everybody a threat. Sometimes even the term 'insider' makes people uneasy. Security leaders should position the concept within the organization properly, incorporating the language of the objective that clearly communicates the tangible risk for the enterprise. Any compliance requirements related to the program can facilitate the implementation process, since organization members understand industrywide compliance measures are a normal part of the business processes and are therefore more accepting with that perspective in mind.

Maintaining the program value focus. Important elements regarding the safety of intellectual property, and other benefits from the program having organization-wide impact, should also be communicated. In addition, it's strongly recommended that it be clearly presented as an organizational program, not just an initiative mandated by the CISO, and pushed as just another security regimen being implemented. These considerations help to establish and promote a cooperative groundwork early on in the program's development, and facilitate success by managing possible resistance before it has a chance to take root and gain momentum.

Prudent technical planning. Targeting the solution gaps that need to be filled and identifying the appropriate solutions to fill those gaps is a first phase of the process. Proof of concepts (POCs) are traditionally part of solution vetting at this stage. Effectively integrating new and existing technology solutions, instead of tearing everything down and building from the ground up, is a proven strategy for success. Identifying current capabilities, along opportunities to utilize plugins, or input un-siloed big data for holistic security analytics are beneficial considerations. Recognizing the emerging factors and influences of both on-premises and cloud environment requirements, and the need to implement comprehensive controls across all the organization's global domains, is part of the early planning. In addition, recognizing the benefits of a phased solution adoption approach has proven benefits in logistical implementation, budget expenditures and cost controls.

A broader view of engaged commitment and responsibility. Most members of an organization realize that security is not just one person, one department's job. It applies across the entire organization. A security initiative's success often requires the combined effort of a broad range members within the organization, and in many cases at all levels. Cooperative collaboration is a key value for success. CISOs may share the role responsibilities with IT counterparts, or take the lead, yet because of the significant

> *Most members of an organization realize that security is not just one person, one department's job. It applies across the entire organization.*

technology element involved in adopting new security solutions, a complex integration of people, products and processes must be taken into account. New software and new areas where security solutions are being implemented may impact the normal workflow of an organization. Organization members will look to information technology, cybersecurity officers and CISOs, to provide a thoughtful balance of leadership and partnership to shepherd the success of the initiative. Cross-organizational support and implementation lies at the heart of this blueprint for success.

Emerging standards and certification requirements

As mentioned above, communicating the requirement for meeting certain mandated security standards may be involved with proactively changing the corporate cultural perspectives, as well as being part of the process of organizational integration for a new security initiative. Encouraging more mindful awareness of cybersecurity needs and requirements is key to successful adherence to these standards. It is important to maintain a comprehensive perspective of the requirements of these standards and the holistic security needs of an organization. However, meeting all the requirements does not ensure complete security.

Compliance and certification: a starting point, not an end goal. Payment card industry (PCI) data security standards, FISMA (Federal Information Security Management Act) certifications, and other regulatory or self-directed standards, for example ISO 27000, are all created to ensure protection from a host of known (natural or man-made) threats. Usually organizations are worried about non-compliance, so they focus intensely on compliance. But to lose sight of the other emerging risks, outside the purview of these standards is a mistake. Some years ago, when there was a credit card breach, Visa's public statement often used to be: "The organization was not PCI compliant at the time of the breach." If one thinks about it, it would be a true assertion. Yet because people focus so much on compliance, those requirements only represent a snapshot in time. For example, there may be 250 controls that need to be implemented to

> *...to lose sight of the other emerging risks, outside the purview of these standards is a mistake.*

ensure the system is in compliance. But what if there was an update made following the certification, and that update introduced a vulnerability or exposed sensitive data? What if a system was considered out of scope or exempt from the compliance but ended up with the sensitive data and gets breached?

Incorporating risk-based thinking with compliance adherence. While auditors annually certify an organization, one subsequent update after certification leaves organizations just one change away from being non-compliant. And, what happens if there is a breach during that time? While a critical part of the security picture, these certification frameworks cannot function with omniscience. One of the biggest problems security leaders face is that security criteria and other sets of factors are evolving so quickly that compliance requirements can't possibly keep up with them. They're not addressing all of the risks; nor will they ever be able to. When a security program is primarily or solely based on a compliance focus, an enterprise may be compliant, but they may not have covered all of their risks. There will be gaps for emerging risk areas. Out of necessity, forward-looking security leaders are now changing their thinking to one that incorporates a risk-based approach.

Accounting for the risk of unknown for abuse cases. As responsible security leaders identify new threat vectors, they can't wait until a law or standard mandates a change in their controls to respond effectively. Many security practitioners and CISOs know they should have their primary security focus on a risk-based approach program, rather than primarily, and in some cases only, on standards to meet compliance requirements. Compliance is important for its assurance value, yet it should not be seen as the ultimate or only goal. Many organizations believe that if they are compliant, they're good to go; they have fulfilled their obligation and responsibilities. Yet, just because they may be compliant, security leaders, and the organizations they support, must not be lulled into the belief that their due diligence for holistic security has been achieved. Compliance is really only the beginning of comprehensive security hygiene.

Innovations and changing perspectives in organizational culture

People, process and technology are often intricately intertwined with the successful implementation of any new advanced strategic security initiative in today's fast-changing environments. Ideally, the advantages of greater productivity, higher efficiency, broader capabilities, and lower cost, are associated with the value of these strategic adoptions. Despite vendor assurances of ideal functionality and utility, however, when new solutions are presented that are ultimately revealed as difficult to use or integrate, or they

> *In some cases, the simplest and easiest to use solutions mask long-term limitations in the solution for robust capabilities and the expanded flexibility required for future solution growth with the environment.*

adversely impact the processes of corporate culture, in the end, they may not be cost effective. These solutions must be vetted and challenged for their de facto ultimate value. In some cases, the simplest and easiest to use solutions in the short term mask long-term limitations in the solution for robust capabilities and the flexibility required for future solution growth with the environment. The POC phase of any strategic security initiative is essential for vetting the prospective solution's unique requirements within the customer environment.

Solution providing heightened context. An example of an innovation available from select advanced security analytics vendors is the self-audit. Its impact on process and people is striking, providing high value, with comprehensive detailed and accurate results. From a technology perspective it is a component of a preexisting solution which is simple to use. Its value to security teams is that it delivers virtually zero false positives. From the user's perspective, it is something like a periodic credit card statement sent to every employee, showing their activity for the last week or month. With the recipient's unique knowledge of their own activity, their context, they're able to immediately flag any activity that is anomalous, enabling prompt remedial action, if needed. Organizations adopting this innovative solution have found it not only improves security effectiveness, but it has changed the culture of an organization in a positive way, where employees feel a sense of partnership, and join in protecting the organization.

Added efficiencies can elevate employee involvement. In the self-audit scenario, solution customers have reported it changed their employees' and contractors' behavior as it related to proactively enacting security procedures, such as readily updating their passwords and increasing their strength. They now had a visibility into their organization with a heightened understanding of the importance of proper security hygiene. That knowledge included the appreciation and understanding that all members of the organization should do their part to help keep the environment secure and free of malicious activity. A growing number of organization members felt they had a tangible stake in maintaining the welfare of the enterprise, and a responsibility in participating in the protection of the crown jewels. When you deputize your end user as part of your security solution, in effect making them partners, it changes their attitude and approach to security.

Verifying depth of engagement with adoption. One instance, shared from a colleague whose company delivered the self-audit feature, was quite revealing regarding the success of their program. The solution provider wanted to test the effectiveness of the self-audit, to see if employees were

> *They sent private self-audit reports to the entire employee base, and in doing so, sent counterfeit reports to 200 people. Within an hour, 150 tickets were opened with IT...*

really checking their activity. They sent private self-audit reports to the entire employee base, and in doing so, sent counterfeit reports to 200 people. Within an hour, 150 tickets were opened with IT from the 200 select employees, stating there was fraudulent access on their accounts. It was quite revealing the depth these people were involved with the self-audit program, which turned out to be a great success for the adopting company.

Expanded efficiencies with the self-audit. Some self-audit customers extend the functionality of the solution feature, to deliver added efficiencies by taking it to the next level of operational integration. Adopting the 'trust, but verify' concept, the employee's manager, or a project team leader, also receives a copy, to see if there is any anomaly. The managers and project leads have the context of what activity the team member should be involved with, and with that context are able to filter the information more effectively than a system administrator or security analyst. As well, the employee's motivation to align with requirements and expectations is strengthened with the knowledge that other members of the team at a higher level are reviewing the information too. In other cases, the self-audit was deployed as a supplemental revenue stream for an enterprise.

Considerations on adoption resistance within the organization. It's only natural for users to prefer the path of least resistance with their use of technology. One simple example is the previous iOS version for an iPhone had a passcode with four digits, and later versions had a six-digit option, for greater security. People would say they didn't like it and they didn't want to have the passcode at all, that the phone should always be on. This was how they managed their own devices. They felt entitled to this convenience. This sensibility of entitled convenience is so engrained in our day-to-day psychology, that the minute something adds a few clicks, or additional steps, people don't like it. Unfortunately, that attitude carries itself into the professional work environment. Education and awareness must be in place to redirect users' understanding that one wrong click in this setting can mean a serious compromise or a damaging breach that can impact the entire organization, and they may be seen as being responsible for the breach.

Security context and perspective for users to understand. The circumstances of users in an organizational setting might be compared to a TSA pre-screening check before you fly. When you travel in the post 9/11 world, the circumstances are entirely different. They demand adherence to security policies

> " *The security procedure may be perceived as an inconvenience, but there is no shortcut for safety and security.* "

based on very real threat scenarios. While people may complain about the inconvenience of removing their shoes, it is an undeniable fact that a terrorist in real life tried to blow up a commercial airline jet with a shoe bomb. This is also true in the enterprise environment setting. Very real and serious consequences are forcing organizations to continually evolve preventive measures. The security procedure may be perceived as an inconvenience, but there is no shortcut for safety and security. It's not about trying to take away someone's privileges, or freedom, but to maximize the safety and protection of the organization.

Shared protection comes from shared responsibility. Sometimes people have the feeling that it's the security team's job, with the perspective: "It's not *my* job to protect the organization." This is where the culture, from the top down, and from the bottom up, must begin to understand that it is truly a collective responsibility. Anyone can literally be just one or two clicks away from malware being downloaded and you've got a major incident in an organization. The end user at all levels must be aware that they have enormous power at their fingertip and in their clicks. If they all don't become mindful of security, it's not going to work. This is where the tagline almost all security departments, both physical and cyber, use: "Security: It's everyone's responsibility. *Sec_rity* is incomplete without *U*."

The CISO's critical role in contributing to organizational policy

I feel fortunate to have been in a security practitioner role for decades. Throughout that time, continuing to the present, one theme has been close to my heart, which is that the CISOs still traditionally do not have a seat at the table of corporate governance. It's important to understand the reasons behind this, what the implications are, and possibly offer a proactive thought leader vision for a path forward. Information security is no longer just an information technology issue. It is an organization-wide culture and value that must be adopted in the same way as the ethics, integrity and trust code of conduct provides the foundation for any enduring institution or enterprise. We do not need to wait for major debacles like the world-famous Enron, and others, to enact laws after the damage is done. We've seen too many examples of breaches where the CEO had to step down and the CISO/CSO position was vacated with replacements that followed. Cybercrime is one of the top global risks and will require significant resources and change of culture.

Security mandates seen in conflict with the bottom line. While numerous professional security certifications exist, security itself is not yet a standardized profession, and still quite new to some companies. Many organizations view information security as a cost center and a budget burden. For some outside the security infrastructure, it feels as if they're being forced to buy unwanted insurance which doesn't contribute to a company's bottom line. When push comes to shove, cool new product features almost always win out over prudent security planning. Making matters more concerning, some companies don't really pay too much attention to security until something happens. Then the fingers start to point, and the blame game begins.

New kid on the block. Because of its comparative late arrival to the corporate structure, exactly where CISOs sit in the hierarchy of companies and organizations remains unclear. It is still common for CISOs to report to a CIO or even lower within the IT group. In the healthcare industry, they often report to the CIO or CCO (chief compliance officer). Traditionally security leaders occupy director level positions, often two steps below the executive C-level. From an operational perspective, this means the CISOs' security goals often get lower priority than the objectives of the executives they report to.

Lower prioritization of mandate delivers higher risk to the organization. The differences of priorities for the CIO and CISO boils down to IT traditionally getting the lion's share of budget and resources for technology initiatives, while security needs are deferred or disassembled and re-prioritized. Throughout the industry verticals, most CSOs and CISOs struggle for recognition, funding and resources. Security planning, readiness and capabilities are minimized and suffer as a result, leaving security teams only able to respond tactically and reactively to challenges rather than strategically and proactively.

> *Security planning, readiness and capabilities are minimized and suffer as a result, leaving security teams only able to respond tactically and reactively to challenges, rather than strategically and proactively.*

Selected sectors support the CISO agenda. In more regulated industries, for example, financial services, CISOs roles have risen in importance out of necessity. Government and the high-tech vertical also put a high value on the CISO's mandate. As well, the size of an organization and its focus on research and development can influence the CISO's effectiveness within an enterprise. Yet as long as CISOs are embedded in the lower layers of management, without direct visibility to the top tier of management, the ability to effectively communicate the priorities of their mandate and evolving challenges remains compromised. This directly impacts their ability to get the budget and resources they need to build an effective cybersecurity program to protect the organization.

Status quo remains unchanged. In 2012, when I worked with *SC* magazine on an article relating to this topic, they cited a survey that indicated more and more CISOs were being heard in the boardroom and contributing more to organizational strategy. The survey findings were optimistic six years ago, encouraging a view that tangible progress was underway. With that trend observed in a setting where cybersecurity and threats are gaining continuously heightened awareness, one would expect by now a distinct and observable change in organizational dynamics at the executive level to be evident. I am afraid, however, that projection expressed in the survey does not reflect the reality I see today. Generally, CISOs are still in the back seat. Not much has really changed.

Reality check for future CISOs and their organizations. No matter what, the volume, variety and sophistication of threats will continue to rise, posing increasing risk for organizations. CISOs must be able to articulate the risks in business language to facilitate understanding at the C-level. This includes using metrics wherever possible to support the budget request, to avert the risk of disasters and cyber-attacks, and to demonstrate the value of a prospective security investment. The sobering alternative is that these threats can significantly impact the business. As we have seen with a large number of notable breaches in recent years, these issues can't be ignored. Organizations must view the head of cybersecurity with the caliber of importance reality demands, and provide enough authority, resources, budget, and visibility at the highest level in the organization. An operational independence should be part of this change, so that crippling conflicts of interest are removed from the dynamic. The very survival of an enterprise may depend on it.

CONCLUSIONS & TAKEAWAYS:
Priorities of insider threat programs

Devin Bhatt's experience with a range of public and private sector security challenges gives him a unique perspective. As well, he understands the value of security professionals sharing information, along with recognizing the dangers of those exceptions where executives may think that hiding breach information helps protect their image in the marketplace. In fact they're endangering a company's livelihood. Especially critical is the need for the executive level to recognize the importance of the CISO's mandate. While it may not be a profit center, it should be seen as a profit protection center, and provided with a completely justifiable budget allocation. And with the new EU GDPR mandate in play, which requires all multinational organizations controlling the personal data of EU citizens to be able to report breaches within 72 hours, or suffer a 4% fine of their global revenue, supporting a CISO's objectives from the entire executive level is critical for a company's well-being. In some cases it will be a matter of survival. Evolutionary thinking of the executive board is required. Full standards compliance does not mean the environment is secure.

Insider threat programs are a significant component of the CISO's charter. Bhatt's insights cover not only the technical elements required for a successful insider threat program, but also include the way the program is staged within the organization. Every element of insider threat programs, from inception to implementation and evolving maintenance, must be approached with the end goal in sight: the long-term effectiveness and success of the program. This includes acceptance at all levels. On this point, the self-audit feature, available with a select number of advanced security analytics vendors, has been shown to not only deliver low false positives, but also engender an organization-wide sense of partnership with the insider threat program.

In any event, Bhatt recognizes that the age of manual security monitoring has passed. Meanwhile, privileged access entitlement management, data-centric security and controls are needed, and the requirement for perpetual due diligence continues to rise, with the need to place identity as the new threat plane at the center of a CISO's security strategies. IAM systems are no longer capable of addressing the security requirements alone. To address these challenges, a strategic shift to the adoption of security analytics driven by advanced machine learning algorithms, drawing comprehensive context from big data, accounting for the gray areas and blind spots, bringing identity closer to the data, is the only viable option at this point from the technologies that are available to organizations today.

In the following *Borderless Breach Flashcard*, one company faced a virtual threat to its survival from the results of an insider breach, and then it got worse. Moreover, this initial breach took place after the company thought they had performed all the correct due diligence and taken all the proper security precautions. In the following chapter, the factors of identity, access risks and access outliers will be examined in relation to their critical importance in Borderless Behavior Analytics.

BORDERLESS BREACH FLASHCARD *Stealing the Wind*	
CATEGORY	Data theft, economic espionage by foreign powers.
WHO	**The target:** American Superconductor Corporation (ACC), wind turbine high-tech component manufacturer.
WHAT	American Superconductor partnered with Sinovel, a small Chinese firm partly owned by the government. Sinovel manufactured the skeleton hardware for the turbines, while ACC supplied the proprietary sophisticated control technology and computer code to run them.
WHEN	2011
WHERE	USA, China, Austria, transnational insider breach, followed by cyber-attacks thru social media.
WHY	Economic greed, market control.
HOW	Already aware of China's reputation for theft of American intellectual property, ACC took extensive security precautions to protect their technology with encrypted protocols and kept the IP off the internet. Unable to reverse engineer the technology, the Chinese used classic entrapment spycraft and recruited an Austrian employee of ACC who had privileged access to the proprietary software. Once turned, the Chinese gave the insider a shopping list of items, including source code to the technology, and then put it into production. Later, when ACC engineers were testing the next-generation of software in the turbines in China, they discovered their new software was already installed. Once the breach was discovered, ACC brought a lawsuit against the Sinovel. In turn, the Chinese military's cyber-espionage Unit 61398 launched a phishing email attack against ACC. It succeeded and gave the Chinese complete access to all of ACC's legal strategies.
HOW BAD?	ACC lost their lawsuit against Sinovel. ACC's total economic loss is well over a billion dollars, with a workforce reduction from 900 to 300. Adding insult to injury, Massachusetts, ACC's home state, later purchased these windmills with the stolen software in it using U.S. federal stimulus funds.
HOW COULD IT BE AVOIDED?	If UEBA had been in place, it is likely that data exfiltration would have surfaced as anomalous behavior with unusual downloads of sensitive intellectual property. In addition, an unusual concentration of access requests targeted on the Chinese lawsuit within ACC's legal department would also have likely raised alerts the security team could respond to.

Identity, Access Risks and Access Outliers

The Thresholds to Cross, The Gaps to Fill

How far must enterprises go to assure their access plane is risk free?

It is no longer enough for companies to merely shore up defenses against general dangers. Evidence-based knowledge — drawn from context, mechanisms, indicators, implications and actionable intelligence — can help leaders prepare for precise strikes against IT or information assets. Concurrently, forward-thinking CISOs recognize that identity — as a core element of access — represents a serious potential threat plane to the environment. Yet with that recognition, another reality rears its ugly head. Manual processes and legacy roles driving identity and access management (IAM) today leave far too many open doors. In addition, the ubiquitous advent of hybrid and on-premises data centers, integrated with a range of cloud applications, represents a widening surface area as the complexity of access increases with technology innovation.

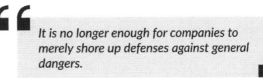

> It is no longer enough for companies to merely shore up defenses against general dangers.

The practice of periodically rubber-stamping certifications for compliance in no realistic way resolves access risks. Instead, it is an ineffective waste of time and broadens the access risk plane. Consider, for example, a small enterprise environment with *100* users, with *10* accounts each, plus each account has *10* entitlements (*100 x 10 x 10*). That totals *10,000* entitlements. Then consider compliance certifications are required quarterly, and you must manually manage *40,000* entitlements per year for only *100* users! That's just one slice of the access complexity beyond human capacity to analyze. Add to that all the other entities, devices and applications operating within the environment, and the magnitude of potential for identity-based access risks then expands to a sobering scale for any CISO.

These are access entitlements that IT is theoretically aware of, but there are also instances of privileged access entitlements that occur which are unknown to IT. Some experts say as much as 50%, or more, of an organization's privileged access is unknown. That's a lot of access. More accurately, that's a lot of unmanaged access and unknown privileged access. To

> *To manage risk across the access plane, how can an organization achieve that if it doesn't even know who has privileged access entitlements?*

manage risk across the access plane, how can an organization achieve that if it doesn't even know who has privileged access entitlements?

A new approach to security is essential. Just as importantly, it must be a smart approach. This approach must have the right phases and steps that address today's known challenges, to effectively position an organization to manage the unknown threats of tomorrow, and to scale with the evolving requirements of the future. The core focus of the solution to this challenge lies in a functional merging of identity analytics (IdA) with UEBA (user and entity behavior analytics).

The disquieting discovery gap of access in privileged access in IAM and privileged access management (PAM) solutions is closed by the fusing of IdA and UEBA capabilities. For a UEBA solution to monitor and analyze privileged account abuse, it first needs to know where privileged access resides, and this comes from IdA. Legacy methods of identifying privileged accounts with tags, prefixes or other traditional approaches, have resulted in missing more than 50% of privileged access, much of it having been granted over time at the entitlement level via privilege escalations.

Compatible with IAM/PAM solutions, identity analytics improves with the ability to ingest and analyze data from their varied environments (including hybrid) to deliver a risk-based solution for identity access management from the analytics made possible by integration with UEBA. IdA removes rubber-stamping and access cloning, provides risk-based certifications, detects access outliers, cleans up access for dormant and orphan accounts, and reduces workload with dynamic access provisioning.

IdA is a major evolutionary phase for empowering IAM/PAM. The leading IdA solutions reside in a few best-of-breed UEBA vendors that provide identity analytics through machine learning models. The advantages of a UEBA-IdA solution adoption for reducing risk within an organization's environment continue to become apparent. For example, as a first empowering step, an organization can drastically reduce its identity attack surface area before integrating a UEBA component of the solution that will detect behavior-based anomalies. Gurucul's best practices for advanced security analytics solution installation recommends a discovery and deactivation process (using IdA) of targeting all inactive, orphan or dormant accounts and misaligned or excess entitlements.

In one real-world Gurucul case, a financial institution implementing this process reduced their potential internal access risk plane of accounts and entitlements by 83%. They took their world of identity-based access risks and minimized them in one straightforward and comprehensive project step. Only the required users and entities that remained within the enterprise had up-to-date access permissions and entitlements. At this phase in the adoption of advanced security analytics, using IdA first, the planned implementation of UEBA was measurably streamlined and optimized.

From this point in a solution adoption, the ultimate goal for security and risk teams implementing IdA would be to maintain risk-based access only when, where and how it is appropriate, to the right individuals. Then the enterprise would have a more effective UEBA monitoring solution to look for the unknowns, the behavior anomalies that might indicate a compromise and a possible breach.

By leveraging a risk-based approach, access is no longer defined or constrained by hard and fast static rules of access control. The evolving challenge remains how to continually improve controls on access and optimize comprehensive 360-degree monitoring. How do you reliably maintain the surface area of access?

> *How do you reliably reduce the surface area of access?*

One IdA solution component entails refining the context of access controls. For example, with someone working in a high-tech R&D department, why might they need access to sensitive information while on vacation in Hawaii, unless they had indicated their plan to do so ahead of time? What kind of device might this engineer be attempting to access with? Is it out of the ordinary? This enhanced context insight into identity and access risk is empowered by IdA risk scoring. Making sure users and entities have access to assets only when and where they need it is a core mandate of IdA consolidated with UEBA. In the case with the engineer in Hawaii, their ad hoc access request would leverage risk scoring for approval.

With the implementation of IdA and UEBA — drawing from data science and machine learning, which supports the evolving and deep system knowledge behind every identity — the prospect of rapidly and confidently targeting

> *With... IdA and UEBA – drawing from data science and machine learning, which supports the evolving and deep system knowledge behind every identity – the prospect of rapidly... targeting access outliers and access risks on the identity risk plane becomes eminently more manageable.*

access outliers and access risks on the identity risk plane becomes eminently more manageable.

Through baseline definitions built and defined for each identity, account, access and activity — analyzed against peer groups — a 'living' persona of 'normal' is created to detect anomalies. It is performed through continuous self-learning and self-training machine learning models. This comprehensive UEBA-IdA solution capability enables security teams to reliably spot privileged access risks, to proactively reduce access risks and monitor risk-scored behavior from a single view. This keeps access risks clean for the access rights provided, as well as providing monitoring for behavior-based anomalies and threats. The two sides work holistically together.

If a high-risk-scored behavior anomaly occurs, a SOC knows the exact details and avoids wasting time. For example: *what's* happening and *when* (e.g., an unusual volume of prioritized data is being accessed); *who* is performing it (actions that might be completely contrary to their user's identity use profile); *where* the action is taking place (which might be remote and unsanctioned); and *how*, on *what* device (an atypical one, which might also trip alerts).

Two practical use cases exemplify the utility, functionality, and value of a UEBA-IdA solution:

- A software development company needs to ensure an application developer has access to the production environment to do his work. The enterprise's leadership team is concerned that different developers with the same permissions can get into the same production environment and make changes in the code that are unwarranted or unsanctioned. IdA facilitates removing high-risk or shared access risks and provides intelligent roles for users based on the context of accounts, access and activity. Now controls are placed on particular files with risk-based access certifications on who can check them out.

- A company's payroll system contains sensitive information, and as a matter of course, issues can arise with its functionality. A help desk ticket is opened and the issue is forwarded to the support professional who is on call. By opening the ticket, the individual is requesting temporary access permission from a PAM system. IdA would validate the access is privileged when used and would provide a risk score on this access. As the support team member is given special access into the payroll system to work on resolving the issue, UEBA would monitor the identity, account, access and activity for abuse, compromise and anomalies during the workflow. When the support member has completed his work, he checks the ticket back in. With it, his access to the payroll system

> **IdA would validate the access is privileged when used and would provide a risk score on this access.**

closes. The enterprise systems accessed by this support team member are only enabled in direct association with the help desk tickets he is assigned to and only for the period of the support action response itself into which IdA and UBEA maintain full visibility.

None of this is possible unless an enterprise knows who the individual is, so that systematic assessments can be performed based what their defined roles are, as well as, the context of the activity by user. Clearly, modern enterprises represent a range of sizes and business models. As a result, they have different uses and requirements for UEBA and IdA.

In the following section, CIO Teri Takai shares her perspectives and insights from her broad range of experience in government and enterprises. They relate to how IdA and UEBA's advanced security analytics address the challenges of managing identity, access risks and access outliers in a broad range of emerging cloud and hybrid cloud network environments. Following this, we'll share additional observations on her insights about the Borderless Behavior Analytics story.

BORDERLESS EXPERT INSIGHTS

Teri Takai*
CIO at Large

Currently a Senior Advisor for the Center for Digital Government, Teri Takai recently served as the CIO and EVP of Meridian Health Plan. Prior to that, she served as the Department of Defense Chief Information Officer (DoD CIO). In this capacity, Ms. Takai was the principal advisor to the Secretary of Defense for Information Management/Information Technology and Information Assurance, as well as non-intelligence space systems, critical satellite communications, navigation, and timing programs, spectrum and telecommunications. She provided strategy, leadership and guidance, to create a unified information management and technology vision for the DoD. As Chief Information Officer for the State of California, she led more than 130 CIOs and 10,000 IT employees spread across the state's different agencies, departments, boards, commissions, and offices. Prior to these positions, she was a Director at the Ford Motor Company, serving the company for over thirty years.

A member of Gurucul's Executive Advisory Board, Ms. Takai has supplied instrumental support in the company's planning, development and strategy for the organization's solution development and market approach with a special focus on identity and access intelligence analytics and management. In this chapter she provides her expert insights on the challenges of identity access management with organizations facing the challenges of migrating from legacy environments into the cloud.

Overview

Identity is a new perimeter and threat plane that CIOs, CSOs and CISOs must address to reduce risk, protect resources and detect threats. Identity is a plane that intersects with virtually every data source within the IT infrastructure and its importance only increases with cloud adoption. Many organizations still rely on declarative legacy roles, rubber-stamping certifications and manual processes to manage identities exposing them to excess access risks and access outliers. External threat actors compromise identities to evade detection from existing defenses while insiders work under the radar to access data for exfiltration. Analyzing access, activity and alerts with identity-centric behavior analytics provides a new defense for a new perimeter.

---

* The views and opinions expressed by Teri Takai in this book are her own, and do not necessarily reflect those of her current, or any of her previous employers.

Evolving perspectives on identity as a new perimeter

In the past, a first order of business for chief information officers was focused on protecting their data at the perimeter. Today, many continue with this traditional perspective and there are multiple ways of doing that. They have implemented new

> *It's quickly reaching the point... where it's impossible for organizations to keep up effectively with the threat vector.*

technologies in terms of next-generation firewalls, and other solutions designed to protect the perimeter, all of which remain a necessary part of the IT infrastructure. It's quickly reaching the point, however, where it's impossible for organizations to keep up effectively with the threat vector. CIOs, CSOs and CISOs must realize that a shift in thinking is in order to face the new challenges of what happens if someone is in their networks and how they then protect their data.

Recognizing a new reality of the perimeter. The second element of this new priority perspective is that as we migrate to the cloud, we're usually not taking our entire infrastructure to the cloud. Instead, organizations are using cloud providers that effectively support a particular area of the business but are nonetheless connected to their networks. That trend highlights this second vulnerability which is increasing and growing as it poses three crucial questions: What is the perimeter? What's protecting the perimeter? Is that protection effective?

> *What is the perimeter? What's protecting the perimeter? Is that protection effective?*

Risks posed by partners in the environment. The third priority involves the recognition that going forward, enterprises will need to engage with external partners on an expanding basis. While this trend is not new, its impact has become much more acute and the factors behind it are changing and evolving. Clearly, the notorious Target data breach of 2013 received a great deal of attention in headlines. However, it has not necessarily raised appropriate awareness of the serious security concerns behind that story. Many times in the past under legacy environment frameworks, partners engaged with file transfers. Now as use patterns move more towards APIs, and more active exchange ensues, this opens all the participating organizations to the vulnerabilities of all their partners.

The essentials of protecting the amorphous new perimeter. These new realities compel the security community to expand and reform their concept of what it really means to protect at the perimeter, which is continually changing. The essentials of this challenge boil down to two crucial certainties. The first point is that it's important for us to have tools that effectively show what is happening in our network. The second point says that relying on personnel to continue to manually monitor the networks is no longer a reliable security practice. The scope and volume of data, users, and systems is simply too vast. The only realistic approach now is to move into a machine learning environment where comprehensive visibility, monitoring and analytics can be

> *The only realistic approach now is to move into a machine learning environment where comprehensive visibility, monitoring and analytics can be set up, based on the behaviors observed and reliable effective alerts can be provided.*

set up, based on the behaviors observed, and reliable effective alerts can be provided.

Insider risk, the hidden time bomb

The next element of delivering network security assurance centers on having a clear understanding of what constitutes the insider risk. This subject has been the topic of paramount concern in government circles, especially the Department of Defense (DoD) at the time the WikiLeaks challenge occurred. This was exacerbated by the 2013 Edward Snowden incident. What's critical to understand is that these cases did not necessarily involve threat actors who planned to do intentional harm. However, this is the way many traditional enterprise SOCs think of and approach the problem.

> *...these cases did not necessarily involve threat actors who planned to do intentional harm. However, this is the way many traditional enterprise SOCs think of and approach the problem.*

Unintentional bad behavior remains a serious risk. With the workforce changing, and being accustomed to having access to all types of information, it becomes increasingly difficult to ensure secure data. In many cases the insider risk turns out to be unintentional. Numerous organizations, including my own experience in state jobs, at the DoD, and also at a healthcare company I worked for, was to run drills to show people what would happen when they inadvertently clicked on links in emails they shouldn't have clicked on.

Valid and compromised identities represent risk. Identity is clearly a new perimeter. While compromises and breaches are not always driven by malicious motivations, they still represent a threat plane of serious risk for any organization. Security leaders should keep this in mind when planning the next generation of security assurance in their networks.

IAM controls access

Identity and access management (IAM) has been the main focus to control access, but this traditional approach no longer addresses the security demands of today's sprawling perimeters. A key requirement is to assure organizations have the analytics in place to be able to understand what activity is occurring in the network for the access granted. To achieve this, security leaders need to know about both what the next generation of identity is, as well as the next generation of identity management controls.

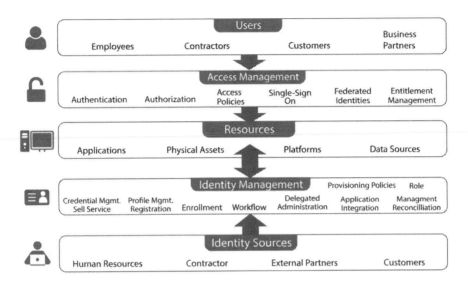

IAM Controls Access
Figure 5.1

Traditional identity management's increasing challenges. The illustration above depicts the identity and access management issues in greater detail. At the top, the user base itself represents a range of different issues and challenges with employees versus contractors, versus customers and business partners. Historically, in addition to protecting at the perimeter, IT teams tried to control access with access management policies through identity management solutions.

New complexities compound the difficulties. The security assurance problem is more clearly illustrated when you examine the details in the access management box. It calls out a range of security access processes. In the box above are the different resources, such as various applications and platforms. All of these come with an accompanying array of complexity. Network experts logically ask, "How do you

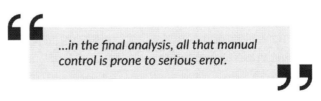

...in the final analysis, all that manual control is prone to serious error.

actually do that?" Managing this through provisioning, policies, registrations, and so on, can only be achieved if organizations commit a significant amount of headcount to manually control all that access. Yet in the final analysis, all that manual control is prone to serious error.

The urgency of recognizing new requirements in security. When one considers the number of applications, the number of legacy applications, as well as the systems administration rights — and the difficulty with being able to administer all of that across the numerous users and the various identity sources — it quickly becomes clear this requirement for reliable network access security can only be achieved with robust analytic support and machine learning. Recognizing the need to respond and adapt to this profound growth in network access risk is critical for the CIO's and CISO's organizational survival and success.

Data expansion in modern networks

Data continues to expand with increasing velocity and variety. This is the challenging new normal facing CIOs, CSOs and CISOs. IDC Research (International Data Corporation) observes that data is growing so quickly that it will reach 44 zettabytes by 2020. And an interesting fact conveyed from the PBS special — *The Human Face of Big Data* — cites that humanity ingested the same volume of data in their lifetimes during the 16th century as they would in two days of modern times. However, there's an important extension to these observations which impacts network security today.

Legacy systems facing evolving technologies. Even as one views the technologies of 2013, security experts recognize that a majority of legacy systems, both from government and commercial sectors, date back well before 2013. While it's interesting to look at the 16th century, the pertinent exercise is to view the mid-1900's, which provided the framework of thinking where so many of these legacy systems originated. The network architects' priorities at the time were all focused on mainframe, file transfers and controlled access to data. They could in no way anticipate, or account for, the sophisticated access and staggering data volume that IT organizations face today. They never conceived of their networks being accessed by the general public or by someone in a different geographical area. When you correlate that infrastructure model with the way data are growing, it clearly indicates there must be a new and different approach to how we're protecting that data.

> *The network architects... could in no way anticipate, or account for, the sophisticated access and staggering data volume that IT organizations face today.*

Government priority on revamping security. Today there's a great deal of focus in the federal government on what to do about securing legacy systems. The former Federal CIO, Tony Scott, put a great deal of attention on the renovation of those legacy systems to ensure they are secure. Anyone can sign up for *Federal Computer Week's* daily email (https://fcw.com/). There, you can see the government's approach regarding how they protect their systems and how they achieve that with the old legacy systems still occupying a sizable footprint in network technology.

Data + Access = Threat Surface

When engaging in next-generation thinking beyond the constraints of traditional legacy environment perspectives, security leaders need to recognize the new challenges posed by identity. The first element is the existence of the insider risk. The second involves external partners who need to access an organization's data, in turn creating access outliers that may or may not be known by the system owner. The third component addresses the challenge of being able to keep up with this onslaught of data on-demand, to see, or allow others to see, the data safely and effectively to run the business. The complexity of these challenges centers on a pure and all-encompassing access management framework. Data and access are linked, opening up the surface area for access risks centered on these essential points:

- Compromise and misuse of identity is at the root of modern threats.
- Identity is also a perimeter with excess access risks and access outliers.
- Security cannot be assured unless organizations know: who has access, when was the access, and whether the identity should have access.

Complex access management requirements. While organizations must provide the access to whoever needs it, when they need it, as well as the level of access required, they also need to be able take it away whenever necessary. This is a key point. People within a company may be moving to other positions within the organization, and in doing so, no longer need particular access rights. Those unrequired (and fundamentally unsupervised by the original owner) access identities accumulate within an organization; the risk associated with each one grows as well. Access management policies and processes must be quicker to respond, to close the gap between what access is really needed and what organizations are continuing to allow reflexively.

Accelerating access complexities. Here's a case in point regarding the challenges managing access entitlements: Workforces have different access needs, at different times, plus levels of data management expertise. Identity aggregates multiple accounts and entitlements per user or entity. So if an organization had *1000* users with *10* accounts each, that would equal *10,000* credentials to manage. Then add in *10* permissions per account and that would equal *100,000* entitlements to manage. That's a considerable access risk and threat surface area.

Realistic controls on access required. This example, while seemingly dramatic, actually represents a reality within organizations. It encourages security leaders to step back and think about the number of users in a company, think about what these users (and entities) need access to, and even within that, what permissions they need. This highlights the challenge of how an organization actually manages that, and how that organization realistically controls what individuals have access to.

The consequences of failed access management

Organizations and their workforces face growing threats through breaches of their identities. Hijacked accounts enable intruders with full access rights of the employee. Security leaders

> Security leaders must now assume that external actors are in their infrastructure. This urgently reinforces their prime mandate: protect your data.

must now assume that external actors are in their infrastructure. This urgently reinforces their prime mandate: protect your data.

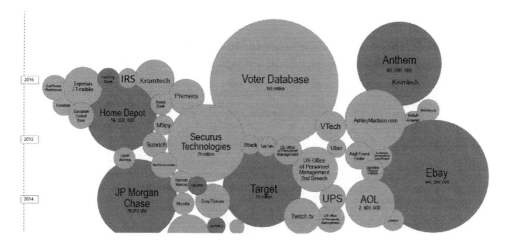

The World's Biggest Data Breaches
2014 to Mid-2016
(Source: http://www.informationisbeautiful.net/)
Figure 5.2

Breach trends growing. The illustration above provides a vivid example of how widespread data breaches have been over the last two years and the magnitude of the damage. While many are probably known to the majority of readers, seeing the range of impact within a correlating context is instructive. These breach

> ...many organizations just feel overwhelmed and they don't really know what it takes to ensure they have the best security possible.

trends are becoming far more visible to the senior management of organizations, up to the board level. A problem, however, is that many organizations just feel overwhelmed and they don't really know what it takes to ensure they have the best security possible. This is a growing issue where the government may need to expand control and requirements of standards for disclosure. As well, there are contributing factors to these breach trends that security leaders should keep in mind.

Training is insufficient. Training is no longer adequate to address identity threats and account hijacking. As it relates to the insider risk and the insider management, while virtually every company does training and periodic drills, it's insufficient. We now live in a world, depending on the particular demographics of any company, where people are just used to being able to click on things and feel secure to do so. Attackers today are devising ingenious ways to encourage people to believe their email link is legitimate. It is highly unlikely that anyone reading this has never clicked on something at least once that they shouldn't have. So the takeaway is that it doesn't mean there shouldn't be training, but training alone will not deal with the dimension and the size of the problem.

Workforces change constantly. New hires, departures, part-time and remote workers are part of the constant ebb and flow of the modern workplace. These new, departing and terminated employees are high-risk groups who require special focused analysis. In addition, high privileged access (HPA) accounts are also a high-risk group often with accompanying account sharing which compounds the risk element. Another element of the emerging workforce transformation that organizations are contending with is the use of a growing number of contract resources, some of whom may work remotely. While that contract resource may come in for days, weeks, months, or ultimately become a permanent part of the enterprise, the organization remains dependent upon whoever they have contracted, to ensure the access to the network is secure. This is a characteristic of the new 'gig economy', where more and more people will be serving for short-term engagements, and the trend will likely only increase over time. Moreover, access to the network often doesn't end with the end of the engagement. This may be unintentional, but the risk of this open access is real.

Unchecked expansion of a range of access. As organizations move into engaging that kind of broad range of individuals, while still maintaining a core employee workforce, it becomes increasingly more difficult to control access through our existing identity management solutions. If you consider the scenario mentioned earlier that resulted with a hundred thousand entitlements, think how that will change on a daily basis. It fully exacerbates the problem to the point where it is fundamentally uncontrollable.

The importance of detecting access risk or access outliers

If they haven't already, CIOs must realize that they will be breached. It's just a question of when, and how badly. In late 2016, *IT Security Guru* cited a survey which reported that,

> *If they haven't already, CIOs must come to the realization that they will be breached. It's just a question of when, and how badly.*

"65% of IT leaders expect a serious data breach to hit their business within the next year." This is a frightening statistic. Whether that's on purpose, whether it's inadvertent, regardless of where it comes from, there will be individuals accessing information in networks who shouldn't. Particularly with the insider threat, that's an important concept for all security leaders to keep in mind.

The criteria of visibility. Once CIOs acknowledge the inevitability of a breach of some magnitude, it then becomes critical to ensure comprehensive visibility. This entails first being able to set ground rules around what SOCs want visibility of, then to have visibility of it. After this, and most importantly, they must have the machine learning capability to continually iterate on the data and context to facilitate threat and risk analysis, recognition and response.

The balance between human requirements and efficiencies. With these visibility objectives in mind, here's an example of the challenges many CIOs face with selecting and integrating new solutions into the security mix. In this case it relates to solutions we were considering at the Department of Defense. Many of the early user behavioral analytics tools required a significant amount of analytic time from individuals looking at data in order to detect the anomalies from false positives. We decided it was prohibitive to even think about implementing the tool, not because of the tool's cost, but because we couldn't afford the manpower to do the analyses with the tool.

Enhanced efficiencies with next generation UEBA. With the next generation of UEBA tools, the human resource requirement is changing. CIOs don't need the same levels of staff or high analytic expertise as before. A majority of the analysis can be done using the tool that will learn from itself. These advancements are exactly the advantages we were seeking at the Department of Defense. Unfortunately, they did not yet exist in a robust, mature and reliable form. However, the older generation of UEBA tools, which lack the efficiencies of real machine learning, are still also available on the market. Organizations must exercise prudence when considering an adoption of this kind.

> *With the next generation of UEBA tools, the human resource requirement is all changing. CIOs don't need the same levels of staff or high analytic expertise as before.*

The impact of cloud applications on IAM

Simply put, cloud applications change identity management dramatically. During my Ford Motor Company experience, one of the initiatives Ford performed over time, was to build our own very large application systems. We put in what we felt were very sophisticated identity management and access management solutions. These were ultimately linked to active directory and a common email.

Yesterday's environments working with tomorrow's solutions. Now CIOs are faced with two challenges. The first is they want to supplement their homegrown systems with a software as a service (SaaS) solution, for example, a CRM (customer relationship management) tool, which sits outside the original network perimeter. The second is that the control and configuration of SaaS solutions are different. The CIO's desire is to integrate one of those CRM tools into the legacy systems that have information necessary to manage the customer. The current access management and identity management schemes, however, don't provide the control needed to ensure comprehensive security.

A multitude of access points. To begin with, the advent of cloud applications means CIOs are dealing with more than one access management approach. For one particular data access scenario, users must come through the SaaS provider, then they have to go to legacy data, or the legacy application identity management solution. That means it becomes increasingly difficult to accurately control that access and assess risk. Within this rising complexity, CIOs must be able to both control access and monitor the access in near real-time, to see where the anomalies are. That is why a tool like a mature UEBA solution integrated with identity analytics (IdA) is so important as a supplement to today's access management capabilities.

Visibility across the IT and SOC domains of responsibility. UBEA with IdA provides a holistic perspective addressing access risks and detecting unknown threats. Historically, CIOs might not have seen it that way, where the IT side of an organization would be responsible for access, while the security side looked for threats. In too many cases in the past, however, both sides considered them to be completely separate priorities. In doing so, they might have been missing a critical access risk aspect of the identity threat plane.

An old problem with new insights. While everyone's heard more about Target than they've cared to, there's still another angle to consider with this case. It's remarkable that there are organization leaders who don't understand the organized crime threat and how identity has been leveraged for malicious ends. They don't see that their data might represent an identity management access threat or a privacy concern. These adversaries have become sophisticated in

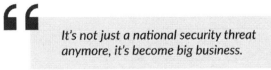

It's not just a national security threat anymore, it's become big business.

terms of being able to piece data together from different sources to produce lucrative results. It's not just a national security threat anymore, it's become big business. Organizations face a new form of competition, which is ruthless, unethical and targeted on the crown jewels of the enterprise: their data.

Surpassing IAM capabilities

With this evolving rich complexity of identities and access privileges, the ability to holistically control access through IAM has passed. Traditional declarative roles and groups lack the flexibility for today's needs. Active directory (AD) and other directories often have access conglomeration and group proliferation.

> "With this evolving rich complexity of identities and access privileges, the ability to holistically control access through IAM has passed."

IAM challenges include:
- Dealing with multiple identities
- Dealing with multiple accounts
- Managing many manual tasks
- Coping with ill-defined business processes
- Expectation to make the IAM a data synchronization engine for application data
- Getting all stakeholders to share a common view of solution objectives, priorities and responsibilities
- Lack of leadership and support from sponsors
- Deploying too many siloed IAM technologies in a short period of time
- Lack of consistent architectural vision

Manual management of identity is outdated. Any of the bullet points above represent a checklist of its own. There could be paragraphs of insight around what each means and why it exacerbates the identity management issue. But in summation, taking all of these factors into account, the idea of being able to deal manually with the multiple identities, accounts and access entitlements becomes virtually impossible. The only logical deduction you can arrive at is that a new approach is required.

Symptoms of struggling identity management

The first symptom that companies are struggling with identity management is rooted in the fact that a large number of organizations have an enterprise architecture that has become outdated, obsolete. Consequently, the value and utility identity management solutions deliver vary based on when they were adopted and their suitability to the context of today's environments. In addition, they are different at the platform level as well. As a result, the ability to standardize how an organization performs pure system administration at the platform level becomes a serious challenge.

Status quo equals status 'no'. Technology does not sleep, and of course, security leaders must keep their eye on an evolving market and the next generation of identity management. Hoping the current legacy identity management solutions will continue to serve an organization is unfortunately

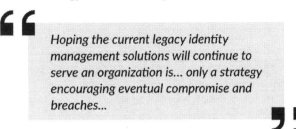

Hoping the current legacy identity management solutions will continue to serve an organization is... only a strategy encouraging eventual compromise and breaches...

only a strategy encouraging eventual compromise and breaches which will likely be discovered only months later. This scenario benefits no one, including those on the IT staff.

Evolving technologies and growing challenges. Another symptom of struggling identity management is at the application level. CIOs remain hard-pressed to control the way applications are rolled out to ensure they have consistency of identity management across all their solutions. Add into this rich mix in the environment the newer technologies needing to drive through APIs, along with enterprises wanting to accommodate external customers and business partners. These are all areas where these problems have grown significantly and they represent a major challenge for the CIO.

Accurate visibility of risk plane restricted by traditional tools. Too many elements of the hybrid environment are nebulous and changing quickly so that it is not humanly possible to manage them all. The resource cost is prohibitive. As a result, it is equally challenging for any CIO or CISO to be expected to know exactly what their identity access risk and threat plane is from the view available through traditional legacy access management. When you add to that the desire for businesses to have more control over who has access, where it's actually out of the hands of the CIO, the imperative to have a different perspective on this entire mounting problem becomes even more critical.

New solutions should support existing solutions. One key point to keep in mind, however, is this new perspective is not about replacing the identity management solutions organizations have today. There's nothing wrong with them within their functional context. They still service a crucial part of the environment. They just lack the comprehensiveness to close the awareness gap of what access has been provided and how the access is being utilized. They need to go to the next generation. However, until that next generation of identity management is fully developed and mature, which in many cases means replacing aging legacy systems, organizations need to supplement the system with identity analytics driven by machine learning. This means security leaders should have different tools and different approaches which deal with the access environment the CIO has today to be able to move forward successfully. Any mature UEBA solution with identity analytics fills an awareness gap as an integrated part of the tool suite. It offers a risk-based approach of identity access management for organizations that was not originally provided by their solution framework.

How do CIOs and CISOs achieve security assurance? The pressing questions for CIOs and CISOs are: How do they get to where they are confident their long-term security decisions are risk-based? How do they use the right identity analytics to reduce excess access and access outliers, along with user and entity behavior analytics solutions to detect unknown threats, beyond rules, signatures and patterns? In this rapidly evolving world, most are recognizing they can't do it alone. Before, they only had to identify and manage the red and green — the bad and the good activities. Now they must also manage and monitor the massive amount of gray in their environments — the unknown unknowns.

> *Before, they only had to identify and manage the red and green – the bad and the good activities. Now they must also manage and monitor the massive amount of gray – the unknown unknowns – in their environments.*

Partnering with solution providers who 'Get it'

Facing the imperative to implement productive change to ensure network security, CIOs and CISOs face a range of solution vendors. Many are quick to point out what's wrong with the CISOs' environments and what needs to be changed or replaced. More mature solution vendors approach this prospect and discussion from more of a partnership perspective that communicates, "Yes, in fact you have a problem with your legacy systems, but we understand replacing them is a long, lengthy and ugly process. Until you can replace them, how are you going to be able to understand who's accessing those systems, how they're being accessed and who's actually utilizing the information? We have that experience and customers who can verify that. We can help you." What this means is the solution must supplement, and perhaps modify the access security strategy, not replace it. These solution providers must be able to complement the current protection of the identity perimeter, and protection of the data, and delivering the ability to see who actually is accessing the data.

> *What this means is the solution must supplement, and perhaps modify the network security strategy, not replace it.*

Ease of use after adoption. When considering these security solutions, CIOs should also take into account their workforce's productivity. While some CISOs may believe they are adopting a technology that secures and manages access, if it is too painstaking to work with, it will result in employee frustration. Some of the workforce may even try to find a way to skirt the new system to make their jobs easier. This creates a new access risk and threat plane. Adopting organizations and solution vendors must take these factors into account together to assure the solution is one that can be institutionalized and supported over the long term by all involved. Lack of support will likely lead to solution failure.

Final perspectives on identity management and UEBA providing identity analytics

With the title of this book being *Borderless Behavior Analytics – Who's Inside? What're They Doing?*, the intended message is targeted at organization leaders and security professionals who do not necessarily see identity analytics and user and entity behavior analytics as being involved holistically to address access risks and unknown threats. Security teams often focus on detection and response within SOCs. However, if the identity access plane is loaded with excess access, access outliers and over-provisioned from years of rubber-stamping certifications and access cloning, the reduction of these access risks is paramount to the success of the SOC mission. Add in industry's adoption of cloud technologies and we face a hybrid environment where identity is the attack vector. With this realization comes the recognition there is no longer a perimeter, there is no border. To achieve holistic security in this borderless environment, today's SOCs must now look at identities from the access risk side, the threat side, and integrate everything together for a risk-based approach to be predictive and eventually prescriptive in response.

Fundamental security objectives remain the same. With this recognition of a need for transformation, certain traditional security priorities and methods do not change. This means don't throw out what you have. For example, the firewall is important, but it must compliment the solution array to the point where it achieves the seamless and holistic coverage made possible by mature UEBA, identity analytics and machine learning. This is not a substitute for what CIOs are doing today. It's an augmentation that addresses a need that exists because of the evolving state of an organization's infrastructure and applications.

Patterns of complexity will grow. This insight also includes the acknowledgment that things are going in and out of environments much more often, as opposed to in the past, and this pattern will only continue to increase. It's almost impossible today to find an organization with zero cloud access. There would be some application hosted online, whether it's Salesforce.com, Box, Dropbox, an FTP server, or any of the document sharing facilities. Their presence in an organization all fortify the view that change is inevitable, and required, and stakeholders in this world must pay attention to this trend and its implications.

The new normal. While security leaders are continually trying to implement improvements, they are simultaneously and constantly being barraged by the technology landscape. They're constantly required to make those adjustments to that reality. Given their constrained resources, and the rapid pace of technology evolution, there's

> *There is access in their networks that they don't know about.*

only so much they can do to protect their environments with status quo thinking. They *will* be breached. It's only a question of time and magnitude. There is access in their networks they don't know about. The question remains: What tool will they use to supplement what they have today, to be able to know what they control and who's in their network?

Essentials of identity analytics for identity management. The first priority is closing the awareness gap to understand who is in your network, what their access entitlements are and their associated activity accessing data and applications at any point in time. This awareness gap has been a serious challenge for IAM solutions. The second priority is for the user and entity behavior analytics component to have the ability to establish baselines via machine learning. They must then highlight anomalies with risk scoring, enabling a SOC team to inspect and potentially take remedial action.

Targeted and granular risk scoring capability. A popular use case is using UEBA to analyze privileged access abuse. However, you need identity analytics to learn and locate privileged access first as legacy methods to track privileged access are ineffective. Too often the status quo is at the account level using naming prefixes, tags or an access management solution that reports on what has been recorded. It is not uncommon for identity analytics to find 50% or more of unknown or hidden privileged access. They are frequently entitlements that have escalated to privileged access within standard accounts. For UEBA to be effective for privileged access abuse as a use case, it requires identity analytics to locate privileged access accounts and entitlements. The new mandate is risk scoring down to the entitlement level. This is a perfect task for machine learning and a futile one for humans.

Suitability of UEBA solutions and ranges of maturity. The requirements for sound identity management today are profoundly complex. Any identity management solution that has not incorporated identity analytics along with user and entity behavior analytics, and machine learning, into its security strategy is at a disadvantage. Expect partnerships between leading

> *Expect partnerships between leading IAM and PAM solution vendors and UEBA solutions with identity analytics to close the awareness gap... and discovery gap...*

IAM and PAM solution vendors and UEBA solutions with identity analytics to close the awareness gap between access and activity, as well as the discovery gap to locate unknown privileged access, migrating to a risk-based approach for identity access management. This enables risk-based certifications, detection of excess access, access outliers, cleanup of access for dormant and orphan accounts, and reduced workloads with dynamic access provisioning. In addition, intelligent roles replace legacy roles with reduced risk and more accuracy for users and peers.

The security leader's mandate. CIOs, CSOs and CISOs need to keep doing what they're doing, to be aware of where new developments exist, where innovation is going, with the realities of their organizations continuing to expand their world into the cloud. In addition, as business partners get savvier, they will want organizations to open up data in different ways than ever before. Through all this, security leaders must be aware of where the industry's going in terms of next-generation identity management and how IdA and UEBA augments confronting the challenge of identity as a new perimeter and attack vector.

CONCLUSIONS & TAKEAWAYS:
Critical strategies for filling the gaps in security through identity analytics

To reduce risk, protect resources and detect threats, CIOs, CSOs and CISOs must recognize identity as a new perimeter, access risk and threat plane, a borderless perimeter. Insider threats, partners, customers, devices, entities and applications must be accounted for in evolving identity management strategies. CIO at Large Teri Takai shares the essentials of protecting this continually changing amorphous new perimeter. Addressing this challenge boils down to two essential points: 1) it's critical to have tools to effectively monitor activity in the network; 2) relying on personnel to continue to manually monitor the networks is no longer a reliable security practice. The scope and volume of data, users, and systems is simply too vast for human management. Within this challenge lurks the insider risk. Here, unintentional, as well as valid and compromised identities, all represent serious risk. Traditional IAM, as the conventional focus of access control strategies, no longer addresses the security demands of today's sprawling perimeters. Takai observes that security leaders must understand this next generation of identity and employ a new generation of identity management controls. Without that, the perimeter will continue to expand in unmanageable complexity, resulting in an even broader access risk plane of alarming magnitude.

As data and the multitude of access points expand in modern environments with increasing velocity and variety, identity is the singular plane that intersects with virtually every data source within the IT infrastructure. Its importance only increases with cloud adoption. *Data + Access = Threat Surface*. As workforces change constantly and the unchecked expansion of a range of access increases with no prospect of abatement, the importance of detecting access risks and access outliers resonates with increasing urgency. Privileged access abuse stands at the top of this hierarchy of unaddressed risks, where over 50% of organizations' privileged access risks are unaccounted for. One cause of this discovery gap in unknown privileged access risks is there are far too many entitlements for humans to manage or assess.

Realistic, robust and effective controls on access are required. Core requirements include comprehensive visibility across the hybrid environment into access and behavior. With the overwhelming volume of data, this has only been possible recently with advanced machine learning drawing from big data. With the advent of widespread cloud adoptions there is no other realistic option to manage risk effectively. Threats can no longer be considered only the work of individual attackers. It has become big business, and the strategic objective of nation states. External threat actors compromise identities to evade detection from existing defenses while insiders work under the radar to access data for exfiltration. Analyzing accounts, access, activity and alerts with identity-centric behavior analytics provides a reliable new defense for an emerging amorphous perimeter. With these advanced security analytics solutions in place, using risk-based analytics, organizations are more effectively able to provide the right level of access to whoever needs it, when they need it, and maintain the capability of taking it away whenever necessary.

All of the preceding chapters have led up to and supported the realization that we need a new approach in security, managing identity, and detecting unknown threats. The next chapter will explore security innovation in greater detail, along with the key drivers behind that imperative. The next *Borderless Breach Flashcard* highlights an instance in the growing trend of potential insider threats and the seismic impact these risks pose to organizations.

BORDERLESS BREACH FLASHCARD
For Sale: Keys to the Kingdom

CATEGORY	Hacktivism by a suspected NSA insider, or an alleged Russian operation.
WHO	**The target:** National Security Agency (NSA).
WHAT	The NSA's super-secret hacking tools appeared on an online digital auction, with samples of classified NSA documents, and were offered for sale to the highest bidder.
WHEN	2013
WHERE	Onsite or possibly cyberspace: Suspected NSA insider breach, while allegations of Russian espionage persist.
WHY	Political activism, economic gain, or alleged espionage.
HOW	In August 2016, a group calling themselves the Shadow Brokers stated that they possessed a "full state-sponsored toolset" of "cyberweapons," designed to break into computer systems and networks, and offered them online for auction via Bitcoin bid. A number of sample classified NSA files released by the group were deemed authentic by ex-NSA members of the agency's Tailored Access Operations (TAO), their elite hacking unit. The logical route for this exfiltration would be either through misuse or highjacking of insider credentials for high privileged access (HPA). While accusations of Russian involvement have been voiced, expert opinions refute that. They observed the logical likelihood of insider involvement, with the files dating back to five months after the Snowden breach and his escape to Hong Kong.
HOW BAD?	Two nation states reconfigured the stolen malware and weaponized it for political purposes, causing widespread business disruption and impacting enterprises globally. Continued potential compromise of this cyber toolset remains a serious concern. As well, a loss of confidence in the NSA's own security capabilities has occurred. As long as the flaws that the toolset exploits remain unpatched, it enables attackers from anywhere around the world to gain access to countless critical computers to steal data, plant malware and cause chaos.
HOW COULD IT BE AVOIDED?	Alerted to the possibility of additional Snowden-like breaches, if the NSA had a mature UEBA-IdA solution in place, HPA account anomalous behavior would have likely identified unusual downloads of highly classified sensitive intellectual property. This would have enabled them to identify the threat actors, deny access and take remedial action.

We Need a New Approach:
Key Drivers

Recognizing a time of change is at hand

How do you recognize innovations in security that can advance your objectives and mission?

The annual *Data Breach Investigations Report* (DBIR) from Verizon is a much-anticipated release of critical findings for the security community. It's comprehensive, analytical and a bible of insights for security leaders to help them to understand their evolving worlds, to recognize new emerging areas of concern, and to help map the road ahead of them. They use this independent data to reference when developing their strategies going forward, and to have the metrics for known risk when proposing new security initiatives for their environments to management. Constructive change begins with one voice articulating the challenges at hand to management, accompanied by the severity of the problem, the solution options, the assessment of which solution is the best, along with the costs and logistics required to implement that solution.

The 2016 *DBIR* report (the ninth year of its issuance) shared trends which highlight the importance of identity as a threat plane. The percentage of data breaches breaks down to 83% external actors and 17% insiders. This remained consistent over the past three years. Insider threats are relevant and not going away soon. But there's more. A new trend in the financial services sector with Web App attacks involves credential compromise to commit financial fraud. It ranks at 82% where it was 31% the previous year. For threat action types, phishing leads the pack along with hacking, malware and

149

social media as the primary methods of attack. Hacking with stolen credentials ranked #2 next to malware for command-and-control (C2) communications (#1) and malware to export data (#3). What does this mean? We have financially motivated external threat actors using phishing attacks to steal credentials to install malware for C2 and data export. The burning question this brings to thoughtful security leaders is whether they focus on the polymorphic response for every changing malware, or, whether

> *If there are blind spots for access risks and identity misuse or compromise, how can they be detected?*

they focus on the account compromise and hijacking. If there are blind spots for access risks and identity misuse or compromise, how can they be detected?

A number of industry leaders have observed the concerning number of privileged access instances which reside outside organizations' identity and access management solutions' purview. Gurucul's Craig Cooper, Chief Operating Officer is one of them: "Most Fortune 500 companies have more privileged access outside the vault than inside." That means those privileged access entitlements are unaccounted for, off the radar screen. That's a serious threat plane. Meanwhile, many organizations still rely on manual methods to manage privilege accounts and credentials through IT, without any coordination with SOCs. A number of accounts still have default passwords, and most organizations lack an approval process to create privileged accounts. Some security leaders are asking if they can live with these risks given identity is the new attack vector and the most valuable accounts to compromise are privileged. Others already know the answer to that question, and are actively seeking the solutions to a problem that is only getting more complex and acute over time.

The complexity and density of today's hybrid environments has grown beyond queries, filters and pivots to search for threats. With no current and future-proof security strategies in place to understand exactly who is in your network, and what their access entitlements are, how can there be any semblance of a prudent security policy in place? A number of solutions already in place should be assessed. Many IAM (identity and access management) and PAM (privileged access management) now need advanced security analytics support to maintain secure management of access. They can't do it alone anymore. Returning to the *DBIR*, the statistics are discouraging:

- Time to compromise is getting faster due to phishing, credentials compromise and quick installation of malware for C2 and data export — all achieved in a matter of minutes.
- Time to detection is slightly better, but still remains a matter of months, and dwell time persists as a large time gap.
- Phishing effectiveness continues with 30% of recipients opening phishing

emails, 12% clicking, and the median time for a first user to open was 1 min 40 secs, while the median time for the first click was 3 mins 45 secs.

- Only 3% of targeted individuals reported phishing emails.
- 63% of confirmed data breaches involved weak, default or stolen passwords.
- Privilege misuse ranked #2 for reported incidents and #4 for reported data breaches.
- Miscellaneous errors and privilege misuse are the two highest frequency items for incident classification.
- Stolen or default credentials are key to POS (Point of Sale) attacks where 97% data breaches featuring stolen credentials leverage legitimate partner access.
- POS vendors are a key target to then attack their customers using stolen credentials.

What does this mean? Humans click, passwords fail, time to infection is minutes, while detection takes months. Detecting account compromise, hijacking and misuse from an identity-based behavior perspective changes the game for defenses. New gray areas exist. It's no longer just good or bad. There are good people with inadvertent actions and misunderstood behaviors. While training is helpful to face the challenge, it is inadequate to resolve the overall problem. The goal for CISOs is to move to the front of the kill chain, to detect compromise, versus confirming the data was stolen at the end of the kill chain. Clearly there is a need for security innovation.

> *New gray areas exist. It's no longer just good or bad. There are good people with inadvertent actions and misunderstood behaviors.*

While a number of CISOs and CIOs have indeed recognized the sea change for security defenses and processes — a transformation is at hand — some nonetheless remain committed to the status quo of legacy perimeter defenses for various reasons. Our expert contributor Robert Rodriguez, founder and president of SINET, has hosted the annual SINET 16 Innovation Awards, which enlists a panel of CISO judges to select the top security innovations each year. Drawing from his vast range of first-hand experience in both the public and private sectors with the challenges of information security, Rodriguez shares his seasoned insights on security innovations and the context for user and entity behavior analytics and identity analytics. His observations include the influences behind solution adoption and the future of innovation in the cybersecurity industry.

BORDERLESS EXPERT INSIGHTS

Robert D. Rodriguez*
Chairman/Founder, SINET

Robert D. Rodriguez is Chairman and Founder of the Security Innovation Network™ (SINET) — an international community builder whose mission is to advance innovation and enable global collaboration between the public and private sectors to defeat cybersecurity threats. SINET connects the ecosystems of the entrepreneur, academia, science, private industry, investment banking, system integration, policy, innovators, venture capital and the federal government to include the civilian, military and intelligence agencies. After serving 22 years as a Special Agent with the United States Secret Service, Robert retired. He currently serves on the Board of Advisors for The Chertoff Group, as Director Emeritus for the San Francisco Kraft Fight Hunger Bowl and the National Cyber Security Hall of Fame Board of Directors.

A member of Gurucul's Executive Advisory Board, Robert has provided invaluable consultation in the company's journey through its dynamic growth and evolution of predictive security analytics. He lends his qualified insights into the innovations and developments in cybersecurity along with behavior analytics' invested future in it.

Overview

In this module, Rodriguez observes the recent trends in cybersecurity and the impact of hybrid cloud adoption on cybersecurity requirements. As a solution element of these challenges, he observes past behavior's predictive utility in identifying future anomalies. This solution factor is most effectively incorporated when the realities of establishing and managing identity in the environment are optimized. Strategies for managing excess access are also discussed. Program trends for insider threat detection are examined as it is weighted against the challenges of balancing the human effort against the critical mass of growing data. Rodriguez also shares his insights on the solution optimization trends targeting today's security gaps. Rodriguez provides his analysis on why advancements in cybersecurity are incremental and lack dynamic innovation. He concludes with his perspectives on private companies' partnership with government agencies and behavior analytics' place in that relationship.

Recent trends in cybersecurity

Since 2011, we've seen CISOs sharing more information than ever before. They're collaborating with a spirit of partnership in their own trusted communication channels

* The views and opinions expressed by Robert Rodriguez in this book are his own, and do not necessarily reflect those of SINET, or any of his previous employers.

and environments. The focus on the importance of holistic enterprise risk, versus compartmentalized risk, has been part of that dialog. Boards of directors and CISOs are having constant communication. If cybersecurity is not number one, it's in the top three priorities of every board of directors meeting.

CISOs with multiple strengths in demand. These CISOs have moved from being primarily a technical leader, to an executive leader role, able to articulate to the executive management team, along with the CEO and board of directors, the issues and priorities relative to cyber. Compensation and demand for talented and qualified CISOs has grown markedly. The job shortage has also increased. Instead of filling these important roles, we're seeing larger gaps and voids because of the lack of qualified talent.

Research and investments on the rise. The research and development community, the academic community, and the grant opportunities on cybersecurity, have all increased significantly over the last five years. The dynamics of mergers and acquisitions has also grown significantly. In addition, the amount of venture capital for the last five years has risen to massive amounts. Many changes have taken place over the last five to ten years, even from the policies perspective.

Government's priority focus on cybersecurity. Part of the policy evolution and change includes the national framework we now have, with the creation of the White House's role of Cybersecurity Coordinator in 2009, and Rob Joyce currently holding that post. The numerous information sharing bills, the security versus privacy bills on Capitol Hill, and the debate of cybersecurity versus privacy — Apple vs. FBI — are part of the security industry's response to the changing face of cybersecurity in the world today.

Data overload in today's environments. The amount of data overload is staggering, crippling some organizations. The bottom line is we simply can't afford not to have innovative solutions address this challenge. It's impossible to keep up with the deluge of data. Imagine all the military drones sending photographs of rocks in the middle of the deserts of the Middle East, to the analysts — millions and millions of photos. Which one do they pay attention to? The technology needs to be able to say, "This rock moved, and that's the one we need to focus on and prioritize."

A haystack of needles. The same circumstances of overwhelming data are true with present-day cybersecurity in hybrid cloud environments. We've moved from finding the needle in the haystack, to finding the needle in the haystack of needles, and then prioritizing and making that information actionable.

> *We've moved from finding the needle in the haystack, to finding the needle in the haystack of needles...*

Enduring importance of insider threat. Regarding insider threat, during my tenure with the Secret Service, studies were done in 1999 through 2002. *CSO* magazine and the Secret Service collaborated, interviewing chief security officers to understand the emerging threat plane. Insider threats were the chief concern. It's still either number one, or at the very least, in the top three today, and it's not going away. From the malicious component to the non-malicious, mistakes by people just trying to do their jobs, insider threats are a constant priority concern.

Big data solutions meet the challenge. Virtually all security experts say the amount of data and the growth of that data has become so exponentially high that security organizations can no longer keep throwing headcount at the problem. Qualified and experienced companies like Gurucul, with big data user behavior analytics solutions, address this challenge by delivering the ability to closely monitor anomalous human behavior, providing predictive risk scores to detect access risk and unknown threats. These advanced security analytics, empowered by innovation, driven by mature machine learning, and plugged into big data, are critical to provide a comprehensive part of the behavior-based solution.

UEBA minimizes human touch points. It's acknowledged you can never eliminate humans from the security equation, nor would you want to. While they must remain a critical part of the process, security teams can no longer completely cover the gargantuan expansion of manually managing the data. We must minimize the amount of touch points by humans because it just doesn't scale. That's the importance of UEBA and IdA technology as part of the solution.

Best-in-breed solutions and reliable results. Forward-thinking CISOs know they have to utilize the best from this new breed of solutions which are coming out today. These solutions can bring the needles to the top of the haystack, as well as pick out the most critical ones, and send them off to the specialists who need to take a closer look.

The impact of hybrid cloud adoption on cybersecurity

The impact has been seismic on the security industry. This move between traditional on-premises solutions to cloud-based solutions has changed the rules of engagement. Organizations continue to adopt some sort of a cloud-based play — from AWS, Office 365, Box, Dropbox, or solutions like Salesforce.com, and a range of SaaS, PaaS, IaaS (software as a service, platform as a service, infrastructure as a service) options — so that the security challenge has transformed into a different scale and complexity than ever before. Not only do you have to continue to perform your on-premises security in the way you were, but you now also need to understand your cloud worlds and integrate effective cloud security in each one. Then, you must seamlessly stitch it all together.

The inevitability of expanding cloud adoption. It's interesting to look back to

2010. The conversations were all about, "Can we trust the cloud?" Today's discussions observe that data might be even be more secure in the cloud. Yet the provocative question persists,

> *...the trends tell us we've swung the pendulum of the word "trust." The government and other commercial entities are entrusting their data in the cloud.*

"But, *really*, how secure is the cloud?" While that debate continues, the trends tell us we've swung the pendulum of the word 'trust'. The government and other commercial entities are entrusting their data in the cloud. Anyone who looks at ASW — Amazon — knows they're dominating the web services market. Their revenue growth indicates there's definitely a path moving forward in the IaaS direction and it will continue to change the dynamics of all cloud solutions. This is especially true for the rising importance of targeted cloud solutions offering unique values over others.

Cloud innovations add security requirements. Cloud definitely brings a wave of innovative concepts that have been game-changing influences for some companies. Their growth has enabled them to turn the corner of success. No longer do companies need to overpay for infrastructure resources they're not utilizing. Instead, cloud's new options of utility empower flexible growth to match the entire spectrum of how fast or how slow an organization might go. Cloud's elastic pay-as-you-go provisioning reduces CapEx and maximizes the value of OpEx expenditures. These cloud innovations deliver greater efficiencies and effectiveness while reducing cost. Nevertheless, hidden within the agile complexity of the cloud's advantages lies the fundamental requirement to reliably protect everything in the environment.

Outdated security strategies fail to secure the environment. In the past, some CISOs were unable to understand the concept of the paradigm shift in proper perspective because they remained ingrained with the perimeter concept of security for the corporate environment. At the time, the domain was so secure that they knew about anything coming in or going out, while on the outside it was the wild world. This had been the standard model of focus: protect the perimeter and give support to keep the bad guys out and the good guys in. But now with cloud, that old solitary concept has no place in the minds of forward-looking CISOs.

The potential threat of employee devices. This new normal compels security leaders to retool their thinking when they examine their on-premises environments, with people coming in and out, there are a completely new set of factors to contend with. Employees are bringing their own devices (BYODs), IoT (the Internet of Things) is

> *...people are jumping the perimeter all the time. Most are good people, with legitimate behavior – but not all – and that's where the danger lies.*

expanding, and people are jumping the perimeter all the time. Most are good people, with legitimate behavior — but not all — and that's where the danger lies.

The goal: hybrid cloud as secure as on-premises. An additional factor CISOs should keep in mind when considering their evolving security requirements is that the typical tenure of an employee has declined markedly. It has shrunk from multiple years to a few months in some cases. One or two years are quite common nowadays. In the past, companies used to have people work for decades within a single organization. This 'gig economy' circumstance creates a situation where organizations must keep giving new people access to data, yet also make sure all of that remains secure, just as it has traditionally been with their on-premises environments. That is the CISO's goal and challenge: to make their hybrid cloud solutions as secure as their on-premises solutions were. As CISOs start to rethink the right way to approach this objective, some are also seeing that the way cloud is managing security might even provide some of those innovations for their on-premises environments. These new capabilities allow customers to pay a cloud fee for an identity management as a service (IDaaS) solution, meaning elements of on-premises security requirements are eliminated with a significant cost savings.

Past behavior's role in identifying future anomalies

Beyond what the potential cloud security solutions offer, the variable that needs to be taken into account is an individual's behavior within the network. We're all creatures of habit. Just think about how you operate every day, or every week. How you type. That's intelligence, and that's also a critical part of identity which is defined by behavior. I have a colleague in the UEBA space who likes to say: "You can steal somebody's credentials, but you can't steal their behavior." That's the giveaway right there.

Behavior defining identity. Here's what's behind identity through behavior: when you see someone comes into work every morning, badges into the building at 9:00, logs onto his computer at 9:10, checks emails at 9:15, makes morning calls, interacts with a certain category of documents, uses cloud services in a certain way for a particular purpose — he has a distinct behavior pattern. This is all part of that person's identity defined by their behavior.

The fingerprint of behavior. At times, while someone else might succeed in stealing someone else's credentials, their ability to mimic that person's behavior is next to impossible. The distinct behavior for access and actions are like fingerprints that give away the attacker. It quickly flags the action as an anomalous behavior, ready for the next step, risk scoring. The anomalous behavior pattern is

> *The distinct behavior for access and actions are like fingerprints that give away the attacker.*

conspicuously outside the baseline behavior profile established by the user's earlier use patterns as well as those of his peer groups.

Balancing priorities of identity management with UEBA. While there is a rising awareness of the benefits of user and entity behavior analytics, and its importance in emerging technologies, an equally important element of security success relates to identity management. Too often, identity management is in the purview of IT departments, while security monitoring belongs to the SOCs, creating two separate silos of responsibility. This disconnect represents a serious vulnerability.

Establishing and managing identity in the environment

Identity management in cyber is a persistent challenge. It's becoming more acute while account compromise continues to grow as an effective method of penetrating an environment. Along with organizations having a solid identity analytics solution in place, one broader idealized concept would involve not only having a national identity management enrollment and authentication program, but a global program. If you consider that we register vehicles, and we're able to get a driver's license, a social security card that enables us to get a passport, we need to get there. Until we do, we'll have a higher level of risk, which lowers the level of correct and timely attribution. We need to know, with the highest level of precision possible, who's out there on our landscape.

A call for more comprehensive identity standards. Some privacy advocates may disagree, but we need, at a minimum, to have national identity management and multi-factor authentication to include biometrics. Therefore, whatever that consists of needs to augment identification and to make it the most robust and user-friendly technology advance to identify who's who. In my previous career with the Secret Service, I was issued something called the commission book. In my commission book, I had a badge, a photo, and a document certifying I was a United States Secret Service agent. The only way to get it was to undergo a thorough background check, polygraph, and dozens of interviews. You still have to go through that because the nature of the job enrollment was extensive. We need an element of this process to get proper identity management. In an ideal world, having a global or even national identity, would address quite a few challenges.

The complexity of a single identity in many systems. Looking at the realities in present day hybrid network environments, nothing's ever this simple and straightforward. When we look at any corporate environment there

> *Sometimes, just to establish identity becomes tricky because there are so many handoffs, so many proxies, so much masking, and all the required procedures to make sure you are able to have the right attribution.*

are so many different systems, so many different infrastructures. Sometimes, just to establish identity becomes tricky because there are so many handoffs, so many proxies, so much masking, and all the required procedures to make sure you are able to have the right attribution. All of this is to assure, "This action is being performed by this person, and based on their behavior profile built in correlation with peer groups, and other data, we can see that what this person is doing is normal."

Strategies for managing excess access

Organizations must think seriously about access and how they grant it. In the past, some IT groups issued access to a new employee based simply on cloning the access of someone else who happened to be on the team the new hire is joining. The hazard is that the IT group might end up giving far too much access to this person than their position requires. Elimination of cloning access and rubber-stamping certifications should be a first order of business for security leaders.

Too much access. The following scenario exemplifies the problem. Bob has been in a tech company for nineteen years. He went from engineering, to support, to special projects, and after almost twenty years he accumulated a great deal of access which was never properly closed off when he moved from department to department. He's currently in special projects. Then, a new person joins the team and IT says, "Okay, just give him Bob's access profile." What IT did at that point was provide this new person too much access, much of which he won't pay attention to while he is primarily focused on his new special projects activities. Every piece of unwarranted additional access an organization gives represents an access risk which could be hacked or compromised. Multiply this scenario, and a host of others where privileged access entitlements are granted

> "Every piece of unwarranted additional access an organization gives represents an access risk which could be hacked or compromised."

and unaccounted for across a global enterprise, and the scale becomes staggering.

Excess access elimination. The goal is reducing this access risk plane, including eliminating excess access, or access outliers, as requirements. It can be achieved by implementing two methods. One involves using identity analytics for a risk-based approach to identity access management (IAM) removing excess access, cleaning up the access plane to reduce access risk. A second involves the creation of intelligent roles from machine learning models that reverse engineer role access from the entitlement level back into peer groups. Intelligent roles replace legacy roles defined by manual processes and rules. Going forward, from a clean access plane status, risk-based certifications and access requests and approvals keep things in check.

Insider threat detection program trends

Here's a testament to the importance of analytics. If you look at the number of companies that have been funded and grown over the last four years or five years, the number one area that's covered are the analytics-based companies because knowledge is king. Intelligence trumps all. Whether it is business intelligence, or threat intelligence, or market intelligence, people pay a great deal of money for that specialized, timely and accurate information.

Unmanageable data overload. Based on the growing challenges facing organizations today, you can't understate the importance of innovative analytic technology solutions to help advance the field. It is a new normal of total, massive, unmanageable data overload of digital exhaust. This data excess is continuing to get worse. Only solutions with advanced analytics, powered by machine learning and leveraging big data for context, can provide the visibility into identity risks and the monitoring of user behavior for unknown threats that is needed across all an organization's hybrid cloud environments.

> *Only solutions with advanced analytics, powered by machine learning and leveraging big data for context, can provide the visibility into identity risks and the monitoring of user behavior for unknown threats that is needed across all an organization's hybrid cloud environments.*

Resiliency and recovery priorities. The cybersecurity trend is also moving toward the importance of resiliency. CIOs and CISOs know the bad guys will get in and they can create harm. Now they need to ensure they can operate if harm comes. This circumstance reflects an attitude that the likelihood of a breach occurrence is high. For security leaders it's just a matter of, "What severity will it be, and how do we respond to it?"

The challenges of balancing human efforts against the growing data

A starting point for addressing the new approach is with the recognition of the overwhelming volume of data that can no longer be realistically analyzed by humans. In some quarters, however, a bias remains that this is still a viable option.

Vested interests in the status quo. An illustration highlighting some of the characteristics embedded in the challenge of innovation adoption is exemplified by system integrators, the SI model. It's designed as a billable service model. A number of business minds are locked into that framework as a sensible, profitable, and sound business approach. Yet when you have a billable service model, it's inherently designed to suffocate innovation while inflating budgets.

Lower efficiencies and higher risks. A number of organizations today, as well as the People's Republic of China, are inclined to throw headcount at a challenge like this. That's simply the wrong approach, with diminishing returns in efficiency. The further anyone

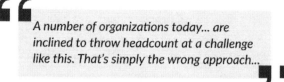

A number of organizations today... are inclined to throw headcount at a challenge like this. That's simply the wrong approach...

ventures along this strategic path in a setting of such rapidly evolving technology and complexity, the more unnecessary cost and risk they instill.

New technology model required. To evolve successfully, organizations must move from the 80% bodies and 20% technology model, to 80% technology and 20% bodies. Today's cybersecurity requirements simply no longer scale with the majority of the work being performed by humans. The imbalance is growing daily. It will not solve our hard cybersecurity problems. It can't give us the intelligence and knowledge we need to effectively do our job and deliver the appropriate levels of security.

Priority focus on data. As security leaders come to accept that technology is needed to support their needs, they also begin to identify their wish list of features and capabilities. My colleagues in the security industry have observed how CISOs are increasingly saying they want their cybersecurity analysts, their data scientists, or any of the intelligent people in their organization, to focus only on the right data. They want technology to help their specialists pick out exactly what that data is. They should not be bound by chasing down alerts that ultimately turn out to be low priority or false positives. That results in the analysts missing the forest from the trees when it comes to the criticality of assessing priority anomalies efficiently and being unable to keep on top of details that require the most attention.

Solution optimization trends targeting today's security gaps

While automation of different sets of tasks has been widely recognized for its advantages within different security solutions, this advancement represents the first building block of empowered efficiencies within a holistic environment.

From automation to orchestration. A critical recognition among many CISOs is that of the need to move from automation, to orchestration, to facilitate more effective central decision-making. This means having the ability to integrate all of the varied automated components of an advanced analytics security solution, supplying simple transparent holistic controls to enable monitoring, analysis and response from a comprehensive solution with flexibility for future needs.

Emerging requirements for remediation and attribution. The orchestration capability helps the CISOs do their job to assure comprehensive remediation. Eventually, some form of attribution should be included because a number of industries and corporations are battling with this challenge. Nevertheless, in order to do proper attribution, it must become clearly mandated within the cybersecurity industry.

Larger organizations are early adopters. While a few vendors are developing these solutions, it is an area that needs to trend upwards, with wider customer adoptions, which supports solution capabilities development for a broader base of customers. The select companies that are currently in need of this generation of solution tend to be the larger organizations with the budget. The size and complexity of their hybrid network environments warrants the development and adoption of this kind of solution. While a wide range of organizations could benefit from these solutions, lower awareness of the proven value, and budget constraints, are currently inhibitors to wider adoption. This is a hard problem to solve, and an important one at the same time, especially with certain government agencies. The challenge too is that the solution must be viable and scalable.

More innovation needed in cybersecurity. In terms of other trends, the restraining factor is the frustrating limitation of the conservative incremental advances of innovation. It is disappointing that we are not seeing more disruptive innovation in cybersecurity. I haven't seen anyone discovering fire or the light bulb. Meanwhile, it's a cat and mouse game. Sometimes we're staying ahead of the adversary, and other times we're not. What's needed are solutions that reflect thinking from an intel perspective, with components reflecting an understanding of weak points of defense, attacker strengths and likely scenarios.

> *...it's a cat and mouse game. Sometimes we're staying ahead of the adversary, and other times we're not.*

Why advancements in cybersecurity are incremental and lack dynamic innovation

First and foremost, we essentially built an information highway, as a DARPA (Defense Advanced Research Projects Agency) project, which was not originally designed for critical business or financial utilities. It was not constructed to be ultra-secure, but instead to facilitate exchanging and sharing information. Its architecture was ad hoc and designed to be resilient. Over the decades, there was never a real master plan, and for better or worse, its structure grew organically as the use cases for it continually changed and evolved with remarkable speed. By the time we arrived in the nineties, it was identified as a future cornerstone of commerce. Because it's so porous, we're now trying to re-frame, strengthen and shore up the digital highway.

Absence of original plans intensifies challenges. In an ideal world, the infrastructure for this digital highway would have been built with high quality ingredients in the first place — the best cement and asphalt available. There could have been standards established determining the requirements and regulations to assure the highest grade materials were used to provide a safe, resilient, robust, strong, secure, trusted freeway. It could have been planned and developed by seasoned civil engineers working with a unified purpose and vision. But organic and dynamic innovation does not always work that way. Use cases rise in popularity, evolve and change drastically, as has been demonstrated by the original Facebook model and what it has become today. Multiply that dynamic phenomenon exponentially, and you have today's internet. Now we're trying to go back in and fix a framework that has too many porous holes in it. Moreover, we're chasing a moving target. Better cement and better asphalt will always need to be developed.

A higher calling motivating innovation. This uncharted development legacy makes inspired leaps of innovation in cybersecurity difficult. Nonetheless, entrepreneurs dream. They dream of flying to Mars. They dream of solving the world's hardest problems. Most of the cultures of these entrepreneur companies are wonderful, very mission focused. They have a sense of purpose and commitment and sometimes of collaborating with the government. They realize that we all have a shared hard problem to solve. They're entrepreneurs who are making solutions that are perfecting the national security and economic interest of our respective nations. There's a lot of personal commitment. Because of national interests and economic interests, as well as privacy and personal rights, we all have a higher calling. That certainly motivates innovation.

Conflicted priorities inhibiting progress. Some companies often funded and backed by private or venture capital, may be too focused on making money at the expense of dynamic innovation. In addition, it seems at times that when capitalism comes into play it can get in the way of the path forward towards productive game changing dynamic innovation. These people start thinking about their exit strategy early on versus solving the real hard problems. Frankly, these players are rarely a source of dynamic innovation.

Additional factors stagnating innovation. Another factor influencing a stagnation of innovation is about how people tend to be scared of changing, or making wholesale modifications. While you have a new and completely different solution which might seem to meet current needs, people may still be cautious. They feel, "This is my security portfolio and I'm turning it upside down. There could still be unseen liabilities with it. It's probably best if I wait and see later versions of the solution to be sure it addresses all my needs. Then I'll think about adoption." This hesitant cautiousness in a community considering forward-looking solutions stifles innovation.

Accepting some level of risk in new solutions is required. A fundamental reality remains: we must move from being conservative, or too risk averse, to taking risks. We need more early adopters in the buyer community. If we don't take risks we'll never really truly be able to rebuild this digital highway or to alter the world. That's one of the challenges of not taking risks: we're going to continue to fall further behind the adversary. The buyer community is also a partner in this. I'm looking for change agents who are not afraid to lead change, but to embrace change, and move forward with it.

Factors influencing early adoption in security technology

Inherent risk takers, versus risk-averse people that depend on legacy systems, are early adopters. These change agents are willing to take that risk. They drive the spirit of early adoption. Part of the challenge, however, and especially in the government, is that there's no reward for failure. There is no profit margin or shareholder value, no driving motivation to deliver more for less. As a result, there's no reward for taking risks. So the culture there is different than in the commercial world.

Organizational pain defines urgency. An additional factor that might influence someone who was originally inclined to be a late adopter, to ultimately become an early adopter, is that they may have gone through a compromise or a breach. It boils down to the amount of pain the organization's suffering. If there's a lot of pain and uncertainty about the quality of a system's security assurance, and if the existing solutions clearly are not addressing the pain, CISOs need to adjust their strategy.

Regular exposure to innovators strengthens insights. Another influence is when CISOs are exposed to and surround themselves with the innovators, the risk takers, the early adopters. Those change agents are a key influence. Listening to and understanding their forward-thinking, and the way they approach challenges, is part of building a platform of strategic change targeted on the needs, goals and objectives of an enterprise's next generation of security assurance solutions.

Fast-tracking knowledge via experienced communities. In Sydney, Australia, SINET is taking U.S.-based forward-thinking CISOs to share insights from their innovative projects with the Australian CIO and CISO communities, as they exchange their knowledge in turn. Thought leadership means sharing

> *...a group of security leaders... know they can gain knowledge from colleagues who've already gone through their own versions of trial and error adoption cycles.*

at a high level. The U.S. CISOs have different perspectives towards the big problem involved with hybrid cloud challenges based upon their years of hands-on experience with cloud. With the country's recent 'cloud first' mandate, Australia's CISO culture is undergoing an unprecedented and accelerated nationwide adoption pattern with unique insights apart from the U.S. culture in terms of state-of-the-art cybersecurity technology and practices. The takeaway in this context is that this is a group of security leaders who know they can gain knowledge from colleagues who've already gone through their own versions of trial and error adoption cycles. In doing so, U.S. and Australian peers' experience helps each other streamline their own paths to adoption of certain solutions, with knowledge and processes that have been proven in the field. Moreover, adoption of best practices developed elsewhere can speed implementation at a lower cost.

Newer infrastructure encourages earlier adoption. In this context, it's also interesting that with their cloud first mandate, Australia is moving much faster than the rest of the world. The adoption of cloud services in Australia is growing rapidly with compound annual growth rates (CAGR) of 23-24 percent (per Melbourne IT study) against a global average of 19.4% (per Forbes.com). It appears that because they were newer, and some other adopters before them have established a number of proven best practices, that they have less to lose, or risk. This might be one of the factors causing them to be adopting at a quicker pace. Experts observe the benefits Australia will experience with these solutions represent a possible 30% savings for taxpayers in government spending.

More legacy physical infrastructure complicates adoption. One additional perspective on that idea is when we look at physical infrastructure. Changing our telephone systems in the United States was difficult to go from landlines to mobile. On the other hand, we are seeing other countries where there was not as much infrastructure already in place. They're adopting mobile phones at a much quicker pace because it's easier to set it up, as opposed to the legacy technology solution of digging trenches and managing other cumbersome infrastructure requirements.

Individuals, not industries, determine solution trends. While some wonder if there are any specific industries that encourage early adopters, aside from organizations depending on legacy systems which would compel late adoption behavior, it essentially depends more on the individual security leader than it does the sector. In today's world, these sector independent security leaders drive innovation and adoption.

UEBA, IdA and perspectives on private companies' partnership with government agencies

When I transitioned from the public to the private sector in 2004, I rebooted to become an entrepreneur and a venture capitalist on a mission. As an entrepreneur, I became focused on advancing innovation to defeat global cybersecurity threats and providing a platform for the business of cyber to take place. I founded SINET (Security Innovation Network) as a super connector. We connect the investor, the builder, the buyer and the researcher.

Shared interests and goals. Part of my mission and activities also included a deep involvement with the Secret Service Electronic Crimes Task Force (ECTF). ECTF is a nationwide network of participants who provide support and resources to field investigations of crimes such as bank fraud, virus and worm proliferation, access device fraud, telecommunications fraud, internet threats, computer system intrusions and cyber-attacks, phishing/spoofing, identity theft, and more. It's more of a human model, a collaboration model, than technology. The beauty of it is when you bring together investors and government, security professionals, entrepreneurs, and large corporations, the opportunity to collaborate on shared hard problems increases dramatically. It's a great alternative to working in silos, and only focusing on your own respective path in society.

The value of a public/private partnership. The ECTF model has proven to be highly successful. It's based on trust. It's based on a community and a sense of purpose and commitment that we all have a hard problem together. The public/private partnership is essential to the success of that model. Nevertheless, the private sector needs to lead. The mandate is on industry, the owners and operators of critical infrastructure. The onus is on them to take more of a leadership role and facilitate more participation in these collaboration models.

Innovation leadership from the private sector. The government can't do everything. The participation by small, medium and large companies several years ago, and with the DHS (Department of Homeland Security) supported by the White House, formed a security cooperative. It started in various cities like Washington DC, San Diego, and a number of cities in Texas, that participated in building out the framework on the Internet of Things. Their topics of interest addressed cloud as well. This organizational framework provides a well-reasoned, foundation for possible regulation — a precursor to official government regulation — that has already been developed and vetted by a national group of recognized and qualified security experts. Indications are that the market will be regulated. Like the path of the automobile, the automotive industry at least had input on that framework, and on

...the White House... formed a security cooperative... that participated in building out the framework on the Internet of Things.

those policies, versus the government working with no input from the private sector.

Proven experience in on-premises and hybrid cloud required. A last point is quite important in terms of the ecosystem of a public/private partnership. We must promote an awareness of innovative solutions that could ultimately protect the military command and control systems and our nation's critical infrastructures. Innovation, in its most simplistic form, is just having an awareness that comes with advanced security analytics solutions from enterprises like Gurucul that exist so that it can better society.

CONCLUSIONS & TAKEAWAYS:

Implementing productive change in advanced security strategies

Observing that the internet has evolved in an organic way, by spurts of innovation, taking it in new unforeseen directions, Robert Rodriguez notes its original design was not created to service the robust business applications and sensitive information being managed and transmitted across today's networks and within hybrid environments. Factoring in the rapidly multiplying digital exhaust, which doubles every year, he states it is time to recognize the need for change in security strategies.

Government has responded to these concerning trends, establishing new initiatives to cope with the new challenges, including the White House's role of Cybersecurity Coordinator. All the while, the data overload in today's environments continues to mount. Rodriguez observes: "We've moved from finding the needle in the haystack, to finding the needle in the haystack of needles, and then prioritizing and making that information actionable." As this circumstance endures, it does so with the recognition that the issue of insider threats, whether malicious or not, has had an enduring sense of importance for both government and private organizations. Rodriguez calls for the need of machine learning to handle the sprawling digital exhaust, which is now far beyond human capabilities to manage. The impact of cloud adoption and the emerging growth of hybrid environments have made that urgency even more acute.

Yet innovation within government is not driven by the same profit motives as private enterprises, and risk-taking is not rewarded. Advancements in cybersecurity in both the public and private sectors are incremental and too often lack dynamic innovation. Outdated security strategies fail to secure the environment as some organizations continue to see the business case as a systems integrator model, and to futilely commit more human resources to the challenges. As attackers continue to innovate, Rodriguez calls out the need for private and government organizations to find more common collaboration points to partner and strengthen strategies and security solutions. A critical component of this initiative is to promote solution development targeted more at the 20% human engagement and 80% technology ratio, where he observes the reverse ratio is prevalent in too many organizations today.

At the core of success in these future initiatives lies the requirement to achieve a single identity risk profile across all systems, as well as the comprehensive management of identity through a risk-based approach. Achieving these goals facilitates the significant reduction of the access risk plane. Without this, and machine learning with big data to draw from, effective user and entity behavior analytics programs cannot be realistically effective to detect unknown threats. For those who have adopted the next generation of advanced security analytics, they are looking toward the automation of various security analytic functions along with the optimization of the entire solution across a hybrid environment. The leaders for adopting these next-generation solutions are ultimately found among those whose acceptance of innovation is part of their personality versus their organization profile or a particular industry they might work in.

With the need for a new approach in security being recognized, the next chapter examines the evolving technology of machine learning and big data which makes advanced security analytics possible. The next *Borderless Breach Flashcard* portrays an instance where, faced with clear signs that they were a ripe target for a major malicious attack, they chose instead to focus their strategies on developing new products and easy-to-use services, instead of bolstering their security. This decision resulted in what some experts described as the largest breach in history.

BORDERLESS BREACH FLASHCARD	
Notoriety on Steroids	
CATEGORY	Stolen user data – one of the largest breaches of its kind in history.
WHO	**The target:** Yahoo and its customers.
WHAT	Hackers allegedly backed by a 'state-sponsored actor' compromised over 500 million passwords and other information from Yahoo's server.
WHEN	2016
WHERE	USA, online.
WHY	Economic gain and notoriety.
HOW	In July of 2016, notification that vast amounts of personal data originating from Yahoo were posted online for sale. Yahoo responded by investigating their network to see if indeed any claims of these might be true. They discovered that over 500 million of their customers' personal information had been compromised. The final count surpassed one billion. This breach occurred four years following the massive Aurora cyber assault by Chinese military hackers, who breached a number of prominent high-tech companies, including Google. Unlike Google, who prioritized security to a high level, Yahoo instead focused on developing new products and services, placing security at a lower priority. Yahoo saw security more as an inhibitor of customer retention, where products were slower and more difficult to use (the internal name for Yahoo's security team was 'The Paranoids').
HOW BAD?	Named by some as the largest intrusions into a company's network, FBI and SEC investigations followed. The company also faced numerous lawsuits. One specifically cited Yahoo for reckless disregard because they had not strengthened their security, after promising to do so, and they knew they were a prime target for attackers. The cost per remediation of each breached identity is estimated at $232, representing an astronomical expense. In addition, Verizon was in the middle of acquiring Yahoo for 4.8 billion dollars. Yahoo's final acquisition price suffered a loss of 300 million dollars.
HOW COULD IT HAVE BEEN AVOIDED?	Yahoo was clearly forewarned of their company's risk, and did not have a mature UEBA-IdA solution in place. If it had, the anomalous behavior would likely have been identified, allowing their SOC team to respond effectively years ago to remediate the threat. The cost of doing so would have been a fraction of the cost of remediating this in 2016.

Discovering the Unknown:
Big Data with Machine Learning

Machine learning's road through big data to advanced security analytics

Why was predictive and advanced security analytics comparatively late to the game in machine learning?

Eric Schmidt, Executive Chairman, Google observed: "From the dawn of civilization until 2003, humankind generated five exabytes of data. Now we produce five exabytes every two days... and the pace is accelerating." While a number of experts quibble with the accuracy of that statement, it still rightly calls out the rapid speed of the expanding world of big data. The PBS special *The Human Face of Big Data*, and its accompanying teaching materials, portray the vast range of new possibilities emerging from big data. Elephant seals equipped with antennas on their heads help to map the oceans. Satellites target mosquitoes to support a better understanding of malaria. An SMS (system maintenance service) solution prevents the sale of counterfeit medicines in Ghana. Smartphones predict you're going to get depressed. Credit cards know two years before you do that you are headed toward divorce. Pills transmit information directly from your body to your physician.

Joe Sullivan, past CSO of Uber observed in an earlier chapter, "As I researched it more deeply — seeing that every company was storing increasingly more data — I came to realize that the future was in big data." But big data is nothing without machine learning. Big data is something like a vast field of wheat that needs the farmer to harvest, the mill to process it, and the baker to mix the flour with the right ingredients and then bake it to produce a gourmet pastry you might consume at a coffee house. Big data is the raw material. It is nothing without the right tools

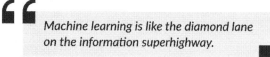

Machine learning is like the diamond lane on the information superhighway.

and process. Machine learning is like the diamond lane on the information superhighway.

From 1952, when Arthur Samuel wrote the first learning program to play checkers and improve the more it played, the 'game was on'. The research and scientific applications are well-acknowledged for their importance. Since then, the evolution of machine learning witnessed a shift in the 1990s, where the knowledge-driven approach shifted to a data-driven one, and the business applications in machine learning began to offer an entirely new world of potential. In business, machine learning analytics driven by algorithms have been adopted with great effect and value, in a range of market verticals including finance, manufacturing, marketing, and, of course, behavior analytics.

The benefits machine learning deliver to all these endeavors are:

- Accelerated time in model development, model testing and delivery of actionable insights
- Delivery of an optimal balance between predictive accuracy, performance and cost
- Utilization of streaming data to deliver real-time analytics
- Reduction of risk with enterprise-grade machine learning
- Acquisition of best insights in model performance and outcome

The age of advanced analytics had arrived, which meant organizations had solution capabilities that were much less reliant on human knowledge to build and maintain the solution. This solution set gave organizations the ability to detect patterns and predict outcomes across a wide range of variables far beyond human capabilities. This delivered a capability to analyze vastly greater amounts of data, which included unstructured data alongside traditional structured data found in transaction application systems. This unstructured data included elements such as text, log, social and machine data. Within this sea of raw information, machine learning has provided the ability to adapt to changing conditions through continuous learning.

Within this sea of raw information, machine learning has provided the ability to adapt to changing conditions through continuous learning.

Financial organizations, such as FICO (originally Fair, Isaac and Company), have used it in fraud detection where their solutions employ an input layer (with the raw data), 'hidden' layers that process and link the inputs, and an output layer that produces a score indicating fraud risk. Machine learning (ML) use cases extend into property, casualty, life and health insurance, and more. Manufacturers have used ML to facilitate resolution of machine outages or assembly line disruption. Utility businesses use machine learning to manage service interruptions to their customers. Businesses have employed ML to enhance the logistics of delivering goods and services. Sales and marketing organizations leverage ML to analyze a massive number of factors contributing to a consumer's purchasing considerations, such as demographic and location data. This data, along with purchase and browsing history, helps predict a consumer's preferences and buying actions. Included in this capability, ML analyzes vast repositories of disparate data found in social sources, web logs, transaction systems, and geospatial sources to deliver a scalable predictive solution that provides distinct advantages for today's marketing and sales requirements. Internet giants like Amazon Web Services (AWS) now offer their own ML solution. All have used ML to bring together disparate information to deliver accurate forecasts which had before been impossible to render.

Predictive and advanced security analytics had a steeper curve to climb for one simple reason: accuracy. The challenge to accurately identify verifiable risk amidst a sea of complex data in near real-time defined its core requirement. If errors occurred in marketing analytics, or logistics in manufacturing or service deliveries, it represented an inconvenience or diminished productivity. Predictive security analytics had a higher bar for proving value. Failures in security analytics held the potential for impacting an organization's bottom line due to data exfiltration, espionage or regulatory fines. Security teams needed to see the unassailable proof points and were hesitant to adopt unless relevant solid results could be shown. Their requirement was the highest detection rate with the highest validation. For example, noisy alert systems

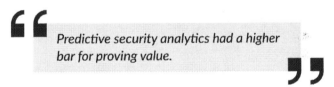

Predictive security analytics had a higher bar for proving value.

delivering 5 detections out of 100 high-scoring alerts, versus 8 out 10, were considered to have low value to security teams.

The other issue of requesting absolute proof in results drives analysts to use rules of known threats versus uncovering the unknown with machine learning. To be predictive and absolute in results is something of an oxymoron.

As recently as 2010, some analysts created a misperception that predictive analytics, powered by machine learning, was not feasible for the foreseeable future. Generally, their concerns boiled down to a few areas:

- **_Outlier detection_** – With machine learning considered better at identifying similarities than finding outliers, outlier detection was viewed as a classification problem. The lack of a perfect model of normality was a constraint.

- **High cost of errors** – With intrusion detection, the cost was too much noise. Administrators in turn, dialed it down. Factors like spam detection generated a highly unbalanced cost model creating unacceptably high false negatives or misses.

- **Semantic gap** – The challenge of transferring results into actionable reports and the problem of defining the difference between abnormal activity and attacks were considered unresolved.

- **Diversity of data and network traffic** – Basic characteristics such as bandwidth, duration of connections and application mix, exhibited immense variability, with large bursts of activity being common, were considered too large a challenge to overcome.

- **Difficulty with evaluation** – Where evaluation of the data produced was considered more difficult than building the detector because of data difficulties.

While this may have been the perspective of some doubters in 2010, concurrently the market-leading vendors in UEBA had already been making significant inroads in their solutions, working at all of these quality challenges. 2014 was a breakout year for the advanced development of these solutions. Decisive strides were achieved in establishing this next generation of proven and reliable UEBA capabilities with mature machine learning. Evolution continues. Leading vendors in the UEBA space are targeting new challenges, to strengthen their prescriptive user and entity behavior analytics capabilities into platforms, while some are moving on further to provide prescriptive capabilities. It is instructive, however, to consider the evolutionary context in the development timeline of UEBA and IdA, to have an understanding of how the UEBA venders addressed the analysts' concerns of 2010.

- **Outlier detection** – Reliable models of normality have become well-established through self-learning and self-training models of users and entities over the course of 30 to 35 days, and much faster with ingestion of existing history of users. Linking their behavior with static and dynamic peer groups further refines the modeling and eliminates the issue of bad behavior in baselines. Identity analytics (also using ML) has helped to drastically reduce the number of unaccounted for access risks.

- **High cost of errors** – The comprehensive ability to classify users, entities and their behavior across

> *The comprehensive ability to classify users, entities and their behavior across the broad spectrum of hybrid environments, applications and devices has robustly addressed misclassification issues.*

the broad spectrum of hybrid environments, applications and devices has robustly addressed misclassification issues. False positives and negatives have also been demonstrably reduced, with critical context from big data and increasing the number of models for specific use cases.

- ***Semantic gap*** – The gap between UI (user interface) and API (application program interface) has been closed by virtue of numerous innovations. The UI experience has become enhanced with color-coded graphics which include business and user friendly descriptions of anomalies that facilitate speed and ease of use. Accurate and normalized risk scores (0-100), with thresholds for specific alerts, in a number of categories within a UEBA solution, provides precise actionable intelligence and clearly defines the difference between abnormal activity and attacks in a range of relevant categories. Analytic response codes (ARC) with risk scores, instantly categorize what type of anomaly it is, and its severity, communicating directly to the solution in the API relationship, facilitating accuracy and optimal automated risk response times.

- ***Diversity of network traffic*** – Mature solutions have migrated to big data supporting both structured and unstructured data. They include predefined data connectors for ease of data ingestion. They enable customization and addition of new attributes with flexible metadata. In essence, a mature UEBA solution can ingest any data for any desired attributes.

- ***Difficulty with evaluation*** – The advancement of the normalization and correlation of data has enabled shorter proof of concept cycles, along with using historical data to speed-train models for faster time to value for the use cases of UEBA and IdA. More mature UEBA solutions with experience in hybrid environments have learned on-premises data is often more varied, as well as 'dirty', however, while cloud data is less varied and cleaner.

While machine learning may have arrived late to the game of advanced security analytics, its journey has been filled with initiatives making the solution more mature, comprehensive and robust. It now stands in a position of delivering extreme value in a broad range of security use cases. Our expert contributor Leslie K. Lambert, CISO at large, with a vast range of first-hand experience in information security, will share her seasoned insights on machine learning and its benefits in user and entity behavior analytics and identity analytics.

BORDERLESS EXPERT INSIGHTS

Leslie K. Lambert*
CISO at Large

Former CISO for Juniper Networks and Sun Microsystems, Leslie K. Lambert, has over 30 years of experience in information security, IT risk and compliance, security policies, standards and procedures, incident management, intrusion detection, security awareness, threat vulnerability assessments and mitigation. She received *CSO* magazine's 2010 Compass Award for security leadership and was named one of *Computerworld's* Premier 100 IT Leaders in 2009. An Anita Borg Institute Ambassador since 2006, Leslie has been mentoring women across the world in technology. Leslie has also served on the board of the Bay Area CSO Council since 2005. Lambert holds an MBA in Finance and Marketing from Santa Clara University, and an MA in Experimental Psychology.

The chair of Gurucul's Executive Advisory Board, Leslie has supplied instrumental support in the company's planning, development and strategy for the organization's solution development and market approach. In this chapter, she provides her expert insights on machine learning in advanced security analytics.

Overview

In this module, Ms. Lambert observes the impactful way in which machine learning is reshaping security. She explores the manner by which machine learning helps meet the challenge of social engineering attacks, as she also provides insights into low and slow insider threats and how machine learning detects abuse by trusted users. She then lends critical insights into data exfiltration through remote access malware and the detection of IP theft with machine learning. As misconceptions of machine learning are common, Lambert provides real-world perceptive context on this topic, especially in reference to UEBA and IdA. Common UEBA utility scenarios are provided which are followed by real-world case studies in UEBA, empowered by machine learning. These brief case studies include citing the distinct benefits security leaders see with this caliber of security solution. At the conclusion of her section, she explains notable misconceptions around machine learning in advanced security analytics, as well as shares thoughts on the future of it.

Machine learning is reshaping security

At the 2016 RSA Conference in San Francisco, it was virtually impossible to find a security solution vendor not claiming to use machine learning. Both new and

---

* The views and opinions expressed by Leslie K. Lambert in this book are her own, and do not necessarily reflect those of her current, or any of her previous employers.

established companies were touting machine learning as a major component of the data science being used in their products. What is machine learning? Is it really reshaping cybersecurity?

The pervasiveness of machine learning. We'll define machine learning as the science of getting computers to act without being explicitly programmed. Over the past decade, machine learning has enabled self-driving cars, practical speech recognition, effective web search, and it has vastly improved our understanding of the human genome. Machine learning is so pervasive that we use it dozens of times a day without knowing it. Many researchers believe machine learning is the best way to make progress towards human-level artificial Intelligence (AI). The incredible power of machine learning and its application to analytics is reshaping cybersecurity, as we know it.

Machine learning and UEBA. In particular, applying machine learning to user and entity behavioral analytics is profoundly improving our ability to make sense of the volume of data generated by security products in the enterprise. When machine learning concepts like automated and iterative

> *...applying machine learning to user and entity behavioral analytics is profoundly improving our ability to make sense of the volume of data generated by security products in the enterprise.*

algorithms are applied to learning patterns in data, we can probe data for structure, even if we don't know what that structure looks like.

Relationships in data nodes. In the past, security products attempted to correlate data to discern patterns and meaning. We now know better. Instead, today we perform link analysis to evaluate relationships or connections between data nodes. Key relationships can be identified among various types of data nodes or objects, things we might think of as organizations, people, transactions, and so on.

Extracting meaning from digital exhaust. Machine learning is what enables us to bring together huge volumes of data which is generated by normal user activity from disparate, even obscure, sets of data — digital exhaust — to identify relationships that span time, place and actions. Since machine learning can be simultaneously applied to hundreds of thousands of discrete events from multiple data sets, 'meaning' can be derived from behaviors and used as an early warning detection or prevention system.

Iterative data reprocessing to discover patterns. The ultimate test for a machine learning model is error validation on new data. In other words, machine learning is looking to match new data with what it's seen before, and not to test it to disprove, reject, or nullify an expected outcome. Since machine learning uses an iterative, automated approach, it can reprocess data until a robust pattern is found. This allows it to go beyond looking for known or common patterns.

Machine learning and social engineering attacks

How can analytics prevent IP theft after a successful account compromise? Real-world use cases from Verizon's 2016 *Data Breach Digest: Scenarios from the Field* illustrate potential ways machine learning can be used to detect or prevent similar incidents.

Industrial espionage discovery. In one example, a manufacturer's designs for an innovative new model of heavy construction equipment were stolen following a social engineering attack. The company was alerted when a primary competitor, located on another continent, introduced a new piece of equipment that looked like an exact copy of a model recently developed by the victim company.

Targeted spear phishing. The attack employed a scenario familiar to forensic network security analysts. The threat actors identified an employee who they suspected would have access to new product designs they were after — the chief design engineer. They targeted their victim via a spear phishing campaign based on the fictitious LinkedIn profile of a recruiter. The attackers began sending emails containing fictitious employment opportunities to the victim. One contained an attachment with a malware file embedded in the document. When opened, the malware began beaconing to an external IP address used by the threat actor. The attackers then installed a backdoor PHP (hypertext preprocessor) reverse shell on the chief design engineer's system. From there, exfiltration of all the pertinent data the threat actors required was achieved.

Security breach forensics. When viewing this scenario from a perspective of maintaining the goal of stopping the breach before the damage is done, an InfoSec analyst would seek to identify what intercept points might have been used to uncover the anomalous behavior occurring with the chief engineer's account. One is the presence and availability of multiple log files containing rich information about what data had been transferred, when, by whom, and to where. This data is available from intrusion detection logs, NetFlow data, DLP logs, firewall logs, antivirus and malware reporting. Because this data was underutilized, the victim company left itself wide open to several types of compromises.

> *Because this data was underutilized, the victim company left itself wide open to several types of compromises.*

Correlating expanding unwieldy data. It is an unfortunate fact that not all organizations are capable of making sense of complex data from multiple sources. The volume and speed at which this data is produced can seem unmanageable. In addition, the ability to correlate dissimilar data in a normalized and comparable manner may be unavailable to an organization. When this situation occurs, it's time for more advanced analysis with sophisticated mathematical support. This entails data normalization, analytics, and the application of machine learning.

Comprehensive visibility of data and user behavior. Using machine learning in circumstances like these can provide a more holistic view of the combined log data and expose suspicious activity. In addition to revealing malicious command-and-control traffic, machine learning models reveal who is accessing, storing and using data in uncharacteristic ways when compared to normal and peer group behavior. However, according to Sommer and Paxson's *Outside the Closed World: On Using Machine Learning for Network Intrusion Detection*, detecting account compromise via machine learning also poses unique challenges.

Outdated security methodologies and tools. Security professionals typically expect an extremely low false positive rate from network security tools. This has given rise to the popularity of 'whitelist' and 'blacklist' approaches which are too rigid to adapt to account compromise threats like the one described above. When scaled to an enterprise of 2,000 users, a one percent daily false alarm rate per user translates to 20 false alarms a day. Eventually, a tool generating this many false positives will be ignored. That's basically what happened with the infamous Target breach referenced earlier in this book.

Analysis accuracy strengthened by proven techniques. When an account is compromised, bad logins are typically sparse and mixed with good behavior in such a way that an algorithm or human operator may miss bad behavior among the preponderance of good logins. The expectation maximization (EM) algorithm approach addresses this problem by treating the compromised account as a two-user model in which sessions may either be produced by the original user or a new user. This method causes benign sessions to fall out of the likelihood calculations, so they do not sway a mix of good and bad sessions toward being evaluated as good overall.

Security gaps without machine learning. In this particular incident, if the victim company had employed machine learning to analyze the data already in hand, they likely would have been alerted to several suspicious activities including who was accessing the designs, where the files were being stored, how and where they were being moved, non-typical access to sensitive data repositories, and several other possibilities.

> *...if the victim company had employed machine learning to analyze the data already in hand, they likely would have been alerted to several suspicious activities...*

A valuable supplement to security strategies and practices. Most organizations have multiple security tools in place producing meaningful log data. Applying machine learning algorithms to these information sources to profile user access and behavior is a logical next step and will certainly deliver critical security data.

Low and slow insider threats: Detecting abuse by trusted users

In the preceding section, I discussed how machine learning could be used to detect phishing-based account compromise attacks using a real-world use case from the 2016 Verizon *Data Breach Digest*. Here we'll examine how to detect insider threats using similar techniques.

Insider spying with 'borrowed' credentials. This Verizon example involves an organization in the middle of a buyout that was using retention contracts to prevent employee attrition. To find out what other employees were being offered, a middle manager acquired IT administrator credentials from a colleague who was also a friend. He used these credentials to access the company's onsite spam filter and to spy on the CEO's incoming email. The abuse didn't stop there. The same credentials were also used to browse sensitive file shares and conduct other unauthorized actions.

Compromise leads to multiple breaches. This scenario is rife with information security issues. These include social engineering, unauthorized and inappropriate use of privileged access credentials to access files including the confidential email archive on a spam-filtering appliance. Why wasn't the company able to detect this activity until an after-the-fact forensic investigation, despite having ample data to support its clear and direct discovery?

Flaws in privileged access security policy. It's apparent the victim organization was unaware of the illicit activities of this specific IT administrator. In fact, they were not monitoring the access patterns and behaviors of elevated privileged accounts. While it's unclear what the IT administrator's specific job function was, we know the access privileges assigned to his user account were wide-reaching and powerful, spanning the gamut of file shares, from email archives to spam filtering infrastructure. Meanwhile, the access privileges were poorly configured, as he was able to traverse several different types of systems with just one set of credentials.

Context criticality. What makes it difficult to detect insider threats like this one is context, or more accurately, the lack of it. The mind-numbing volume of log files and outputs from security tools are typically standalone, siloed sources of data. Rarely are these rich sources of intelligence correlated with one another to achieve greater understanding of what access and activities have taken place.

> What makes it difficult to detect insider threats like this one is context, or more accurately, the lack of it.

Leveraging existing data for critical insights. Security teams need to be able to examine these access patterns and behaviors in a way that allows them to see important relationships between multiple sets of activities, possibly taking place in different locations concurrently. This is where data science and machine learning is invaluable. In this case, machine learning could have been used to analyze the data already in hand. This would have revealed suspicious activities including accessing inappropriate files (that belonged to others), how and where they were being moved or copied, and non-typical access to the spam filtering infrastructure and confidential email archives.

A new normal for IT and SOCs. IT technology and know-how has moved far beyond verifying the simple heartbeats of IT applications and infrastructure servers. Organizations need to know who, what, where and why, and they must know it virtually in real time. Machine learning overcomes the seemingly insurmountable challenges of creating links between mountains of dissimilar and disconnected data sources. In this case, being unaware of the online activities within an organization, and not monitoring access credentials in a vigilant manner, reflects a lack of ownership for the basic responsibilities of security professionals. It demonstrates a deficiency of due diligence for the organization they support.

Mandated security procedures deliver results. In contrast, within Lockheed Martin's *Cyber Kill Chain®* model, the 'Exploitation' phase is where security professionals are mandated to perform systematic examination of rich data sets that exist inside the organization. What better way to do this than via link analysis techniques used in machine learning that enable us to proactively detect and prevent persistent threats?

Data exfiltration through remote access malware: Detecting IP theft with machine learning

In this section, we'll look into how remote access threats can be exposed with the machine learning techniques we explored in earlier sections. I like to call it catching a RAT (Remote Access Trojan) by the tail.

Phishing email delivers stolen credentials and privileged access. In this next Verizon example, a manufacturing company experienced a breach of a shared engineering workstation in its R&D department. A phishing email resulted in a RAT backdoor being downloaded onto the system, which enabled the threat actors to escalate privileges and capture user credentials for everyone who had used the system. By the time the breach was discovered, a significant amount of information had been leaked out via FTP to a foreign IP address.

Evolving cyber-attacks bring greater risk. Most companies understand that data breaches are inevitable. It's no surprise that spending on cybersecurity tools has expanded from traditional 'prevent and protect' technologies to include post-breach 'detect and respond' solutions in an attempt to

> *..spending on cybersecurity tools has expanded from traditional 'prevent and protect' technologies to include post-breach 'detect and respond' solutions...*

control and manage unavoidable cyber-attacks. In addition, cyber-attacks are becoming more targeted, resulting in companies experiencing more damaging compromises that have a bigger impact on their business. These attacks aren't limited to specific vertical markets, though healthcare and financial services seemed to be the favorites in 2016.

Compromised identity a growing concern. The Identity Theft Resource Center (ITRC) has been tracking security breaches since 2005, looking for patterns, new trends and information to educate businesses and consumers on the importance of protecting identities and personally identifiable information. From 2005 through April 2016, the ITRC recorded 6,079 breaches, covering 862,527,023 identity records. That's a lot of compromised identities! Moreover, these are only the ones reported!

Attackers favor identity theft. Today's attacks compromise identity as a primary vector to pull sensitive information from an organization for both financial gain and social notoriety. These attacks are sophisticated, better funded, more organized than ever before, making it imperative for organizations to immediately analyze potential threats and risks related to anomalous and suspicious behavior.

A range of data sources to monitor. In addition to monitoring how identities are being both used and managed, other critical data sources within an organization's computing environment should be examined to provide more context beyond who and what. Some data source examples include network access, event and flow data, DLP data, sys logs, vulnerability scanning data, log files from IT applications, etc. In many cases, this data may already be consolidated into a log event management or SIEM solution.

Rich context needed for advanced security analytics. This vast array of data, when combined with information on how identities are being used by both humans and machines, creates a rich source of context that can be mined using threat analytics and anomaly detection. When we view identity as a threat plane, hundreds of attributes can be modelled in machine learning algorithms to predict and remediate security threats.

Rules no longer apply. Machine learning is a force multiplier. Rules-based detection alone is unable to keep pace with the increasingly complex demands of threat and breach detection. This is primarily because rules are based on what (little) we know about the data, and in turn generate excessive alerts. Since humans lack the ability to predict what future cyber-attacks will look like, we can't write rules for these scenarios. In contrast, machine learning and statistical analysis can find anomalies in data that humans would not otherwise recognize or detect. For example, they can leverage useful and predictive cues that are too noisy and highly dimensional for humans and traditional software to link together.

Pervasive RATs. Going back to our Verizon *Data Breach Digest* example, let's consider how machine learning could detect a RAT. First, let's clarify what we're talking about. A Remote Access Trojan is malicious malware software that runs in the background on a computer and gives unauthorized access to a hacker so they can steal information or install additional malicious software. Hackers don't even have to create their own RATs; these programs are available for download from dark areas of the web. Trojans have been around for two decades. The term 'RAT' is relatively new.

Masked downloads install malicious malware. RATs usually start out as executable files that are downloaded from the internet. They are often masked as another program or added to a seemingly harmless application. Once the RAT installs, it runs in system memory and adds itself to system startup directories and registry entries. Each time the computer is started, the RAT starts as well.

Machine learning's ability to detect atypical activity. How can machine learning help here? RATs generate anomalous data conditions from several system resources. Machine learning algorithms would detect this activity as atypical, since they represent system services or resources that are not 'normally' running. In this case, machine learning algorithms can perform anomaly detection for machine-, not user-, based access and activity. Machine learning models can even compare 'self-versus-self' and 'self-versus-peer group' access activity for machines and users. They do this by using historical baselines to determine anomalies with high accuracy. If it's not a normal condition, it's an anomaly, and machine learning will uncover it and catch the RAT by the tail!

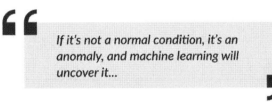

If it's not a normal condition, it's an anomaly, and machine learning will uncover it...

Misconceptions of machine learning

While numerous UEBA vendors tout their machine learning capabilities, their ability to demonstrate this in a POC (proof of concept) might be problematic for a number of reasons. The first is if the POC is short-term, for example five days, and the customer wants the solution vendor to find a smoking gun with the presumption it will be done via machine learning. Real ML, however, takes time, needs context and is deeply data adjusted. The models must train with baselines to do the work. That takes time for the models to self-learn and self-train — a lot more than five days.

Threat hunting vs. demonstrating ML in POCs. If the objective is to find anomalies in this short term, the only likely way a vendor will be able to do that is by threat hunting, to run a collection of rules and causalities, and they may indeed succeed in finding anomalies. But that's not machine learning, nor is it repeatable. Anything that shows up within a few days is almost certainly rules-based.

Use cases demonstrate machine learning capabilities. More mature customers of UEBA and IdA are learning to ask for use cases where only machine learning can solve a problem, such as finding access outliers or privileged access risk and abuse. The main use cases require risk scoring of entitlements that could be in the millions and far beyond human capacity. If customers understand the benefits of ML, and plan to adopt it for its long-term value, they must give the solution a true ML test. This means commit the time required to vet the worth of the solution and the breadth of its capabilities. As the old adage goes: "A shortcut is the fastest way to get somewhere you don't want to be." Short-term threat hunting simply can't provide any meaningful insight into a vendor's ML capabilities. In some cases, vendors say they have machine learning, when they really don't. They have merely rebranded their solution to respond to the awareness trend of ML's popularity and perceived value in predictive and advanced security analytics.

Self-learning models that optimize in a month. Contrasting the rules-based model, user behavior-based machine learning uses clustering to find outliers or anomalies from the normal for self-versus-self, self-versus-static peer groups, and self-versus-dynamic peer groups (where the machine learning determines the peering for more accuracy in outlier detection). Once an anomaly is found, predictive risk scoring machine learning models factor in time-based norms and deliver feedback to score accurately, with low false positives. These models are self-learning and self-training. They optimize over 30-35 days of data ingestion to create baselines for behaviors. Access to historical data can speed the learning curve of models to a few days. Keys to success are the magnitude of access to ingest data sources into big data infrastructure, as well as, the proven compute scale for the data science math within the machine learning models and the resources provided.

> ....historical access data can speed the learning curve of models to a few days.

Context from big data lakes. The causality scenarios demonstrate that more context is crucial to get a useful perspective of the total risk in the hybrid environment. Here, machine learning evolves on context and it integrates effectively with big data lakes to provide the critical ability to analyze data over a length of time, not just an instance. Visibility extends across both on-premises and in the cloud.

Holistic visibility of accounts, entitlements, access and behavior. Machine learning comes in various disciplines. Identity analytics focuses on identifying access risks, excess access and access outliers. UEBA, on the other hand, focuses on anomalous behavior from insider threats, data exfiltration and access abuse. Both disciplines use clustering and outlier ML analysis, however for different outputs. These outputs can be used together and holistically for improved security. For example, and as previously noted, to detect privileged access abuse, you must know where the privileged access is with identity analytics. This is a critical solution element, since industry experts cite over 50% of privileged access entitlements lay outside an organization's directory and vaults. If the UEBA ML does not know where to look, or is missing 50% of its target, it can't be effective. To address that challenge, IdA uses ML to provide holistic visibility of privileged access risk and runs in concert with UEBA models to look for abuse.

Common utility scenarios for machine learning in security

The following three examples represent familiar, yet risky, circumstances for a majority of enterprises today. These scenarios illustrate common identity-based access risks and threats, which highlight the importance of combining machine learning with contextual behavior analysis that includes peer group access and activity comparison, cloud access and activity monitoring and the ability to correlate access and activity against identity data stores like HR applications, IAM solutions, directories, and more.

Data exfiltration with departing employees. A sales employee plans to leave the company to take a job with a competitor but has not yet made his intentions known. Before resigning, he wants to gather as much competitive information as possible. This is information the employee would normally have access to for their job role. However, the new actions of downloading more data than usual are suspicious. When compared to that individual's dynamic peer groups, these risk-scored actions reveal this is the only sales person performing this volume of activity. The machine learning risk models give the identity a high score for the recognized anomalies, indicating the actions must be investigated.

Stolen credentials from phishing attacks. A set of login credentials belonging to a customer support representative of a financial company are stolen in a phishing attack. The attacker logs into the on-premises support application account with all of the authority of the original genuine user. The intruder accesses many of the same contact and support account records as the legitimate user normally would do. However, the attacker does this with more frequency and with increased volume of data downloads than for a normal customer support analyst. This activity is quickly spotted as something outside the norm, and the company is able to suspend the account until an investigation can be conducted.

> *This activity is quickly spotted as something outside the norm, and the company is able to suspend the account until an investigation can be conducted.*

Misuse of unmanaged cloud resources. A contract worker had been working with a company for many years. He worked at home and performed his job via VPN for remote access. For all practical purposes, he acted like an actual company employee, with the access rights and privileges of an employee. When his contract was terminated, he was deprovisioned in the HR systems. Nonetheless, login credentials for Salesforce.com were overlooked for termination. He still had access and continued to login to siphon off customer information to provide to a competitor. This behavior was detected through analysis of the current HR data correlated to the contractor's current activities.

Case studies in UEBA machine learning: The broader benefits

While the scenarios above represent common events many organizations might face where UEBA and machine learning are engaged to provide a fundamental security solution, the use cases below present a deeper insight into how UEBA and IdA combine to deliver broader crucial benefits to an organization. These field cases are from Gurucul's portfolio of customer delivery success stories.

Organizational security fortification through risk scores. An insurance customer needed to disrupt external intruders by adding step-up authentication based on machine learning risk scores for user behavior. When a user logs into an account, the authentication system performs a real-time call to the user behavior machine learning solution that provides a current risk score. This risk score is fed into the authentication system which then determines the authentication challenges for the user. A high-risk score can result in two or three security challenges to successfully login while a low-risk score may result in one or no challenges to login. If an account has been compromised, the external intruder is highly likely to raise the risk score due to abnormal behaviors as compared to the normal user. The high-risk scores result in additional authentication challenges which the external intruder may not be able to provide thus locking them out for the present time. The employee may also become more security aware by seeing an increase in the number of authentication challenges required to access their user account.

Attack surface reduction enhanced with targeted identity roles and privileges. A financial services customer employed machine learning models to analyze access and activity for employees to highlight excess access. With this intelligence, they reduced accounts and entitlements by 83%. This lowered the vulnerable surface area of identities open to phishing and social attacks. Machine learning models enabled the determination of the right person, data, time and place with more accuracy than human processes could, reducing both group and role proliferation. Machine learning also produced new intelligent roles for eleven departments, replacing legacy roles created from manual processes and rules. Gartner analysts estimate that machine learning models will determine 50% of roles and privileges in the next two years.

Rapid discovery of industrial espionage via compromised credentials. A leading manufacturing enterprise was concerned about protecting intellectual property, knowing that unethical nation states and espionage are common threat vectors exploited in their industry to gain technology advantages. The customer had modern security defenses in place for known bad threats using signatures, patterns and rules. They understood that targeted phishing and social engineering attacks could compromise account credentials. The customer deployed a user behavior analytics machine learning model solution, which extracted historical access and activity data to accelerate analysis by the models. On the second day of use, the SOC team detected two highly privileged research accounts that had been compromised. Further analysis revealed an unethical nation state as the intruder. What the enterprise suspected came to light in a few days using machine learning to detect abnormal account behavior that common security defenses looking for known bad indicators had missed. Without machine learning, normal patterns of discovery and response cycles for this type of attack would be in the range between months and years, with standard intruder dwell time cited by most analysts as well over 200 days.

> " *Without machine learning, normal patterns of discovery and response cycles for this type of attack would be in the range between months and years...* "

Self-audit feature flags nefarious activity. An insurance company sought to raise security awareness by providing employees with self-audit reports once a week which furnished risk-scored access and activity data from machine learning models. One employee spent a Wednesday out of the office to be in support of a sick child. That employee did not access her high privilege accounts on that day. The following self-audit report she received on Friday, however, revealed account login and activity for Wednesday. Having her own unique context, the employee quickly recognized this was not possible. Upon investigation by the security team one of the high privilege accounts was found to have been compromised for over 3.5 years by an external intruder. The context of the self-audit report with machine learning risk scores and visibility into access and activity data added new eyes beyond the SOC team's capabilities where they would have likely overlooked this activity. Machine learning models aggregate multiple accounts, access and activity under one identity for an employee to quickly assess their activity and any possible risk-scored anomalies, much in the same manner as reviewing a credit card statement.

Clear benefits delivered by machine learning and UEBA. All four cases above were Gurucul customers who experienced clear-cut benefits to their businesses, along with numerous enhanced security monitoring efficiencies that have continued long-term.

Perspectives on the future of machine learning in security

As I mentioned at the beginning of this module, a majority of UEBA security vendors are touting their solutions as being driven by machine learning. However, *caveat emptor* — let the buyer beware — not all machine learning is created equal. There's more information in Chapter 13 of this book on the range of machine learning in UEBA solutions as well as the specific requirements for machine learning in mature UEBA solutions.

Machine learning's continuing evolution. The important thing to keep in mind is that while its impact as seen in other industries has already been profound, we are just getting started with machine learning in security. With cutting-edge advanced security analytics vendors, predictive analytics is expanding to include prescriptive capabilities. The new realities in today's expanding hybrid environments require machine learning's support now. Continuing to employ the inefficient, ineffective, futile human efforts using rules, patterns and signatures to cope with a growing amount of data that is doubling year over year can no longer be considered a feasible strategy for security experts to detect the unknown. Data science is needed and machine learning is the answer.

CONCLUSIONS & TAKEAWAYS:
Machine learning's continuing journey in advanced security analytics

The age of big data has arrived, with machine learning supporting analytic processes across science, business and a range of other settings and applications. Its irreplaceable value provides higher accuracy, delivers substantial cost savings, offers broader performance capabilities far beyond human scale, and many more benefits. Machine learning's arrival at predictive and advanced security analytics has been somewhat slower than other channels of analytics due to the high-stakes importance of reliable accuracy. 2014 represented a breakout year for machine learning's capacities on a broad array of functionalities. Now, analysts view machine learning as providing an invaluable contribution to an organization's complex security risk prevention capabilities.

Award-winning CISO at large, Leslie K. Lambert observes how machine learning is reshaping security. She also notes, however, that all machine learning (ML) is not alike. While some vendors claim their solutions are ML, they are in fact manually driven by a rules-based process, dealing entirely with known bads. On the other hand, mature machine learning uses automated and iterative algorithms to learn patterns in data, and probes the data for structure that may be new and previously unknown. This enables machine learning to perform link analysis to evaluate relationships or connections between data nodes, things such as organizations, people, transactions, etc. This complex iterative data processing discovers patterns and extracts meaning from the vast ocean of digital exhaust. As a result, machine learning identifies relationships that span time, place and actions, on a potential scale representing millions of access entitlements within an organization.

Instances of real-world breaches are examined where machine learning might have discovered the behavior anomaly associated with the malicious activity in a timely manner. They include an industrial espionage case where targeted spear phishing was employed to compel the victim to open a file containing a malware file embedded in the document. Another case depicts an insider using 'borrowed' credentials to spy on executives through their email accounts. This was an instance of privileged access abuse that was poorly monitored by the victim organization's security team. The final scenario cited involved data exfiltration through remote access malware — a Remote Access Trojan (RAT). All of the cases examined by Lambert were well within the capabilities of machine learning, with predictive and advanced security analytics, drawing from big data via UEBA or IdA, to neutralize a potentially severe risk.

Lambert goes on to observe how compromised identity is a growing concern, as attackers favor identity theft to compromise account credentials. To address this challenge properly, a broad range of data sources must be monitored comprehensively and with a responsive speed to inhibit attacker dwell time as much as possible. With the rich context, this machine learning process produces required advanced security analytics.

Lambert then examines misconceptions of machine learning and how some vendors try to demonstrate their value during POCs with swift threat hunting, and showing results. Mature machine learning, however, takes more time to ingest data to be able to produce valuable results. The best method to demonstrate machine learning capabilities is through use cases, which employ both self-learning and self-training capabilities. This is a marked contrast to manually driven threat hunting driven by rules and causalities that may not be sustainable over time.

Finally, Lambert presents three examples of common utility scenarios in machine learning for advanced security analytics. These are: data exfiltration with departing employees, stolen credentials from phishing attacks, and misuse of unmanaged cloud resources. She then cites four case studies from Gurucul's solution delivery roster which have delivered definitive value for their customers. They are: enterprise threat detection through risk scores; identity access surface reduction for accounts and entitlements; rapid discovery of industrial espionage via compromised credentials; and a self-audit feature flags nefarious activity. Lambert then shares her observations about the future of machine learning in predictive and advanced security analytics, which is growing and evolving, keeping pace with emerging technologies and attacker innovations.

One of the challenges of effective machine learning in advanced security analytics is how organizations manage their big data. The next *Borderless Breach Flashcard* is actually a success story of one bank that saw the crippling risk of unwieldy big data on the horizon, and adopted a smart solution to deal with it. The following chapter ventures much deeper into the story of big data in advanced security analytics, with critical insights into the data lakes, the sources of big data, and more.

	BORDERLESS BREACH FLASHCARD *Dodging a Security Big Data Gridlock*		
CATEGORY	Overwhelming amounts of big data across an array of global SIEMs placed a multinational bank in peril of being non-compliant with regulators and facing the prospect of being barred from trading.
WHO	**The target:** Barclays Bank.
WHAT	After an internal study, Barclays Bank assessed it generated 44 billion security events per month, growing quickly to 65 billion per month due to recent acquisitions. An array of SIEM solutions, across 12 global data centers and 60 servers, were not integrated holistically nor supported analytical requirements. The SIEM solutions were far beyond conventional capabilities which topped out at 500 million events per day. The security data from each silo of information was not integrated. Querying retained data was impossible. Big data gridlock loomed with a vast threat plane unaddressed by uncorrelated security data.
WHEN	2013
WHERE	Globally.
WHY	With big data across multiple regional management centers and data silos, no comprehensive capability of extracting the data, or providing comprehensive security monitoring and analysis, using proper real-time security data to identify threats was virtually impossible. A new class of solution was required to address this growing problem which threatened to cripple the bank's earning capability.
HOW	Barclays adopted an advanced security analytics solution, which replaced the need for SIEM solutions. They met their complex regulatory requirements, which had to satisfy 176 regulators worldwide. The new solution also highlighted a number of previously unknown problems without having to purchase additional security solutions.
HOW BAD?	It's more like, how bad could it have been? Stephen Gailey, the head of security services for Barclays, observed: "We wouldn't be doing this if we weren't getting value out of it... It's keeping us from being fined... Without... (it [the advanced security analytics solution]), we might be taken out of the market... or stopped from trading altogether."
TAKING STOCK	This is one case where prudent decisions, made in a timely manner to allow proper adoption and integration practices, put the company ahead of the security analytics curve. The question is, what other organizations should be taking similar steps to avoid big data gridlock?

Big Data in
Advanced Security Analytics

The tipping point of digital exhaust

A number of professionals in high tech enjoy the sci-fi perspective, especially references to *The Matrix*. In its dystopian future everyone is controlled by machines with infernal consequences. Some observers, like Elon Musk, correlate that chilling model with evolving trends they see emerging in technology today, predicting a dire future, where the dark side of artificial intelligence (AI) portends a paradigm shift, where the balance of essential controls within society's infrastructure shifts decisively away from human influence and to that of machines. It's almost as though the entire world becomes a single brain. Pragmatists applying a more optimistic view assure us this is unlikely, yet they acknowledge that the sea change of technology's influence is a new normal and already a significant part of our daily lives.

This rapid evolution of technology has influenced our quality of life in ways we've never anticipated. The impact continues to grow. In a sense, our iPhone's control our behavior with a never-ending variety of interruption-driven calls to action. Facebook's first president, Sean Parker, observes how the founders consciously exploited the way people fundamentally think and behave with its "social-validation feedback loop." Automation compels us to forgo thinking in the performance of certain manual actions (like autocorrect in typing), or engaging particular mental functions (like online shopping choices). "Let the machine do it," has become an ingrained attitude for many. Google Maps shows us the shortest route to a destination and when the best time to drive is to ensure we're traveling in the shortest time possible. Amazon, and a host of other online-based enterprises, post ads in your online applications or send you emails based on your browsing history with their websites, as they strive to influence and streamline your purchase decisions which are customized based on their understanding of your preferences drawn from analytics of your previous purchases and online product research. Manufacturers, shipping companies, financial services companies — along with an expanding range of business enterprises and government agencies — all leverage big data analytics for tactical and strategic objectives.

These analytics mine and process a vast array of diverse data varieties. The burgeoning accumulation and totality of all this information, 90% of which was created in the last two years, represents big data and the concept of digital exhaust. From a security perspective, the volume, velocity and variety of data that organizations must contend with has crossed a threshold where humans can no longer manage it effectively. Traditional approaches in security analytics no longer suffice, can no longer cover all the requirements to ensure an environment's security. Something more is needed that must contend with the sprawling and growing volume of data. That next

> Something more is needed that must contend with the sprawling and growing volume of data.

generation in security capabilities is advanced security analytics.

For advanced security analytics, this expanded capability is only possible with mature machine learning, drawing invaluable context from big data. Vendors in this space can't just claim they do machine learning; they must be able to show the data science behind it and demonstrate the business value. How organizations respond to this impactful set of developments, where the realities of big data demand change, may determine their success or failure, their very prospects of survival.

But how did we get here? What *is* big data? When and how did big data cross this upper limit, which represents a point of no return? What solutions exist to address the challenge today?

Big data refers to large and complex data sets that traditional data processing application software cannot process effectively because of its volume, velocity and variety; its three-dimensional nature. This was documented as a part of big data's original definition (from Laney in 2001). Over time, however, those three 'V's have since been expanded by other experts to include three more.

In all, the six *V's* of big data are:

- **Volume** – The quantity of generated and stored data. The size of the data determines the value and potential insight and whether it can be considered big data or not.

- **Velocity** – The speed data is generated and processed to meet the requirements of availability in real-time, as well as demands and challenges that that might impact or impede its access for efficient utility and analytical development.

- **Variety** – The type and nature of the data, both structured and unstructured, which expands the choices and options which facilitate analysts to effectively draw from the range of critical context to produce useful resulting insights.

- **Veracity** – The quality of raw or refined captured data can vary greatly, affecting accurate analysis.

- **Variability** – Inconsistency of the data set can hamper processes to handle and manage it.

- **Value** – What benefit data delivers by virtue of comprehensive control of big data's massive volume.

Acknowledging these defining characteristics associated with big data, experts grapple with the associated challenges of digital exhaust, which include capture, storage, analysis, data curation, search and mining, sharing, transfer, visualization, querying, updating and information privacy. These complexities continue to multiply, creating increasing difficulties and complications, as well as opportunities for those with the right solutions to face the challenges.

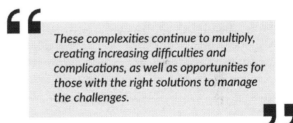

These complexities continue to multiply, creating increasing difficulties and complications, as well as opportunities for those with the right solutions to manage the challenges.

But, of course, it wasn't always like this. In 2002, the threshold of the digital age was crossed. While digital information existed well before that, the tipping point came when digital information surpassed 50% of all information in existence, and from that point on it ballooned and will continue to do so for the foreseeable future.

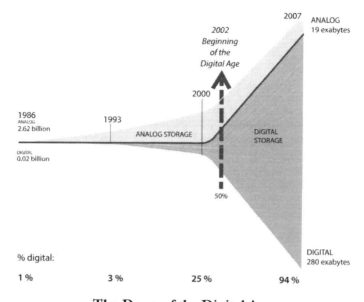

The Dawn of the Digital Age
(Source: http://www.martinhilbert.net/worldinfocapacity-html/)
Figure 8.1

Since that time, with the advent of mobile devices, social media, and all the other factors in our digital world — where even the ringtone on our iPhones is data — data is undergoing an active and continuous growth. While this statement is not a shock to many, it's helpful to understand why that phenomenon is occurring. As an example, people used to have one laptop or desktop computer where they would access online banking; it used to be only one device. Now it's common that three different devices might typically be used to log into that same bank account.

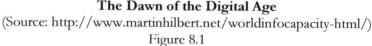

...data is undergoing an active and continuous growth.

Another example is Skype. When you receive a Skype call, it can come in on two, three or four different types of devices, and you choose which device to pick up the call on. That's all data at work. This example highlights how the number of users' electronic devices has multiplied three times, four times. Now it's assumed everyone by default has two or three computing devices, some have more. Add to that the advent of the cloud with its staggering entirety, and we're witnessing continuously growing data volume. It's everywhere. The beauty and the benefit is that today you can access the data from anywhere. The concern is, of course, with all that global access, increased risk inevitably occurs.

The ubiquitous data on-demand model creates copies of your data too. Dropbox, for example, gives you a copy of a file from the cloud, and makes a copy of it in the process. These online applications are all the same. It's the same process with your pictures, your iTunes, Box.com, and others. The way these tools have matured, they also automatically allow you to sync data. At times you don't even know your data is being synced somewhere else. That creates security concerns, having all of those processes at work in the background adds to the data, constantly expanding the world of big data, and with it, more targets for nefarious actors.

Online enterprises like Google and Facebook perform this type of data syncing all the time. If you create a dummy account, just by your usage, and the fact that you're using the same devices, you're still signed on using one account, even if you're using another account. These device IDs, and behavior tracking, can tie all your activities back to you (one identity). All of this is a part of big data. The lists of existing data that are constantly expanding continue to grow exponentially. While Google and Facebook have well-funded, sophisticated and continuously evolving security strategies to protect their data, most other organizations do not. Then there are the categories of emerging data which are fast approaching on the new horizons of technology.

> *While Google and Facebook have well-funded, sophisticated and continuously evolving security strategies to protect their data, most other organizations do not.*

Technology innovations such as self-driving cars, and the mapping and navigation systems that make them possible, are only a small element of what's quickly approaching in the immediate future. This applies in each technology field, everywhere in the world. The result is there's now a burgeoning load of digital exhaust to be dealt with, and that's the bull elephant in the room. What has happened because of this rapid development, very logically, is the data related to security has ballooned. Now it's simply too much data for humans to process, no matter how many skilled resources you add to the task.

While many people talk about artificial intelligence (AI) as having arrived in the security technology landscape, that's not really the case yet with advanced security analytics. Mature machine learning represents the framework of technology that advanced security analytics leverages to process and analyze big data today. While the more data ingested by an analytics solution which is driven by machine learning, the smarter it gets, yet, it still does not think for itself like AI. Not yet at least. The rules of this game remain in a state of flux. In the following section, Nilesh Dherange, Gurucul's CTO (chief technical officer) shares his insights on the state of big data in advanced security analytics today and where it's headed in the future.

BORDERLESS EXPERT INSIGHTS

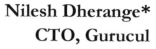

Nilesh Dherange*
CTO, Gurucul

Nilesh Dherange is responsible for development and execution of Gurucul's technology vision. Dherange brings a wealth of experience in inventing, designing, and building software from inception to release. Dherange has been a technologist and leader at three software startups, and at one of the largest software development companies in the world. Prior to co-founding Gurucul, Dherange was an integral member of a company that built a Roles and Compliance product acquired by Sun Microsystems. Dherange was also a co-founder and VP of Engineering for BON Marketing Group where he conceptualized and created BON Ticker — an innovative patented bid management system which used predictive analytics to determine advertising bids for PPC (pay-per-click) marketing campaigns on search engines like Google, Yahoo, MSN, etc. Dherange holds a B.A in Social Science, B.E in Computer Engineering from University of Mumbai and M.S in Computer Science from University of Southern California.

Overview

Dherange first explores big data and the threat plane evolution, observing how SIEM (security information and event management) solutions were originally thought to be a comprehensive answer, which was eventually overshadowed by a paradigm shift in security. This change relates to limitations with early generation cybersecurity solutions and their inability to manage the explosion of data volume, this also includes IAM and PAM (identity and access management and privileged access management), as well as, DLP (data loss prevention) and firewalls.

He then focuses on the drivers for next-generation security analytics, which address identity as the new threat plane. Other factors include siloed environments and partitioned security data, the accelerating volume of big data, the expanding array of devices and applications being accessed from everywhere, hacker innovation, as well as the lack of privileged access oversight and management. With advanced security analytics identified as the most suitable solution set for these challenges, Dherange then discusses the critical data sources for these analytics which incorporate: SIEM, IAM and PAM solutions, DLP, Active Directory (AD), endpoint detection and response (EDR), secure web gateways and secure email gateways (SWG/SEG), cloud access security brokers (CASB), NetFlow network devices, as well as, other IT, business and security data sources. He then shares the objectives of fast data capabilities within big

* The views and opinions expressed by Nilesh Dherange in this book are his own, and do not necessarily reflect those of his current, or any of his previous employers.

data and advanced security analytics, along with the issue of separate and unintegrated data silos and the challenge this presents for holistic and comprehensive advanced security analytics.

Dherange then provides an overview of data lakes, including the characteristics of data lakes and the robust enhancement of capabilities they provide to advanced security analytics driven by machine learning. He also shares a catalog of the major data lake platforms which include: Apache Hadoop, Cloudera, MapR, Hortonworks and The Elastic Stack. Dherange then explores perspectives on data lake adoption, varieties of data lake models, data lakes from the analytics standpoint, as well as data storage challenges for advanced security analytics. He then provides reference architecture for the advanced security analytics framework and the data ingestion process within that framework. After providing an overview of Gartner's top three UEBA (user and entity behavior analytics) vendors, Dherange offers perspectives on the journey to next-generation advanced security analytics and the need for perpetual innovation in security.

Big data and the threat plane evolution

Observing the emerging trends in big data technology, a question comes up among those CISOs striving to gain the right contextual understanding of big data's impactful influence on their own industries and organizations. They ask, "Is big data advanced security analytics traveling on the same journey as SIEM solutions?"

The be-all and end-all that really wasn't. A decade and a half ago, SIEM was supposed to provide definitive value and it evolved into the central data warehouse for security information. But more recent and rapid developments influencing the security industry created a new reality where that's no longer the case. Now CISOs are looking at solutions to security challenges from the perspective of advanced security analytics and big data. Some even believe it could be an alternative to SIEM. Yet, are there lessons we learned during the previous journey that might prove useful here? What are the parallels, what are the similarities? And, what are the differences when it comes to this new technology trying to solve the problem? There certainly is a scale issue. As big data exploded onto the scene, it exacted a seismic transformation of everything in the process.

A de facto paradigm shift in security. Different factors should be taken into account to correlate these two classes and generations of security solutions. In one way, clear parallels are difficult to draw because of traditional security analytics' and SIEM's origins as an older technology framework developed within a different paradigm. It was good at the time when SIEMs were in play as a security mainstay;

> *The security concerns an organization had back then are entirely different from the security concerns they face now.*

they were great for the use cases they were targeted for. But with a gap of almost a decade between the inception of two solution models', the environmental and technological dynamics have changed rapidly and dramatically. The security concerns an organization had back then were entirely different from the security concerns they face now. Hybrid cloud infrastructure is the contemporary anchor model for environments. The computing environments companies had back then were completely different, simpler, more on-premises-centric than what exists today. There was virtually no cloud, no mobility, no BYOD (bring your own device), no IoT (the Internet of Things), nor 24/7 users accessing computing networks and data from everywhere in the globe, as well as a host of other factors. Data volume, variety and velocity have changed the game, and with it, a seismic expansion of the threat plane.

The relativity of data volume. When it came to managing threat data, the volume was comparatively huge for SIEMs at the time. Yet the scale was entirely different. The volume of security data SIEMs must contend with today dwarfs the volume model from earlier years. Back then, a user would likely have one device interfacing with sensitive data on-premises, behind a fortress of physical and logical firewalls and other safeguards. Now, a user might have four or five devices, most of which are mobile and typically exist outside the organization's physical environment. This represents a flood of access and activity security data that SIEMs were never designed to deal with. In the near future, a user might have ten or more devices, use is more ubiquitous, including the IoT and other related emerging technologies, such as your car as a device. What we know is the security community is observing the reality that data volume is big data, yet data volume is relative as is the volume of anything. What is *a lot* of data? What is it compared to? Whatever that volume and variety is, advanced security analytics must account for all of it.

Limitations with early generation cybersecurity solutions

While all the security solutions described in this section remain critical for an organization's current security perimeter, their ratio of value has diminished markedly in the face of the rapid growth of big data, hacker innovation, the new factors of mobile devices, IoT and BYOD, as well as, ubiquitous cloud use from members of an organization, or its customers, from anywhere, at any time. The fundamental limitations of these solutions are examined below. The gaps in security, stemming from these limitations of legacy technologies, represent the areas advanced security analytics solutions must fill for a credible organization to maintain a viable security perimeter.

SIEMs. A decade ago SIEMs were the standard for large organizations, and the perception of that solution set's critical value persists. The earlier confidence in these solutions, however, can no longer be relied upon in the same measure. Some security leaders drove adoptions of this technology as the be-all and end-all answer to their challenges. Now, some years later, they're learning the hard way that new challenges have manifested themselves in cases which SIEMs cannot possibly address effectively. Manual efforts to threat hunt or find security anomalies via query, filter and pivot efforts, have become problematic as the need to improve detection response ratios, to lower false positives and improve incident response, continues to rise. The breadth of data to drive machine learning can be costly due to SIEM indexing fees and expenses. SIEMs can no longer address these security challenges alone. While some SIEMs are integrating UEBA features, they are far from full maturity and are traditionally targeted only on the data silo of the SIEM itself. Few have adopted an identity analytics (IdA) component on their roadmaps, which is a core capability to apply a pre-processing tool and methodology to dramatically reduce the access and activity threat plane.

IAM and PAM. An expanding awareness gap exists between what access rights have been provided by IAM and PAM solutions, and how the rights are being utilized by users. Years of compliance-driven rubber-stamping and access cloning can no longer be an acceptable practice because they perpetuate a serious and unknown access risk plane. IT leaders must now justify to management and CISOs their actions of importing data from a legacy and outdated identity access plane that was based on manually defined roles and legacy rules, thus putting 'garbage' into the system. Using the same roles and same definitions simply makes no sense for addressing the rapidly expanding excess access and access outlier problem. Even the new best-of-breed IAM solutions may not provide all the capabilities required to move to a risk-based approach. In addition, the inability to discover privileged access risk at the entitlement level, and within applications, is a liability for PAM solutions. For this reason, experts note that 50% of this privileged access lies outside of existing lists or PAM vaults. In addition, privileged access entitlements are emerging as a prime target for hackers. This

> *...privileged access entitlements are emerging as a prime target for hackers...*

trend is growing because users with privileged access have 'normal' use patterns for their roles that exhibit a wide range of atypical behavior, as compared with traditional users in an organization. As a result, it is difficult for SOC analysts to identify malicious activity effectively because of the high volume of incidents with false positives, creating a high value access target and tactical opportunity for hackers.

DLP. While some cloud vendors have begun to build in DLP capabilities into their environments, it's only a partial element of the solution. The real challenges emerge as organizations have on-premises DLP deployed on their endpoint devices, plus DLP integrated with a cloud storage environment, yet they aren't connected. As a result, SOC teams must write policies multiple times for the numerous scenarios. No overreaching DLP solution exists to consolidate and address these disparities, leaving concerning gaps in security.

Firewalls. Advanced firewalls cannot address the unique challenges of hybrid environments. They can't provide all the event logs in a viewable manner nor in real-time. These incomplete and outdated security solutions cannot cope holistically with the emerging challenges networks face today. They deal only with known bad patterns or signatures of specific malware. And while their repository of known bad signatures is constantly being updated — which is critical data to maintain and incorporate in a more comprehensive security strategy — they alone can never account for the unknown bads, the vast gray area of risk that is growing as a threat plane in most organizations today.

The drivers for next-generation security analytics

Beyond the six V's of big data (*Volume, Variety, Velocity, Veracity, Variability* and *Value*), forward-looking CISOs are recognizing new de facto additions to the descriptive list for big data, as their criticality increases relevant to the success of the current landscape of hybrid environments. Officially documented in this publication for the first time, they are *Venue* and *Vector*. These two new 'V' attributes of big data highlight the challenge

> *...CISOs are recognizing new de facto additions to the descriptive list for big data... they are* Venue *and* Vector...

of big data in silos within the organization's environment. With the separate and unintegrated silos (the *Venues*), come the gaps — the *scotoma* or blind spots — in a security perimeter. *Vector* relates to the channels by which data flows and is ingested into data lakes and elsewhere, as well as its effectiveness and cost. As long as IT groups and CISOs are at odds regarding access and identity policies, which are disconnected from risk-based activity monitoring, the challenge will persist, no matter how well a data lake is set up. These two new attributes' importance will only become more acute in the future. Meanwhile, hackers seek out these opportunities, the blind spots. Examining the drivers of next-generation security analytics in greater detail in relation to big data bears value to target the elimination of blind spots.

Identity as the new threat plane. Analyzing the access and activity data of a user for their accounts and entitlements is ground zero for predictive risk scoring. Activity alone fails to provide enough context and visibility. The identity gap with access must be closed to effectively evaluate risk. Chief risk officers understand this issue and now demand risk scoring down to the entitlement level, while also understanding the benefit of uncovering hidden privileged

> *Activity alone fails to provide enough context and visibility. The identity gap with access must be closed to effectively evaluate risk.*

access through IdA and thus which activities to analyze for access abuse.

Siloed environments and partitioned security data. SIEM, IAM and CASB (cloud access security broker) solutions represent vertical silos which too often pigeonhole critical security data. These solutions all provide critical data sources of analytic responses, with risk scores utilized on a horizontal plane, yet which are isolated and separate from identity. A customer choice for a solution silo should not restrict the machine learning analytics available, nor should data be held hostage within closed solutions. A holistic risk-based approach, with comprehensive monitoring across all horizontal planes of an environment, is required.

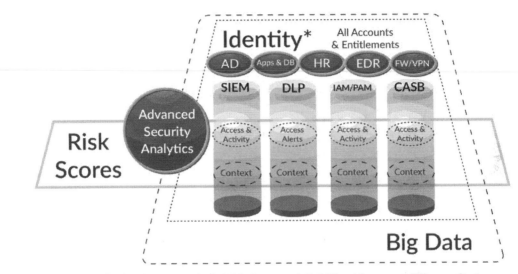

*Additional silos include: SEG/SWG; Network/DHCP and Documents/File repositories

Advanced Security Analytics and the Horizontal Planes
Figure 8.2

Accelerating volume of big data and growing need for fast data. The reality of perpetually expanding data, doubling every year, including security data, makes it decisively clear that manual management of security data, in a timely manner, no matter how many human resources are committed to the challenge, is simply no longer possible. *Fast data* is needed, which represents active security data, immediate status, unlimited scalability and availability for ongoing purposes. Only mature machine learning algorithms, which have been proven for their effectiveness and value, can be reliable in big data security analytics solutions, and delivering actionable intelligence with fast data.

Expanding array of devices and applications accessing from everywhere. The ever-increasing amount and variety of devices and applications gaining access to an organization's hybrid environment has exploded. This trend will only continue to grow, with increasing speed and with no anticipation of diminishing. The newly defined identity threat plane expands with it.

Lack of privileged access oversight and management. The issue of targeting by malicious actors, as well as the growing concern for insider threat via privileged access entitlements, is something organizations are only now beginning to understand and appreciate. Often, what appears first as an insider threat issue may indeed be revealed later as an external attacker who is likely exploiting an insider's identity and user account. Organizations today are finding as many as 70% of the privileged access entitlements in place in their environment were unknown and unmanaged before employing identity analytics.

Hacker innovation. Our adversaries continue to devise creative ways to hack into and laterally traverse our environments. An example of this mindset was revealed in a Forbes.com article where hackers used an internet-connected thermostat from Google-owned Nest to provide an access venue to gain control of other IP-based devices in the home. In a similar fashion, thieves can use access to a thermostat to establish when the occupants are home or not, by the fluctuation of temperature settings. These are just small examples of perpetual hacker innovation going on wherever data is flowing, and CISOs must stay on top of all of it. The era where data can remain partitioned, secluded and fortified has passed. Identifying new access opportunities as they arise, and incorporating them into an organization's security strategy, is key to proper security hygiene.

Advanced security analytics – The critical data sources

As the core component elements of advanced security analytics, UEBA and IdA collectively draw from a broad range of data sources to provide holistic monitoring and behavior analytics for a risk-based approach. This entails visibility into all access and activity for accounts and entitlements across all horizontal planes of an identity within an organization, to properly deliver accurate risk scores. The broad variety of data

> *...UEBA and IdA collectively draw from a broad range of data sources to provide holistic monitoring and behavior analytics for a risk-based approach.*

from various security solutions include, but are not limited to, the data sources below.

SIEMs. A SIEM solution's primary function is to aggregate the data relevant to monitoring and managing privileges of users and services, including directory services, system-configuration changes and log audits. SIEMs gather, analyze and present information from network and security devices, IAM applications, vulnerability management and policy compliance tools, operating systems, database and application logs, as well as external threat data. Capabilities include: data aggregation of various logs from a wide range of sources; correlation of common attributes as it links events into meaningful clusters; alerting automated analysis of correlated events; dashboards for insight into patterns of questionable activity; compliance for governance and auditing processes; retention of long-term data to support correlation over time (which is critical for compliance and forensic analysis requirements).

IAM and PAM. IAM manages an individual's proper and timely access to approved resources within an organization. IAM controls identity information about users on networks which includes authentication of a user's identity and provides insight into a user's access and activity authorizations. Descriptive information about a user, along with how that information can be accessed and modified, and by whom, are typically a part of an IAM solution's capabilities. Managed entities in IAM include users, hardware and network resources and applications. PAM specifically deals with the challenge of privileged access management within an organization. Privileged users hold the keys to the kingdom, and any compromise of their credentials can be catastrophic for an organization.

> *Privileged users hold the keys to the kingdom, and any compromise of their credentials can be catastrophic for an organization.*

DLP. DLP solutions either provide alerts on, or prevent, potential data breaches and exfiltration transmissions by monitoring, detecting and blocking sensitive data, while the data is: *in-use* (endpoint actions*), in-motion* (network traffic), and *at-rest* (data storage). DLP also deals with data leakage incidents of sensitive data, which flags unauthorized parties whose actions stem either from malicious intent or inadvertent errors in use. Sensitive data includes private or company information, intellectual property (IP), financial or patient information, credit card data and other information.

Active Directory (AD). AD is a directory service and set of processes developed by Microsoft for Windows domain networks. Most Windows Server operating systems include this feature. AD was originally designed for centralized domain management and later became an umbrella title for a wide range of directory-based identity related services. Active Directory Domain Services (AD DS) authenticates and authorizes all users and computers in a Windows domain type network. A server running AD DS is known as a domain controller and it also assigns and enforces security policies for all computers and installing or updating software.

Endpoint detection and response (EDR). EDR software employs advanced threat detection technology on endpoints (computers), which focus on detecting suspicious activity on hosts and network PCs. Combined with an engine based on artificial intelligence, EDR software is reactive in detecting and stopping threats (malware, virus, zero-day attacks and advanced persistent threats [APTs]). EDR's AI self-learns and does not have a requirement for an internet connection to update databases.

Secure web gateways and secure email gateways (SWG/SEG). A SWG is traditionally an appliance-based secure Web gateway that uses real-time code analysis technology, URL filtering and antivirus scanning to prevent malware and Web-based threats. A SEG is an email security solution that protects against spam and data leakage. It also provides reporting, analyzes inbound and outbound content, and assists with policy control.

Cloud access security brokers (CASB). A CASB is a technology solution that arbitrates data between in-house IT architectures and cloud vendor environments. Its capabilities traditionally include the ability to encrypt or manage data so it is more secure in a cloud environment. A CASB resides between internal and external systems for securing outbound data. CASB solutions often provide features such as auditing, data loss prevention, encryption and monitoring. CASBs help protect enterprise systems against cyber-threats with features such as malware prevention and data security that render data streams unreadable by outside parties. An example of a CASB technology is the cloud encryption gateway which takes data at the point of egress and encrypts it for security purposes.

> CASBs help protect enterprise systems against cyber-threats with features such as malware prevention and data security that render data streams unreadable by outside parties.

NetFlow network devices. Developed by Cisco, NetFlow is a network protocol for monitoring and collecting network traffic flow data produced by NetFlow-enabled routers and switches. NetFlow-enabled routers export traffic statistics that are gathered by a NetFlow collector (either a hardware appliance or software application) which performs traffic analysis determining direction and volume. Regarded as an industry standard, NetFlow is supported by non-Cisco platforms which include: 3Com/HP, Dell and Netgear (*sFlow*); Alcatel-Lucent (*Cflow*); Ericsson (*Rflow*); Huawei (*NetStream*) and Juniper (*Jflow*).

Additional security data sources. Added to the solutions above, SOCs must also maintain monitoring visibility of commercial applications and databases, HR information, social media, as well as Dynamic Host Configuration Protocol (DHCP), SaaS/IaaS solutions and document files. In addition, different organizations have different security needs, based on size, organizational complexity and business model. Other sources of data may be required as well.

The objectives of *fast data* for security analytics. The volume, velocity and the variety of the data are staggering for some organizations. One of Gurucul's customers has reported 25,000 events per second. Taking into consideration the wide range of voluminous data described above, the objectives of achieving *fast data* capabilities in security analytics are given clearer context. *Fast data* is the rapid application of mining and analyzing structured and unstructured big data into smaller data sets, in near-real or real-time, to deliver timely actionable intelligence. With this in mind, the criticality of

Venue and *Vector* comes into sharper focus. For *Venue*, when all the critical data resides and is maintained in an agnostic data lake, that's clearly beneficial. Yet when it is isolated and cordoned off into silos, that's where security problems can be hidden.

The challenge of data silos for security analytics. Too often, big data is kept in separate silos, controlled by different groups within an organization, usually IT and security. Relating to data flow, or lack of it, *Vector* underscores the movement and direction of big data into a centralized data lake, facilitating its analytic utility applications from that venue versus going into separate silos, resulting in big data fragmentation, and hence severely diminishing the capability for comprehensive visibility and monitoring of identity and access activity. If the data is not aligned with a proper and all-inclusive ingestion process, from all silos, it cannot provide the critical contextual value its potential represents. As well, some solutions may be able to store data at high rates, but fall over when they are expected to validate, enrich, or act on data as it is ingested. The challenge security leaders now see with greater clarity is that the siloed nature of data is a problem that if not addressed by a mature security analytics solution, it will leave unknown unknowns unaddressed across a serious and expanding access and activity threat plane. A single vast, comprehensive

> " If the data is not aligned with a proper and all-inclusive ingestion process, from all silos, it cannot provide the critical context value its potential represents. "

and agnostic continuously updated repository for all data, processed at scale during ingestion, is needed to alleviate the challenge of silos, to provide a single source for data mining and analytics. This is but one reason for the rise in popularity of data lakes.

Big data technologies – The data lakes

Commonly called data lakes (a term coined by James Dixon, CTO Pentaho), these are not to be confused with data warehouses, which by nature have their data organized for a particular purpose, traditionally modeled for reporting. This means any data found in a data lake has been imported by design; it fills a purpose which is to be used for a particular analytic function. Data is generally highly transformed and structured when stored in a data warehouse. A more recent technology development, on the other hand, a data lake is more like a large body of water in its natural state, where all data streams flowing into it are unfiltered, unprocessed from source systems. This raw and untransformed, unstructured, data is critical. The more the better. From there, users sample, examine or process the 'muddy' data into pristine data for a particular goal or purpose — analytics. The more data in a data lake, the more potential for analytics to extract knowledge deeply via machine learning. The more data you feed to the analytics, the smarter it gets. This vast realm of data, therefore, is predominantly the domain of data scientists who have the skills and tools to access, explore, transform and process the raw data to reveal meaningful and predictive patterns and to extract insights as needed.

Launching the petabyte sorting and storage race. Google has been a leader in cloud research and the inspiration for data lakes began there. One paper published in 2004, building on an earlier one, represents the starting point of this innovation: *MapReduce: Simplified Data Processing on Large Clusters.* The paper inspired Doug Cutting, working at Yahoo! at the time, to develop an open-source implementation of the MapReduce framework, which he named after his son's toy elephant: Hadoop. MapReduce is a programming model for running multiple processing frameworks and generating large data sets. Programs written in this practical format are automatically adapted for running on parallel processing systems and executed on a large cluster of commodity machines. This is the foundation of today's data lakes.

Characteristics of data lakes. The first aspect in contrast with data warehouses, where data warehouses are exclusive in their data storage, is that data lakes are all-inclusive of their data, which for all intents and purposes is retained permanently. This means some data that enters the data lake may ultimately never be used. The hardware technology of big data lakes utilizes cheap and readily available storage, making scaling a data lake to terabytes or petabytes far more economical than traditional data warehouses, or even security solutions like SIEMs. This is made possible by virtue of a data lake's capability of allocating various virtual storage nodes — which are not tied to a single server or a single location — for expanding storage as needed. This represents a tightly controlled cost, since customers are only charged only for the storage space they need, when they need it. Data lakes are data agnostic, storing all non-traditional and traditional data, regardless of source and structure (structured or unstructured), in its raw form, until required for use. Unlike data warehouses, which are rigidly designed, data lakes support deep analysis of factors that emerge over time, and where supporting data for analysis is natively available within the larger set of data. This capability also represents far more flexibility and adaptability in analytics for data science users.

A robust enhancement of analytics with data lakes. Because of all the factors listed above, possibly the largest advantage of data lakes is that they facilitate faster and richer insights. For canned reporting capabilities, drawing from established criteria of targeted data, data warehouses are a suitable choice. For three-dimensional and evolving deep analytic capabilities, data lakes are becoming a much more critical component of enterprises today seeking a decisive advantage in

> *For three-dimensional... analytic capabilities, data lakes are becoming a... critical component of enterprises today seeking a decisive advantage in their operations and strategies.*

their operations and strategies. Some organizations implement data lakes alongside their traditional data warehouses for a hybrid approach to optimal reporting and analytics. In many cases today, however, organizations are implementing their own next-generation analytics solutions on top of data lakes.

Apache Hadoop. The original data lake, and typically referred to simply as Hadoop, it is considered the main and foundational player in the data lake world of offerings, and the fountainhead of many other major data lake solution platforms which originated from the Hadoop domain. While it provides broad agnostic data lake repository capabilities (*Hadoop Distributed File System* [HDFS]), which is the core of its framework, Hadoop has developed other platforms as well. It can also support data warehouse requirements with *Hadoop MapReduce* which implements the MapReduce programming model for large scale data processing. Also under the Hadoop umbrella are *Hadoop Common* — with libraries and utilities — and *Hadoop YARN*, a platform that manages computing resources for scheduling users' applications. Various software *Apache* branded packages are offered within these platforms. Hadoop's popularity is empowered by virtue of the fact it is a collection of open source projects which means that development and advancement occurs at a rapid pace, compared to traditional software developed by a single enterprise. Hadoop's reliance on open source software and commodity hardware make it compelling from both a cost and features perspectives for organizations evaluating either a new data platform, or planning to replace or upgrade a legacy system. Considered a standard for data lakes by many, Hadoop has the widest adoption within the industry at this point; half of the Fortune 50 use Hadoop.

MapR. An Apache Hadoop distributor, MapR offers their version of HDFS, a database management system, a set of data management tools, and related software. Combining analytics in real-time with operational applications, its technology runs on both commodity hardware and public cloud computing services. The company contributes to Apache Hadoop projects, and in 2011 supported an EMC-specific distribution of Apache Hadoop (a leading data storage solution manufacturer, EMC is now part of Dell, Inc.). High profile adoptions have increased MapR's prominence in the market. Amazon chose MapR to deliver an upgraded version of their *Elastic Map Reduce* (EMR) service. Google selected MapR as a technology partner where MapR broke the minute sort speed record on Google's compute platform. MapR has a number of supporting solutions including their MapR-DB document database management system which is marketed as *NoSQL*.

Cloudera. Founded by three engineers from Google, Yahoo and Facebook, who had deep Hadoop and MapR experience, the company provides open-source Apache Hadoop distribution *CDH* (Cloudera's Distribution including Apache Hadoop). *CDH* incorporates the core components of Hadoop (mainly MapReduce and HDFS) that deliver scalable distributed data processing of large data sets, along with additional enterprise-focused modules offering security, high availability, and

> " 50% of Cloudera's engineering work is contributed to Apache-licensed open source projects. "

integration with hardware and other software. Cloudera offers a number of additional software, services and support for more targeted customer requirements including: *Cloudera Manager, Cloudera Navigator, Gazzang, Cloudera Navigator Optimizer,* and *Impala.* 50% of Cloudera's engineering work is contributed to Apache-licensed open source projects. While Hadoop is an open-source project for storing large amounts of data, the free version of Hadoop is not easy to use. A number of companies have created more user friendly versions of Hadoop, and Cloudera is considered the leader in this niche.

Hortonworks. Yahoo!'s venture capital investment in Hadoop production applications helped found this enterprise. The *Hortonworks Data Platform* (HDP) platform incorporates Apache Hadoop as a main data lake player and is used for storing, processing, and analyzing large volumes of data. The platform is designed to deal with data from a wide range of sources and formats. The platform includes HDFS, MapReduce, and additional components: *Pig, Hive, HBase,* and *ZooKeeper.* Hortonworks collaborated with Microsoft Azure and Windows Server for Hadoop distribution in 2011. In 2015, Hadoop acquired Onyara, whose engineers were engaged with an NSA software project that later evolved into Apache NiFi, a top-level domain open source project. Hortonworks has partnered with software-related companies, including for business service management and automation (BMC Software), data integration (Attunity and Cleo), and for cloud, database and virtualization infrastructure (SAP, VMware and Stratoscale). Inspired by Hadoop, the source of the company's name comes from another elephant, Dr. Seuss's *Horton.*

The Elastic Stack (previously known as: The ELK Stack and Elastic ELK). Originating from an entirely different technology framework than Hadoop, the Elastic Stack is comprised of **Elasticsearch, Logstash,** and **Kibana,** which are platforms under the Elastic umbrella that were developed to integrate and work with each other efficiently. Each component is a separate solution powered by the open-source vendor Elastic. *Elasticsearch* delivers search and distributed computing capabilities, while *Logstash* normalizes a wide range of time series data, and *Kibana* is a visualization tool, all of which collectively deliver a holistic analytics tool. *Elasticsearch's* JSON-based (JavaScript Object Notation) query language is considered easier to use than more complex systems like Hadoop's MapReduce. Its JSON-based Domain Specific query Language (DSL) is simple and powerful, making it the de facto standard for search integration in any web application. Elastic originally appeared on the market as an enterprise search platform and has evolved into a more comprehensive solution.

> *Originating from an entirely different technology framework than Hadoop... (and) because of its ease of use and simplicity, the Elastic Stack is growing in popularity.*

Because of its ease of use and simplicity, the Elastic Stack is growing in popularity.

Microsoft Azure's HDInsight. Built to the open HDFS standard, *HDInsight* is a fully managed Cloud Hadoop offering that provides optimized open source analytic clusters for Spark, Hive, MapReduce, HBase, Storm, Kafka, and R-Server. Designed for redundancy and high availability, providing head node replication, data geo-replication, and built-in standby *NameNode*, HDInsight offers resilience to critical failures not delivered in standard Hadoop solutions. It supplies cluster monitoring and enterprise support backed by Microsoft and Hortonworks.

Amazon's Data Lake Solution. Nested within the broad array of AWS Cloud offerings, and more specifically in *Amazon Simple Storage Service* (S3), the company announced their data lake solution in late 2016. The AWS Cloud solution suite includes managed services that help ingest, store, find, process, and analyze both structured and unstructured data and it is integrated with Hadoop with MapReduce modeling for large-scale data processing. While data is stored in S3, the metadata is stored in both *Amazon DynamoDB* and *Amazon Elasticsearch Service* (Amazon ES). Storing data in S3 allows a durable secure data storage in any format. Data in S3 integrates with other services, such as *Amazon Redshift* for data warehousing, *Amazon QuickSight* for data visualization or, *Amazon Machine Learning* to build machine learning models. In addition, the Amazon Data Lake solution integrates with third-party tools to facilitate customers provisioning the right tool for their needs.

New data lake vendors. Competition is relentless in this space, and newcomers are always jostling at the starting gates, striving to provide competitive value at attractive rates. At printing, a few of the newcomers bloggers are watching include: HVR, Podium Data, Snowflake and Zalonie.

Perspectives on data lake adoption

While all data lakes are theoretically the same in their function, how organizations use them differs widely. How data lakes are planned, organized and set up is an important consideration for any security leader. One way to look at the variety and model variance is from the inventory management perspective. Target has a physical warehouse; Walmart has a physical warehouse; Amazon has a physical warehouse. Every physical warehouse would have a different way to store their products and manage them, yet it's essentially the same set of products. Walmart or Target stock their merchandise in their physical stores, with aisles, storerooms, distribution hubs, etc. Amazon, meanwhile, likely has your favorite soap stacked right beside a popular book. Their distribution has an on-demand model, not one consisting of stocking shelves based on projected sales. The

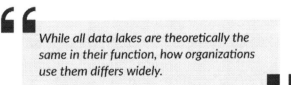

While all data lakes are theoretically the same in their function, how organizations use them differs widely.

products are still the same. It's just how the physical warehouse and distribution models are organized that makes them vastly different.

Varieties of data lake models. The Target/Walmart versus the Amazon conceptual framework is similar to the flexible planning perspectives applied to big data lakes as well. Even if one organization is using a data lake solution from Hortonworks and another is on MapR, which both deliver the same fundamental utility, it does not mean these organizations would organize the data in the same format as the other. In the simplest terms, it is the same as if you have a 10 x 10 storage space, but the way one might organize 100 items that need to be stored there will be different for one individual organization versus the other. This is all based on the needs in the present, those perceived for the future, and the perspective of the data scientist serving as the data lake architect. That's basically the flexible perspective needed for how one organizes data in a data lake. The data lake architect would work in partnership with the CIO and CISO. The storage space would, of course, be vastly more complex than a 10 x 10 storage space and storing only 100 items.

Data lakes from the analytics standpoint. With a data lake in place, the objective is to optimize it and ensure you know you'll get maximum value out of it. There might be certain use cases you're running, where you're targeting different variables, such as date, identity or activity, across all silos and environments. Amazon has been dealing with these challenges for years, and is constantly evolving their approach to their analytics, how they arrange data, and how these variables apply to big data through machine learning. The same is true for advanced security analytics. It's always evolving with machine learning. The more data it ingests, and the more data the model processes, the smarter it becomes. At the preliminary phase, the most challenging aspect is harnessing the data correctly.

Data storage challenges for advanced security analytics. While the prospect of a data lake represents a decisive advantage for organizations, how they are architected is a critical consideration. Without the right planning ahead of time, the full benefit of a data lake might not be realized. On some occasions, organizations seek experienced third parties, such as an advanced security analytics partner, to assist them with a proven data schema to help them build out their own data lake, to align properly with precise goals and objectives for an optimal adoption. Critical considerations include:

> *While Hadoop data lakes are schema-less, organizations must still organize the structure of data stored in them.*

- *Schema-less design* – While Hadoop data lakes are schema-less, organizations must still organize the structure of data stored in them. Directory structures for data loaded into HDFS, data processing output and analysis, as well the schemas of objects stored in systems such as *Hive* (for additional data management functionality) and *HBase* (additional data access functionality), must be accounted for.

- ***Data storage formats*** – Hadoop data lakes support a number of file and compression formats, each with specific strengths suited to different formats. Along with HDFS for storing data, a number of systems are integrated on top of HDFS, such as *Hive* and *HBase*. Systems such as these must be taken into account as well.

- ***Multitenancy*** – Supporting multitenant clusters often involves hosting multiple users, groups, and application types within these clusters. Planning how data will be stored and managed in these multitenant clusters must take these factors into account.

- ***Metadata management*** – Descriptive, structural and administrative metadata related to the data stored in the data lake can be as critical as the data itself, to facilitate optimal management of this essential resource. Understanding these concepts and making the right decisions related to metadata management are crucial for security analytics success.

Reference architecture in the security analytics framework. Different organizations have different approaches to their reference architecture as it relates to analytics. IBM provides a good model to refer to exemplify the scope of this challenge and requirement. While IBM's is designed for a business model, the applications for security have a direct correlation of relevance.

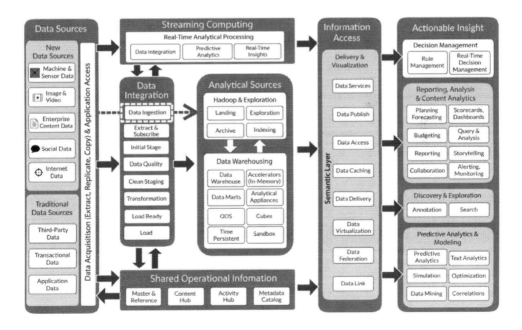

**Data Ingestion and the IBM Big Data and Analytics
Reference Architecture**
(Source: *IBM Big Data & Analytics Reference Architecture* V1, eBook, *2014*)
Figure 8.3

Data ingestion within the framework. Understanding and properly managing the complexity of the ingestion of new and traditional data sources for advanced security analytics requirements is essential for success of a data lake adoption. IBM's model is fundamentally a machine learning framework, containing the data source layers and where the data, from a range of sources and technologies, is coming from: this is the big data. With the ingestion layer (see dotted line and arrow in illustration above), these various technologies of data must be

> *With the ingestion layer... these various technologies of data must be transferred in their unadulterated form to be staged and properly loaded into the data lake.*

transferred in their unadulterated form to be staged and properly loaded into the data lake. Within this infrastructure, there may be different platforms or mechanisms which include tens of NoSQL databases, all which must all be harnessed correctly, to facilitate holistic monitoring for risk-based access and activity security analytics.

Evolution of the data lake is inevitable. As more data is added to the data lake, its size and richness continues to grow. Drawing value from a data lake can be accomplished through analytics and the tableaus of reporting, visualizations and user interfaces. Each point in this layer may have different flavors of components that must be set up. Also, when it comes to big data, every company or organization will have its own way to create data, manage data, as well as how they choose to deploy their entire data infrastructure. It's expected some sort of data lake standardization will occur in the near future, as was the case with data warehousing tools. There are multiple ways in how an organization can create and shape the new data lake 'warehouse'.

Gartner's top three UEBA vendors

Drawing context from big data lakes, advanced security analytics utilizes both UEBA and IdA to deliver value by virtue of their range of use cases. Gartner has been studying the UEBA field for a number of years. In 2015, their *Market Guide for User and Entity Behavior Analytics* observed 20 vendors worthy of inclusion. In 2016 their UEBA market guide narrowed the field to 15, where over a half supported only one or two use cases. The

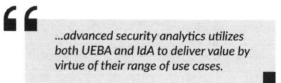

> *...advanced security analytics utilizes both UEBA and IdA to deliver value by virtue of their range of use cases.*

2017 Gartner *A Comparison of UEBA Technologies and Solutions* (Technical Professional Advice) report observed the horse race had narrowed down to only six vendors that are capable of at least six use cases. This is a key indicator of versatility and the widest utility for customer requirements. Quite a reduction and sorting out in a short period of time. For purposes of reference, the top three in this category represent the best vendor capability criteria of qualified solutions that occupy this space. This metric also supplies insight into the vendor's solution delivery models. (**Note:** For full disclosure, Gurucul is one of the top three vendors described below.)

Vendor A. This vendor's UEBA model, with their six use cases, is not based on true machine learning, but instead on query rules (which often demonstrate results in short-term POC trials). This factor, of course, limits the depth and breadth of their solution's ability to find the unknown unknowns and the hidden and expanding access and activity threat plane. Vendor A only recently migrated to an open-source big data platform, and this vendor's profile in Gartner's report observes significant consulting services and customizations are "highly advised (if not truly mandatory) for a successful deployment." Adoptions where two consultants were needed for over a year for the customer to facilitate the solutions operational functionality have been reported within the industry. This security product does not have an IdA component, meaning any claim to advanced security analytics is strained. Per the Gartner report, the vendor is changing its core UEBA focus, custom coding for a SIEM solution framework as part of its move to compete in the highly competitive SIEM market.

Vendor B. This vendor profile notes a low price for an easy-to-use tool; it also comes with limitations for data collection and custom use cases. Per the Gartner report: "...some customers with heavy application and non-IT data analysis use cases typically chose other tools, quoting lack of flexibility with collection and custom model development." Vendor B also recently moved to a big data platform, yet it still currently relies upon rules for the SIEM solution space, and it is not a true machine learning solution, contrary to this vendor's claims. The company does not have an identity analytics component, and as a result is unable to monitor an organization's access entitlements in a holistic risk-based approach.

Vendor C. The one vendor platform in this Gartner group bases its analytics framework on true machine learning to gain invaluable context from big data. Vendor C's analytics platform solution focuses on machine learning models from the identity vantage point, as they have run on big data infrastructure since the inception of data lakes. As a result, they have an advanced metadata model for attributes, sub-attributes and within a hierarchy. This company is agnostic to customers' data. Replacing a SIEM solution is not their objective, but instead to optimize its (as well as IAM and PAM) capabilities, and to make them smarter. Vendor C offers over thirty use cases. While some professional services are required for deployment, this is to enable API integrations, as the broad range of ready-to-use use cases are well vetted for common utilities. Its use cases and capabilities, beyond Gartner's diminutive six use cases, have helped to establish the vendor's technical leadership in the market for its broad capabilities that also include offering custom use case development, along with automated risk responses and closed-loop deployments, which the competition is currently unable to provide.

Perspectives on the journey to next-generation security analytics

CISOs must target realistic security gains in their strategy execution, not ideals. Perfection in security is the enemy of good enough. Good enough brings regular and reliable results, while seeking perfection is a misplaced ideal in the security realm. Far too many false positives exist, and the quest for perfection, within the relentless light-speed pace of digital business, is counterproductive.

> *Perfection in security is the enemy of good enough. Good enough brings regular and reliable results, while seeking perfection is a misplaced ideal in the security realm.*

The need for perpetual innovation in security. CISOs must recognize their opponents have a wide array of strategies, tactics and methods to break into their environments. In response, security's overall mandate for IT protection has evolved. There will always be a push-pull dynamic, which is the law of cyber-nature. The question is how much CISOs push versus how much they can pull. The key is to recognize their target is always moving, and their innovations must also keep moving. The instant any sense of perfection might be achieved in security, it is obsolete a moment later.

The prospects of 'predictive' and 'prescriptive' in maturing security analytics. We're all familiar with the Google Maps application that gives real-time traffic conditions, suggesting optimal routes to one's destination and offering a prediction of drive time based on continuous updates to their data base. That type of predictive capability is certainly a goal of advanced security analytics, and a realistic one. Meanwhile, next-generation UEBA vendors are already offering prescriptive capabilities. Data growth is still exploding. We're only at the tip of a continually morphing and growing iceberg. Even today we're seeing the ever-changing exponential aspect of data. Where in the past, it was based on a per human focus, now when you add IoT, a plethora of applications, ubiquitous 24/7 global access, and other factors into the equation, it is no longer correlated on these per human calculations. There is a multiplication factor where one percent represented one IP address, or one machine ID, and now one percent might be associated with 1000 machine IDs. This only underscores the fact that CISOs must master the eight V's of big data, and recognize we're just at the initial phase in terms of big data. There will be so much more in the near future, expanding by leaps and bounds, where industry experts may need to find a new term for it, something like *Megascale Data*.

CONCLUSIONS & TAKEAWAYS:
The continuous evolution of big bata

With an expansion of the six "V's" of big data (*Volume, Velocity, Variety, Veracity, Variability, Value*) to include two more (*Venue* and *Vector*), Dherange notes the ever-evolving nature of big data on all fronts, along with the need for *fast data* capabilities and advanced security analytics to keep pace with that evolution. Keeping pace also involves choosing the right data lake and aligning with the needs of the organization, while remaining up to date with the state-of-the-art developments in data lake technology. As the established technology players continue to consolidate and expand their offerings through innovation, new players are constantly striving to stay nimble and inventive, to jump ahead with a next generation of technology development that might tilt the game in their favor within the marketplace.

Meanwhile, the community of threat actors is constantly on the lookout for blind spots, and they are poised to leverage any tactical or strategic innovation to give them a ruthless competitive edge. With all of this perpetual innovation, unending and exploding data volume, constantly expanding users and vectors of access, perfection in security can never be possible. But maintaining a constant vigilance with the right advanced security analytics solution, drawing critical context via machine learning, to maintain a quality of good enough, and always being ready to evolve to the next tier of requirement in dynamic security hygiene, is the key to organizational survival.

The next *Borderless Breach Flashcard* depicts what may ultimately be judged to be the most damaging breach in history. Its impact on cybersecurity will certainly be felt for years to come. The following chapter explores the next generation of innovative security controls being developed to face the challenges of continuous technology advancements and the ceaseless evolution of threat actor tactics and strategies.

BORDERLESS BREACH FLASHCARD	
The Tipping Point in Cybersecurity	
CATEGORY	Opportunistic hacker exploitation of inadequate security policies.
WHO	**The target:** Equifax, a consumer credit reporting agency.
WHAT	An unpatched Apache Struts vulnerability was exploited in a breach that compromised the personal data of over 145 million U.S. citizens.
WHEN	2016 to 2017.
WHERE	USA.
WHY	Inadequate security planning and failure to employ established best practices by IT leaders and cloud security architects.
HOW	A critical unpatched Apache Struts vulnerability was exploited, breaching Equifax's website. This web application vulnerability represents only larger fundamental security concerns for Equifax. It was revealed that prior to this mega breach, they had other reported security weaknesses which were not addressed completely or in a timely manner.
HOW BAD?	While it isn't the biggest data breach in history, it may be the most damaging. Experts now openly question the viability of social security numbers as having continuing value, while others demand a complete revamping of organizational security strategies. Senator Mark Warner, Vice Chairman of the U.S. Senate Select Committee on Intelligence, called on Congress to reframe data protection policies, to discourage businesses from creating large, centralized pools of highly sensitive data which represents a mother lode of data to fuel a plague of nefarious activity. A major spike in identity theft and fraud is predicted which could extend for years. Equifax's stock has dropped significantly, to a one year low. As well, the company's CEO, CIO and CSO have suddenly 'retired'. A huge cascading impact on customers, partners, the company's reputation, trustworthiness and business has been observed.
HOW COULD IT BE AVOIDED?	While many pundits assess the "what" of this story, and technical minds seek to know the "how" of it, possibly the crucial perspective to explore is the "why" of it. That achieved, responsible security leaders, and their bosses, are in a better position to understand "what's next" and hopefully take measures to address the challenge as effectively as possible. The "why" of it is if executives do not commit budget and full support to invest in advanced technology solutions, then the "what's next" is more breaches, with increasing systemic damage to businesses and a compromising of the fabric holding modern commerce together.

9

Unconventional Controls and Model-Driven Security

The Evolution of Unconventional Controls and Model-Driven Security

Seasoned CISOs seeking to enable their business enterprises to move at the speed of the customer across channels, while improving risk management practices, find unconventional controls are essential for changing the rules for threat adversaries. They've discovered model-driven security solutions that drive frontline security controls in real time represent unconventional controls which improve the consumer experience, while making it more difficult for threat adversaries. This combination of benefits to the consumer and the enterprise is changing cybersecurity control capability maturity. CISOs who study threat actor tactics and adjust controls accordingly have ventured beyond the traditional conventional controls defined in risk

> *Seasoned CISOs seeking to enable their business enterprises to move at the speed of the customer across channels... find unconventional controls are essential for changing the rules for threat adversaries.*

frameworks, to designing new control capabilities using emerging technology solutions. That's why unconventional controls, and specifically, model-driven security (MDS) controls, have a rightful place in security planning for the foreseeable future. Understanding how these types of security controls evolved is helpful, since the innovative process that created them is embedded in the conceptual framework of forward-looking security professionals today.

As a primary responsibility, a majority of these experienced security leaders learned the foundational practice of demonstrating due diligence to regulators, auditors, security assessors and stakeholders. They used risk frameworks with conventional security controls by focusing their energy on the alignment of business and IT practices, with the specific control standards required in the risk framework of choice (i.e., ISO 27001 and NIST 800-53). A handful of them began intensive research into threat actor tactics using multiple sources of security intelligence and sharing information through sector-based information sharing and analysis centers (ISACs). The more they made adjustments to their controls the more they improved resiliency by making it more difficult for the threat actors. Their study of the evolution of threat actor tactics encouraged them to experiment with unconventional controls that weren't part of an established risk framework from authoritative sources. Several of them chose to work with early-stage security solution companies who were more nimble and responsive to a unique set of innovative requirements. As the speed of threat actors changing tactics increased, the larger the percentage of unconventional controls grew in the enterprise and the results included higher levels of resiliency.

Adding to the landscape of their responsibilities and priorities of focus, these pioneering CISOs often needed to pull disparate groups together, creating a cohesive cybersecurity program, while striving at the same time to develop and align workable security strategies to face emerging challenges. Not a simple task. More often than not, vendor procurement processes and evaluation criteria required significant adjustment. Market share and financial resiliency became less of factor versus the demonstrated ability to attract technical talent and pivot on a new design idea.

Compliance with federal and state regulations is traditionally included within the CISO's portfolio of responsibilities. For financial organizations, this represents a rigorous requirement. Failure to be in compliance can mean the cessation of business activity, revenue streams becoming paralyzed. In early days of cybersecurity, the stakes were high, and the rules of the game constantly changing every month. Jim Routh, a now seasoned CSO with Aetna, described what his inaugural week involved as the first CISO at a major financial services company. He discovered on the first day of his tenure that he was required to immediately produce an enterprise-wide strategy of cybersecurity for review by a federal regulator from the Office of the Comptroller of the Currency (OCC), one of the most rigorous financial regulators enforcing cybersecurity controls.

Routh was fortunate in that he had been referred to a deeply experienced former CISO, who, when getting the call, arrived onsite at Jim's office with two additional highly qualified CISOs from competing financial services firms. They all helped Jim Routh prepare for the impending OCC review. They developed the presentation material and then had Routh present it back to them so they could coach him on what to avoid saying to the OCC. The following day, the OCC presentation went smoothly, thanks to the coaching and rigorous preparation led by the CISOs who helped Routh.

Here, in his first job in security as a CISO, Routh learned the criticality of building professional relationships and information sharing, as well as the importance of conventional control models.

> *...in his first job in security as a CISO, Routh learned the criticality of building professional relationships and information sharing, as well as the importance of conventional control models.*

Routh also learned that helping an industry competitor lifts the resiliency of the industry as a whole, and is in the best interests of consumers and the financial services industry. The CISOs who helped Jim followed a tried-and-true formula of choosing an industry risk framework, aligning practices with the control standards in the framework and then having a third party attest to the effectiveness of the controls. This formula represents the foundation of cybersecurity audit and governance practices built on conventional controls, which are well known, established and effective. All audit and regulatory practices use the same foundation for determining the effectiveness of cybersecurity programs and enterprise resiliency. All third-party governance processes follow the same conventional controls. All key stakeholders, senior management, board members, regulators, internal and external auditors and CIOs bought into this model of conventional cybersecurity controls. Similar to his peer security practitioners, Routh learned how to utilize conventional controls in his introduction to security fundamentals.

In this scenario, the only stakeholder who refused to buy into this framework of conventional controls was the threat actor, who preferred to discover methods to circumvent these controls and then share that information with other criminals. In response, as criminals adjusted their tactics, risk-driven security programs (those programs that studied threat actor tactics and made adjustments) generated experimentation of control capabilities that ultimately gave birth to unconventional controls based on innovation and emerging technologies.

Meanwhile, the solid foundational precepts in conventional control frameworks represented the cornerstones for modern enterprise security programs and remain core to any CISO's perspectives today. Yet keep in mind Routh's initiation into the CISO role took place fifteen years ago. And as Devin Bhatt observed in Chapter 4, *"...compliance does not automatically equal security. Compliance only represents a snapshot in time, and a partial one at that."* Hacker

> *Risk-driven security programs, not compliance-based security programs, evolve controls based on changes in threats or threat actor tactics.*

innovation and tactics leveraging technology advances are perpetual. In response, this is where the demand for a continuous evolution of a CISO's thinking, based on emerging conditions and challenges, comes into play. A case in point: encrypting all data at rest is a conventional security control that does little to protect data if the encryption keys are compromised. Risk-driven security programs, not compliance-based security programs, evolve controls based on changes in threats or threat actor tactics. This emerging trend has opened the door for unconventional controls.

An example of a recent real-world experience exemplifies how all enterprises can be impacted within the span of a few weeks. A nation state obtained sophisticated malware created by the NSA, the most advanced cybersecurity expertise in the world (for more details on this story see the *Borderless Breach Flashcard* on this story: *For Sale: Keys to the Kingdom*, preceding Chapter 6. This hostile state reconfigured the stolen malware and weaponized it for political purposes, impacting enterprises globally. Enterprises large and small across a range of industries, meanwhile, grappled to repel such attacks to avoid massive business disorder. Then, two weeks later, another nation state executed a similar attack for different political purposes, causing significant business disruption in healthcare, logistics and other industries.

Very few enterprises today possess the level of sophistication and resources to withstand this type of cyber-attack every few weeks. Due to threats of this magnitude, complexity and potential for seismic damage to an organization, CISOs entering the realm of cybersecurity today have a broad host of new factors to consider which impact their strategic thinking as they face a new breed of emerging threats. This is where solutions like model-driven controls, emerging from risk-driven security programs, come into play.

> **Very few enterprises today possess the level of sophistication and resources to withstand this type of cyber-attack every few weeks.**

As a frame of reference on the factors influencing the need for innovative thinking in the CISO world, it's helpful to look at the experience of Wafaa Mamilli, a CISO who arrived very recently to the security field as a CISO for a multinational pharmaceutical company. With research and development facilities located in six countries, clinical research conducted in over 55 countries, manufacturing plants in 13 countries and products marketed in 120 countries, Mamilli faced the same mandate as Routh: to build a world-class information security program. But, as we saw above, the world of cybersecurity had changed. New lessons needed to be learned and new best practices had to be adopted. Undergoing a similar process of reaching out to experts in the field — one of whom was Routh — for security framework recommendations, and incorporating those insights with the tribal knowledge of information security experts within her company, Mamilli developed a plan containing similar foundational steps as Routh.

These foundational steps consisted of:

- Choose a risk framework and underlying set of control objectives and standards (in this case NIST)
- Assess current maturity level and identify gaps aligned with risk tolerance
- Build a roadmap to address the gaps exceeding risk tolerance
- Execute and then iterate the assessment

Add to that the collective experience of over a decade of facing security challenges and responding to threat evolution, the team of CISO peer advisors emphasized the need to share information with peers through an ISAC (a conventional approach) along with the need to invest in unconventional controls, and specifically, model-driven security. Today, these two points are the foundation of innovative thinking for CISOs and security leaders responsible for creating resilient environments for their enterprises. The first point relates to seeking information on what the threat actors are doing every day, comparing notes on which tactics and strategies are most effective to counter the compromise of IT and security in an enterprise. When security professionals do this, in settings such as FS-ISAC (Financial Services Information Sharing and Analysis Center) and NH-ISAC (National Health Information Sharing and Analysis Center), the potential for balancing the scales with the hacker community has a greater prospect of success.

Exploring the last point in greater detail, while a standard control framework is a necessary requirement, it is not sufficient to avoid major security breaches. The threat landscape is evolving too quickly. Threat actors respond to changes in controls, invest in innovative ways to bypass controls, and share information in criminal forums. They seek any blind spot to capitalize on. Building business

> *...while a standard control framework is a necessary requirement, it is not sufficient to avoid major security breaches. The threat landscape is evolving too quickly.*

resiliency requires innovative adaptability, speed and agility in cybersecurity controls. Jim Routh refers to these innovations as 'unconventional controls' which are designed and tailored to meet a range of emerging threats powered by malicious tactical and technology innovation. This term aligns with the perspective of risk-based priorities, as opposed to compliancy requirements. This is the foundation and framework from which model-based security evolved.

Model-driven security emerged when unconventional controls evolved to leverage automation and machine learning to amplify their effectiveness, and are now a critical part of our future in security. If an organization adopts the strategy of implementing unconventional controls as supplements to conventional controls, the framework of model-driven security has already arrived. This is a core requirement for enterprises striving to move at the speed of the online consumer and those that wish to have some reasonable level of resilience against the most sophisticated cyber weaponry ever created. In the following expert section, Jim Routh, CSO of Aetna, will examine the world of unconventional controls and model-based security in greater depth.

BORDERLESS EXPERT INSIGHTS

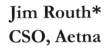

Jim Routh*
CSO, Aetna

Jim Routh is the Chief Security Officer, leading Global Security for Aetna and the Chairman of the NH-ISAC Board. A former board member of the FS-ISAC, he also served as the Global Head of Application and Mobile Security for JP Morgan Chase. Prior positions include the CISO for KPMG, DTCC and American Express. He has over 30 years of experience in information technology and information security as a practitioner, management consultant and leader of technology, analytic and information security for global firms. He has won numerous industry awards including: the 2016 Security Alliance Award for Innovation, 2016 ISE Luminary Leadership Award (for the Northeast), the 2014 North American Information Security Executive of the Year for Healthcare, the 2009 BITS Leadership Award for outstanding leadership of the Supply Chain Working Group (in collaboration with NIST the U.S. Dept. of Treasury), and the 2007 Information Security Executive of the Year for the Northeast. He is a co-author of the FS-ISAC white paper on 3rd Party Software Security Controls and several other industry white papers.

Overview

Routh begins by observing the importance of innovation in security to face a sea change of new requirements. Part of this involves effectively integrating the three *T's* of a cybersecurity program: *Top talent, Tools* and *Techniques.* Routh stresses how techniques are essential and a key to realizing unconventional controls as a critical game changer in security. Expanding on this theme, he examines the evolution of the demand for unconventional controls, observing emerging needs to define new requirements in security, noting the fundamental limitations and risks of conventional controls which are too often rooted in compliance requirements.

Among the emerging risks enterprises face, Routh examines the prime threat of phishing scenarios. Those fraudulent practices break down to: domain spoofing; look-a-like domains; email spoofing; compromised email accounts. He also outlines the existing unconventional controls that are in place for these types of phishing attacks, as well as where new controls are being developed for one area, which remains unaddressed at the time of this writing. Routh also focusses on unconventional controls for privileged access management. Incorporating a risk-based approach and employing machine learning to extract context from big data are key to the effectiveness of privileged access management as an unconventional control, which is increasing in

* The views and opinions expressed by Jim Routh in this book are his own, and do not necessarily reflect those of his current, or any of his previous employers.

importance for enterprise-wide security. Using algorithms to identify online behavior that does not match an established pattern enables enterprises to revoke privileges when an unauthorized party attempts to use someone's credentials for a privileged entitlement, all without human intervention.

Routh then explores the objectives for next-generation authentication, noting tactics used to bypass conventional binary authentication controls, including focus on the hacker methodology of credential stuffing and its impact. Routh observes the de facto transition away from conventional password controls and the growing adoption of emerging continuous behavior-based authentication. With that, Routh shares his fundamental perspectives of model-driven security with its goal of balancing security and facilitating the customer experience by utilizing automation and machine learning. In this specific case the consumer/user experience improves (no need to remember a password), while the security capability (ongoing authentication based on models with higher reliability versus passwords) also improves. He observes the growing momentum of model-driven security and the advantages of early adoption for enterprises with next-generation security tools.

Routh discusses the challenges for auditors given the emergence of unconventional controls and the impact on traditional auditor assessment models in facing a sea change in responsibility, which involves reconciling conventional and unconventional control auditing. To address this challenge of assessing control effectiveness, Routh describes the need to evolve auditor skillsets in the age of machine learning. Data science is a fundamental component of next-generation emerging security programs which entail a range of viable approaches to model-driven solutions. With this breadth and variety of security solution development, Routh observes the broadening mandate for qualified security expertise in the field, with an expanding role and need of data science knowledge for security professionals, including auditors. The critical mass of development and innovation, in Routh's view, strengthens the key objective of moving at the speed of the customer, where the best response rates differentiate new leaders in security.

Routh concludes with the 2017 Equifax mega breach and its implications as a tipping point event, which has led to a paradigm shift in security requirements. The only viable response to these types of mega breaches requires continued innovations in data science and behavioral attributes which strengthens the objective of moving at customer speed and presents the potential for a new standard in security models.

The importance of innovation in security

Innovation is essential for the successful CISO today. Fifteen years ago, CISOs chose a risk framework, implemented controls and measured them against the effectiveness of the established risk framework. That's how a mature and resilient security program was measured. Today, however, the increasing rate of change in security controls, plus the use of unconventional controls, represent critical differentiators for empowering the resilient enterprise.

A sea change of new requirements. With comparatively few changes in the business, security strategy used to be stable. Now, however, dynamic changes to the business, combined with continuous technology and hacker innovation, require enterprises to constantly adjust and modify in response to those developments. The challenge with conventional controls is they are largely driven by regulation and precedent. All this is good, and needed, yet at the same time they are insufficient tools for today's CISO to develop a resilient enterprise. Being compliant in no way guarantees reliable security. A resilient enterprise today must employ unconventional controls. Innovation is essential to realizing that goal of resiliency.

> *The challenge with conventional controls is they are largely driven by regulation and precedent. All this is good, and needed, yet at the same time, they are totally insufficient tools for today's CISO...*

The CISO's route to achieving the prime objective. CISOs are regularly working to change the rules for the threat adversaries, creating friction to deter them. Today, however, those rules are stacked in the hacker's favor. It's too easy to be a cybercriminal. In response, CISOs must continually seek new and effective ways to make it more difficult to be a criminal by creating a great deal more friction for them in the environment. That means investing in unconventional controls which come from innovative ideas, and once systematized, automated, and often rooted in machine learning, become the foundation of model-driven security.

The three T's of a cybersecurity program. At the heart of any model-driven security strategy are the three T's of security: *Top talent, Tools* and *Techniques*. While many people believe talent is the most important of the three T's, ultimately techniques are the most critical. Talent is always attracted to learning innovative techniques which improve their professional capabilities and credentials. Focusing on teaching techniques, and allowing experienced hires to choose where they want to live, will give CISOs access to the best talent. As well, focus by the CISO on innovative techniques, including unconventional controls, is the decisive differentiator to ensure and evolve an effective security strategy going forward.

Unconventional controls as a game changing technique. As CISOs strive to maintain a resilient enterprise, they must balance their investment in technology, in developing talent, and in the techniques they use. A growing number of CISOs today are assessing the advantages of

> *A growing number of CISOs today are assessing the advantages of unconventional controls as an investment in innovation, to fundamentally change the landscape, to rewrite the rules for the threat adversary.*

unconventional controls as an investment in innovation, to fundamentally change the landscape, to rewrite the rules for the threat adversary. This enables environments to become more resilient. While these CISOs recognize security breaches will always occur, they understand the recovery and response to the business impact of a breach will be differentiated by the establishment of a resilient enterprise and an effective incident response plan, as opposed to a status quo enterprise security strategy that may crumble when a major breach occurs.

Criteria of a successful security program. From a CISO's perspective, of the three primary elements required for any enterprise to achieve a secure hybrid environment, the first and foremost is to ensure the security program is risk-driven, not compliance-driven. While a privacy program is traditionally compliance driven, a security program *must* be risk-driven. This requires an understanding of the threat landscape, investing in security intelligence, as well as consistently altering and adjusting controls based on changes in threat actor tactics. Regulations will always lag. Threat actor tactics are a leading indicator of which risk-based adjustments are required, not regulations. It is essential to be able to quickly adjust a security strategy based on threat actor tactics. This is done by the enterprise through the consumption of security intelligence from multiple sources and validation of the intelligence through ISAC members. Today, the alacrity and quality of the decisions made by a CISO related to shifting the tactics of threat actors will have more impact on an enterprise's security posture and resiliency than the effectiveness of conventional controls from a risk framework.

The importance of unconventional controls. The second element of a sound and secure hybrid environment strategy is to recognize that innovation — and investment in unconventional controls — is essential for any resilient enterprise offering products, services and capabilities across the digital landscape. Innovation in the techniques, the technology, and how we use them, may mean the difference of a breach having a major impact and crippling the business, versus an enterprise that can sustain a breach and have no measurable negative business impact.

Metrics versus KPIs of a security programs core functions. The third consideration to keep in mind is that while it's easy and common to measure particular processes, metrics aren't what's critical in security. Measuring statistical trends is important, in the right context. However, assessing the key performance indicators (KPIs) of the core functions of a security program,

> *...assessing the key performance indicators (KPIs) of the core functions of a security program, and determining the health of those core functions, is more important than metrics.*

and determining the health of those core functions, is more important than metrics. Measuring the health of core business processes, and underlying security controls, is what gives security leaders a critical baseline to determine the health and resiliency of their security program. CISOs don't own key business processes, so they must imbed security controls within those core business processes instrumenting business leaders with the information (KPIs) to make essential business decisions. There are techniques to do this while lowering the total cost of IT ownership at the same time and improving the consumer experience.

Evolution of the need for unconventional controls

Fifteen years ago, applying a risk framework with conventional controls and getting an attestation of the control maturity was standard practice, and was sufficient to demonstrate enterprise resiliency. While this remains an essential element of a security program, largely for the value of demonstrating due diligence to certain stakeholders (auditors, regulators, 3rd party governance functions for enterprises, board of directors, etc.), the formula for applying a risk framework of conventional controls is no longer the primary foundational component to enterprise resiliency.

Outdated perspectives of security leaders. Ingrained in traditional CISO thinking was the perspective that the number of changes to control standards was directly correlated to the maturity of the overall security program. More changes to controls meant less resiliency, while few changes meant maturity and higher program resiliency. The underlying assumption had been that the more change in control implementation, the less mature the program. In other words, if control standards changed continually, it was the result of an immature program that was 'fixing' or remediating the practices to align with the control framework. Yet, what security professionals like Routh learned early in their careers is not sufficient to avoid major breaches today, even if they are in compliance with regulatory requirements.

Emerging needs define new requirements in security. There was high value in the adoption of a standard risk framework in the past, and there continues to be value in the adoption and implementation of an industry standard risk framework today, as a foundation to build on. Alone, however, it's simply no longer sufficient to rely exclusively on this original risk framework to avoid major breaches. Fifteen years ago, an enterprise security policy was likely to be a document of 20+ pages describing control objectives and policies for data protection. It was supposed to be updated annually, yet in reality the document was usually updated by a single author every two or three years. No one read the newly-revised version nor remembered what the updates were. Today's enterprises, on the other hand, add new controls, or change existing control procedures, daily. Many of these changes, driven by shifts in threat actor tactics, involve control standards or procedures that are not well documented, if at all, simply due to the challenges of real-time updates to risk frameworks. The cyber threat landscape continues to change more rapidly than at any other time in our history. And, over time, changes in security policy and procedure began to take place within organizations, organically at first, and more at a grassroots level.

Necessity and hands-on experience driving security innovation. In some cases, senior cybersecurity leaders who moved from one organization to another, bringing their experiential security knowledge with them, often increased the amount of changes to control standards and practices within their new organizations. In doing so, they initiated a proactive transformation of the security program under their leadership. Once the new controls and practices were implemented, the program maturity took hold with alignment of practices to control standards, and recertification or subsequent assessment confirmed the improvement in enterprise resiliency. Now, in contrast with older traditional CISO perceptions, the number of changes to control standards today is actually an indicator of growth and maturity, not immaturity. Unlike the past, making consistent changes to control standards today is actually an indicator of improved resiliency in a program. Consistent modifications to

> Now, in contrast with older traditional CISO perceptions, the number of changes to control standards today is actually an indicator of growth and maturity, not immaturity.

control standards or procedures can indicate active responses to changes in threat actor tactics, resulting in higher resiliency and greater maturity for a cybersecurity program. This has evolved as a required response to the increased level exhibited by innovative threat actors and the relentless success of particular malicious intrusion strategies.

Conventional controls for primary threat actor tactics. In recent years, phishing emails have been the dominant threat vector for criminals and nation states. On average, it takes just over a minute for any phishing campaign to trap a victim who clicks on the wrong link or attached file. Intelligence sources point to phishing as the root cause of the majority of data breaches today. Conventional controls recommended by most authoritative sources involves educating enterprise users and consumers on the types of phishing lures used, with the goal of improving the user's level of resiliency, and reducing their susceptibility to click on fraudulent phishing emails. Enterprises spend time, money and resources to educate end users to trust email less and to recognize the characteristics of a phishing email. Tools that create benign phishing lures for enterprise users to learn from are prevalent in today's enterprises, giving users who click on the bait an educational opportunity to learn how not to trust specific types of emails.

Limitations of a conventional control. At an RSA Pre-Conference Workshop a few years ago, four CISOs described the punitive results for employees who clicked on a phishing lure more than three times. In each case the user was identified to the enterprise, and in one case the CEO personally called them up to terminate their employment on the spot. Results shared by the CISOs revealed positive trending in a reduction of employees who clicked on test phishing emails. If we consider this technique of how we're educating enterprise users, we must recognize that we're teaching users not to trust email messages. Email, however, is part of the fabric of virtually all enterprises today and is used as a critical means of communication. In most cases it is an essential business process. It appears, therefore, that this approach may not be sustainable

> *The adversary, however, is always changing tactics. Conventional controls are simply not enough.*

in the long term, simply because the end result is it requires a lack of trust in email which is an integral tool for most organizations. This is an example of how a conventional control is effective for the enterprise as long as the adversary doesn't change tactics. The adversary, however, is always changing tactics. Conventional controls are simply not enough.

Security requirements beyond the traditional framework. Security leaders must recognize that the conventional controls defined within a framework alone will likely be inadequate to manage risk in a sustainable way. This is not because the frameworks are no longer effective. The reality is that the threat landscape is more diverse and changes more rapidly for any framework to keep up with. Most meaningful changes to policy frameworks come about over time, as a consensus among subject matter experts influences the need to update the standards. Risk frameworks with annual changes and updates are about as frequent as is practical. This pace of change, although admirable given the difficult work of codifying changes, is misaligned with the evolution of the threat landscape. Security practitioners must evolve their practices driven by the changes in threat actor tactics. Keeping up with the changes to risk frameworks alone is insufficient, leaving threat actors free to thrive in their constant search for vulnerabilities in an organization's environment. This is where unconventional controls are needed to meet the challenge.

A core objective of unconventional controls. Cyber threat actors seek the most efficient way to achieve their objectives with the least amount of effort. If enterprises respond by consistently changing their controls, they can create friction for threat actors who are forced to continually adjust their tactics. Today, significant changes occur every day in the policy, practices and measures of enterprise residual risk. We measure our enterprise risk trends daily and share them with senior executives to help them understand what influences represent changes to risk. One of the most interesting aspects of this daily pace of change is that the majority of the changes in controls are in unconventional categories. Ensuring that an enterprise is a less attractive target is about as good as it gets for a CISO, and is dependent on the organization's level of agility in making adjustments to unconventional controls.

Biological model comparisons and process impact on a wider scale. Unconventional controls mimic another highly resilient framework of defense and protection known as the mammalian immune system, which includes humans. Antibodies that automatically respond to threats are essential to the human immune system. Models driving unconventional controls are becoming more and more essential to the enterprise. With this objective in mind, the use of an unconventional control in response to changes in threat actor tactics has significant implications for determining the

> **Security professionals need to evolve control standards and procedures in response to shifts in threat actor tactics...**

effectiveness of the control. Conventional risk frameworks, however, don't offer much in the way of guidance for the auditor of unconventional controls. Security professionals need to evolve control standards and procedures in response to shifts in threat actor tactics, which means enterprises must change how they build and deploy technology architecture, which in turn creates more challenges for the auditors dealing with these essential model-driven controls. This evolutionary process impacts all stakeholders in the security process and lifecycle.

Phishing scenarios requiring unconventional controls

Reducing vulnerability to email phishing requires security professionals to know there are four types of phishing tactics and that controls exist for most of these types. Each is an unconventional control that injects trust into email, versus reducing trust by educating users not to trust email. To consider an unconventional approach to the problem of phishing, security leaders must first understand the fundamental challenges and mitigation solutions for the four types of phishing emails, each of which uses a different technique to compel an end user to click on a URL or link. A phishing email taxonomy would traditionally include:

- Domain spoofing
- Look-a-like domains
- Email spoofing
- Compromised email accounts

THE CHALLENGE: Domain spoofing. The most common tactic is to send an email that appears to come from a legitimate and trusted email domain (for example, 'trustedemail.com'). The threat actor uses trustedemail.com to appear on the visible portion of the email as the sending domain (i.e., *good-guy@trustedemail.com*), yet they are spoofing or fooling the header record with a fraudulent domain that is not seen by the end user. The email message appears to be legitimate, so the end user treats it as legitimate.

THE SOLUTION: Domain spoofing unconventional control model. Domain spoofing has been used for a decade and is the most common tactic used for both phishing and fraudulent email or spam. Two dimensions to this tactic impact an enterprise: out-bound and in-bound email. If an enterprise wants to eliminate the potential use of spoofing of their respective domain by criminals, then the enterprise must enforce a DMARC (Domain-based Message Authentication Reporting & Conformance) protocol policy for all outbound email sent by enterprise users or vendors on

> *The enterprise effectively tells all ISPs... to only deliver email from enterprises... authenticated by the ISP.*

behalf of the enterprise. This is accomplished by centralizing the domain registration process for the enterprise to ensure all domains are configured consistently and the DMARC standard is enforced. The enterprise effectively tells all ISPs (Internet service providers) to only deliver email from enterprises originating from specific email servers authenticated by the ISP. The ISP then drops all emails purporting to be from the registered domains, according to the DMARC published policy, and the end user never sees the phishing email in their inbox. The implementation and publishing of a DMARC policy by an enterprise has evolved in the past eight years. Today it is no longer an unconventional control since it was adopted into the NIST standards as NIST 800-177 Trustworthy Email. It evolved to a conventional control as more enterprises implemented it, so this process is likely to be more common going forward for other unconventional controls.

Added advantages of the domain spoofing control. This technique offers a number of benefits. First, it eliminates the possibility of a threat actor sending a phishing email from the sending domain of the enterprise, which protects the consumer or institution sending the legitimate email. Second, it adds trust into the email system, preventing fraudulent email from reaching the consumer. An added benefit is that all legitimate email sent from the enterprise receives an increased response from the consumer. In one implementation, we measured the before-and-after effect of implementing DMARC. Email campaigns after the DMARC implementation registered a 10% increase in click-through rates annually. Sometimes the major competitors in email campaigns are the perpetrators, and spammers, so eliminating this tactic adds trust into the email system requiring no additional effort from the consumer or end user.

The in-bound perspective on protection. It is also possible to benefit from DMARC on the in-bound side of the enterprise, protecting its users from this phishing tactic. Aetna employs an unconventional approach that analyzes all in-bound email by its sending domain. We apply a machine learning model (applied to all email sent to over a hundred enterprises) on in-bound email that separates legitimate email domains from emails originating from

> *We apply a machine learning model... on in-bound email that separates legitimate email domains from emails originating from known bad sending domains.*

known bad sending domains. We then drop delivery of email from known bad domains using domain filtering in real time. The machine learning models improve with the volume of email domain data collected, and the result is another unconventional control (using DMARC as an attribute) that adds trust into the email system for the end user. This application of machine learning is a supportive step in the model-driven security taxonomy.

THE CHALLENGE: Look-a-like domains. These are registered domains that appear to look like a popular and recognizable domain, but often have one letter off, which the user does not recognize when reading the email message — for example '*ACCME.com*'. Threat actors must go through a domain registration process to execute this kind of attack and these domains are often taken down within days. This 'quick hit' technique is common for spammers and for sophisticated threat actors with available resources.

THE SOLUTION: Look-a-like domain countermeasures model. The tactic of using a look-a-like domain can be addressed by using brand protection services which provide crawling engines to search for domains similar to the ones belonging to the enterprise and which initiate takedown services when they are discovered. Another effective technique is to drop all email coming from domains registered in the preceding 48 hours, by writing a script that extracts a daily intelligence feed of newly-registered domains. The script then flags email messages from any of those newly registered domains and directs the email gateway infrastructure to drop the message or not to deliver it to the end user. Most look-a-like domains are registered and used immediately by criminals for fraudulent purposes to bypass reputation-based spam filters. Legitimate businesses often test their domains for weeks before sending legitimate emails. This is another unconventional control

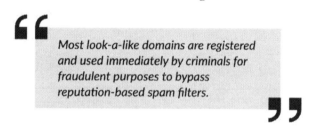

Most look-a-like domains are registered and used immediately by criminals for fraudulent purposes to bypass reputation-based spam filters.

that adds trust back into the email system and is relatively simple to implement.

THE CHALLENGE: Display Name Deception. This tactic involves the creation of email messages with a forged name of the sender. This phishing technique has grown in popularity since so many end users read email from their mobile devices that do not display the entire sending domain, plus reading the sender's complete email domain requires more inconvenient clicks for the typical mobile device user.

THE SOLUTION: Display Name Deception countermeasures model. It is feasible today to use machine learning algorithms applied to in-bound email for an enterprise that uses attribute information about the sending email domains to determine if their respective reputation for sending legitimate email is high enough. This essentially divides sending domains into those that are trusted based on past history, and those that have a history and reputation for sending fraudulent email messages at scale. Algorithms determine which category the sending domain is and if the email is coming from a domain known for sending fraudulent email, the email may be sink-holed or not delivered. All of this takes place in real time and helps the enterprise improve the veracity of emails that are received and reduce the level of phishing.

THE CHALLENGE: Compromised email account. This technique represents the fastest growing tactic today, due to the billions of compromised credentials from email providers that have been breached. Phishing emails come from legitimate email accounts and email domains that are trusted by spam and phishing filters, and, in turn, the email is delivered unencumbered to the unsuspecting end user. This tactic represents the biggest challenge for enterprises today.

THE SOLUTION: Compromised email countermeasures model. The fourth tactic is the one with no unconventional control available at the time of this writing. An unconventional control for this type of phishing email is currently in development. Originally, this tactic was not used frequently because it was dependent on a criminal gaining access to a legitimate email account. Unfortunately, the billions of user's credentials now available on the dark web (many coming from email providers) are contributing to the increased frequency in use of this attack vector. With the advanced development phase of an unconventional control for this specific tactic, and the security community is hopeful it can be implemented successfully in the near future. This is the nature of unconventional control evolution. First the problem is identified, and then security experts work to develop the effective solution.

The importance of unconventional controls against phishing. Each of the methods used by criminals or nation states requires different security countermeasure techniques by the enterprise that is willing to employ unconventional controls. Conventional controls emphasize education, reducing trust for the end user. Unconventional controls are designed to protect the consumer, or user, and add trust to the email system. The people

> *Conventional controls emphasize education, reducing trust for the end user. Unconventional controls are designed to protect the consumer, or user, and add trust to the email system.*

factor, in terms of phishing, will always result in some impact. How CISOs manage that, determines resiliency of the enterprise, and that's where the evolution of unconventional controls come into play. When these unconventional controls mature and are empowered with automation and machine learning security analytics, they represent an emerging set of model-driven security measures.

Evolving unconventional controls for excess privileged access entitlements

Two recent security incidents across industries impacted countries around the world. They were the direct result of the release of highly sophisticated malware designed by some of the top cyber minds in the world, which were stolen and employed by two nation states. These two attacks used advanced cyber weapons created by the NSA, which were hacked, stolen, or leaked by unknown parties, then auctioned and published by a group known as the Shadow Brokers. These events represent a decisive paradigm shift in threat actor tactics which have significant implications for the private sector. Enterprises in the private sector must now assume that attacks of this nature will continue. The tradecraft used takes advantage of vulnerabilities in commercial products to gain root access to users in the enterprise with the highest access privileges (domain and server administrators) using cyber weapons designed to make their malicious activity look like normal administrative activities in log files. This tactical nuance has critical implications for how enterprises must protect privileged administrative accounts.

The absence of a risk focus in compliance-driven programs. Many enterprises reduce the number of individuals with full-time privileged access by requiring all administrators to request privileges for specific actions and present a password to a vaulting solution that expires the privileges according to security policy. This represents a conventional control and an effective one. Many controls from established risk frameworks recommend sending log files for privileged users to the security operations center (SOC) staff to analyze for potential anomalous patterns. This conventional control

> This conventional control for privileged access from a security perspective offers limited protection since SOC analysts lack the time and the context to do anything with the log files from what a DBA (database administrator) does on any given day.

for privileged access from a security perspective offers limited protection, since SOC analysts lack the time and the context to do anything with the log files from what a DBA (database administrator) does on any given day. What might be suspicious anomalous behavior for a normal user might very well be justified and work-related behavior for a privileged user. Filling up log files for a SOC analyst to investigate without context for the logged activities makes little or no sense. It is clearly a conventional control, but not one that adds risk mitigation for external threat actors who are using compromised insider privileges.

Unconventional controls incorporating the risk factor. In 2016 Aetna implemented a new approach to privileged user monitoring that is clearly unconventional and offers a set of controls that significantly improves protection for privileged users and their enterprises. Managers of the privileged user receive immediate alerts when actual behavior for the privileged user does not match prior behavior, creating an anomalistic event. Managers have the context to know what a DBA should do, as well as how and when they should do it. This represents a more effective security approach, delivering virtually no false positives. In privileged access analytics (PAA), which combines identity analytics (IdA), and user and entity behavior analytics (UEBA), this is referred to as a manager anomaly assessment. Individual users can also be deputized to review their own activity in risk-scored self-audit reports. Because these types of reports are automated and driven by machine learning, drawing context from big data, this would also be an example of MDS (model-driven security).

Components of privileged access analytics. The starting point for this type of advanced security analytics is a data lake, fed with source data from entitlements (*see graphic below*), web browsing logs from the web proxy, data loss prevention (DLP) logs from the DLP tool of choice, and physical access data. Specifically designed machine learning algorithms applied to the data uncover behavioral anomalies which are shared with the manager so they can determine if a specific set of behaviors represents legitimate activities. These algorithms are behavioral risk models which create patterns of use for every person or account that has been granted privileged access for a temporary period of time. The user patterns are derived from four sources of data:

- Entitlement data
- Web browsing data from the web proxy
- Email usage data from the DLP log data
- Physical access data

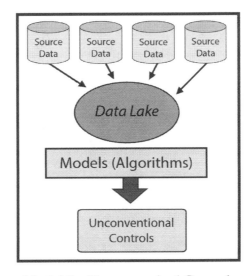

Model for Unconventinal Controls
Figure 9.1

Actionable risk intelligence. In machine learning, risk thresholds determine one of two required actions. If the behavior score is within a specific range of tolerance, an email is automatically generated to the privileged user's manager asking them to confirm whether the anomalistic event is reasonable or not. If the manager's response to the email is 'no' (via a large red button), then the security operations center is notified to begin intrusive monitoring. If the behavioral risk score is high and above the threshold, then the specific entitlements are automatically revoked for the privileged user, without human intervention, and an incident ticket is created in real time. The security operations center is notified, as is the manager of the privileged user. Essentially the effectiveness of the primary control is tied to the behavioral risk model. The more data describing the behavior of the user, the better the model performs. If the manager's response is 'yes', the models are updated and no alerts for this behavior occur in the future.

The growing need for closed-loop response capabilities. This flavor of MDS is referred to as closed-loop automated risk response. Every registered user of the network has a behavior pattern captured, and all online activity and access data is compared against the user's existing pattern, so when behavior changes dramatically, the model can trigger a remedial action, if required. This unconventional control may represent the new table stakes in modern security programs given the propensity of sophisticated cyber weapons enterprises face now and in the near future.

The impact of new and widely adopted unconventional controls. Unconventional controls are not easily identified within the most commonly used risk frameworks and represent innovation, either in the technology capability being applied or in the techniques being used by the security practitioner. Unconventional controls often result in either a new control standard or, at minimum, new control procedures and audit requirements. This circumstance has significant implications and challenges for auditors and security assessors of controls. This is discussed later in the chapter.

Objectives for next-generation authentication

In 2016 over 3 billion credentials (login IDs and passwords) were harvested by criminals in the U.S., according to Shape Security. That's a lot of credentials, given that the U.S. population is approximately 350 million. This situation represents a prime target for evolving threat actor innovation, as every organization must deal with a growing diversity of highly skilled threat actors today. The tools available to the threat actors are evolving and getting more effective all the time. One example of this is credential stuffing, which to all indications is a threat actor tactic whose use will continue to grow.

The method and impact of credential stuffing. The way credential stuffing works is when criminals obtain legitimate credentials from the dark web that originated from a variety of data breaches and use the credentials on other domains. A tool such as Sentry MBA makes it easy for the criminal to use credentials on other websites at scale to attempt

> The criminal using credential stuffing can double their odds of success by adding a prefix to the password... which will yield 400 accounts per 10,000 credentials...

authentication. This tactic works about 2% of the time, meaning a criminal with 10,000 sets of login ID credentials will gain access to approximately 200 accounts using this credential stuffing method. The reason this works is because users generally have access to many websites and mobile applications, and the reuse of passwords from one site to the next is common. The criminal using credential stuffing can double their odds of success by adding a prefix to the password (e.g., *AcmePassword123*) which will yield 400 accounts per 10,000 credentials or 4%. Since there is no limit to the availability of credentials for criminals today, there are few constraints preventing them from using credential stuffing as a tactic for account takeover.

Additional tactics to bypass conventional binary controls. Threat actors have adjusted their tactics, taking full advantage of the wealth of data available to them through illegitimate sources such as the dark web, and are using the data to bypass binary controls. Crawling engines provide demographic information to bypass security challenge questions. Social Security numbers (SSNs) are illicitly obtained from the many small providers of quality healthcare services and are then used to exploit financial sites by passing password reset functions to gain control of accounts. Last year 145 million consumer records were exposed in a single breach of Equifax. Because of all these malicious hacker innovations, multi-factor authentication (MFA) is more of an effective deterrent than single factor authentication, a common conventional control today.

Transitioning away from conventional password controls. One can easily understand that conventional password controls are nearing obsolescence. In fact, binary authentication controls are approaching end-of-life (EOL) for the enterprise. Authentication today is largely an event that initiates online access. Once authenticated to the network, presentation of the correct user ID and password authorizes access to the application and the user is trusted. If not, you're not allowed in and are untrusted. Multi-factor authentication takes this process a step further with the requirement of another binary authentication factor (e.g., PIN over text, a token, biometric attributes, or security questions).

The criticality of continuous behavioral-based authentication in security. A number of security professionals are now moving beyond passwords to deploy behavioral models using numerous attributes of online behavior to create a signature pattern for each user across mobile and web channels. The behavioral attributes are collected during account registration and refined during additional online account usage.

> *A number of security professionals are now moving beyond passwords to deploy behavioral models using numerous attributes of online behavior to create a signature pattern for each user across mobile and web channels.*

This generates a risk score (standard deviation) to which the application can react to in real time so the actual authentication event is integrated into the user lifecycle of the application rather than at the beginning of the lifecycle. The relative sensitivity of the application ties its authorization of the user to the user's behavioral authentication risk score, providing the level of access commensurate with the risk score at any point during the user's experience within the application.

Emerging behavior-based technology for authentication. The next generation in authentication involves the migration away from authentication as a singular event, to become an integrated and continuous part of the process of online activity, from the beginning through the end of interaction by the consumer or user. The attributes used are diverse, many coming from the combination of the device, the channel, and ultimately, the user. The attributes themselves are benign and don't represent privacy challenges (for example, how you hold your phone when texting) and are simply matched to an established pattern. Deviation from the established pattern requires additional authentication (swipe or a PIN via text), depending on the risk score and the sensitivity of the application. This approach is called behavior-based authentication, where the many attributes are matched to an established pattern, and a deviation in behavior triggers additional security controls. Whatever biometric authentication is available on the device (touch ID or equivalent) is included as an attribute in the risk score which notifies the application what level of access to allow. All of this occurs in real time, with behavioral models used by a risk engine that constantly determines the user's authentication score based on a combination of attributes.

> *All of this occurs in real time, with the behavioral models used by a risk engine that constantly determines the user's authentication score based on a combination of attributes.*

Advantages and requirements of model-driven security. Continuous behavior-based authentication, which improves control effectiveness and consumer experience, needs behavioral models in numerical form that represent and compare past behavior with current behavior to produce a variance risk score which is fed to an integrated authentication application. Behavioral attributes don't need to be stored or processed, thereby optimizing privacy. Use of unsupervised machine learning improves these models and drives frontline security controls at a higher level of productivity than SOC analysts performing inefficient manual analyses on a mountain of raw data. Model-driven security control design must be imbedded into cloud provisioning capabilities to address any evolving compute platform transformation.

Fundamental perspectives of model-driven security

The growing perception of how machine learning helps enterprises achieve higher resiliency is based on the idea that the digital exhaust from new security tools requires machine learning to process and allocate resources to cyber threat hunting far more effectively. In reality, machine learning is also creating a critical impact on security controls at the frontline. In any application, behavioral models are changing the way we design security controls, which include binary authentication and behavioral authentication. The

> Authentication is no longer a singular event, but an engaged process that persists throughout the user's experience within the environment.

more models, the better; the more data, the better. Authentication is no longer a singular event, but an engaged process that persists throughout the user's experience within the environment. Operating security controls online in real time requires models and unsupervised machine learning. Using models to constantly monitor the online behavior of privileged users, with the ability to revoke privileges when anomalies are detected in real time, is an example of an unconventional control that can and will prevent the destruction of data across devices in seconds.

Balancing security and facilitating the customer experience. Managing new privacy paradigms and maintaining an ongoing level of trust with consumers will remain an evolving challenge for enterprises going forward. Consumers don't trust large commercial enterprises or governments. Yet, establishing a brand based on consumer trust is essential for success and survival in the marketplace. Technology advancements offer the potential to go well beyond consumer trust and privacy thresholds, yet the devil is always in the details. Incorporating a mature advanced analytics solution with identity analytics, along with user and entity behavior analytics (IdA and UEBA) at its core, to protect consumers and build better online experiences, is a worthwhile investment. With an array of well-chosen and proven security analytics solutions, the prospect of straddling the line of trust is decisively empowered. As well, the breadth of model-driven security controls represent more than what is defined in the UBEA category of products.

> ...the breadth of model-driven security controls represent more than what is defined in the UBEA category of products.

The new normal of constant change in control procedures. The cyber and physical elements of today's security programs are converging, which will result in more and more policy changes. Whenever security organizations change a control standard or, more frequently, a control procedure, it is triggered by a change in practices aligned with a new control requirement or threat dynamic. Almost every control standard has several key performance indicators that measure the health of the process where the control is imbedded and is monitored frequently. One of the KPIs that carries critical weight is how many changes are introduced (control standards, procedures and the corresponding practices), and the average is one per day. A viable risk-driven security program should change security posture measures through the control standards and procedures at the same pace as threat actors who adjust tactics. This year, daily changes may be the more accurate indicator of both maturity and resiliency, but next year it may be one-and-a-half changes daily; the next year, two changes. It will never again be once a month, or once a quarter, or annually.

Cost benefits of unconventional controls. Aetna has implemented an authentication model using behavioral risk scoring from patterns that enables us to make adjustments to authentication controls without changing application code, thus saving millions of dollars every year. Changing authentication controls quickly provides an enterprise with more resiliency to respond to changes in threat actor tactics, avoids the need for developers to write or change application code every time an adjustment to an authentication control is made, and saves on operating costs. This is another positive outcome for pursuing unconventional controls.

Model-driven security going forward. Model-driven security has significant implications with talent management techniques for CISOs. Aetna has over two hundred models in production today driving security controls, so the design, deployment and adjustments to controls are done largely through changing models. Data scientists need to work with cybersecurity professionals since it is becoming foundational for security. Both must understand each other. A basic understanding of data science and machine learning is essential for all security professionals today. This requires a new strategy and development curriculum, along with adjustments to recruit the right security professionals with the right training and abilities for innovation to face future challenges. Auditors and security assessors must gain this understanding, as well. A new auditing practice is evolving to test the effectiveness of machine learning models called CRISP-DM (cross-industry standard process for data mining). It helps the thousands of auditors who must validate the effectiveness of machine learning models.

The advantages of early adoption with next-generation security tools. Tool selection criteria are changing based on the ability to not only address emerging threat techniques, but also to be flexible enough to evolve as tactics evolve. Early-stage product evaluation and adoption is an effective way for enterprises to expand innovation in control design by partnering with advanced security analytics solution vendors, to assure their

> *Early-stage product evaluation and adoption is an effective way for enterprises to expand innovation in control design by partnering with advanced security analytics solution vendors, to assure their product roadmap develops in alignment with the enterprise's needs.*

product roadmap develops in alignment with the enterprise's needs. These needs are centered on model-driven security which enables the business enterprise to move at the speed of the customer across all channels, while improving risk management practices.

Challenges for auditors and unconventional controls

Over the past few decades, the majority of the enterprise control standards for private industry were derived from authoritative sources (e.g., NIST 800-53, ISO-27001, FISMA, COBIT, COSA, etc.). The maturity of an enterprise's security program was directly tied to the results of testing controls to determine if the enterprise practices were aligned with the control standards of the regulatory framework which had been selected and applied. Often referred to as policies, control standards are documented and periodically tested by auditors or security assessors. The traditional view was that the more stable the results of the testing of controls, the more mature the program. Evolving business models and system architectures, however — and even the hiring and firing of people — all led to changes which have had impactful implications for practices that evolved outside the traditional alignment with controls. From the auditor's perspective, this necessitated further requirements for remediation and testing. This supplemental vetting process, however, often represents uncharted territory for many auditors and security assessors. CRISP-DM can help auditors and regulators develop experience testing the efficacy of machine learning models.

Reconciling conventional and unconventional control auditing. Conventional controls are well established within risk frameworks and clearly defined. In addition, the audit testing procedures are mature, well-established, taught to others within the discipline, and are repetitive. When external auditors test for identity and access management (IAM) controls today, the methods and techniques used for sampling and testing control effectiveness are based on decades of practical experience, all of which is well-documented. Auditor skill level is measured and quantified through certifications and ongoing education for industry standards (see ISACA.org), including the American Institute for

> *Outside of those parameters, however, is a different paradigm of due diligence in security.*

Certified Public Accountants (AICPA) certifications. Auditor assessments matter, and the methodologies used are considered mature and recognized as critical and effective within the parameters of conventional controls. Outside of those parameters, however, is a different paradigm of due diligence in security.

Supplemental access controls needed for privileged users. An example of the challenges facing auditors is how conventional controls for monitoring and controlling access for privileged users (those with the entitlement rights to add or delete accounts, such as domain or server administrators) are well-established in all control frameworks, as are auditing practices related to monitoring privileged users. Yet, more and more organizations use unconventional control behavioral risk models for privileged user management due to the need for control objectives of heightening importance. Facts are that all cyber incidents involving data exfiltration required some sort of breach or bypass of privileged user rights. This puts more of a premium on controlling the misuse of privileged user rights or credentials being used by a threat actor to exfiltrate sensitive data. The impactful controls addressing this challenge most effectively are the unconventional ones.

The challenges of assessing control effectiveness. One of the biggest implications with the implementation of this type of unconventional control is not in the integration effort itself (which in many cases is relatively easy to do), but in the auditing of the effectiveness of the unconventional control. Privileged access management (PAM) control represents a growing trend of applying control models to real-time access management, a trend that is accelerating as security practitioners build and implement better and more sophisticated machine learning capabilities. As a result, this trend makes the job of the auditor more complicated and challenging, requiring the testing of control models to determine their effectiveness. Unfortunately, unlike the decades of control testing in practice, with its constituent documentation and processes, no body of data or techniques exist to test these new control models. The use of an unconventional control, like this one for PAM, requires new testing procedures and techniques for auditors.

> One of the biggest implications with the implementation of this type of unconventional control is not in the integration effort itself... but in the auditing of the effectiveness of the unconventional control.

The evolving requirement of auditor skillsets. Auditors must be taught how to assess the control effectiveness of model-driven security controls since conventional approaches will be inadequate and unsatisfactory. Auditors need a greater facility and understanding of machine learning algorithms to test model effectiveness. More and more organizations are bringing data science as an additional approach of their security teams. Data scientists contribute to raising skill levels in data analytics for security professionals, and this has been instrumental to an organization's ability to deploy unconventional controls in response to changes in the threat landscape. Going forward, skills of data scientists are also critical in helping auditors figure out how to test unconventional and model-driven controls throughout the enterprise, and CRISP-DM can help.

Data science in emerging security programs

The preceding examples of unconventional controls in this chapter are not found in any contemporary reference to risk frameworks. Yet employing innovative techniques and unconventional control design represents essential security hygiene for enterprises today. It is supplemental to using a traditional risk framework as a foundation and does not diminish the value of conventional controls or risk frameworks. Employing unconventional controls is a necessary ingredient of enterprise resilience, given the evolution in threat actor tactical innovations. But simply deploying standalone unconventional controls may not be enough, because each control has its own characteristics and requirements that must interface

> *...simply deploying standalone unconventional controls may not be enough, because each control has its own characteristics and requirements that must interface and integrate seamlessly with the overall enterprise security strategy.*

and integrate seamlessly with the overall enterprise security strategy. At times, a CISO must take responsibility for the innovation needed to ensure the alignment with the unique security requirements of an enterprise. Because of these requirements, no off-the-shelf solution may be available. Engaging the most qualified experts in data science, to facilitate security innovation, is critical for success.

Implementing the data science option. In 2015, I brought a chief data scientist into Aetna's security program. The rationale for this decision was the numerous unconventional controls were creating so many new log files that our SIEM capabilities were struggling to keep up with the volume of new data sources and how to correlate them. I assessed the right approach was to build a data lake, dedicated to security, to feed with data sources, and apply mathematical algorithms — machine learning models — to help us determine patterns and identify anomalies worthy of further analysis and investigation. My objective was to be able to derive information that would help us make better decisions in allocating our scarce security resources to the highest risk at the enterprise level, and to do this at scale, across a large enterprise. I hired a highly talented data scientist trained by the NSA, with both cyber and commercial enterprise experience. He built a Hadoop cluster, fed vast amounts of security data into it, and initially built over a hundred machine learning models. These were created to find criminal patterns in payment processes performed by crime syndicates in Nigeria and Indonesia that were using data obtained in W-2 fraud

> *...the numerous unconventional controls were creating so many new log files that our SIEM capabilities were struggling to keep up with the volume of new data sources and how to correlate them.*

schemes to bypass password reset controls in health savings accounts.

The range of viable model-driven solution approaches. The chief data scientist was largely successful in both the design and implementation of the data lake and integrating the models. We have over 200 models in production today. But while that was taking place, there were eight other implementations in production of models that were driving frontline security controls. An example is where we have a privileged user monitoring capability that has been in place for the last year which measures the online behavior of the privileged user for the period of time they have that privilege. Then, if there's any deviation in the behavioral pattern, the model automatically generates an email to the user's manager to determine whether it's a legitimate action or not. If there are several deviations, anomalous events that don't match the model, the privileged access is revoked automatically and a SOC security operations incident is initiated. All of this is done in real time. This capability enables enterprises, to essentially operate in real time with their frontline security controls. There will be more implementations of models driving frontline security controls going forward. That's a fundamental trend I have observed.

The broadening mandate for qualified expertise in the field. The lesson I learned while our data scientist developed our solution involved a recognition that we had eight different examples of model-driven security controls in production, all using different technology solutions for different purposes, largely using the same architectural design. Included in the unconventional controls I described earlier are examples of automated model-driven security controls in production today. With this insight, I realized there was more than one approach to achieve model-driven security or data models that can drive frontline security controls in real time. Point solutions offering specific control designs using data models are, at times, just as effective as building a large data lake architecture, and in some cases they're easier to implement for specific controls and environments. With the breadth of solutions, their requirements continually evolving and the different levels of abstraction involved, one single data scientist is hard-pressed to cover it all effectively. Security professionals must begin to take on elements of responsibility and innovation for these security solutions.

The expanding role of data science among security professionals. Most CISOs say it's difficult to attract top talent and there's a shortage of skills in the industry. Our situation at Aetna, however, is quite different. We cherry pick the best talent in a diverse environment of candidates, hiring much higher than industry averages for women, people of color, and veterans. We attract the best because we teach new innovative techniques in cybersecurity based on what our security professionals want and need to learn. The implication from this talent perspective is that we're teaching our security professionals the fundamentals of data science. Data science is a foundation for both control designs and implementations in security. We have a curriculum in place that we're constantly enhancing, essentially teaching security professionals how to use data science in control design and implementation. This represents the wave of the future for all enterprises and learning techniques for how to drive security controls based on models, is what we and the industry need in the next generation of security professionals.

The context of model-driven security in a broader strategy. Many security professionals predict how model-driven security is embedded in the future for the industry and that artificial intelligence (AI) will be a component of every security product. My experience in recent years is different. Model-driven security is absolutely part of our future in security. If you have embraced the need for unconventional controls supporting conventional controls, model-driven security has already arrived. It is required for those enterprises with the objective of moving at the speed of the online consumer and those

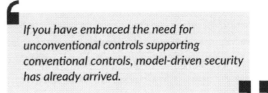

> If you have embraced the need for unconventional controls supporting conventional controls, model-driven security has already arrived.

that wish to possess a reliable level of resilience against the most sophisticated cyber weaponry ever created.

Moving at the speed of the customer

The evolution of a CISO's security strategy is not a process conducted in a bell jar. We learn lessons that inspire innovation from everywhere, beyond security, in a range of business verticals and across the landscape of technology, talent and techniques. As an example, when I moved to a new house I needed another flat screen TV. I went online to research my prospective purchase and looked at various models on different websites. I ultimately chose Walmart's website, where I purchased the TV and was satisfied with the experience. Several months later, I read a case profile in a book about how the Walmart business sponsor for the web application fulfilling customer requests had been adamant that the design must produce a fulfillment request in less than 15 milliseconds. I was intrigued to understand why having speed down to the millisecond was so essential for this web application. Then I learned that to get the correct inventory data, the web application had to pull data from one of two data centers in Bentonville, Arkansas, and the round trip time was 50 milliseconds, or 25 milliseconds each way. What fascinated me was the fact that I could never appreciate the difference between 50 milliseconds and 15, so why go to all that trouble for this web application?

Responsive best speed differentiates. It turns out that speed for an online retailer is everything. In this case, the business sponsor realized that most shoppers online will open several browser sessions with competitors, so the site offering the fastest response had a higher probability of winning the order. Therefore, the Walmart team chose to use inventory data from a regional data center that was accurate 80% of the time, and pay for shipping for the 20% it was inaccurate, simply to accomplish a fulfillment request in under 15 milliseconds. This is an example of moving at the speed of the consumer and this experience influences many different kinds of online interactions across industries.

Customer speed and security. The only way to provide frontline security controls at this

> More and more of our existing security controls will ultimately be driven by analytic models that improve with more data and can be adjusted as threat actors shift their tactics.

level of speed (close to real time) is through models. More and more of our existing security controls will ultimately be driven by analytic models that improve with more data and can be adjusted as threat actors shift their tactics. Criminals and nation states are using models to crack security controls and enterprises need model-driven security to consistently adjust security controls on the frontline with the consumer.

Applications for the next-generation of security. As the resilient enterprise of today adjusts control procedures daily, the resilient enterprise of the future, however, will adjust controls hundreds of times daily, through models that adapt in real time as the data changes. This means retooling our security teams to embrace data science applied to the design and deployment of models. It begins by recognizing that unconventional controls are essential and the organizations that know how to apply innovation to security control design will be the most resilient enterprises.

The 2017 Equifax breach: Implications of a tipping point event*

Everyone in the industry, and country, has been talking about the Equifax mega breach, and the implications it has for security going forward. The first thing to recognize is that the root cause of the data breach was an IT security hygiene issue where they did not have up-to-date patching for the Apache Strut vulnerability, which had been identified and released months before. Equifax was, in fact, two cycles behind. That is not uncommon for a large organization, however, for an organization accountable for sensitive consumer information, it's a relatively basic responsibility. There were other controls that failed as well, and because of that, the criminals were able to manipulate and then exfiltrate a great deal of critical data.

Elements of the tipping point factor. The significant impact for other industries, or enterprises, is that the personally identifiable information (PII) records of over 145 million consumers are now on the dark web and in criminal exchange forums that enable other criminals to use social security numbers, and other unique information relative to consumers, to try to do things like bypassing controls in a password reset function. This data enables a threat actor to answer security questions based on demographic information and social security numbers, so they can take over the online accounts, and then commit other forms of criminal activity for profit, largely fraud. The sheer size of the data that has been released into the criminal domain has an impact on every enterprise employing conventional authentication controls using passwords.

A paradigm shift in security priorities. If an enterprise has a reasonable patch management program in place, that will initially protect them against this type of attack. But that's not enough. The real implication for all enterprises, and certainly for Aetna, is the concern over enabling more consumer data to get into the hands of criminals through exchanges on the dark web. That has a significant impact on the viability of

* To learn more about the 2017 Equifax breach see the Borderless Breach Flashcard at the beginning of this chapter, on page 214).

login IDs and passwords, simply by hackers using either the password reset process, or the account registration process using the demographic and attribute information they've harvested to bypass those controls. A new authentication method is needed now.

Innovations of data science and behavioral attributes. Aetna believes, and we are one of the few organizations moving beyond passwords for all of our consumers, to something we call *continuous behavioral-based authentication.* This model-driven security engages an ongoing process throughout the consumer's interaction, whether it's over the web, or for mobile applications. It uses benign behavioral attributes represented in a mathematical model. The actual behavior is compared in real time against those models, and a risk score is generated. That risk score tells the application how much access to permit throughout the interaction by the user with the application.

> *...we are... moving beyond passwords for all of our consumers, to something we call* continuous behavioral-based authentication... *(which is) ...an ongoing process throughout the consumer's interaction...*

Strengthening the objective of moving at customer speed. The beauty of this method is that it virtually eliminates friction for the consumer, because they don't have to remember passwords. The reality is people have trouble remembering passwords. They use passwords for hundreds of websites and mobile applications. They reuse similar passwords time and time again. That leads to credential stuffing where criminals try out different passwords in different domains, and get a hit two to four percent of the time. That means the threat actors take over the consumer's account. So passwords and binary authentication tools have been standard, have been universal, but they're really reaching and end-of-life. What's necessary is a more of a continuous authentication model, based on algorithms that deliver that capability.

The potential for a new standard in security models. We can use thirty to sixty different attributes for an individual via a mobile application, or a web application, to calculate, throughout the entire interaction, whether that's the legitimate user matching the identity, or not. It's a better security model than what has been in use up to this point, and it's actually less effort in terms of friction for the end user. We're implementing this model next year. And, I believe we're going to see enterprises implementing this aspect of model-driven security more and more going forward and into the foreseeable future.

CONCLUSIONS & TAKEAWAYS:
The emerging wave of unconventional controls

Recognizing the sea change in security, moving beyond compliance-based security programs to risk-based ones is an essential requirement to ensure resiliency in today's fast-evolving world of cyber threats. Model-driven security, which delivers critical actionable intelligence, is here today and represents the future for cybersecurity professionals. As well, the viability of traditional access authentication methods and passwords are nearing obsolescence. As hacker innovation rises with no prospect of abatement, a new class of security solutions must be implemented to maintain parity with the threat. This new class incorporates unconventional controls and model-driven security.

CISOs today, like Wafaa Mamili, have many more security capabilities at their disposal compared to Routh when he started in security fifteen years ago. She has embraced the wave of model-driven security and is using machine learning models deployed supporting her frontline security controls enabling her enterprise to achieve resiliency, despite the evolving threat landscape of today.

Amidst this expanding threat plane, a new focus on privileged access abuse has been observed, and with it the need for advanced security analytics. These analytics draw context from big data to flag anomalous behavior of insiders, as well as outsiders striving to mask their behavior as insiders with privileged access. Getting rid of passwords due to their obsolescence and using *continuous behavioral-based authentication* to both improve the consumer experience and security at the same time is unconventional. This empowers not only access control to the environment, but maintains behavioral visibility through the entire user experience within the environment.

Accomplished data science is the intelligence behind this next generation of security analytics and unconventional security controls. It begins with dedicated data scientist specialists creating big data lakes where the vast sea of digital exhaust resides so that security context can be extracted via advanced mathematical algorithms — machine learning models. Auditors and security assessors must understand these machine learning models and how to test them to stay in pace with the evolving nature of these emerging unconventional controls and model-driven security. With an eye on keeping the evolution of security solutions on pace with customer speed, data science is now becoming the responsibly of the next generation of security professionals, who like Wafaa, embrace the broad variety of security innovations emerging to cope with the rising tide of hacker innovation, and take part in the process of security innovation now and into the future.

The brave new world of hybrid environments, with users and entities connecting from countless wireless devices, from anywhere in the world, 24/7, is the new reality for a majority of enterprises. The next chapter explores this, along with the insights of one CISO who is well along the journey to secure his company's hybrid environment through advanced security analytics. The next *Borderless Breach Flashcard* portrays a case of wide-scale unethical activity within a bank, where employees created millions of accounts without customer knowledge.

BORDERLESS BREACH FLASHCARD *The Virtual Boiler Room*	
CATEGORY	Company-wide high privileged access (HPA) abuse.
WHO	**The target:** Wells Fargo Bank and Wells Fargo customers.
WHAT	Over 5,300 employees were fired from the bank for creating millions of unauthorized checking, deposit and credit card accounts, without the customers knowing about it.
WHEN	2011 to 2015
WHERE	North America branch offices.
WHY	Greed. Overaggressive sales targets? Management pressure?
HOW	To meet aggressive sales targets, a large number of employees engaged in an abuse of their privileged access to customer account information to open over 2 million unauthorized deposit accounts and 560,000 credit card accounts in customers' names. This was done without customer approval or their knowledge. A large number of these accounts incurred annual fees, interest charges and overdraft protection fees which accrued over time. The bank hired a consulting company to investigate after this activity only after it faced a massive law suit from the City of Los Angles for these shady practices.
HOW BAD?	At least one class-action law suit (City of Los Angeles). The damage includes over $185 million in fines, and the largest penalty fee in the history of the Consumer Financial Protection Bureau (CFPB). $3.3 billion have been set aside for legal costs. The states of California and Illinois suspended bond investment in Wells Fargo, representing billions of dollars. The two top executives were stripped of tens of millions of dollars in pay, with the CEO being forced to step down. Serious brand damage includes compromised trust of the institution in the market place. The magnitude of damage, and customer flight, continues to be assessed as a number of criminal investigations are pending.
HOW COULD IT BE AVOIDED?	Since they hired a consulting firm to discover the problem, the bank did not have a working or effective UEBA-IdA solution in place. If it had, the pattern of opening multiple accounts for customers with HPA accounts would register anomalous behavior and would have created timely alerts about the questionable behavior.

Cloud and Mobility:
Unknowns for Identity Risks and Misuse

Strategies for addressing the evolving unknowns

If you haven't been impacted by cloud, when will you? And if you have been impacted, what are the significant adjustments?

One way to look at this challenge is to view the old traditional security strategy as something like what Joe Sullivan observed, how on-premises environments were originally like building a castle, with a moat for protection. That thinking parallels, in ways, with the traditional waterfall model applied to software development, which was popular many years ago. Like castle building in the physical environment, this production model has a highly formalized and unidirectional work flow and promoted monolithic, inflexible development. One way to look at it is in the figure below.

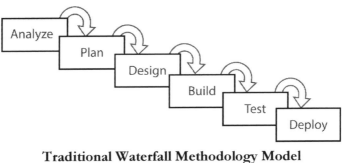

Traditional Waterfall Methodology Model
Figure 10.1

Contrast this model with the newer Agile and DevOps nonlinear methodology which is gaining increasing adoption and popularity. Various graphic conventions have been developed to portray it. The one below distills the concept.

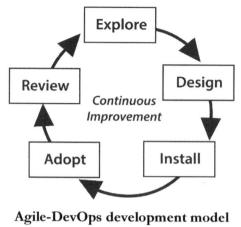

Agile-DevOps development model
Figure 10.2

The obvious difference between the waterfall model and the Agile-DevOps approach is that once the development cycle is complete, it immediately begins anew, initiating a new phase of improvement. Gary Eppinger observed in Chapter 1 how his approach in security solution adoption is not to try to get it perfect, since once it's in place, elements of it will already be out of date. The important objective is that the solution works as planned. Both he and Jerry Archer discussed the benefits of a phased approach. Because of the smaller solution components being implemented, this approach is more budget friendly, and also takes into account the factors of both continuous technology evolution and attacker innovations. Once a phase of a solution has been adopted, it needs to be measured

> *...his approach in security solution adoption is not to try to get it perfect, since once it's in place, elements of it will already be out of date. The important objective is that the solution works as planned.*

against the original design goals. You must also perform an assessment of the solution against the emerging requirements in the environment.

Success in today's hybrid cloud environment demands the acknowledgement that requirements are changing, evolving. Like machine learning, CISOs must be continuously self-learning and assessing their environment's needs and responding with insightful and impactful responses. Adopting this strategic mindset is key to managing the broad array of factors that comprise the unknown unknowns in the security leader's world.

Once that perspective is adopted, the fading perimeter becomes less of an amorphous threat. The prospect of dealing with all the variables of unknowns for identity risks, compromise and misuse become more tangible and workable. Factors like terminated employees with active access rights and privileges, insiders wandering networks collecting data and exfiltrating it, and compromised accounts logging in from multiple locations, all become focal points of a practical advanced security analytics solution that delivers reliable and actionable results. Initiatives like radical reductions in accounts and entitlements due to excess access, access outliers, plus group and role proliferation, producing a net effect of reducing the attack surface area for identity, become a matter of standard best practices and manageable due diligence.

Solutions will be in place for scenarios like cloud users downloading confidential information, concealing it on their devices, and then exfiltrating it from the company network. This is often seen with soon-to-depart employees leveraging a hybrid environment to evade detection. Gaps in visibility, with SIEM (security information and event management) being on-premises and CASB (cloud access security broker) and IaaS (infrastructure as a service) being in the cloud, with limited connection or unified visibility, will be addressed.

Once this paradigm shift in perspective and strategic thinking is achieved, and mature best-of-breed UEBA, IdA and cloud security analytics (CSA) solutions are adopted, CISOs will be able to field and answer the tough questions like: How does cloud expand access risks, compromise and misuse to employees, business partners or customers? How do you ensure you cover all the bases for on-premises and cloud for unknown risks and threats? How is data access and use changing with cloud and mobility? How does cloud and mobility change visibility for defenses? How does the importance of identity access change with cloud applications? What changes for data exfiltration detection are

> Once this paradigm shift in strategy thinking and perspective are achieved... CISOs will be able to field and answer the tough questions...

required with cloud applications? How is identity managed to reduce access risks in the cloud? If cloud identities are compromised, what detects compromise or misuse?

The hybrid environment — bridging on-premises and cloud, along with mobility, BYOD (bring your own device) and IoT (Internet of Things) — currently represents the embodiment of the new frontier of Borderless Behavior Analytics. An early adopter in cloud security analytics, along with UEBA and IdA, Gary Harbison, CISO of Monsanto, is a pioneer in utilizing predictive and advanced security analytics in both cloud and on-premises environments. In the following section he shares his seasoned experience in information security and insights on the benefits of CSA, UEBA and IdA.

BORDERLESS EXPERT INSIGHTS

Gary Harbison, CISO*
Monsanto

As the Chief Information Security Officer for Monsanto, a leading global agriculture company, Gary Harbison leads the Information Security Office (ISO) with global ownership of information security, IT risk management, and protection of Monsanto's critical data. Gary's organization is responsible for the Global Information Security Strategy, IT risk management and compliance, security education and awareness, cyber threat and intelligence, business continuity planning, and governance of the IT Security Controls and Privacy program. Gary and the ISO are focused on managing Monsanto's risks and cyber threats globally, and enabling the business with pragmatic security solutions. He is also a member of the IT Leadership Team helping to define and drive Monsanto's global IT strategy. Gary has over twenty years of IT experience, with seventeen of those focused in the information security domain. This has included multiple global Fortune 500 companies, as well as public sector experience with the U.S. Department of Defense.

A member of Gurucul's Executive Advisory Board, Gary has provided instrumental guidance for the company's path through the ever-evolving and complex path of challenges of facing the company's emergence in the field of UEBA and IdA security. He shares his seasoned in-depth insights into the challenges in emerging world of the hybrid cloud security and machine learning's place in it.

Overview

In this section, Harbison begins with his depiction of the fading perimeter of enterprise environments as a model for securing a company's network and the importance of Borderless Behavior Analytics within this context. He then discusses the challenges with transforming into hybrid cloud security from legacy platforms and also how cloud and mobility changes visibility for defenses and perimeters. On the critical topic of data exfiltration, Gary explores comparisons on change and impact with cloud application security versus on-premises security. Relating to legacy processes, he discusses the future for signatures, rules and patterns within cloud security. He then investigates the impact of cloud API transparency challenges in the corporate network. Employee and user identity in reducing access risks in the cloud, as well as the detection of compromised cloud employee and partner identities in cloud hybrid environments, are examined. Harbison then delves into how machine learning discovers unknown access

---

* The views and opinions expressed by Gary Harbison in this book are his own, and do not necessarily reflect those of Monsanto, or any of his previous employers.

risks, account compromise and detection of unknown threats. He summarizes by giving his observations on the CISO's role with cloud and mobility trends and balancing business goals with network security priorities.

The fading perimeter and Borderless Behavior Analytics

The fading perimeter has been going on for some time. For years companies have had contractors, third parties or partners in their environments, configuring and installing systems. These outside parties might even have had devices plugged into the environment that were not managed by the enterprise IT groups. Security experts have observed this kind of perimeter erosion over the last few years.

Perimeter multiplication and de-evolution. More recently, as capabilities in the cloud became more prevalent, this erosion became even more pronounced. A major influence was the proliferation of devices in terms of numbers and type (including BYOD), as well as the increasing number of different infrastructure environments that now form a company's 'virtual perimeter'. It is this blurring, eroding border, and the lack of effectiveness of the old 'one border' perspective that has accelerated the mindset of CISOs. It reflects profound implications for those changes. This is important, because enterprises must now contend with an increasing number of multiple perimeters and borders in the future.

Moving from legacy platforms to hybrid cloud: The security challenges

As companies migrate platforms to the cloud, the key for security teams is to understand they still need the same capabilities, controls, visibility and protection as on-premises. This objective may consist of the same approach or the same controls. However, it might require entirely different controls, a new approach, or a completely different thought process.

The challenge of visibility across varied environments. In the past, we relied on egress points and standard areas in the network to get visibility. With cloud environments, however, we may not have the same opportunity. As more applications and systems move off premises to the cloud, employees may not always VPN back into their network to access resources. So how do we continue to get the visibility we need and the comprehensive monitoring we require?

The need for innovative resourcefulness in security. With the expanding range of enterprise cloud adoptions, we no longer have one perimeter. This means multiple entry and exit points. The challenge is in understanding how to

> *The challenge is in understanding how to consistently have the same baseline security assurance in each of those environments.*

consistently have the same baseline security assurance in each of those environments. Achieving that same protection, outcome and value — between Amazon Web Services (AWS), Microsoft Azure and Google's Cloud IaaS environment — requires creative thinking within security organizations. As part of the planning process, security design teams will also take into account that with infrastructure or platform as a service (IaaS or PaaS), a majority of the security will be managed by the provider. In this context, a company's security team will serve in a security assurance role, ensuring the controls are in place.

Redundant duplication and rebuilding controls. On the infrastructure side, there is no easy way today to consistently apply control across an AWS, Azure, or Google mixed cloud environment. Security teams often find themselves duplicating and rebuilding controls several times based on what IaaS/PaaS environment they're migrating to. A benefit of going to the cloud, however, is that automation provides the opportunity to ensure all of an organization's

> *Security teams often find themselves duplicating and rebuilding controls several times based on what IaaS/PaaS environment they're migrating to.*

servers (workloads) are configured properly and have passed automated security checks. Segmentation can also be achieved within IaaS/PaaS environments more easily than adding segmentation in traditional on-premises environments.

Cloud's scaling flexibility. One of the variables impacting this new perspective is the ability of speed to deliver infrastructure environments and the agility to scale up and down. This contrasts with the traditional model of building capacity to peak loads on-premises, and having it stand idle when not at that threshold. The cloud's scaling flexibility can also help maximize budgeting dollars.

Innovative security tactics. Security experts are discovering innovative methods of utilizing the capabilities of the cloud to benefit them. An example is refreshing workloads every 48 or 72 hours pulling from the known gold standard build images. From the persistence standpoint of an attacker seeking extended dwell time in their target's environment, this represents a challenge to gain and maintain access for a sufficient period of time to find and exfiltrate the data they're after. This security tactic increases the likelihood of attacker mistakes, which enhances the probability of detection by machine learning models and SOC teams. This method is not foolproof if an attacker succeeds in stealing valid IT administrator credentials through social engineering or other means.

How cloud and mobility changes visibility for defenses and perimeters

As data has become much more portable, and as enterprises adopt cloud-based storage and file sharing/collaboration services, identity and access management becomes critical in maintaining the user experience through federating authentication and using those credentials across the various cloud environments, mobile devices and other entities. Migrating this functionality into this complex collection of systems and elements is a core CIO and CISO objective. This is necessary to provide employees the ability they need to have a more seamless and frictionless experience using the environment.

Achieving visibility across all environments. This functionality is also an important factor in terms of security teams maintaining visibility. As IT systems are spread across those environments, the commonality SOC teams use to correlate comprehensive and reliable visibility is the identity. As long as IT and security teams have implemented a strong federated single sign-on solution with consistent identities across cloud platforms and applications (e.g., Amazon Web Services, Salesforce, Microsoft Office 365 or email, as well as an IT system on an internal network), security teams can then use that identity model to correlate their visibility across those environments. This is where fuzzy logic and nearest neighbor algorithms develop an identity associated with its accounts, access and activity. Orphan and dormant accounts are also called out for remediation.

> " As IT systems are spread across those environments, the commonality SOC teams use to correlate comprehensive and reliable visibility is the identity. "

IdA and UEBA empower hybrid environment threat analysis. Going forward, cloud providers continue to offer better and more robust capabilities for the monitoring of access and activity through APIs and CASBs. In parallel with this, security teams will empower a big data platform with IdA and UEBA machine learning models as they consolidate it centrally to correlate, analyze and identify access risks and unknown threats across all those environments. They'll have an excellent picture of an employee, entity or partner's access and activity, even though it may actually be spanning across five or six different IT cloud environments or on-premises systems, located anywhere in the world.

The impact of mobility and BYOD with DLP transition from on-premises to the cloud

The need to understand the movement of critical data remains unchanged. It goes back to the original function DLP (data loss prevention) provided: visibility into the flow of our data — where it's being sent, how it's being used in the environment, and where it's being saved. It has also allowed us to take proactive control to stop sensitive information from being sent out, or from being copied and removed from our IT infrastructure and endpoints.

Limitations of unconnected DLP. While some cloud vendors have begun to build in DLP capability in their environments, it's only a partial element of the solution. The real challenges emerge as you have on-premises DLP through your endpoint, and DLP integrated with a cloud storage environment, but they aren't connected. As a result, your team must write policies multiple times for the multiple scenarios. This is where cloud security and integration requirements grow in complexity, challenging efficiencies. Unless the vendors start to open up their products and DLP capability to integrate with other products, this drawback will persist. The need to tie DLP together only increases as environments become more complex.

> *The real challenges emerge as you have on-premises DLP through your endpoint, and DLP integrated with a cloud storage environment, but they aren't connected.*

Embedding controls in data. Beyond DLP, the other part of the transition challenge is the need for data protection as it moves through the various cloud infrastructures, endpoints and devices. This is known as containerization, and includes encryption and rights management. CISOs are asking, "Can we reach a point where controls really follow the data as it moves throughout all those different endpoints?" The ultimate objective is to embed those controls (e.g., print, save, access, open) into that unstructured data file so controls stay with the data file as it is in transit throughout the various hosting and infrastructure environments.

Varying BYOD policies for different organizations. Each company will have to determine their own risk profile and policy as BYOD and mobile becomes more of a need and a standard. With mobile devices, you can implement mobile device management and ensure you are able to securely wipe the device. Containerized solutions also keep all the data on a mobile device, or even a laptop, in a controlled secure encrypted container. Without standards and controls in place, BYOD can become a sieve with respect to controlling data.

BYOD functionality evolution. Some security solutions allow you to use applications in the cloud (with a proxy-based CASB), but they can prevent data from being stored locally, downloaded, or copied locally. You can use those enterprise applications within a mobile browser; you just can't save data via downloads. It's all evolving, but within the BYOD space, it will boil down to how much risk a company wants to take on. In addition, the corporation must determine if employees want to use their own device or possibly see this as burden where they must buy and support their own device. Either way, data on the device must be protected.

BYOD access context determining risk levels. Context and scale are other critical factors in assessing BYOD security policy. It's not one size fits all. For example, security teams may allow more flexibility around BYOD within their organization's sales group, versus a product development team or an R&D group dealing with intellectual property. They may not offer the same types of enablements because of the difference in risk. Determining who has access to the data becomes critical.

> *Context and scale are other critical factors in assessing BYOD security policy. It's not one size fits all.*

Data exfiltration: Change and impact with cloud application security versus on-premises environments

Similar to other traditional security controls, as we transition into the cloud, detection of data exfiltration may require a different approach and mindset to be successful. For example, the methodology remains the same to understand data movement in each environment — what 'normal' looks like and what is authorized, versus seeing data activity that doesn't make sense or is an anomaly. Behavior modeling and baselining a user's typical usage patterns, rates, and thresholds, on how much data is accessed and downloaded through those environments each day, helps surface anomalies for users and within peer groups. This offers the ability to quickly investigate those anomalies with rich contextual insight that alleviates false positives — data use that might be atypical, but which is in fact legitimate and required for an employee's work.

Digital exhaust hampers efficiencies. The older, manual ways of approaching security visibility, or non-automated ways, slows security teams down. There is so much digital exhaust to monitor that any realistic prospect of security assurance simply cannot be expected. In this new normal of the hybrid cloud, machine learning and big data are essential to deliver accurate and timely insights to the security analysts. They can quickly understand what actions are required so they can execute appropriate remediation in an expedited manner. This is a critical key in security for successful cloud adoption.

> *In this new normal of the hybrid cloud, machine learning and big data are essential to deliver accurate and timely insights to the security analysts.*

Revelations from deeper data. While enterprises strive to draw the full value from their hybrid environment's data, they invest in security products providing controls and visibility today, where too often it's too little too late. After a SOC analyst sees an alert fire on an incident, and digs into the data, they find the missing clues of what they should have seen was going on for some time. In collecting all the data without user and entity behavior analytics, organizations are not driving the insights they need, when they need them; and they're not getting the full value from their existing investments. UEBA provides analysts with the deep data insights they're not getting today, yet which allows them to drive additional value from their existing data sources.

> UEBA provides analysts with the deep data insights they're not getting today, yet which allows them to drive additional value from their existing data sources.

A force multiplier required for complex hybrid environments. Over time, the industry is learning that to be truly effective at proactively 'hunting' for threats, you must have the right tools. Traditional patterns, rules and signatures are not able to detect more advanced attacks, and 'throwing people at the problem' simply does not scale when you consider the amount of digital exhaust is doubling year over year. A force multiplier is required to pick up the human nuances of behavior that ultimately flag anomalous activity. Machine learning leverages useful and predictive cues that are too noisy and highly dimensional for human experts and traditional software to detect. It has the ability to find high-order interactions and patterns in data for complex problems such as insider threats, compromised accounts and fraudulent cyber activity. Machine learning is the force multiplier whose time has come to support the mounting data volume and variety in hybrid environments for access risk and unknown threats.

Efficient security analyst utilization. With the high demand and shortage of quality talent to detect and respond to advanced threats, it is important that organizations do everything in their power to drive the most value from each employee on the team. Every second those highly talented and qualified resources spend engaged in manual data crunching and correlations, means the true value of their expertise is not being realized. The hazards of data fatigue loom and the security team specialist may grow increasingly dissatisfied with their role and responsibilities. From a CISO's perspective, while they can't fully utilize that resource, the SOC team won't be catching attacks as quickly and as comprehensively as required.

The future for signatures, rules and patterns in cloud security

Signatures, patterns and rules will continue to maintain a role in network security for the foreseeable future, to block the known bads. Most companies face varying types of attackers. Some of the less sophisticated ones will continue to use a selection of the more dated attacks that could trigger a signature. These signatures still play an important role in 'cancelling noise', thus increasing the ability to detect more sophisticated attacks.

Innovative intruders persist. This concept is more focused on the fact that sophisticated attackers watch the security industry very closely, and they have observed a continued focus on stopping malware. For this reason, they are shifting tactics to rely less on malware, and pivot to the use of valid employee credentials (preferably privileged access accounts) that allow for lateral movement in the environment and data access that looks like legitimate employee activity.

Machine learning baselines normal behavior. This is where user and entity behavior analytics plays a critical role. When machine learning understands the normal behavior of an account, it will see when someone else may be using that account for non-legitimate purposes through behavior anomalies. Security teams are observing the rising hazard of the insider threat and of data leaving their environments. This could be a disgruntled employee or a cyber-espionage kind of attack where employees are targeted to try to gain their credentials. Finding that insider attack, using UEBA, requires baselining the employee's and peers' normal behavior and then identifying when they're trying to access data and systems which are either not part of their job or that they typically don't use.

The inevitability of compromise. Most CISOs agree, they can't guarantee there will never be a compromise or a breach of IT systems. To help defend against that probability, security teams need to lower the threshold of noise it takes to detect an attack or an account compromise. Reducing the entire surface area open to attack in a proactive manner also reduces the profile of excess access and access outliers. As a result, an attacker is forced to work harder. They become more frustrated trying to gain access, and in the process they are more likely to generate noise and make a possible mistake. Security analysts will see this occurrence with behavior analytics and be able to address issues early on. It's a two-sided approach of lowering the ceiling of noise for detection and raising the difficulty of access attack infiltration. UEBA and IdA are key disciplines to achieve this goal.

> *....security teams need to lower the threshold of noise it takes to detect an attack or an account compromise.*

Reducing intruder dwell time. A success metric security teams should consider is the dwell time. The quicker SOC analysts see the account compromise occur, the shorter the dwell time. This means that it will be less likely these intruders will be able to succeed in getting data out of the environment and resulting in a breach. While signatures and rules will still maintain a supporting role cancelling noise of known threats, security experts recognize they must expand their capabilities to find the problems quickly, and leverage UEBA to fill the gaps for unknown threat detection, and IdA to reduce access risk.

CASB solutions provide shadow IT visibility and controls

It's important to understand new tools, like a cloud access security broker (CASB), and understand how it fits into your security architecture. Along with delivering functionality in visibility, compliance, data security and threat protection, they provide opportunities to achieve similar capabilities implemented for on-premises environments through a proxy or secure web gateway. In other words, a CASB provides a 'funnel' for centralizing monitoring of cloud environments by forcing traffic entering the environment through a CASB proxy gateway. You can also get visibility and monitoring from a CASB using an API deployment for access and activity of SaaS applications with APIs. Another benefit of forcing some of your egress traffic through a CASB is to gain a deeper understanding of cloud usage and greater visibility into unsanctioned cloud applications, or shadow IT.

CASB form factors. Three types of CASBs exist. They give their customers a range of options for visibility and to control a larger set of cloud applications. They are:

- *Reverse proxy* – Deployed as a cloud gateway, this mode sits in front of a SaaS application, to provide visibility into identity, to authenticate who the users are and where they are going. This monitoring includes data moving in and out of the environment.

- *Forward proxy* – Here the CASB provides a forced control choke point on-premises, in most instances, by routing all endpoint traffic through it, and then updating endpoint DNS settings. Visibility for instances such as BYOD are then monitored by a reverse proxy where DNS settings remain unaltered. On-premises solutions may deploy software agents on endpoint devices.

- *API mode* – This mode enables users to operate on any device at any location with no modifications. It analyzes access and activity via API integration with SaaS, IaaS, PaaS and IDaaS. This mode provides organizations access to native SaaS features, to perform log telemetry, policy visibility and control, as well as, data security inspection on all data at rest in the cloud application or service.

Multimode CASBs. When all the operational modes described above are available in one solution, they are referred to as multimode CASBs. All forward or reverse proxy-based CASBs are important data sources which expedite the delivery of rich context for machine learning models. Cloud, however, is only one data source, and if unincorporated with what users are doing on-premises, this allows machine learning in only one silo and represents limited visibility. To facilitate the breadth of risk scoring needed for accuracy, comprehensive monitoring with hybrid visibility across both cloud and on-premises is required.

API transparency challenges in the hybrid cloud environment

For UEBA and IdA, the importance of APIs relates to the access and visibility they provide into logging data and other information involving movement to the cloud, mobility and other initiatives. Empowered by advanced machine learning, UEBA pulls all the data together. It then centralizes the data so it can be utilized from a comprehensive analytic standpoint. These analytics then deliver the ability to unlock new and broader insights from the data, enabling

> *Empowered by advanced machine learning, UEBA pulls all the data together. It then centralizes the data so it can be utilized from a comprehensive analytic standpoint.*

security teams to see things they had not been able to see before. This delivers the full value of the data.

Uniform visibility across systems and users. The reality of most organizations, however, is that visibility is achieved through many different vendors, partners and infrastructures. While the APIs expose rich data, which can be consumed by those platforms, the challenge is this information from multiple sources needs to be accessible in a simple-to-use, centralized and orchestrated way to truly unlock the value. Vendors and cloud providers are progressing and getting better with that capability. This goal would be further enabled if the industry had an open API standard SaaS applications could adhere to. This would help ensure seamless integration between SaaS applications and behavior analytics platforms. As time goes forward, and network speeds increase, the proxy options of a CASB becomes less attractive. However, for now, it provides SaaS application visibility for those cloud applications lacking an API.

Security solution criteria. As you review most enterprise security architectures deployed at companies today, you will likely still see controls and products provided by various security vendors. Though CISOs have desired a simplified vendor landscape and more integrated product stack, the fact is that to achieve effective controls, a 'best-of-breed' approach is still largely used to achieve success. There's always some work required to integrate the various products and unify the visibility. It becomes even more difficult as you go to the cloud environment where you must rely on the application, infrastructure or platform (SaaS, IaaS and PaaS) provider to expose the data to you. CISOs always have to ask, "Does the solution have an API? And does the data available from the application and infrastructure expose the right mesh required with the data from other providers? If not what's missing, and how do I get it? Am I getting the data I need for security and behavior analytics in my custom environment?"

The importance of identity in reducing cloud access risks

In the future, as enterprises' cloud adoptions expand, recognition occurs that the inside and outside of the network has begun to blur. At this juncture, identity becomes critical for security assurance. This is not just user identity in the traditional sense of how security teams think about it. It's also the identity of employees, partners and third parties, the identity of the endpoints they're using, as well as the identity of different keys automating authentication in the environment.

Context in identity, trust and access. CISOs must start making security decisions based on identity and the context around how much we trust that identity, versus, determinations based on IP addresses and where someone is entering from. If you look at the traditional model of a perimeter where everyone who is inside is trusted — and there may be some segmentation internally — we often make decisions on trust based on what network users were coming from. In the future, enterprises will not have one big perimeter, but many perimeters. For example, each SaaS provider or the cloud hosting environment is itself a perimeter. SOCs can no longer make security and trust decisions based on which network users are connecting from. People will have always-on connectivity, via mobile devices, and as a result, a more mobile workforce will exist, even on their laptops. It becomes critical to make trust and access decisions based on identity and the context of what we know about that identity.

Numerous factors determine context. The following are examples of how UEBA uses context. If Gary Harbison is logging in, is this the normal time Gary logs in? Is he logging in from the work laptop he always uses? Is he logging in from a geo location based on his IP address which he normally uses? Is he trying to access a system he normally uses? Answering all these questions gives us the context that either increases or decreases the level of trust a SOC correlates with this identity. It's no longer just, "Yes this is Gary because he gave the right password and username." It's also, "Do these things look right? Or instead should more information be required to validate it's Gary (e.g., step-up authentication)?" Or should a SOC analyst use this data to understand the context through UEBA and IdA risk scoring and possibly highlight it as a potentially risky connection? In addition, it's not uncommon for an outsider threat to first manifest itself within an environment as an insider threat due to account compromise or hijacking. SOC teams must constantly assess these potential scenarios.

> ....*context... either increases or decreases the level of trust a SOC correlates with this identity.*

Changing trends for establishing identity with passwords and usernames

No one in the security industry would say they're happy with the level of security and assurance provided by usernames and passwords. As attackers continue to target valid credentials, more and more CISOs are moving to multi-factor (MFA) authentication. Single passwords continue to be compromised. With the more sophisticated attackers, their goal is to attain valid credentials to help them move laterally in an environment and access the data they want. Using passwords only to establish trust for an identity is no longer a reliable approach.

Validating identity with context. While two-factor and multi-factor authentication are important, the focus now must also incorporate the context — the broader and richer context in which you validate trust in the identity. Username and password is one way to validate the identity and gain trust. But there is additional and critical activity context to consider around the circumstances of any instance of access to an asset as referenced above. For example: What time is the employee using it? How often or how normal is it that the employee logs into the application? Where are they logging in? What machine are they logging in from? What type of data are they accessing and how long are they using it for? Context details like these aid security teams in truly determining the validity of the individual using the identity. UEBA and IdA provide the force multipliers by assessing this large amount of access and activity data and delivering predictive risk scores to focus security analysts' attention.

Multiple elements determine trust. All the factors above come into establishing trust. It's also possible to take the step-up authentication approach where you may ask for different levels of verification. This means your system starts by asking for a username and password if a lot of the context matches the normal baseline profile. However, if the system sees abnormal behavior, like logging in from a different machine, a different time, or from a different location, or high risk score, you may then ask for a MFA, or some other validation to assure the person is who you think it is and you can trust the identity.

The endpoint and identity. UEBA providing a risk score via API integration with an authentication system can automate step-up authentication and alert security analysts as required. Meanwhile, increasingly, our security focus zeroes in on the identity and the endpoint to drive trust. This is the direction hybrid cloud security priorities are headed.

> *...increasingly, our security focus zeroes in on the identity and the endpoint to drive trust. This is the direction hybrid cloud security priorities are headed.*

New modes of establishing identity for cloud gateway

An increasing number of creative solutions are appearing that capitalize on the fact that people always have their mobile phone (or phones) with them. So whether it means having a token or a SMS (short message service) message sent to them, or whether it's where the phone is within proximity of the machine they're accessing data from, the options are expanding. There are even solutions looking at how people use their phones, or how they enter in information on the phone to validate whether it's actually the owner.

Evolving variables impacting identity in the environment. New products, features and capabilities continue to evolve that will determine the validity of who, what, why, when, where and how. This context around what is normal is an irreplaceable component and makes a big difference in determining how much you trust someone is who they say they are. For example when you log into Facebook, they have 80 plus different variables analyzed by big data machine learning to determine who you are, as they assume your password and phone are likely compromised.

Detection of compromised identities in a hybrid cloud environment

Suppose an attacker successfully gains access to a valid identity, begins to use it in the environment then tries to access data and systems the employee usually does not access. This should be something highlighted by user and entity behavior analytics and require investigation by the security team. It may turn out there's a legitimate reason for the user's behavior when the team investigates it. Advanced machine learning is the key to this capability of highlighting anomalous behavior. With machine learning, this previously unusual behavior would then be correlated into the user's baseline use patterns. This in turn helps to define a unique and living contextual 'persona' of the user and likely will not trip a priority alert for the same behavior in the future.

Accounting for all identities in the environment. All identities in the environment, such as system accounts that aren't tied to one person, and including cloud access keys and similar elements, should be included in monitoring through UEBA and IdA. Moreover, in order for business partners and third parties to provide value to an enterprise, they must also have an identity within the organization's environment. They might be connecting through a secure VPN through a limited subset of systems they are providing services for. Alternatively, they may be logging into more of a virtual desktop environment, so they have segmented access. With UEBA and IdA, they will all have a valid identity in the environment, which is established with a baseline normal behavior within their defined business roles and responsibilities. In some cases, customers may be included on their identity and roles within the organization as well.

UEBA's predictive risk score alerts. When the employee or partner's credentials and identity have been compromised, and there's an attacker moving through the environment in a way that does not match the employee or partner's baseline behavior, the SOC will be alerted to see high UEBA predictive risk scores. The critical importance of delivering a singular and comprehensive picture of a user's identity and behavior across all environments and peers is vital for security. UEBA and IdA have an irreplaceable role in successfully reducing access risks and detecting these identity compromises.

How UEBA and IdA integrate to discover unknown access risks, account compromise and behavior anomalies

One key point should always be kept in mind, which relates to both the CIO and CISO's mandate. That is to facilitate company goals and employee productivity, and balance that productivity with security. Here, as well, identity plays a crucial role. Fifteen years ago employees had ten different passwords to access systems in the different environments they worked in. If that was still the highly inefficient workflow model today, employees would be frustrated to no end. Identity access management (IAM) is the key to maintaining that integrated kind of frictionless experience for employees, to be able to access the system in the way they need to do their jobs and enable the business. There is a benefit to utilizing IAM, from an enabling perspective where it helps employees' quality of workflow and productivity. Its benefits in today's environments, however, are no longer as comprehensive as they used to be in traditional environments.

The gap in security assurance. When it comes to effective monitoring and control strategies, however, one issue relates to how certain organizations handle their threat intelligence mandate. It represents a gap in their approach toward security assurance. This gap concerns the policies these organizations have adopted between their IT infrastructure, IAM access side, and the security monitoring threat detection side. At times, far too many unnecessary accounts and access entitlements are permitted to grow unchecked on the IT side. This only increases the threat exposure.

> *At times, far too many unnecessary accounts and access entitlements are permitted to grow unchecked on the IT side. This only increases the threat exposure.*

Big data and the threat plane. For any large organization, the data lake represents a serious set of challenges. Data haphazardly pushed into big data can create an unwieldy data swamp, thus creating a challenge for UEBA solutions to detect unknown threats and anomalous behavior due to poor context. However, amplify that with an unmanaged growing number of orphaned, dormant, and inactive accounts, plus excess access and access outliers, and it will unnecessarily multiply an organization's access risk and threat plane by sobering magnitudes. The result is that the core requirements for comprehensive and reliable timely monitoring become much more difficult to achieve.

Siloed inefficiencies in organizations. Security experts have observed how in the past some operational sides of an organization remained separate. Their functional perspective reflected that the responsibility for identity comes from the IT infrastructure side, or the IAM and access side, where access is given to employees, business partners and customers. The security side remained focused on monitoring the existing environment for threats. The two group's policies lacked coordination to view identity as a threat and access risk plane.

Inadequate and risky identity management. Industry awareness of identity as an attack vector continues to grow while excess access risks, access outliers and shared privileged accounts are recognized as critical elements of this challenge. Account compromise and misuse are at the core of modern threats. Having a poorly managed identity access plane exposes excess attack surface area for phishing and social engineering threats. By leveraging IdA machine learning, defined intelligent roles, risk-based profiles and dynamic access provisioning, organizations radically reduce the access surface area. This minimizes risk dramatically.

> *Having a poorly managed identity access plane exposes excess attack surface area for phishing and social engineering threats.*

IT and security strategy coordination. Understanding where your most sensitive data is, who should have access to it, and how to control that access properly, helps assure you've built the right security into the environment. When IT and security teams coordinate their strategies with a risk-based approach of identity access management, utilizing risk-based certifications, requests and approvals, the identity surface is greatly reduced. SOC analysts can observe access and activity more closely around employees' behaviors due to a minimized privileged environment. At any time the right focus is applied to the highest risk and highest value assets in an organization. This provides an optimal methodology and capability for effective security control.

UEBA as a platform for on-premises and hybrid cloud

From the UEBA and IdA perspectives, the solution allows enterprises to correlate wide and deep sets of data with a focus on user behavior and their identity for multiple accounts, access and entitlements. The solution set's optimal capability provides a broader view correlated across various devices and hybrid on-premises and cloud environments. If you can stitch together identity, accounts, access and activity, within applications on-premises, SaaS cloud applications — as well as high privileged access to IaaS, or PaaS environments, to correlate these events and logs all together across all of those various environments and perimeters — then you're approaching the threshold of comprehensive security visibility and the 360-degree context. This capability begins to let organizations maintain a holistic view by pulling in big data that's available to start monitoring collectively as one perspective across the identity.

Expanded visibility and monitoring. UEBA and IdA also empower enterprises to maintain and extend visibility, and drive value, because they leverage baseline behavioral profiles and identity access with big data through machine learning. This allows security teams to expand the context of their monitoring, and not just rely on the known bad detection of the signature-based world. This threshold is where security teams begin to truly understand their employees' usage patterns and behavior throughout a normal day and gain insight into where the patterns changes and why. As hybrid environments expand and grow with complexity, the *only* way to achieve holistic user and entity behavior analytics is through the power of proven machine learning models. This leverages big data with validated UEBA and IdA models, to reduce access risks and detect high-risk behavior anomalies. Recognizing that IAM needs machine learning is often overlooked by security teams solely focused on detection and response. For some organizations, IAM needs to be cleaned up and revamped to fully address the issues of identity as a threat plane.

> This allows security teams to expand the context of their monitoring, and not just rely on the known bad detection of the signature-based world.

Network security priorities: The CISO's role of balancing business goals with cloud and mobility trends

There is a range of clear benefits in cloud and with mobility, and for some enterprises they represent a decisive factor for their success in the market. These innovations enable strengthening of their position against the competition. Adopting these new technologies and capabilities, empowers a company's ability to compete in the digital marketplace and meet the needs of their customers. For enterprises to stay competitive, CISOs must be the partner in managing these new risks and deciding what risk is acceptable to the company. For an enterprise to continue to gain share, CISOs must make sure they're able to adopt those types of capabilities in a safe manner that properly manages the risk.

Business goals and security requirements. As technology progresses more quickly than it ever has, the challenge for the CISO is to continue to understand the values and benefits to the business and weigh them against the security requirements. This entails understanding the rapidly evolving

> " ....the challenge for the CISO is to continue to understand the values and benefits to the business and weigh them against the security requirements. "

landscape of capabilities, how they impact the network, and figure out how to employ a holistic and flexible security program that manages the evolving risk properly and enables the company to move forward.

The expanding role of CISOs. Even though security is a specialized technical space, CISO's can't discount the critical importance of understanding the business. They must understand what it takes to run the business, what it takes for the enterprise to succeed within its industry and to gain market share. The more security people maintain this business acumen, as well as support an understanding of what employees and leaders are trying to accomplish, the better security leaders can effectively think through that risk within its proper context.

Experienced insights on security risk. There's also a maturity that occurs over time as experienced security professionals come to better understand the threats. With that comes the knowledge of how security controls are integrated together into an ecosystem to manage those threats. This experience helps develop a contextual perspective to assess the actual risk to the company. Experienced security leaders weigh factors in the right balance while someone newer into

> " There's also a maturity that occurs over time as experienced security professionals come to better understand the threats. "

the space might lack that full understanding.

Risk-averse perspectives. Security professionals newer to the field are often more risk averse because of their concerns about taking on risk in general. They lack the perspective to weigh the impact of an adverse event, and the likelihood of the event occurring, so they lean more to 'no'. A more experienced security leader will apply their perspective to assess how bad it would actually be if this risk materialized, and how impactful it would be to the company. The CISO must ask and answer: "How likely is it to materialize when we compare it against if we don't do what's being requested? What's the impact to the company?"

Security's partnership with business. Security leaders must understand why a project is needed, why it's important, what it means to the company, and understand the risks. They can evaluate those risks holistically, and think creatively about solutions that can be put in place to minimize the likelihood of the security risk occurring. First, a CISO's role should always be as a partner to the business and enable the business to succeed by continuing to innovate and move forward, enhance productivity, and gain market share, while properly managing and balancing risk. That's where experienced CISO's will succeed with cloud and mobility going forward.

CONCLUSIONS & TAKEAWAYS:
Addressing the evolving unknowns of hybrid environments

As technology evolves, so too do the processes involved to implement them, from those emulating the traditional waterfall methodology, to the Agile-DevOps development model. Instead of unresponsive monolithic development, the Agile-DevOps model prescribes continuous improvement, with cycles of explore, design, install, adopt and review, and then begin the process anew. With an ever-increasing ratio of cloud adoptions within organizations, this phased development model is best suited to the emerging hybrid cloud environment.

Monsanto's Gary Harbison observes the perimeter has been fading for some time. More recently, with increasing cloud adoptions and the use of mobile devices by a wide range of individuals to access hybrid environments, the security implications are profound. The old 'one border' perspective no longer has a place in forward-looking CISO thinking. Yet the goal to maintain a hybrid environment with the same security assurance as legacy systems remains the same, however, it is challenging across multiple cloud environments, with various controls. Here, the need for innovative resourcefulness in security comes into play.

Where the clear advantages of cloud adoption deliver scaling flexibility, increased productivity and cost savings, the security requirements to accommodate this often involve redundant duplication and rebuilding controls. Included in these challenges are how cloud and mobility changes visibility for defenses and perimeters. The requirement is to achieve comprehensive visibility across all hybrid environments. Both UEBA and IdA deliver that capability, along with hybrid environment access risk and threat analysis, driven by risk-based scoring.

More protracted challenges exist as well, with the impact of mobility, and BYOD, along with DLP transitioning from on-premises to the cloud. With BYOD, different organizations will be required to define their specific security policies in relation to the level of risk they are willing to take on in their environments. With DLP, an innovation involves embedding controls in data to help protect it as it moves through various cloud environments.

The challenge of data exfiltration remains on the forefront of security leaders concerns as the impact on cloud application security versus on-premises environments becomes more clearly understood. While digital exhaust hampers efficiencies, the revelations that can be derived from big data, and the context gained by deeper data analysis, is why machine learning is required. The depth and breadth of these analytics are far beyond human capabilities. As a result, critical data too often resides within a system that could flag nefarious activity. Without the force multiplier of machine learning, it remains hidden. The risk persists. This class of solution also maximizes valuable security analyst resources.

Signatures, patterns, and rules are being complemented by the use of machine learning, analytics, and the ability to detect behavioral changes and drive insights. CASB is a new cloud-based way to achieve a number of these goals. The CASB form factors are: *reverse proxy*, *forward proxy* and *API mode*. These three offered in single CASBs are referred to as *multimode CASBs*. For UEBA and IdA, the importance of cloud APIs relates to the access and visibility they provide into SaaS, IaaS, PaaS and IDaaS. API-based CASBs provide access and activity data critical to deliver machine learning model context. CASB proxies themselves are also a data source for UEBA and IdA machine learning.

As all the experts observed in preceding chapters, Harbison also calls out the critical importance of identity in reducing access risks, especially in cloud. Contextual baselines in identity establish trust and provide risk-based access. This context can include where a user is logging in from, with what device, when they are active, and what systems are they accessing. Are they all normal? It's no longer a matter of providing just the right password. This is an example of where risk-based scoring is involved. As new products, features and capabilities continue to accentuate that impact on organizations, the ability to determine the: *who, what, why, when, where* and *how* factors that help determine risk become more urgent and essential. These evolving variables will continue to influence the development of identity and access management in hybrid environments.

Harbison also observes the challenge of silos within an environment and an organization. With IT and security, sometimes their mandates lack awareness of each other. IT is focused on providing access, while SOC teams are hunting for threats often caused by compromised access. What lies between is an access awareness gap in IAM, along with a privileged access discovery gap in PAM. These unaccounted for gaps represent a serious access risk plane. This is compounded by organizations that might adopt feature-specific UEBA solutions, tied to a CASB, IAM or SIEM. The combined UEBA-IdA solution, however, provides a platform where the two sides holistically work together, as exemplified in the privileged access abuse use case.

The next *Borderless Breach Flashcard* portrays a case where a hacker breached a healthcare provider for over two years. It highlights the challenges many healthcare organizations face, having arrived comparatively late to the security game, due to a number of factors. The following chapter provides one CISO's insights into those challenges, as well as innovative ways UEBA can help a healthcare organization beyond the traditional security applications.

BORDERLESS BREACH FLASHCARD _A Hacker's Long-Term Access to Vital Patient Records_	
CATEGORY	External hacker breaches access to sensitive patient information.
WHO	**The target:** University of Virginia (UVA) Health System.
WHAT	Hacker gained extended, long-term access to sensitive patient records.
WHEN	2015 – 2016.
WHERE	United States.
WHY	Personal entertainment or ego.
HOW	UVA Health System physician's devices were infected with malware allowing the threat actor to see information the physician viewed on infected devices at the same time. Malware programs are capable of stealing, encrypting or deleting sensitive data, altering or hijacking core computing functions, as well as monitoring users' computer activity without their knowledge. During this breach, extending well over a year, the malicious actor could view all the business the physician conducted on the devices, including accessing medical records with patient data.
HOW BAD?	The hacker had access to the medical records of 1,882 patients, which included patients' names, diagnoses, treatment information, addresses and dates of birth. Social Security numbers and financial information were reportedly not viewable. UVA discovered the breach in December 2017 and reported it to the FBI who discovered the hacker didn't take, use or share patient information. While no sensitive data appears to have been compromised, the length of the breach remains a serious concern. According to a 2017 Ponemon study, the average number of days it took US companies to detect a breach after its initial intrusion was 206 days, the timespan of this breach was 764 days. Had the threat actor been more ambitious, the damage could have been devastating.
HOW COULD IT HAVE BEEN AVOIDED?	UVA Health System announced it will enhance security features for handling patient information. Recognizing that healthcare organizations have been a target due to minimal security budgets and as late arrivals to recognizing the urgency for due diligence in security, a majority of healthcare organizations should see this as a 'canary in the coal mine' warning. Any one of a majority could be next. Adopting an advanced security analytics solution with holistic monitoring capabilities would have addressed this threat in near real time, instead of 19 months.

Applications Beyond Security:
Behavior Analytics and Healthcare

The Emerging World of Security Analytics in Healthcare

After the U.S. government allocated billions of dollars for the healthcare industry to implement an electronic record standard, its ultimate impact was varied, widespread and of seismic proportions. The new standard delivered anticipated benefits, yet also brought an onslaught of unexpected distress for security leaders in healthcare. The percentage of healthcare organizations adopting this mode of record keeping increased from 9.4% in 2008 to 96.9% in 2014. Compared to other industry sectors, healthcare went digital overnight. In the process, information security for this vertical was left behind. Unlike other, more profitable business verticals, such as finance, which grew and evolved over a significantly longer period of time, information security for healthcare did not have the organizational readiness to adopt robust information technologies and secure them at the same time. Management, unfamiliar

> **Compared to other industry sectors, healthcare went digital overnight.**

with what was at stake, and in many cases simply without the proper budget, did not allocate proper funding to cover critical security requirements. As a result of this perfect storm of factors, cyber criminals discovered a highly lucrative target field and the healthcare industry suffered a troubling trend of increasing vulnerability to cyberattacks. In the immediate aftermath, sobering statistics emerged.

A few cases in point include:

- PricewaterhouseCoopers reported an estimated 85% of large healthcare organizations experienced a data breach in 2014, with 18% of breaches costing more than $1 million to remediate.

- The Ponemon Institute cited that the number of healthcare cyberattacks over the five years preceding 2015 had increased 125%, while the healthcare industry became an easy target, as observed by many industry experts.

- A 2016 study by Brookings Institute revealed that, since late 2009, the medical information of more than 155 million Americans has been exposed without their permission, through over 1,500 breaches, with the cost of data breaches being $363 per-record, the highest of all industries.

- In 2016, Accenture forecast cyberattacks would cost hospitals more than $305 billion over the following five years, and that one in thirteen patients would have their data compromised by a hack.

- IBM's 2016 *Cyber Security Intelligence Index 2015* noted that 2015 was "the year of the healthcare breach," when the healthcare vertical surpassed the financial services, manufacturing and government sectors for suffering the most damaging attacks. (In 2014, it wasn't even in the top six.)

- According to a study by Healthcare Information and Management Systems Society in 2016, the Federal Government spent approximately 16% of its IT budget on security, while financial and banking institutions spent 12% to 15%. In contrast, however, healthcare providers averaged less than 6% of their information technology budget expenditures on security.

Reflecting on the last bullet, it's little wonder security leaders across healthcare often highlight the lack of staff expertise and technology as a key reason attacks went undetected. Top executives in charge of healthcare cybersecurity across the country are painfully aware of the growing costs of external cyberattacks. In 2017, $3.2 trillion was spent on healthcare, yet except for large organizations, security budgets still remain slim. Healthcare security has been running to catch up with its peers in other industries, while hacker innovation continues to evolve

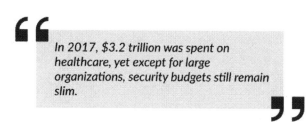

In 2017, $3.2 trillion was spent on healthcare, yet except for large organizations, security budgets still remain slim.

and advance unchecked. Healthcare security leaders have also had their own set of unique complexities and vulnerabilities to contend with.

Beyond the electronic records mandate, mergers and consolidations have been part of the healthcare landscape. These evolving enterprises must often bring together and integrate disparate groups and business technologies to successfully run the overall business. That represents a great deal of additional challenge for the IT and SOC (security operations center) teams to make sure they get everything right. The devil's always in the details and those details are too often the gaps in security. Hackers perpetually hunt for those details, those blind spots. They can sometimes be found when smaller healthcare enterprises buy much of the software to run their businesses from different software providers who are not seamlessly integrated with other solutions in the environment. More gaps. Other complexities include a large number of organizations that have environments on-premises, but are also moving to cloud-based solutions. In many cases, if they're running their own on-premises solutions they're using an external organization to help them ensure reconciliation to compare and align with industry averages. Yet every time enterprises use these services, the software companies providing them may or may not have strong security practices. More unknown blind spots.

The challenges and vulnerability influences in healthcare described above are observed from a high-level perspective. At the core of all their challenges is the sensitive data that must be protected. For insurance providers, hospital systems, and doctors' offices alike, the common challenge for healthcare companies, large and small, is to access and use PII (personally identifiable information) and PHI (personal health information) in a secure manner. Additionally, well over four billion insurance claims are processed yearly in the United States and that sheer volume of transactions, users, and data has emboldened hackers to believe

> For insurance providers, hospital systems, and doctors' offices, the common challenge for healthcare companies, large and small, is to access PII... and PHI... in a secure manner.

they could fly under the radar. And, rightfully so. That was, at least, for the period of time before advanced security data analytics was brought in to confront the challenge.

Yet, even within this mass of data transactions involving insurance providers, hospital systems, and doctor's offices, advanced security analytics cannot be expected to catch every form of healthcare claim fraud; for example, falsifying a patient's diagnosis to justify tests, surgeries or other procedures that aren't medically necessary. That requires a more detailed hands-on forensic investigation. But there are vast areas of healthcare claim fraud where advanced security data analytics can provide critical and measurable results.

Healthcare claim fraud occurs in two categories, those committed by providers, and those committed by members. For purposes of brevity, since the complexity of challenges is extensive, it's useful to focus on claim fraud committed by providers as an example of one category of threats making up the complex set of challenges the healthcare industry faces. There are a number of widespread abuse cases where machine-learning-driven security data analytics can help detect and prevent claim fraud.

A few examples of healthcare claim fraud are:

- ***Phantom Billing*** – This involves billing for services that were never rendered, either by using genuine patient information, sometimes obtained through identity theft to fabricate entire claims, or by padding claims with charges for procedures or services that did not take place.

- ***Upcoding*** – This consists of billing for more expensive services, treatments or procedures than were actually provided or performed. This often involves inflating the patient's diagnosis and code to a more critical condition consistent with the false procedure code.

- ***Service Unbundling*** – A form of upcoding, also called 'fragmentation', this abuse case involves malicious actors billing each step of a procedure as if they were a separate procedure, where normally the set of procedures are performed together as one comprehensive treatment.

In Miami, the capitol city of medical fraud, one doctor fraudulently charged $24 million for medical kits and 1000 power wheelchairs. Also in South Florida, criminals originating from the drug trade have been responsible for hundreds of millions of dollars in healthcare claims fraud. Based out of Central and South America, they fabricated claims from non-existent clinics, using stolen patient-insurance and provider-billing information. When the fraudulent claims were paid out by insurance companies, the mailing address often belonged to a freight forwarder that packaged the mail and shipped it off shore. This category of threats represents only one focal point of medical claims fraud.

While the medical claim fraud examples by providers cited above represent only a fraction of the challenges the healthcare industry faces, each organization traditionally has its own unique problem statement and requirements to ensure their environments are secure. With this critical mass of complexity and vulnerability, healthcare organizations, both large and small, must address the realization that they can no longer reliably protect their perimeter with traditional security strategies.

As organizational management and security leaders in healthcare recognize the lack of expertise and technology in their sector to effectively defend against attacks, it's also time to recognize the opportunity to learn from security leaders in other verticals about what to avoid and where to invest for the best return on security investments. In essence, there's an opportunity to leapfrog past ineffective security technologies and to leverage new security innovations requiring

> *...there's an opportunity to leapfrog past ineffective security technologies and to leverage new security innovations... to deliver higher value intelligence.*

less FTE (full-time equivalent) specialists, to deliver higher value intelligence. For example, why invest heavily in a SIEM and FTEs to hunt for threats when this approach has been proven to be ineffective? In addition, traditional identity access management (IAM) solutions are just not sophisticated enough to do the job anymore.

To close this gap, forward-looking security leaders supplement IAM and SIEM with risk-based advanced security analytics powered by mature and proven machine learning algorithms, drawing context from big data for comprehensive real-time security monitoring. This kind of solution can manage, orchestrate and holistically monitor all the identities within all the systems of an enterprise's hybrid environment. Then the organization knows who has access to what, and what those users are doing with that access. Only then can the fundamental goal of security assurance be achieved. But always keep in mind that basic starting point: you must know who's in your network and what they're doing there. You can only achieve that if you have qualified and up-to-date tools to do the job.

With the volume of digital exhaust simply too large to handle with old, manual and outdated methods, healthcare CISOs can benefit from understanding the advantages of next-generation security intelligence centers that utilize new paradigms of advanced security. In the final analysis, CISOs must learn from their security peers outside the healthcare industry, and narrow the security gaps for their organizations by starting with the recognition that a fundamental change is required to address security challenges, and then incorporate the best and most cost-effective solutions that align with their goals and objective.

William Scandrett is a CISO from a large healthcare provider who has extensive prior CISO experience outside the healthcare vertical. In the next section of this chapter, Scandrett shares his insights on addressing the healthcare challenges of borderless security. As well, he also examines how new and emerging security solutions can benefit the organization's bottom line with optimized operational efficiencies enhancing clinical operations, for both human productivity and apparatus maintenance requirements.

BORDERLESS EXPERT INSIGHTS

William Scandrett*
CISO, Allina Health

William Scandrett is an accomplished information security leader with a proven track record of establishing successful security programs across retail, finance, and healthcare industries. As CISO for Allina Health, Scandrett is responsible for Security Governance, Identity, and Cybersecurity programs, as well as technology compliance and risk management. Prior to Allina Health, Scandrett served as CISO for HealthEast, and held the Information Security Director role at Ameriprise Financial where he led the Identity Management and Governance, Risk, & Compliance (GRC) programs. Scandrett also led the IT Compliance program at GMAC ResCap and consulted at Best Buy through Accenture to help establish their global technology compliance program and software development methodologies. Scandrett is recognized in the information security community for his knowledge, vision and leadership in the areas of Identity, Compliance, and Risk Management. Invited to attend numerous CISO forums and roundtables, he is an active member in many professional security organizations.

Overview

Scandrett begins with observing the impact of how the electronic data standards in the U.S. are forcing a massive change of priorities for security leaders in healthcare who are still struggling to catch up. Increasing security efficiencies in other verticals have left healthcare a prime target for threat actors. Healthcare's wealth of sensitive data and weakness of defenses has offered rich opportunities for hackers. While HIPAA (Health Insurance Portability and Accountability Act) compliance requirements are the regulatory framework for healthcare organizations, compliance does not equal security. Where Allina Health's security's goal is to achieve as close to absolute assurance as possible, behavior analytics delivers enhanced capabilities for effectively managing access to sensitive data.

Observing the challenges of cloud, mobility and IoT for healthcare, Scandrett notes that Allina has adopted some cloud-hosted solutions, and although there are inherent risks involved in adopting cloud technologies, the issues of having a range of new devices in the environment, including unsanctioned mobile phones, represent a tremendous challenge. With the evolution and expansion of security frameworks, Scandrett notes that the enduring value of MFA (multi-factor authentication), frequently used in the financial sector, can provide benefits for healthcare as well.

---

* The views and opinions expressed by William Scandrett in this book are his own, and do not necessarily reflect those of his current, or any of his previous employers.

Meanwhile, forthcoming innovation in security controls must balance risk management with ease of access for legitimate users, while taking into account the growing challenge of insider threat.

Scandrett describes how Allina, in contracted support of their city's hosting Super Bowl LII, used behavior analytics to address targeted controls for authorized and unauthorized access to patient information. Recognizing the various scenarios where healthcare insiders might be compelled to circumvent patient privacy of celebrities and other individuals of special interest, who would be engaged in official Super Bowl-related preparations and activities, was part of the use case development for protecting both PII (personally identifiable information) and PHI (protected health information). Similar use case applications have been observed in other industry verticals, as well.

Emerging ransomware trends, and their implications for medical devices, center around the wide adoption of easily compromised operating systems (OSs) for medical devices, creating a rising vulnerability, where the first ransomware attacks have already occurred. Using UEBA to establish behavior baselines with medical devices supports risk assessments, along with providing a capability to determine causes of device malfunction beyond threat applications. This capability supports operational utilities in medical device maintenance with behavior analytics beyond security, which helps avert clinical risk and enhances physician productivity.

Scandrett calls for the need to expand capabilities in existing defenses, where the current detective strategies must now be integrated with new predictive ones. As well, predictive analytics applied to device performance and reliability has demonstrated value for clinical applications with medical device management. Observing the needs for next-generation hybrid security, Scandrett sees the seamless fusing of UEBA technology, the advanced malware space, and the range of security analytics solutions, as being the key to the comprehensive defense of an organization's environment in the future.

Drawing from his extensive background in cybersecurity, in both the healthcare and finance sectors, Scandrett concludes with his recommendations for new CISOs facing the challenges of the healthcare industry. These include the importance of starting with the basics in security and recognizing healthcare is still catching up with other industries in security. As well, a core value for a CISO's priorities must place the welfare of the patient first, and also align with the goal of moving from being a reactive defense organization to a proactive business enabler.

The impact of electronic data standards in the U.S.

After the healthcare industry adopted an electronics records standard, the industry jumped from an adoption rate of 9.4% in 2008 to 96.9% in 2014. This drastic leap, almost overnight in a sense, represented a seismic paradigm shift in priorities and operational sensibilities for the healthcare industry. It demanded an overhaul from the physical

> " *This drastic leap... represented a seismic paradigm shift in priorities... for the healthcare industry... security ended up being one the last priorities to be addressed...* "

medical record system to an electronic system. In the wake of this initiative, however, security ended up being one the last priorities to be addressed, for a number of reasons.

Increasing security efficiencies in other verticals place healthcare in the crosshairs. Originally, healthcare had the benefit of not being identified as a security target. Security leaders first witnessed initial threats to sensitive data in the financial space, where cybercriminals originally sought to compromise credit cards and bank accounts, because the loss event there was one degree. They compromised the account, they had the money. They got your credit card and they immediately had the funds. Cybercriminals didn't have that much to do; it was easy to monetize their theft. It was in this setting, in an early phase of cybersecurity threats, that the information security space was born. The controls and strategies developed in finance, and some in retail, laid the groundwork for today's framework of security. As those controls grew stronger, the barriers became more robust, making it far more difficult for cybercriminals to succeed at their goal of easy gains. The ROI for a hacker began to change. The controls and defenses were such that it was progressively more difficult to steal and exploit that data. Cybercriminals needed new hunting grounds: enter healthcare.

Healthcare's wealth of sensitive data and weakness of defenses. Hackers came to realize that healthcare holds a tremendous wealth of powerful personal protected health information (PHI), in addition to the traditional PII targets. Not only can this information be used to receive fraudulent medical services, but it's all the information required to facilitate financial events, such as a home or car loan. With the increasing challenges of penetrating defenses in other industry verticals, the tide of cybercrime turned to healthcare. Unfortunately, especially from the provider side, healthcare generally operates between a 2 and 4 percent profit margin. Operating as a nonprofit organization with these narrow margins, too often translates into a lack of funds to afford the standard of security controls that we've had in finance for several years. This stark reality has created a crisis scenario where our data is very valuable, and very easy to get at. There haven't been the funds, nor the staff built up, to quickly integrate any meaningful compensating controls to mitigate these threats. That's the perfect storm of risk factors that made healthcare a target for threat actors overnight.

Response to security challenges remains insufficient. The healthcare industry is now in the middle of addressing these security challenges. Some organizations have been able to adopt responsive solutions fairly quickly, especially the large healthcare systems which have been able to install up-to-date control solutions and are building advanced security programs. Nonetheless, a

> *...a considerable percentage of healthcare provider organizations still don't have a CISO, nor do they have formal security programs.*

considerable percentage of healthcare provider organizations still don't have a CISO, nor do they have formal security programs. As a result, these organizations still don't have the basic blocking and tackling capabilities, such as DLP (data loss prevention) or IPS (intrusion prevention systems) and antivirus applications, that most security leaders from other industry verticals would expect to have in place as basic controls.

Traditional solution pricing lowers, as challenges expand. The benefit for those healthcare organizations striving to catch up and update their environments is that many of these security solutions have been around for a while, and they can now be bought at a discount. What the industry paid for tools such as DLP five to ten years ago was a great deal more than what we're paying for it today (minus inflation). There is an economy of scale and solutions are more affordable, yet healthcare security programs are generally not where they need to be. Organizations like ours that are on the forefront of using solutions like UEBA (user and entity behavior analytics) as a security technology are considered to be quite advanced in our space. It's difficult for a non-profit, with a constrained profit margin to move quickly. They just don't have the budget required to meet the challenge in a comprehensive manner.

The role of behavior analytics with HIPAA compliance requirements for healthcare providers

Healthcare organizations are largely governed by HIPAA as the overarching regulatory framework. From a compliance perspective, especially for us as a non-profit, behavior analytics has tremendous value in that it gives us an opportunity to observe digital network traffic. It provides us with the capability to identify people who are sending PHI, or client information, to certain unsanctioned destinations. The unique user circumstances we have in healthcare are that, as care providers, we are covered entities, and we need to share patient data with other covered entities. This practice is completely normal, understandable and allowed under HIPAA.

The balance of managing access to sensitive data. The challenge for security leaders is: where and how do we draw the line? We must allow individuals within our healthcare network to send PHI to other care organizations, because we're either establishing a preexisting condition for insurance, we're part of a health information exchange, or possibly participating in a contracted research function with the government, and/or with other research bodies. On the other side of the security line are individuals who might be stealing data, or hoping to leverage that data for gain. The gain might be financial, or it might be to acquire privileged information, to learn private details about someone else, likely a patient in our system. That targeted person could be a neighbor, a celebrity, or anyone of interest to the individual seeking to gain unauthorized access to this sensitive data.

Behavior analytics delivering enhanced capabilities for managing access. For the challenge of fortifying where and how that line in security is drawn, behavior analytics gives us an opportunity to understand who's sending what, and where. It's completely normal for a research VP to send information to another organization underneath a pre-approved agreement for research. It is not normal for a nurse, however, to download a collection of patient data and send it somewhere outside prescribed and authorized destinations. Our goal is to use behavior analytics to get as close to an absolute security assurance objective as possible. We want the ability to say we know there is never a case where a frontline staff nurse might have downloaded components of patient data and taken it somewhere outside approved destinations. We have DLP, and similar controls that help us manage the exodus of that data when it leaves the organization. But the actual accessing of that information, and moving it around, even the viewing of it, that's the part

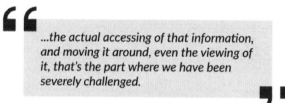

...the actual accessing of that information, and moving it around, even the viewing of it, that's the part where we have been severely challenged.

where we have been severely challenged. We see behavior analytics as providing the realistic answer for that.

The balance of compliance versus non-compliance in security

We all know the age-old adage of security, that compliance does not equal security, and vice versa. I think where the value comes in, or where the crossover for compliance and security exists, is with solutions like UEBA which provide assurances we're doing the basic blocking and tackling every IT organization ought to do, and much more. Ultimately, if all of us were performing all the best practices and doing the right things in the environment, we wouldn't have this major regulatory impact. There'd be no need for federal oversight, simply because organizations would be operating in ways that ensure we're not subjected to the seismic level of damaging fraud incidents and types of events that have been plaguing organizations in recent years.

Security's goal to achieve absolute assurance. The concern about security in the healthcare space is that very little of what we do to meet compliance actually protects the castle. It doesn't really make us safe. It gives us some assurance that our IT organization has matured to a point where we have a level of comfort that we have an infrastructure, or some underlying control structure, that provides fundamental core protections. Yet, in the information security space, we're always seeking the best functionality to provide absolute assurance. We know we'll never attain that goal, so we live somewhere in that *reasonable* assurance space, while we must continue to pursue that *absolute* assurance goal. That's what we strive to do, while at the same time, acknowledge how continuous due diligence in all compliance initiatives remains critical. While they're required and mandated for us in the security space, they are quite literally the lowest level baseline and most fundamental blocking and tackling we can do. Our goal is to build on top of those programs, using them as a foundational framework for a comprehensive, evolving and scaling security infrastructure that meets the challenges going forward.

Requirements of cloud, mobility and IoT security for healthcare

Cloud is one of the elements in our environments that does not represent a source of acute concern for our organization. Cloud isn't a new thing for us. We've had hosted solutions for quite some time. I believe from a due diligence perspective, if we're adhering to proper cloud security hygiene, and we are competent at it, and that the organizations we're doing business with in the cloud have proven and reliable baseline security control postures, with satisfactory SLAs (service level agreements), that our organization is where it needs to be.

The challenges of a range of new devices in the environment. The IoT (Internet of Things), of course, is a big issue for us, especially from the medical device space. Add to this the requirement for healthcare organizations to seriously manage comprehensive BYOD (bring your own device) policies. The added challenges they present to IT are growing and becoming more complex. When you connect to our network from a device you own, we need to have advanced capabilities to see what type of behavior or malware that device might bring into our environment. Are you doing things at home that make your device a higher risk? Do I need to put you in a higher risk bucket based on that? Those are the types of concerns we look at. As well, from the IoT space, how do we balance the safety of wanting to use data points from some of those IoT data sources for clinical care benefits, but at the same time keep the organization safe from those devices that we really have no control over. It's an interesting balance of being able to effectively leverage the advantages,

> *The IoT... is a big issue for us... When you connect to our network from a device you own, we need to have advanced capabilities and see what type of behavior or malware that device might bring into our environment.*

without a great deal of overhead, while also achieving that level of protection where we still feel we're secure.

Unsanctioned mobile phones providing indicators for risk scores. There are examples where UEBA can provide device analytics when someone's connecting to an organization's environment, to deliver insight into whether their mobile phone is jailbroken or not. The status of a device that has been altered to enable software piracy applications, and where games can be distributed for free, might influence the factors determining the risk exposure of that device, as opposed to others. Additionally, it would not only influence the risk exposure of the device itself, but provide insight into the user as well. When we look at behavior patterns of a user who might bring a jailbroken device into our environment, they're usually a higher risk user than someone who buys their mobile off the shelf from Verizon. The user of a jailbroken phone is usually an individual who is technology aware. More importantly, they may have behavior tendencies that would lead them to be more 'creative', indicating they might not necessarily want to follow the rules. They are more risky, by nature. So I might watch that individual more closely. Is it profiling? Yes. Is that wrong? In the context of prudent security procedures to protect a healthcare provider environment, this anomalous behavior indicator is valuable information to help identity and to risk score a potential threat actor in the network.

The evolution and expansion of security frameworks

In the financial sector, the best control we had was a version of MFA (multi-factor authentication), where we could view transactional streams with risk scoring capabilities. We were monitoring a user's activity, or a device accessing something we had not seen before; these controls were really our best protection. Financial services helped pave the way for a great deal of this behavior analysis through a significant portion of the credit protections and controls that were developed at that time. For example, someone used a credit card in Guam; but they'd never been to Guam. On the same day, that individual was in Kansas. How did they get from Kansas to Guam? The financial industry has used step-up authentication on a broad scale to detect that type of anomalous or fraudulent activity for quite some time.

Iterations of innovation strengthen security controls. Building on that original functionality, and going significant degrees deeper in capability, we can use enhanced behavior analytics to get much more specific about the user, or the user's group, with the establishment of a behavior profile. When someone acts outside of that baseline profile, the security side of an organization will take some sort of action in response. Adopting more robust security solutions driven by machine learning and drawing from big data, well beyond those original fundamental conventional controls, numerous enterprises across industry verticals, and beyond finance, are implementing more robust layers of control.

Balancing risk management with ease of access for legitimate users. One innovation provides a risk profile for every user, which is always available to the authentication system. When a user is authenticating themselves, based on what their risk exposure or risk profile is, they might be given no password login access requirement, because they're logging in from the same exact device for the last year, and they're also in their corporate environment. All of that checks out. In a different scenario, however, if they're trying to authenticate from Guam — unless the system has some prior context to validate this activity — then the user would likely have to deal with multi-factor authentication. Or, even further, the user might be denied certain documents or access to resources because they're coming from a completely new location, resulting in their risk profile elevating to a higher level, exceeding the baseline norm, and therefore requiring additional authentication.

> One innovation provides a risk profile for every user, which is always available to the authentication system.

Enhanced capabilities fortify the environment. Clearly, organizations can have a much more granular control over the authentication process, and how people access sensitive information, because we have learned that the traditional controls with login and password are not enough for a motivated threat actor who is attempting to do something nefarious. From the IT perspective of empowering their workforce's productivity, that objective must be balanced against not being too frictionful for legitimate people who are just doing their jobs. Security leaders are striving to find ways to make security more effective, but also make it easier for people who are scored lower in their risk profiles to work productively in their environment.

> ...we have learned that the traditional controls with login and password is not enough for a motivated threat actor...

Applications for the growing challenge of insider threat. Many organizations recognize the need for having insider threat programs. Advanced security analytics solution elements of these programs are often used for early detection systems because the outsider threat is usually first detected as an insider threat, hopefully before it results in the exfiltration of sensitive data. These behavior analytics are invaluable, because with a typical breach, you have a threat actor entering the environment, and by the time they've done their recon of the system, and are attempting exfiltration, they've already tripped up numerous warning alarms with their atypical behavior. Most often, having gained access with a legitimate user's credentials, they can't possibly match that original legitimate user's behavior in every way. With the legitimate user's baseline behavior already in place, the malicious actor's behavior can be detected much more quickly to stop a potential unauthorized exfiltration.

The Super Bowl use case: User behavior analytics applications beyond traditional requirements

At Allina, we recently dealt with compelling use case scenarios due to the fact that our healthcare system was contracted to support the needs of Super Bowl LII, 2018, which was hosted in Minneapolis, Minnesota. This meant all Super Bowl advance personnel who were in the city well before the event itself, might be using our facilities. From celebrities, to players, to individuals of high importance, and even regular folks who've come to town, our healthcare system was one of the go-to resources for their medical needs under the category of essential healthcare services.

Authorized and unauthorized access to patient information. The Super Bowl use case represents a great example where we used behavior analytics to understand how, and possibly why, people might look at someone's healthcare record. Under HIPAA guidelines, authorized healthcare personnel, such as a nurse or physician, have a right to access and review the medical record of a patient they are treating. Healthcare management wants them to do that, because in the interest of patient care, we must be absolutely sure we're prescribing the right prescription, the right anesthetic, whatever it might be that an individual needs from a healthcare perspective. Other legitimate and required reasons for viewing data exist as well. What's not okay is when we have numerous VIPs or celebrities who might be in our care system, and healthcare employees with access to the information, have an invalid interest to see what these VIPs are being treated for, an interest which lies outside their official duties and functions in healthcare.

Circumstances motivating the circumvention of patient privacy. These unsanctioned intrusions into a patient's privacy can be predicated by various motivations and methods. Surrounding the Super Bowl preparation activities, we had a number of individuals who came into our hospitals, per contract, for example with the player's organization, to receive regular care while they were in Minneapolis working on the Super Bowl planning events, weeks before that game. This was, of course, independent of any player injuries. When those high-profile personnel come into our hospital, there can be a great deal of 'chatter' from local news outlets, celebrity sightings, or individuals directly or indirectly involved with that situation. Our nursing medical personnel would naturally talk about who might be onsite at the facility receiving care. That's natural and understandable. However, acting on accessing a medical record based on curiosity clearly crosses the line of medical ethics and legality. On top of that, in these situations there may be interested third parties that come to our hospitals with cash in hand, attempting to persuade hospital personnel to divulge information on those celebrities.

Crossing the threshold of unsanctioned behavior, endangering PII and PHI. Someone with access to sensitive patient data might be incentivized to look at that information with no legitimate reason to do so, which is a clear violation of patient privacy laws. We might also have situations where someone is simply inquisitive. They're not providing direct care for the individual, but these individuals have a personal interest just to see what's going on with a particular patient for various reasons, perhaps a neighbor, or friend of the family.

New behavior analytics capabilities address the challenge. Up to this point, it's been quite difficult for us to truly lock down access controls. This is because we need to remain flexible enough as a hospital to make sure we're providing the right care for that individual, without barriers. But on the other side of that, we must have

> *...we need to remain flexible enough as a hospital to make sure we're providing the right care for that individual, without barriers.*

a method by which we can understand why someone might be performing an anomalous action. Ideally this would occur in real time, so we can interject, if necessary, to ensure our clients and patients are receiving the proper care, and we're protecting their identities as well. UEBA provides that capability, and a great deal more.

Use case development for protecting patient privacy. Now we are working on refining use cases that define where care providers should be while performing their normally assigned duties at a given time during their work day. Based on their job function, and the data they access from different work stations, we can identify if it appears they're demonstrating an interest in accessing a patient's record that lies outside the normal and sanctioned flow of access activity, beyond a specific legitimate clinical use case. We use those rule sets to analyze who's supposed to be in a given location, for what purpose, who's looking up someone's medical record, and whether they should or should not be doing that. It's a remarkably effective way for us to get right to the issue without having to look at some earlier types of security reports that are woefully ineffective because we don't have the manpower to review the overwhelming number of log files.

Similar use case applications in other industry verticals. The objective of maintaining patient or customer privacy aligns with a number of other verticals where similar use cases are being applied. In the financial and banking sector, for example, this same type of use case is gaining expanding adoption. In this context, which is applicable with the top major five banks, a vast number of people, including celebrities, might have an account. An employee of one of these banks, such as a telephone service representative, a bank teller, or someone in another role, will in the course of their responsibilities be looking up their customer's records. This can include seeing how much is in their bank balance or other sensitive information which can in turn trigger unwarranted interest on the bank employee's part. This might occur, for example, when a bank customer comes in to make a withdrawal of some size, and that customer is a celebrity, or maybe even a neighbor of the bank employee. The bank employee, like the care provider scenario mentioned earlier, might be curious to see how much Justin Timberlake, Paris Hilton, or their neighbor has in their accounts, just to satisfy their curiosity. Behavior analytics solutions help prevent that kind of unsanctioned activity.

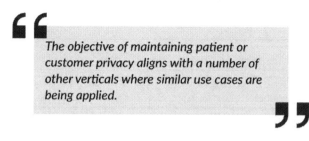

The objective of maintaining patient or customer privacy aligns with a number of other verticals where similar use cases are being applied.

Emerging ransomware trends: Implications for medical devices and the healthcare industry

From a security perspective in healthcare, I believe we are in a growing medical device crisis. Previously, in the healthcare space, we had a degree of insulation, in that medical devices were highly specific. Traditionally, they were built with some version of proprietary firmware or other exclusive features. So, when one assesses the economy of scale for a hacker, the ROI for compromising early-generation medical devices generally wasn't very practical or lucrative. Developing specific ransomware or malware for these unique and specialized devices, on a potential attack surface which is comparatively small, did not scale. With the adoption of standard operating systems like Windows, which is now more widely used today in healthcare, it is a very different story.

Advantages of a widely adopted OS for medical devices. The trend in medical device manufacturing is changing. Now, as manufacturers build cheaper and more scalable medical devices, more systems are running Windows XP (and the like) as their operating system. That fact can facilitate IT organizations from a patching perspective. They get the benefit of using a standard OS which helps them easily patch medical devices, whereas before, they couldn't really do that. This is not only because the operating system of earlier generation medical devices might have been proprietary, there were also risks where installation of antivirus software, or a product agent on a device, would break the devices and/or may void the medical device's warranty.

A sea change in medical device vulnerability. While there are clear benefits to use the common OSs for medical devices, there are drawbacks as well. Now, with the proliferation of standard OSs, the healthcare industry has begun to observe well-known types of ransomware/malware incidents in their environments that were originally only seen on servers and desktops. These attacks now penetrate the medical device space as well. Last year, in 2017, one of the first cases of ransomware on medical devices was reported. This occurred on a Bayer Medrad device — a precision appliance that monitors 'power injectors' which deliver 'contrast agents' to the body, which are chemical, and improve the quality of images for an MRI. This medical device had the *WannaCry* ransomware screen pop up on their LCD readouts, demanding a ransom to unlock the apparatus.

New risk assessments with medical device vulnerabilities. This intrusion trend into the medical device space exacerbates IT's issue of managing and patching medical devices. Do we treat them like a desktop device now? If so, how do we mitigate that myriad of risks? This is especially critical, because for this use case, the stakes are much higher. It underscores a serious problem with ensuring the integrity and reliability of medical devices that are connected to patients, as human lives may be at stake.

Using UEBA to establish behavior baselines with medical devices. From a behavior analytics perspective, the benefits come from applying UEBA's capability to profile the behavior of medical devices and to understand their standard behavior patterns, where we may not be able to patch a device or

> *Through UEBA-specific use cases, we leverage the technology to establish and understand the standard behavior profiles of a device.*

identify what is normal. For example, medical devices all generally have a specific capability. While they may be multi-functional in some ways, they're basically designed for one purpose — such as an infusion pump or an imaging device. Through UEBA-specific use cases, we leverage the technology to establish and understand the standard behavior profiles of a device. Their use patterns are fairly linear and don't change a great deal. Many are set up in one room and service a number of patients per day and may be out of service for a period of time, or they may not be used in the evening.

UEBA's ability to determine device malfunction cause. When we don't have the opportunity to have antivirus software on a device, we can use UEBA to determine baseline behavior profiles. When the device starts to act irregularly, there are basically only one or two causes. Either it's malfunctioning, and it needs to go in for service, or it has been compromised in some way. From a threat perspective, this anomalous behavior triggers UEBA's risk-based alerts that could mean, for example, someone has accessed the device and changed the configuration. It's been hacked. Identifying malfunctioning devices and threat detection, or subsets of these two fundamental cause scenarios, are critical and what security teams see as one of UEBA's emerging benefits in healthcare.

Operational utilities of behavior analytics beyond security

Healthcare providers are generally a network of hospitals which operate with some level of autonomy. Traditionally, there's a healthcare system overlaying the service network which organizes them, facilitates the effective operation of the hospitals, and helps them to employ economy of scale benefits from a finance perspective. Yet, we often see instances where medical devices show up on the hospital network that are unforeseen supplemental additions of medical devices to the healthcare system's planned and established inventory. This apparatus is usually procured by a physician or a hospital organization that might have their own budgets for discretionary purchases of this nature. These unplanned medical devices must now be accounted for and managed, first from a security perspective, and also from a business operational perspective.

UEBA's ability to establish an entity's unique identity. In some ways similar to the general IoT use case that any enterprise would deal with, the medical device use case also has additional critical degrees of complexity and concern. These medical devices are generally managed by the third-party company that installs them, with some type of service contract where a device may digitally report out through the hospital network that it's malfunctioning and possibly requires being swapped out for a new unit. For us, from the IT perspective, that's a device leaving and a new device entering the network. With UEBA, even though that device might exhibit the same behavior pattern as another appliance of the same device model, we now also know its unique identity. Because of this ability to determine the entity's individual identity, we can use this technology almost as a NAC

> " With UEBA, even though that device might exhibit the same behavior pattern as another similar device, we now know its unique identity. "

(network access controller) and learn when a replacement device is performing a function with a somewhat different profile. We also hope to use this technology to help us identify what the various kinds of devices are, and to use behavior patterning to understand where they should live and how they should operate in the network.

Operational utility for UEBA in medical device maintenance. We have also begun to utilize UEBA technology as a form of early warning system to provide us with important indicators that a device is not behaving normally. A device could be compromised and in turn might represent a risk to a patient. Clearly, if a device is malfunctioning, it cannot be allowed to be connected to a patient. Being aware of this critical issue and being able to take action in as near to real time, is essential. In addition, it is also beneficial to understand when a device might be out of rotation. One of the major issues we have in this space is determining when we can safely patch medical devices. There's always a small risk when we patch a medical device for a known vulnerability, where the patching process might take the device down, or might even disable it. As well, it might cause some form of operational or functional issue for the device. There is a need to be extremely careful with medical device patching procedures in healthcare. That's generally why we scan at night or off hours, so we don't disrupt normal patient care or business operations.

Comprehensive utility monitoring for optimal maintenance scheduling. With medical devices, we must always maintain a primary focus on patient care. The IT team can't just go scan a device, because it may be performing a clinical service at that time and be connected to someone providing a critical care benefit. We can also use UEBA technology to help us understand when a device is out of rotation, and when is a safe time to perform maintenance. For example, with UEBA, we may know that between the hours of 8 PM and 6 AM, a particular device is not being used at all and is not connected to any patient. With this capability, we can perform regular maintenance activities during those known 'off hours' so as not to interfere with patient care. This is in contrast to what we would normally do at will with the rest of our IT environment, with servers and work stations, independent of the patient care factor. This also enables us to notify members of our clinical engineering team, for example, with a report on the results of a device that was scanned the previous evening. These reports might indicate the scan didn't go well, that the device is behaving abnormally, which would result in the recommendation that it be pulled out of rotation and be replaced with another device until the cause of abnormality can be identified. Remember, patient care and safety always comes first.

> *With this capability, we can perform regular maintenance activities... we would normally do at will with the rest of our IT environment, with servers and work stations, independent of the patient concern factor.*

Categorizing the medical device fleet for improved efficiencies. Over the long term, we can maximize data analytics for the continually growing baseline of information to build risk profiles for medical device types. With this data, we can assess and categorize scanned devices which appear normal and place them on a safe list. In other cases, with some medical devices, they may act somewhat unusual when they are scanned. These devices would be placed on an unsafe list. This categorization process would also take into account whether they are storing PHI and if they are a lifesaving device. We can get very specific about the way we're managing our medical device fleet to provide security benefits, without introducing clinical risk. When it comes to clinical risk and the prospect of endangering a patient's well-being, there can be no room for error.

Extended UEBA applications as an early warning system. The prospect of a patient possibly being placed in harm's way due to a medical device's faulty behavior is not as farfetched as it seems. The beneficial assurance we gain with the ability to establish baseline behavior risk profiles for medical device types holds great value for healthcare organizations, such as ours. We also see benefit in a clinical sense, where we can work with our medical staff, our physicians, and provide them with data relevant to their operational concerns. Applications can include correlating the baseline data of a medical device group type with the actual data from an individual device. With that, we are theoretically able to provide an early warning system and detect, or even predict, when a device might begin to cause a patient care issue. Depending on how good we get at this, it's not unreasonable for us to consider this type of technology as providing a framework for facilitating the device maintenance process.

Expanding bottom-line value for the organization. This operational functionality of UEBA also helps to bridge the gap for information security, moving from acting as an IT cost center, to performing as a viable business group within the organization and contributing to the bottom line. Prior to this innovation, there have been few cases where we were viewed as a profit center. If we can leverage this technology for true business value, it softens the hard lines where we traditionally look at information security as almost an audit or governance function. We're often seen as a cost center basically selling insurance. We buy numerous solutions with features to provide us with the best security coverage possible. We hope we never have to cash in that insurance policy with a breach event where we would have to use and maximize all those security tools. The current reality is we need to purchase technical elements of security which represent a direct cost to the organization, to protect their assets, yet with no real monetary ROI.

Analytics that help avert clinical risk. As we explore behavior analytics for extended utility and for possible impact on the organization's bottom line, this has game changing potential. If we can provide a direct and measurable value to our clinical staff, to provide risk-based information they might need for their normal data analytics program, to identify when their devices might start to act or behave abnormally, this can arguably protect the organization from clinical risk. For example, the clinical staff would see clear value with a solution providing them data on where a device misbehaves, such as if an infusion pump wasn't providing the correct dosage to a patient. This early warning system enables the clinical staff to be notified that the device is behaving irregularly, possibly malfunctioning, which gives the clinical team the ability to respond to ensure the system is not connected to a patient; and if it is, it should be removed and replaced immediately. As well, it can maximize the use of their budget with better planning for device maintenance that extends the life of medical devices, or predicts when they might fail, and before they become an issue impacting the organization, or a patient, possibly in more ways than one.

> *As we explore behavior analytics for extended utility and for possible impact on the organization's bottom line, this has game changing potential.*

Enhancing improvement of physician productivity. Closely aligning with IT's goals and objectives, part of our mandate in security includes striving to find solutions to maximize physicians' time with patients. We want to reduce any negative impact of technology, so they're not spending time logging on through a keyboard or spending time entering data into EHR (electronic health records). In some OR (operating room) situations, physicians or nurses are gloved, where de-gloving is cumbersome or could possibly break a sanitary field. If we can leverage some of these technologies, such as multi-factor authentication technologies, which UEBA supports, we can also begin to create tangible clinical benefits. Here, we would know what type of access is normal since we know what constitutes normal baseline behavior patterns. We might decide that a certain type of activity by a group of users in a particular medical sphere, or some sort of recovery room, is relatively safe. We might not ask a doctor or a nurse to re-enter their password every time, because we know, based on their physical location and behavior pattern, what they're doing, and why they're there. Why ask for that re-authentication if their behavior baseline is flat? It doesn't necessarily make sense. We start to see, again, where we're providing real business value using these technologies.

Balancing security management demands of personal devices against healthcare data acquisition goals

The objective of providing business value and gaining efficiencies in utilizing data in the most productive way must also be kept in balance with the perspective of prudent security management of personal medical devices that are not part of an organization's official inventory. Healthcare organizations have a certain inventory of ad hoc medical devices, residing within their hybrid IT environment which deliver specific functionality and fulfill particular purposes, yet are outside IT's traditional procurement process. Healthcare organizations either own them or at least have a proprietary control over these medical devices. Because of their associated risk assessment through advanced security analytics, some devices might be on safe list, while others might be on an unsafe list, and, for these unsafe devices, many more controls should be applied to effectively manage them.

The vulnerability of device functionality being compromised. Added complexity for healthcare environments occur where public spaces, set within the same physical location where healthcare services are being provided, are open to people bringing their own personal connected devices, including iPads, mobile phones, Bluetooth-enabled devices, headphones, etc. Many of these personal devices have a potential to be used in ways not originally intended. For example, as was depicted in the news recently, a popular fitness tracking application enjoyed wide adoption with U.S. military personnel. Because of the availability of cloud-stored data, and the ease of accessing the locations of people using these wearable fitness devices via GPS systems, their unintended utility therefore allows these devices to unwittingly track the user as a possible terrorism target, especially when serving overseas. In this case, it was a unique, and nontraditional, application not originally intended for the device, yet it could be misused with sobering consequences. This type of issue will always remain a concern for security professionals in healthcare.

Potential healthcare data harvesting from personal devices. From a healthcare perspective, there are potential applications for personal devices owned by patients within the environment that can be utilized in productive use cases which are not part of their originally intended functionality. This ad hoc utility is a complex issue for us. Generally, from an information security perspective, we strive to keep unknown devices out of the healthcare environment. As part of this general policy, we want to keep wearable technology out of our organization, because we have limited visibility and no control. We don't know where it's been or what the security profile is for those devices. Yet, in a hospital setting, we may actually want some of that data. For example, we may see the advantage of people coming in wearing a Fitbit, or similar wearable technology, because we can scrape healthcare-related information from those devices to provide a better picture of total care. If someone's wearing a Fitbit or using MyFitnessPal, we can look at that data, and leverage it to get a better picture of the patient's health. We'd like to see how many steps they've taken, and what their diet is like. Those types of data points are great leading indicators for us. We currently have a problem statement where we're working to find an effective way to open our environment to these devices without introducing significant security risk.

> If someone's wearing a Fitbit or MyFitnessPal, we can look at that data, and leverage it to get a better picture of the patient's health.

Evolving best practices for providing access and normalization of data. Within the entire IoT space, some components are easier to manage, such as mobile devices, which represent a more straightforward use case for us. When we consider wearable technology, however, and ingesting data from those devices into our environment, these are the questions to be asked: How do you ingest it? What kind of connection is required? What type of handshake is needed? What kind of trust do you build? And, finally, what data is good and reliable? At the end of the day, the bigger issues are data normalization and the requirements of achieving these goals are continually evolving and ongoing. Currently, we don't really know the structure and the type of data that's coming in. So, understanding how to normalize and use the data as part of a patient's health record is the bigger question. I would almost say the security problem is easier to solve than figuring out how to leverage the data from an analytics perspective. It's something we're actively working on to achieve. Once done, it will provide important benefits to our clinical staff and augment patient care.

The need for predictive capabilities in existing defenses

The good news for tried and true security solutions, such as DLP and IPS, is that their pricing has lowered over time, making them more affordable for healthcare organizations with tight budgets. The bad news is that these solutions are simply not enough to contend with the rising tide of threats healthcare faces. We are at a crux, a critical point, where the problem statement can all be boiled down to detective versus predictive controls.

Status quo detective security strategies no longer sufficient. Most of our security controls today are largely detective. We always need a 'patient zero', some type of event to happen where we can generate a signature and then build a defense around that to protect

> *Out of necessity, however, forward-looking security leaders are looking far beyond detective defenses to predictive ones.*

the castle. We will, and must, always be somewhat reactive to known threats. We can block a great deal of hostile payloads through some of our intrusion protection or prevention controls, and other similar solutions, where the work we do — even through our SIEM — is largely detective in nature. This class of security tools will remain a critical part of an organization's array of security solutions. Out of necessity, however, forward-looking security leaders are looking far beyond detective defenses to predictive ones.

Emerging predictive capabilities in security. The trend I see, where I believe UEBA shows great promise, is how the security industry can become predictive in both tools and practices. We can use UEBA to monitor broad traffic patterns, and wide behavior patterns, and extract critical context from big data with advanced machine learning. This provides significant indicators which carry us across the threshold to predictive capabilities which deliver valuable and timely risk-based insights. An example case of UEBA's capability to predict potential malicious behavior is where an employee is visiting job websites, sending themselves emails with process information, possibly accessing data they don't normally work with. They're doing many things indicating the individual will probably leave the company in the near future, and possibly depart with data important to the organization. That's a prediction. Referenced against a behavior baseline of the individual, as well as their peer group, the activity is scored in gradations between either normal or anomalous. An elevated risk score could justify prioritized security monitoring, or even remedial action, especially if the data they're accessing is outside their normal job responsibilities and of a sensitive nature.

UEBA's empowerment of security resources. UEBA's capabilities as a force multiplier for advanced security analysts are invaluable. For example, a user begins behaving oddly, or starts exhibiting behavior we think is anomalous in relationship to their established baseline behavior; an elevated risk score is triggered and an alert is sent to the SOC (security operations center). The behavior could be simply anomalous, or may ultimately end up being scored as malicious, based on the pattern of baseline behavior that establishes risk scores for malicious activity. The prioritized risk-based alert streamlines the SOC process, removing the need to go through countless log files to determine the severity of a user's behavior. The SOC can then take action to engage with that user even before the crime is committed. I believe that's the compelling opportunity we have. And the benefits of these UEBA capabilities are not limited only to the human user use case.

> *...the benefits of these UEBA capabilities are not limited only to the human user use case.*

Predictive analytics for device performance and reliability. The second UEBA use case offering of predictive analytics in healthcare relates to the 'entity' aspect of the solution. It opens the potential to support ROI and profit center objectives for an organization. In this use case, incorporating device behavior as the 'entity', the application addresses not only a security perspective, but also the aspect of operational utility of the device, which relates to its reliability of performance. This enables us to get as close to predictive as technology currently allows.

Clinical applications for device management. The key performance indicators (KPIs) that UEBA analytics deliver represent key bottom line information for any clinical group and the IT group supporting them. In this case, with medical device behavior, the use case objectives are somewhat different for anomalous behavior, in that when a device begins to behave badly, it's usually because an issue has already occurred in the device. Yet, taking baseline analytics for individual devices, and incorporating them with a group of devices of the same class or category, then correlating their behavior and performance along with the age of the device, plus comprehensively measuring utility times, and other factors, delivers valuable metrics for understanding both a given medical device, as well as the collection of devices within a clinical staff's inventory. As well, from the security perspective, the medical device's performance is closely monitored for any anomalous behavior patterns demonstrating potentially malicious activity.

The importance of machine learning and rich context. Once we begin to define the value, I believe the true benefit of UEBA is its use over time. With analytics driven by mature machine learning, we analyze normalized data compiled from big data over longer time periods, and can more accurately identify what type of anomalous behavior is consistent with a certain type of malicious activity. Then we have options. We can define what is erroneous as a behavior pattern, or we can provide analytic value for our other tools. For example, when we see a particular behavior pattern, we add a rule into our SIEM that calls out if it sees a traf2fic pattern expressing an anomalous sequence of events; then a defined type of action should take place. I also see how using this type of data can help enhance other tool sets — DLP, IAM, IDS, IPS, etc. — to bridge the various data silos operating with a single identity-based approach, both for users and devices. Those types of analytics help us better understand what type of precursor anomalous behavior is consistent with malicious activity. Taken to their ultimate application sometime in the future, and using just a touch of imagination, it reminds me of the Tom Cruise sci-fi movie, *Minority Report*, where we can almost identify and convict the criminal, or at least give them a stern talking to, before the crime actually takes place.

The next generation of hybrid security

In terms of the new wave of security technology, taking a wider, more comprehensive view than just UEBA, forward-looking security leaders see a compelling intersection emerging between the elements that come into play to facilitate the comprehensive defense of an organization's environment. UEBA technology, the advanced malware space, and the range of security analytics solutions are three key forms of technologies, when integrated seamlessly together, present a compelling framework for the promise of holistic security. When these work together, we can start to leverage the collective big data from these technologies to get very linear and focused where required. This applies not only

> *...taking a wider, more comprehensive view than just UEBA, forward-looking security leaders see a compelling intersection emerging between the elements that come into play to facilitate the comprehensive defense of an organization's environment.*

to what type of threats are coming in, across industry verticals, but in a more targeted way, to what type of threats we must contend with as a healthcare system, and even more specifically, as my company might be unusually susceptible to.

Triad of solution technologies delivering capabilities for holistic protection. With this comprehensive integration of security solution types effectively integrated, our security and operational capabilities are expanded, creating a new security perimeter framework. If we look at our patch activities, we know if we are good and up-to-date with all our medical devices. If we look at the type of traffic coming into our environment, where we tend to get a lot of email with potential phishing, we have a handle on that. As we look at user behavior, we start to use those data elements from all three security areas together in a tailored way, to become precisely aligned with my company's needs and requirements. That, in turn, raises my security team's effectiveness. That profile for Allina would look very different than it would from a host of other companies in different verticals. We might have different attack vectors; we might have different types of threats. But using those technologies together starts to create a targeted and tailored picture for us, one that is specific to our individual risks and the security needs for our organization. In turn, we address the issue of borderless security.

Recommendations for CISOs new to the challenges of the healthcare industry

I grew up in the GRC (governance, risk management and compliance) space of information security and entered the field around the time of the Sarbanes-Oxley Act. I had been working with consulting firms, such as Accenture, and gained my first exposure to information security practices through the regulatory affairs and compliance space. From there, I transitioned into finance. I've spent most of my career in information security from a finance perspective, running identity and access management programs, GRC programs, and more. My transition into healthcare began with my CISO role at HealthEast, another local Minnesota-based healthcare system. After that I joined Allina, where I've been for about a year and a half. This progression of professional experience provided me with invaluable perspectives, especially having the benefit of a finance background with a strong influence on the strategic approaches and methodologies to information security.

New CISOs should start with the basics in healthcare. If one surveys the history of security in healthcare organizations, they basically have had — for decades — very few security controls, especially on the provider side. My advice for CISOs new to the healthcare vertical is to start with the basics. Start with the things that CISOs should start with in any organization: patching programs, vulnerability management and user access controls. For fundamental high-level security hygiene capabilities, the most effective controls we have are up-to-date patched servers. That's really at the heart of it all. Failure in that essential responsibility was the cause of the 2017 Equifax mega breach. As well, making sure your users are trained and educated to identify phishing, not only in email, but also social engineering attempts over the phone. These are key best practices to ensure fundamental information and organizational security.

The need to recognize healthcare is still catching up in security. From a strategic security perspective in healthcare, CISOs should step back a bit in time, especially if they came from an organization that had advanced security controls, such as the finance industry. For a productive healthcare perspective, CISOs should think about what they might have done about five years ago in finance. That would likely be a good starting point. The second point is that CISOs must understand the true uniqueness of the healthcare provider space. They must understand the way the clinical world works and they must understand how security can either enhance or compromise patient care. That reality is truly unique to our industry.

> **For a productive healthcare perspective, CISOs should think about what they might have done about five years ago in finance. That would likely be a good starting point.**

CISOs' priorities must be aligned with the welfare of the patient first. CISOs can't afford to misunderstand the significance of the clinical realities of their role, nor to underestimate, ignore or undervalue them. It is so much more critical than from a finance perspective. In finance, if there's a security event, and dollars are lost, the organization can usually make a client right. They can make the impacted party whole; they can repay the money. Can they restore identity? Possibly not. But the victim of financial fraud can fundamentally be made whole again in a monetary sense. In healthcare, however, there are too many scenarios where you might not be able to guarantee that wholeness for a patient. If we have security risks and someone is held hostage in their hospital bed, or if someone is connected to a medical device that is compromised, and that device ends up delivering a lethal dose of a drug, you can't necessarily make the afflicted parties right again. You can't recover that patient, or the loss to their family. So, if they think about the healthcare space, CISOs must understand the tremendous responsibility a healthcare security leader has, far beyond other industries.

Aligning with proactive business enablement. With all of this understood, CISOs must maintain these perspectives within the context of their goals and objectives to support the transformation of information security from a reactive type of defense organization, to a proactive business enabler. This is one reason why advanced security analytics holds the key for the future welfare of healthcare organizations.

CONCLUSIONS & TAKEAWAYS:
Catching up and moving beyond with UEBA

Ever since the electronic data standard for healthcare in the U.S. went into full effect in 2014, security teams in the healthcare vertical have been struggling to catch up, while threat actors have capitalized on systemic weaknesses in the industry's defenses. The prize has been healthcare's wealth of sensitive data, invaluable across a range of financial activities. While HIPAA compliance requirements drive assurance of privacy for PII and PHI in healthcare, compliance rarely, if ever, equals security.

Considered to be ahead of the curve in the adoption of strategic healthcare security solutions, Allina Health's goal is to achieve absolute assurance in security, where UEBA provides advanced capabilities for effectively managing an identity's (human or device/entity) access and activity with sensitive data. Integrating innovation in security controls must balance risk management with ease of access for legitimate users, while taking into account the growing challenge of insider threat.

Scandrett describes how Allina — contracted as the designated healthcare support provider for their city's hosting of Super Bowl LII — used UEBA to provide protection and targeted controls for the authorized and unauthorized access to patient information. Recognizing the various scenarios where healthcare insiders might be compelled to circumvent patient privacy of celebrities and other individuals of special interest, was part of the use case development for protecting PII and PHI, as similar use cases apply to other industry verticals.

The emerging ransomware trend of exploiting newer medical devices using older and weaker OSs has created serious vulnerabilities in healthcare security. Scandrett employs UEBA to establish behavior baselines with risk assessments for medical devices to address this rising threat. Expanding capabilities in existing defenses, where the detective strategies must incorporate newer predictive ones, Scandrett leverages UEBA's capabilities beyond the security mandate, as well. Using UEBA to establish behavior baselines with medical devices not only supports risk assessments, but also provides an ability to determine medical device malfunctions with operational utilities in medical device maintenance, which helps avert clinical risk and enhances productivity of medical personnel (doctors, nurses, technicians, etc.).

For next-generation hybrid security, Scandrett sees the seamless fusing of UEBA technology, the advanced malware space, and the range of security analytics solutions, as being key for the comprehensive defense of an organization's environment in the future. And, for the new wave of CISOs in healthcare, it remains critical to start with the basics in security, recognize healthcare is still catching up with other industries, and that their enduring core priority must always place the welfare of the patient first.

The following *Borderless Breach Flashcard* provides a cautionary story about the perils of skipping fundamental best practices when adopting a new cloud solution. This concern is part of the complex world of the hybrid cloud architect, which is the topic of the next chapter. In it, Jairo Orea, with extensive hybrid cloud architecture experience with the Cloud Security Alliance, and UnitedHealth Group, shares his seasoned insights on this topic.

BORDERLESS BREACH FLASHCARD	
One-Click DB Exposure to Rampant Hacking	
CATEGORY	Threat actor exploitation of inadequate NoSQL security settings.
WHO	**The target:** Organizations adopting MondoDB.
WHAT	Organizations using the MongoDB failed to perform due diligence in authentication configuration practices with solution integration leaving their databases (DBs) open to a rash of threat activity. Over 33,000 databases were hacked, soaring ransomware attacks resulted.
WHEN	Summer of 2015 through to today.
WHERE	Globally.
WHY	Inadequate security planning and lack of established best practices.
HOW	With rapid application development and the convenience of plug-and-play and one-click installations, many developers and IT administrators made bad configuration assumptions about MongoDB, a new open source NoSQL database. By ignoring documentation outlining a critical manual configuration ensuring proper security hygiene, they aided malicious activity. Named *MongoDB Ransack,* the attack consisted of hackers capitalizing on an insecure configuration in MongoDB, which by default listens on TCP port 27017. Knowledgeable attackers found the vulnerable data by performing a search with the Shodan search engine, which finds any type of device connected to the internet. This enabled hackers to connect as a privileged user, with heightened access. Serious damage was comparatively easy to inflict on target enterprises.
HOW BAD?	Many cases of entire databases being deleted were reported, followed by ransomware extortion, even though the data couldn't be restored by the hackers. Over 1.1 petabytes of data was exposed due to misconfigured MongoDB databases, which also included additional NoSQL platforms.
HOW COULD IT BE AVOIDED?	The criticality of the cloud architect, developer and administrator roles in any cloud solution adoption cannot be overstated. Applications of prudent planning, best practices and the proper steps for integration into the environment must be assured. Also, if any of the enterprises impacted had a holistic advanced security analytics solution in place, providing a risk-based approach to all the siloes within their hybrid environment, this would not have occurred, especially if automated, closed-loop risk response capability was integrated with authentication.

Hybrid Cloud Environment
Architecture

The identity intersection with horizontal planes in big data, vertical solution silos, blockchain and more

The pressing topic of rethinking security strategy has been a fundamental theme for every contributor throughout this book. Industry analysts and leading security leaders observe how emerging technologies represent a sea change in enhanced and robust productivity, as well as, demanding broad new security requirements. To meet this challenge, an optimal paradigm shift of strategies must be achieved by security leaders and their organizations. As has been observed by earlier contributors, with the advent of the borderless world, old frameworks of on-premises security strategies no longer apply. As more security leaders focus on the cloud, the hybrid cloud, IoT, BYOD, mobility, 24/7 global access, and a wide range of entities and users, CISOs are faced with an overwhelming number of factors that must be taken into account to ensure reliable security in their hybrid environments. Innovation

> **Innovation has drastically changed the security playing field and it compels responsible mindsets to change perspectives. It's sink or swim.**

has drastically changed the security playing field and it compels responsible security professionals to change perspectives. It's sink or swim. Once that change in perspective has occurred, and the right solutions are identified, CISOs must partner closely with chief information security architects to bring it all to fruition.

The core questions CISOs and hybrid environment architects face are: When do you recognize and understand the change and its impact? How do you effectively adjust future plans? Early innovation often shows up in start-up vendors, or as a dynamic new feature within existing solution silos, typically within a year or more on a product roadmap following their initial release. The problem with big data and machine learning analytics solutions, even within the realm of security, is that they do not provide effective or comprehensive value when integrated only within one solution silo. When applied correctly, however, advanced security analytics, driven by mature machine learning, can provide a game changing solution for organizations.

Analyst reports examining advanced security analytics observe the subsets of user and entity behavior analytics (UEBA): identity analytics (IdA), cloud security analytics (CSA), and privileged access analytics (PAA), which represent the broader capabilities sets of this solution class. The vertical silos of traditional security analytics solutions identified by analyst acronyms (i.e., SIEM, IAM, CASB, PAM, DLP, etc.) present a clean, cataloged and organized set of solutions, yet they no longer provide adequate nor effective value on their own. This compartmentalized method of review, sometimes limited only to the specifics of UEBA standalone applications, compromises the ability to recognize the full potential and impact of the entire innovation set of advanced security analytics. The comprehensive capabilities of these types of advanced security analytic solutions — available as a vendor agnostic platform — provide holistic risk-based visibility of access and activity across an enterprise's entire environment, for on-premises and the cloud. The need for an advanced security analytics platform delivering this breadth of capability rises every day. Hybrid security architects, meanwhile, grapple with the need for flexible solutions that accommodate the perpetual evolution of technology within their environments.

Here's the all-too-familiar challenge today within an enterprise's hybrid environment: How do machine learning models share analytics between a SIEM (security information and event management) vendor solution, an IAM (identity access management) solution, and a CASB (cloud access security broker) solution? A use case in point is privileged access abuse, requiring all three of these vendor solutions to interoperate within a hybrid environment. Forrester notes there are more than 50 vendors in its SUBA (security user behavior analytics) report, demonstrating the breadth of the

> ...*critical influencing factors such as hacker innovation taking advantage of the resultant security gaps are constantly evolving in substantive ways, at light speed.*

innovation, variety of vendor choice, and the impacted solution silos. Gartner, meanwhile, considers behavior analytics as a mainstay of UEBA which only lightly ties in with IAM and CASB via machine learning. Beyond the compartmentalized views of respected analysts and analyst organizations, however, there remains an urgent need to recognize the emerging realities of sprawling and unincorporated security data silos which are a growing problem, which should become an essential part of CISO thinking going forward. In addition, critical factors such as hacker innovations, taking advantage of the resultant security gaps, are constantly evolving in substantive ways, at light speed. (See Chapter 8, *Big Data in Advanced Security Analytics*, for more information on the wider range of data silos beyond the SIEM/IAM/CASB example discussed here.)

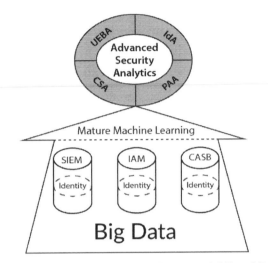

Horizontal Intersection of Big Data and Siloed Identity
Figure 12.1

The reality recognized by forward-looking CISOs and hybrid security architects is that big data is a horizontal plane where its volume and variety provide supportive context for machine learning models, enabling them to deliver meaningful analytics. This leads us to the concept of 'data democracy', enabled by vendor solutions with API access to data, and is not restricted in its utility to a single siloed solution. Without this context, the customer is held hostage from anything but isolated analytic value. SaaS (software as a service) applications also need a standard API with a reasonable SLA (service level agreement), and the Cloud Security Alliance provides the best model for that. CSOs and CISOs, in partnership with hybrid security architects, must first inventory key data sources to feed machine learning algorithms to produce analytics, and to validate all vendor solutions' feeds and the access to them. This may also include the use of bidirectional APIs to enable automated risk response.

Closer examination of behavior analytics underscores another critical horizontal plane that must be acknowledged: identity. Analyzing the access and activity of a user for their accounts and entitlements is ground zero for predictive risk scoring. Activity alone fails to provide enough context and visibility for useful security analytics. The gap between activity and access must be closed to evaluate risk. CROs (chief risk officers) understand this issue and now demand risk scoring down to the entitlement level. They understand, as well, the critical importance of uncovering hidden and unknown privileged access through IdA, and thus what activity to analyze for access abuse. What good is an IAM solution that isolates access rights data and prevents its analysis, which must then be combined with activity data for risk-based assessments by machine learning models? Gaps may appear between the different focus areas of CIOs and CISOs, such as how they view identity and access management data, especially when security teams may be performing analyses at cross purposes in separate silos and exposing the conflicts between them.

> *Activity alone fails to provide enough context and visibility for useful security analytics. The gap between activity and access must be closed to evaluate risk.*

Using separate vertical solution siloes for big data and analytics is dysfunctional, as the most effective solutions involve maintaining a holistic horizontal plane perspective. This approach has not yet been adopted by the majority of CISOs and CIOs. Early adopters have discovered the advantages of migrating to big data lakes in order to store data for long-term value at the lowest cost. To maximize that benefit, analytics should then be run on top of customer-selected big data lakes to avoid reading and storing the data more than once. As a targeted example of this widespread challenge, separate SIEM, IAM and CASB solutions provide data inputs to a data lake while receiving analytic responses with risk scores working on a horizontal plane. Customer adoption for a solution silo should not restrict the machine learning analytics available, nor should data be held hostage within closed solutions.

In the past few years, more than 90% of all data in existence has been generated. We've entered a dynamic new era, where environments struggle with rapidly expanding quantity of digital exhaust, where the analysis of online behavior can reveal identity, access risks, unknown threats, and integrity issues through machine learning models, but only if security leaders have a horizontal and holistic view of the contextual data. With that perspective in mind, CISOs and hybrid environment architects must seek advanced security analytics platforms that can accommodate all these requirements. These platforms must be able to optimally mesh UEBA, IdA, CSA and PAA together, with vendor agnostic efficiencies, across the entire multi-siloed hybrid environment, to deliver holistic visibility and risk-based analytics.

Additional security innovations are available across the landscape of hybrid security. Hybrid environment architects must evaluate their capabilities and impact to ensure they can be configured and integrated into the correct array of impactful solutions that maximize the security they provide. As well, these solutions must be able to scale and grow within their environments. As they do, an amplified focus on integrity has occurred — one of the core pillars of information security's CIA triad (confidentiality, integrity and availability). Going forward, solutions being adopted must now have heightened capabilities to ensure this key attribute. Some solutions have roots in an earlier generation of network security, while others have emerged more recently, and their importance and value

> "...these solutions must be able to scale and grow within their environments. As they do, a heightened focus on integrity has occurred – one of the core pillars of information security's CIA triad (confidentiality, integrity and availability)."

continue to expand. Solutions with origins in earlier technologies, yet which continue to be effective today, include: file integrity monitoring (FIM), network segmentation and containerization. A more recent technology, which is still actively evolving in its utility, is blockchain.

File integrity monitoring. While not undergoing any drastic innovative technology change since it first appeared on the networking scene in the early 1990's, where it was originally employed for Sarbanes-Oxley (SOX) certifications, FIM continues to maintain its relevancy as a critical security component due to its fundamental functionality. This solution offers an internal control that validates the integrity of both data and application software files. It does so by providing verification between the current file status and a known, true baseline. This comparison method traditionally entails a calculation of a known cryptographic checksum of the file's original baseline and compares it with the checksum of the current file under review. File integrity monitoring is automated and can be performed randomly, at defined intervals, or in real-time. Discovering changes in integrity is key, since those changes may be indicators of a breach in progress. A range of file attribute changes may also be included in integrity monitoring. Those categories include: credentials, privileges and security settings, content, core attributes and size, hash values or configuration values.

Network segmentation. Early examples of network segmentation appeared as the demilitarized zones (DMZs) to establish security buffers to isolate internal enterprise resources from the internet. This provided an increased security for assets requiring a higher level of protection. As requirements expanded with the advent of the cloud, this solution evolved to offer 'defense in depth', with zones or internal enclaves — groupings of similar resources or data — within the datacenter for web, application and data servers, as well as production facilities and the entire enterprise environment. This enhanced separation of zones allows specific operation and communication through them while ensuring proper security capabilities. A best practice in creating zones to protect data is to base their creation on data sensitivity, rather than by organization, and to avoid the reflex to over-segment into zones.

Two critical areas of emerging priorities include:

- ***Software defined and virtualized data centers*** – Mobile and temporary servers, with infrastructure as a server (IaaS), software defined networking (SDN) and network function virtualization (NFV), all challenge original datacenter network designs. They require robust capabilities to manage constantly evolving complexities from an organizational and operational perspective. This includes microservices that drive more ad hoc communications and east-west traffic between same-tiered servers.

- ***Advanced threat sophistication*** – Single safeguards no longer ensure security. With multi-vector attacks on the rise, and strategies of execution becoming far more varied to accommodate deeper threat defense, greater sophistication and separation of critical assets and activities is required.

Other areas driving requirements for network segmentation in hybrid environments include global and merged operations, where enterprises expand into new regional locations, or mergers with new organizations, create new complexities. While vital to enterprises, OT (operational technology) and IoT devices represent a risk and need appropriate segmentation. PCI compliance necessitates credit

> *...areas driving requirements for network segmentation in hybrid environments include global and merged operations, where enterprises expand into new regional locations, or mergers with new organizations, create new complexities.*

card and payment data to be isolated from the rest of the enterprise network to ensure adherence to compliance certification requirements.

Containerization. A solution for end-to-end container security, and machine-learning-based application containerization, is a virtualization method to run distributed applications without the need to launch an entire virtual machine (VM) for each application. It runs at the operating system level. Multiple isolated systems are run on a single control host. Automation and threat intelligence are component elements of this flavor of microservices security. Operative areas include:

- ***Access control*** – This functionality defines and enforces policies governing user access to native orchestration engine tools.

- ***Security analytics and vulnerability management*** – The capability to scan container images for vulnerabilities in code errors and misconfigurations is critical. Vulnerabilities may exist in application frameworks, customer application packages, registries, development workstations or on production servers. The scanning tasks are integrated with existing processes to enforce standard configurations, employ best practices and utilize optimal deployment templates to facilitate compliance with industry or company policies.

- **_Runtime risk defense_** – Monitoring activities for anomalies and policy violations, this functionality protects containers against exploits, compromises, program mistakes and configuration errors, plus facilitates remediation.

Blockchain. As the volume of data and transactions expand within the digital world, the concern over the potential for manipulation rises. Maintenance of the master record of events by a 'trusted' third party to monitor and curb data manipulation has fundamental limitations. Unregulated fee inflation of the third parties, non-compatible controls, and the threat of the third party being a target for manipulation, are serious concerns for judicious security leaders. Eschewing the singular nodal approach, blockchain is a paradigm shift in security perspective, engaging an open

> *...blockchain is a paradigm shift in security perspective, engaging an open and public network collective of digital checks and balances, to assure the veracity of a transaction.*

and public network collective of digital checks and balances, to assure the veracity of a transaction.

A blockchain solution consists of an interlocked string — a chain — of blocks, each of which contains records of a transaction between peers on a network. The blocks are created sequentially with each transaction, and linked to a preceding transaction through a series of cryptographic hashes that function like a signature. Any transaction occurring within a blockchain network is visible to all members of that network. Each can verify the transaction's validity against a collective trusted history.

Organizations use blockchain for data or application integration, as well as, management of databases, records, identity and business processes. The strength of a blockchain solution is that it's the network-defined truth — the distributed ledger of transaction records. It does not reside in a central location, nor is it controlled by a single party. A blockchain solution offers capabilities to provide an open, public, immutable ledger of transaction history. Each instance has its own unique and easily verifiable signature which resides on a transaction network which is quite difficult to manipulate. The challenge is there are many vendors (over 70 at the time of this writing) on the market, each with its own strengths and weaknesses, where no leader has yet emerged to define the gold standard.

Similar to other solutions, hybrid security architects face a host of options, choices and possibilities for blockchain technology. All of this must be assessed, accepted, and finally configured within their hybrid environments to produce a seamless array of security that incorporates all solution categories mentioned above, in an optimal manner, and likely more. This includes assuring holistic identity, activity monitoring and access management using a risk-based approach and leveraging big data for context with machine learning. With that, the goal of ensuring comprehensive configuration and integration of all security solutions within a hybrid environment, and having them all perform optimally, is a first priority.

Deeply involved with the Cloud Security Alliance, Jairo Orea is an accomplished hybrid security architect and CISO with the Fortune 500 company, Kimberly-Clark. He shares his hands-on insights about the security challenges and innovations within hybrid environment architecture in the following section of this chapter.

BORDERLESS EXPERT INSIGHTS

Jairo Orea *
CISO, Kimberly-Clark

Jairo Orea is currently the Chief Information Security Officer at Kimberly-Clark. He previously held roles as Chief Information Security Architect and VP, of Security Consulting at UnitedHealth Group (a Fortune 10 company); Chief Information Security Architect at ING; Head of Data Management and CISO at ING Insurance. Orea holds master's degrees in Information Technology and Business Administration (ITAM, Mexico) and Networking and Information Systems for Business (ENST, France). He also has a bachelor's degree in Robotics and Information Technology Management from the University of Atemajac Valley, Mexico. Orea was awarded Harvard Business Journal's Top 40 under 40 Years of Age (2005), University of Atemajac Valley's Award to Professional Merit (2007), and Latin America Information Security Professionals Executive of the Year (2004). In addition to his current position, Jairo serves as Chief Architect for the Trusted Cloud Initiative (Cloud Security Alliance), Education Director for the ISSA CT chapter, Board Member for the Latin America Information Security Professionals Association, Microsoft CISO Council, and the Wall Street Security Council. He is also the founder of the Security Architecture Forum, along with being involved with other boards.

Overview

As Orea compares cloud and on-premises security, he notes the importance of holistically incorporating numerous and disparate vertically siloed solutions to assure comprehensive security. Orea then analyzes the architectural factors driving successful cloud adoption, which includes application containerization, microservices security and the acceleration of services rollout through the use of templates (also known as 'patternization'). He then goes on to explain the phases in cloud and hybrid environment adoption. Success in this arena demands a critical understanding of the interrelationships of the core elements within the hybrid Triad schema which are: data, identity and infrastructure (also known as the construct). The key to security success is in managing identity and its evolution within the emerging security perimeter of the hybrid cloud. Pulling the elements of the Triad together requires incorporating user and entity behavior analytics, identity analytics and leveraging the force multiplier of machine learning in big data, all of which represent advanced security analytics. Orea then observes the expansion of the developer's role in hybrid cloud environments and importance of optimizing cloud adoption with proven best practices. He also notes,

---

* The views and opinions expressed by Jairo Orea in this book are his own, and do not necessarily reflect those of his current, or any of his previous employers.

with caution, the critical influence of developers and their 'one click' empowerment in cloud services development, as well as noting the expansion of self-service capabilities in cloud development.

The impact of mobility on data access for cloud and hybrid architecture is a growing concern, along with the expanding scale of data. Emerging hybrid security strategies must also implement closer controls on data to account for structured and unstructured data security requirements. Included in these observations, Orea explores the disappearance of the perimeter and the demand for a progressive security strategy. This includes supporting the need for evolving controls and segregation as a fundamental access security requirement in hybrid architecture. With this in mind, and the objective of protecting the data, the critical importance of understanding behavior on a holistic scale is essential for a successful security strategy.

Acknowledging that identity is the new threat plane, Orea observes that part of successful security planning in hybrid architecture must holistically address personal identity, as well as service and system IDs, in hybrid cloud security. Only with this accounted for, is effective threat behavior analytics possible. Orea discusses the role of IAM and identity analytics in a hybrid environment and the need for federated application access, along with holistic risk-based monitoring of identities, across all silos in an organization's environment. He then examines hybrid environment elements beyond data, identity and infrastructure. Orea discusses information services domain's central management for security and then delves into the establishment of the right identity access controls and the complexities of privilege management issuance. Privileged access requires a two-tiered perspective which must also incorporate insight into the complex realities of cloud tenancy. Orea then calls out the criticality for internal development groups to align with security patterns and how innovations in development require new patterns, or templates.

Noting the role of API's with cloud security brokers and other elements of hybrid infrastructure, Orea underscores the need to understand the impact on the environment of different firewalls to facilitate the consolidation of hybrid cloud elements. Part of this involves the proper selection of compatible service components in the Triad while taking into account the scale of enterprises and the impact of cloud innovations. Some of these innovations include the ubiquitous controls on data, evolving automated risk response capabilities, database brokers with application firewall controls, along with application decoupling and structureless code. Looking forward, Orea highlights the goals of software defining a single security perimeter and the need for a convergence of development groups and security. Part of this perspective also includes insights into the future of IT security, technology acceleration's impact on security groups, as well as the evolutionary nature of the security professional's mandate.

Comparing cloud and on-premises security

The debate continues over comparing solution frameworks and the effectiveness of cloud versus on-premises security. On-premises infrastructure was not designed to control or enable services from anywhere to anywhere. The only security presence for the data on-premises is that which exists in the physical environment before it goes out into the cloud. Beyond that space it's a different world. In the past, the focus for security in the on-premises world was more on the preventative side because that's where more controls over the environment were integrated. Then, you could prevent a wide array of threats. With the inside locked down, security leaders could be more confident. Now, with the advent of the cloud, that's no longer the case.

A perspective incorporating numerous vertical models. Earlier in my career, while performing security consulting, while also serving as a chief information security architect, I created a database reference architecture for the Cloud Security Alliance (CSA) which is used by several Fortune 500 organizations. This gave me a critical exposure to the needs and requirements of the healthcare industry, and it also drew from my background in the financial services and software development industries. Contrary to a prevalent perception in the security community, the takeaway from my interaction with these different vertical industries was that, at times, the cloud environment may be significantly more advanced than many organization's on-premises environments.

Demonstrable maturity of cloud service controls. Cloud providers have evolved dramatically to allow organizations seamless management of their environment with a high degree of maturity in their technology. Enterprises can adopt a cloud services provider that may offer a fixed 'security as a service' plan, with a certification of their environment, that provides an adequate control level for an organization's operation. Many of these cloud solutions are certified with ISO (International Organization for Standardization) controls, delivering high trust in addition to supporting SOX (Sarbanes-Oxley) controls. These cloud providers offer maturity in their services that deliver a spectrum of features that can be used by an enterprise. They may be even more mature than a well-established enterprise's own environment.

Cloud security design, beyond general features, defines value. The cloud ecosystem is designed to allow the necessary functional interoperability to make it as sturdy and secure as is generally needed at the application layer, the virtual machine layer, as well as the construct, or infrastructure layer. Yet customized security controls, accounting for the unique requirements of each

> It's the successful adoption and integration of specific elements... of solution design that define the quality of cloud security as it measures up against the... traditional on-premises environments.

organization, are usually needed for comprehensive prevention of compromise. Therefore, the prospect of cloud security is simply different. Cloud is generally not necessarily more secure than on-premises. It's all about the hybrid architect's approach to making the environment secure. Most often, attackers come from the inside, whether it's legitimate insiders, or attackers posing as them. However, if the cloud component is designed correctly, it can be more secure than on-premises. It's the successful adoption and integration of specific elements and nuances of solution design that define the quality of cloud security as it measures up against the more monolithic framework of traditional on-premises environments.

Architectural factors driving successful cloud adoption

The main drivers for most global enterprises are to consolidate infrastructure and standardize platforms across the organization. As competitive pressures increase, companies should enable and empower their developers as the enterprise expands services. This translates into opportunity costs for IT and the host organization. From the infrastructure implementation perspective, the server architecture, application architecture, and the network architecture, must all utilize patterns or templates to optimize adoption efficiencies. When global companies standardize on cloud-based services, it translates into faster deployed services and provides redundancies that facilitate quicker access to compute in the cloud. The main architectural drivers for a successful cloud adoption also include application containerization (which I also refer to as 'patternization'). This provides a foundation for one approach to addressing the requirements of a hybrid environment architect.

Application containerization in microservices security. Application containerization is a virtualization method to run distributed applications without the need to launch an entire virtual machine (VM) for each application. A solution for end-to-end container security, it runs at the operating system level and is machine-learning-based. Multiple isolated systems are run on a single control host. Automation and threat intelligence are component elements of this type of microservices security. Application containerization is required to ensure security at the

> *Application containerization is required to ensure security at the broad range of user endpoints that proliferate in an expanding cloud environment.*

broad range of user endpoints that proliferate in an expanding cloud environment.

Acceleration of services rollout through patternization. Patternization means the ability to develop patterns or templates that accelerate the rollout of services. This involves identifying the capabilities of an organization's technologies portfolio — what they use in the cloud. Best practices should be developed from this patternization, which include integrating security and resiliency into the templates or patterns. Once achieved, the delivery of solution components into a given service for the enterprise is simplified, optimized and accelerated.

Status of technology stack standardization impacts TCO. Standardization of the technology stack, acceleration using existing patterns or templates, and leveraging industry knowledge around enabling these services, are key elements for cloud adoption success. Many times, the technology stack provided by the main cloud providers also includes a large professional community of qualified developers. This is in contrast with many legacy platforms where the increased complexity and diversity in the technology stack translates to higher TCO (total cost of ownership). This community, along with containerization and standardization, means faster and more efficient deployment of a new service, which drives more effective TCO for the enterprise.

Volume of cloud provider adoptions streamlines technology. Another factor of successful cloud adoption is how the influence of supply and demand comes into play. As more organizations adopt, and successive versions of cloud solutions mature, their technological advancements facilitate increased reliability, along with ease of implementation. Then, organizations need effective management of these solutions which also includes assuring how security requirements translate into the overall environment. Here, the traditional framework of security thinking must change. A critical consideration on this topic is the vanishing security perimeter, which must now be holistically accounted for within a new and evolving security paradigm.

Optimizing cloud adoption with proven best practices. While the capability of elasticity and on-demand compute power allows organizations to expand and contract as needed, this can only be optimally achieved when expert recommendations and best practices are applied. Only then can organizations effectively balance the cost versus the benefit. One reason compute power might be challenging is if developers need to substantiate various services. That may quickly become a serious challenge, so the factor of elastic compute power represents a main driver. Many companies have decided they don't need to continue to develop traditional data centers because they're going entirely into the cloud. This facilitates reducing challenges in data center management through the use of cloud service provider capabilities, so organizations can focus on their substantial application architecture requirements.

Collaboration within organizations required for cloud adoption success. To make security controls persistent, out to the endpoints of an infrastructure, requires a sense of partnership and business alignment within the organization, especially with investment commitment for the capabilities needed to deploy across the enterprise. All these participating organizational elements are

> *...it is the unique characteristics and needs of each group within an organization that must be taken into account for a secure hybrid environment.*

essential for success. So, while the cloud was generally designed with common organizational requirements in mind, it is the unique characteristics and needs of each group within an organization that must be taken into account for a secure hybrid environment. As a result, ensuring holistic security really depends on the practitioner, the hybrid environment architect, in partnership with the CISO, CIO, and their teams, as well as other groups within the enterprise.

Business requirements creating potential new threat planes. If a lesser skilled practitioner is going into the cloud, hoping to have instant security, it won't happen. While the cloud provider has certain responsibilities, traditionally described in their SLA (service level agreement), the tenant is accountable for whatever they create in the construct. While the provider will deliver the cloud computing fabric, tenants must take care of their own constructs, or anything they create inside them. With new variables created by an organization's business requirements, new risk sectors are created, without bad or malicious intent, but which represent a serious threat plane that must be addressed. The 'one click' empowerment of hybrid cloud developers, discussed later in this chapter, is one element of this concern.

Phases in cloud and hybrid environment adoption

The first phase of hybrid cloud adoption begins with a clear understanding of what the organization wants the cloud solution to do for them. From there, organizations need to first tie their different requirements to the type of provider offering the best match to fulfill those needs and the most mature adoption tool to achieve that.

Due diligence and standardization before adoption. Once an organization understands the drivers taking them to the cloud, they must choose the right provider. A process should be in place that ensures the provider can deliver the services as originally represented. Once done, the hybrid architect, with his or her team, must make sure they become deeply familiarized with the provider's environment. They should establish, from the beginning, a standardization process for cloud orchestration and governance tools to assure the organization can maintain a reliable inventory of solution components which interoperate seamlessly.

Streamlined adoption efficiencies through established patterns. When cloud providers speak with prospective customers, they often ask: "How will you control the consumption of the cloud?" They know if organizations are not careful, within months, the adopting enterprise can experience robust and unplanned cloud usage patterns. Hybrid architects must be cautious about this possibility and establish the right guardrails for the process to facilitate their developers so they can migrate safely to the cloud. This

> *When cloud providers speak with prospective customers, they often ask: "How will you control the consumption of the cloud?"*

traditionally entails providing an orchestration platform, and making sure cloud brokers are integrated to extract and enable patterns to facilitate collection and connecting the dots between the different sources. This involves optimizing the holistic integration of the data, all aspects of the identity, as well as comprehensive insights and controls on the constructs.

Focus on storage and bandwidth consumption. Organizations may migrate from private to public clouds. In doing so, the developers may adopt CDM (Continuous Diagnostics and Migration) applications to safely enable more content. This content is expensive to host because the bandwidth consumption and storage are pushed onto the cloud. Here developers must become familiarized with these cost factors of cloud adoption, which contrast with traditional infrastructure. As developers gain a better understanding of the types of cloud components and create an informed adoption architecture, along with patterns within, they are able to more confidently ensure the choice and optimization of the right kind of cloud services.

Ensuring tight integration of key elements in the cloud environment. Most importantly three key elements must be integrated seamlessly: identity, infrastructure and data. Identity should be managed by the organization, possibly with a SaaS provider, with an identity broker for the cloud. For infrastructure, the governance platform often requires enabling secondary controls partnered with developers. These partnerships consist of the security teams and infrastructure teams collaborating with the development community. All of these efforts are integrated to ensure optimal utility and security of the primary element: the data.

The hybrid cloud's Triad perimeter framework and the evolution of identity in the emerging security perimeter

While a number of hybrid environment architects still see only two perimeters in the hybrid cloud environment, the reality of a third has been gaining deeper and expanded recognition within the discipline. Identity is the new perimeter. Without this key element integrated properly, any security framework for risk is incomplete. The three perimeters form a triad of sorts.

Data security priorities in the cloud. Traditionally, the first perimeter has been the data access element, which requires a collection of specific controls. This includes data controls tied to privileged information, the most sensitive data. CISOs and hybrid architects need to identify where the crown jewels are, so they can properly prioritize their solution objectives to ensure their security. Security leaders, however, cannot ensure protection of everything on the cloud and must choose their battles. They can change controls; they can have fewer application controls used by the organization for the cloud. Yet they must still maintain those controls, or raise the bar on the controls for the data, to bring the controls as close to the data as possible.

Identity security priorities in the cloud. The second, and emerging, critical element in this new triad framework for the matrix of cloud controls, is identity. This encompasses all data and the full access of the data, where identity is the cornerstone for prudent security hygiene. Security planners must understand who has the identity. This means in some cases, whoever the entity is that owns the identity, will also 'own' the ecosystem as a threat plane. As a result, organizations must be cautious regarding who owns the identity being used for developing new operational constructs on the cloud. For example, if an organization has been hosting an inter-cloud environment, where services have been consolidated over a number of years, this will create a challenge, because new identities may have proliferated. Hybrid architects must determine how they will maintain a lean approach for identity so they don't propagate these through their directory. Security planners will also require better controls for understanding access and activity with the person-to-person identities, the personal IDs, as well as, behaviors of service IDs or system IDs. These types of machine-to-machine IDs must be accounted for in comprehensive advanced security analytics.

> *Hybrid architects must determine how they will maintain a lean approach for identity so they don't propagate these through their directory.*

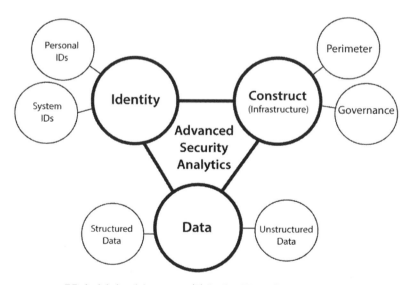

Hybrid Architecture Triad – Key Components
Figure 12.2

Construct security priorities in the cloud. The third element of the Triad is the construct, or infrastructure element. When organizations go to a hybrid environment they often need a cloud broker. Yet there will be certain shared services that will not make sense to place with the cloud provider. These may need to be created somewhere in the internal environment, or delivered by a third party that can tap into the same presence within the cloud provider. These solutions can enable identity services so organizations obtain each element of key cyber defense controls they require.

The criticality of understanding elemental interrelationships in the Triad. The Triad concept, with security for the construct, for the data, and for identity, represents an essential planning framework for hybrid architects. Connecting the three of them, with identity as the cornerstone, sustains the structural architecture of security. It's important to maintain a high level of conceptualization for this model to understand how security gets impacted or altered. Understanding the interrelationships within the Triad helps security leaders in planning for the evolving needs of their environment.

Advanced security analytics at the core of cloud security. Knowing how all these components are interrelated within their collective context, and equipped with the right metadata, enables CISOs to detect abuse when it's happening, and also define what type of portfolio of controls they need for their multiple siloed identities. Forward-looking CISOs and hybrid architects recognize that big data is a horizontal plane intersecting all the identities within separate silos, such as SIEM, IAM and CASBs. Without mature machine learning drawing context from big data through advanced security analytics at the core, it's not possible to gain, maintain and utilize the entire critical context from these silos. The scale is simply too vast for humans to manage, no matter how many resources are committed to the challenge.

The expanding role of developers in hybrid cloud environments

From a traditional perspective, organizations must add elements of resiliency into the application layer. This allows them to reduce costs and expand the opportunity to empower developers. Hybrid environment architects see models emerging within DevOps because developers' work is having an increasingly direct impact on the organizational infrastructure. As developers enable services, they create everything they need, from the user story, to the network, and even to the security components. While all that code is originally written to set up independent environments, developers must, at the same time, maintain these separate environments to interoperate effectively with many different areas across IT.

The 'one click' empowerment in cloud services development. An emerging concern that's having a significant impact on new cloud architecture is where a solution architect can be enabled with a single click. This factor, originating from a single source, can have a wide-reaching effect on the environment. This capability empowers them to focus more on developing reusable components and a framework of capabilities beyond the typical solutions. With this

> *An emerging concern... is where a solution architect can be enabled with a single click. This... can have a wide-reaching effect on the environment...*

streamlined ability to assemble architectural components, they can create a shell to support a key set of services. To achieve that, they establish and select service elements that are foundational for their cloud requirements and ones needing to be defined by niche requirements within the enterprise. The concern is that while this method of empowered and swift automation can deliver important improvements; it may also create unintended and unwanted complications.

Expanding self-service capabilities in cloud development. As hybrid environment architects review a cloud service's existing catalog, they identify whatever supplemental services are required and these in turn become part of the needs list from a development perspective. Developers, in turn, concentrate on creating more self-service elements and capabilities for the cloud which can operate as code or work directly through the API, and up through the GUI. This trend reveals how support programs and the expectations around support have changed. In the past, whenever a robust solution was offered by a vendor, it came with the presumption that a strong and comprehensive support organization would be behind that solution or product. Now, it's self-service along with an expectation that the user should be able to do almost everything on their own. While there may be cases where a user might engage live support, this is more outside the norm than it used to be.

Variances in developer utility profiles. Developers can utilize configuration management services, but the organization must contain the selection of technologies they use. Along with that, they should enable the tools inside the technologies to facilitate the necessary patterns or templates, or the recipes, they work with. This model is generally effective for 95% of the developers in the hybrid cloud environment. Yet not all developer profiles are the same. For example, if a developer is working in a DevOps model, this places them with the other 5%, the innovators. That 5% of developers may have to create new services. If they do, it is usually possible to create shared recipes. In doing so, they should implement the right configuration on the assets they need to be using for security. For example, they should be using the organization's predefined, multi-zoned templates for firewalls.

Priorities of cloud development focus. These trends reinforce the understanding that organizations must invest their developer's engineering talent in a solution to facilitate an experience where customers can directly jump into the solution and be effective on day one. There must not be too steep a learning curve required in new platform solutions offered to customers.

The impact of data access for cloud and mobility in hybrid architecture

Security architects are overseeing and managing a revolutionary paradigm shift in priorities for addressing the new evolving risk and threat plane in their hybrid environments. Originally, all security solutions were created with the traditional on-premises perimeter in mind. It was something of an eggshell approach, with a hard perimeter and a soft inside. Anything inside was secure and anything outside was the wild world. The perimeter strategy was all about continually striving to fortify it, to make it thicker, stronger, and bigger. Now, with cloud and mobility, that concept has been diluted, and even more so with the Internet of Things (IoT).

> Security architects are overseeing and managing a revolutionary paradigm shift in their priorities...

The new normal in hybrid environments. With the cloud, mobility and IoT, we're now putting things on the network that were originally never designed to be there. This adds a concerning factor to any comprehensive security solution strategy, where some security leaders are patching in ad hoc solutions to address the immediate need as they see it. As a result, the risk aspect becomes excessive. The evolving challenges and the diminishing effectiveness of these feature-based point solutions grow apart, lacking a platform strategy, leaving serious security gaps and a widening threat plane.

The expanding scale of data. Considering the limitations of feature-based point solutions, when security architects assess the prospect of thousands of servers, and the reality of millions of endpoints and millions of IP addresses, the issue of scalability presents considerable challenges in security. It represents a sprawling amount of growing data. The most realistic method security architects see to manage this kind of volume is with machine learning. Human resources cannot manage this any longer, and the gaps in security effectiveness will only grow with adherence to status quo strategies. As the security perimeter's disintegration progresses, becoming increasingly porous, and the volume of data continues to rise, security architects in hybrid environments see the urgency for integrating holistic and efficient platform solutions to keep up with this challenge. Many seek the most effective next-generation approach for their unique environments; the majority sees a machine learning approach as the best option for their security strategy.

The perimeter: Security strategy evolution. By necessity, the concept of the perimeter has evolved significantly for security architects. They recognize that scale, data access, and the eroding perimeter, are all directly related. One critical component of being successful in protecting the hybrid environment requires 'control persistency'. Controls must be placed much closer to the data. This requirement is complicated by a range of perimeter elements, because of the need to get controls closer to the data for each instance. Not only do controls need to get closer to the data, but also especially closer to the sensitive information, to ensure that controls are persistent. In addition, mobility and the IoT escalate the complexity of this requirement, as users or developers may access the environment from smart devices, 24/7, from anywhere. That accentuates a challenge when the original controls were primarily based on the physical on-premises perimeter. CISOs have to review the desired policies for each perimeter, with each type of supporting control, and then migrate, adapt and match them into the cloud.

Evolving controls needed. Security leaders must also ensure that their matching data controls will grow with the data itself, which is the essence of control persistency. Regardless of connector, disconnector, on the cloud, on-premises, in the hybrid model, private cloud, public cloud, it doesn't matter. Those controls should persist in the environment of the data, no matter where that data resides and be independently resilient to protect that data. That is a primary objective for the concept of control persistency.

> " Security leaders must also ensure that their matching data controls will grow with the data itself, which is the essence of control persistency. "

Factors influencing hybrid architectural planning. Security architects must consider many issues as they relate to widespread global data access. Even though data is stored on certified cloud environments, it's not enough protection, because the perimeter is fundamentally gone. Employee owned devices, microservices, or cloud services like Box, are factors intensifying the porous nature of the perimeter. With these types of services, where users can exchange data, collaborating with each other, doing that with millions of records on their smartphones or tablets, multiplies the potential access risk and threat plane to sobering proportions. Compounding the challenge is a growing percentage of data that resides in cloud environments owned by parties other than the enterprise.

Segregation: A fundamental access security requirement in hybrid architecture. The first objective, regarding data access security architecture planning, is to ensure there is an ability to segregate who has access to what data, and where the data resides. To guarantee the quality of segregation for environments may require having contextual controls for the type of user or entity accessing the data. This could address a regular user, a service, a service ID, or a system ID, fixing the large amounts of data. In addition, security architects should to be able to monitor security patterns for those users and entities, so they can identify when something atypical from their established behavior patterns has occurred. This could possibly be malicious, necessitating the need to ensure SOCs are able to respond in an effective and timely manner. As a result, the need for a new generation of advanced security analytics or identity threat analytics, drawing from big data, with machine learning to gain critical context for behavior, is plainly apparent to a growing number of forward-looking security architects.

Privileged access: A two-tiered perspective. Especially in the cloud environment, security architects must think on two levels for privileged access. Privileged access has a construct level, where an enterprise's developers create services, along with what IT is implementing and modeling in the cloud or with the cloud services provider. In addition, the controls for privileges of

> *These controls must also comprehensively account for data access for users with privileged access entitlements beyond the administrators in an organization.*

the administrators at the application level for the cloud service must be accounted for. These kinds of controls should enable the kinds of usage where the administrators can access from the host, or virtual machines, and initiate a memory dump as required for their various roles and requirements. These controls must also comprehensively account for data access for users with privileged access entitlements beyond the administrators in an organization. This is why verifying controls closer and closer to protecting the data is critical. Gaining those controls contextually for the users, depending on the type of user, will help to mitigate the potential security risks in the cloud.

Complex realities of cloud tenancy. Security architects are especially concerned about the implications of operating in a multitenancy environment. They must contend with this new normal condition of being a tenant in an environment, where they don't own the infrastructure. They are responsible for knowing who accesses the enterprise's data in this environment, knowing that the data is encrypted, and at times, depersonalized as required. A number of technologies support this requirement, which include key management, or indexing the data in a way that involves tokenizing the data, so that the core records, the PII (personal identifiable information), are rendered unusable. This makes the rest of the data irrelevant because only the application and the end user will understand how those elements are connected within the tokenization of their data. But the main focus is to have those controls as close as possible to the data. Additional security control elements may also be needed. Multifactor access from many cloud providers will deliver data controls from within their ecosystems, delivering additional context for behavioral analytics.

Closer controls on data and the impact on cloud environment effectiveness

There are several elements associated with establishing closer controls on data. The first involves depersonalizing sensitive data, such as PII, in a way that is scrambled. This is possible with an indexing service tying the depersonalization to the real records. An alternative option involves employing a tokenization solution. Even when the volume of data increases, the data attributes, the PII data, and the data thread itself, are now protected inside the barriers within the environment. One of the fundamentally constraining factors at the enterprise level is

> " Even when the volume of data increases, the data attributes, the PII data, and that data thread itself, are now protected inside the barriers within the environment. "

that CISOs tend to encrypt data in the SIEM as a strategy to support the security required for the data use, and in some cases, for the file system realm. Now, forward-leaning CISOs and hybrid environment architects are exploring elevating that capability to enable the necessary encryption controls for data in transit.

Data encryption objectives. The operative concept in these security controls is that only legitimate individuals who should see the data, will be able to see it. In reverse, this entails decrypting the data, or using a token, to decode the indexing of the actual record they need. This requires a specific set of keys to access the data. Meanwhile, if the data itself gets compromised, it's useless to the attacker if they don't have the actual keys for the data.

Structured and unstructured data security requirements. Another example, relating to structured data that resides in a fixed field within a record or a file, is the need to maintain logging and monitoring wherever and whenever this data is accessed. This includes examples such as employee salary information, which is important to keep protected. With unstructured data, controls are available for data such as sales files with millions of records that can be accessed from vaults through a variety of endpoints, such as on a smart device that allows the secure use of this data with specially designed control services. Organizations can enable the controls and encryption for sensitive data along with authentication capabilities into those services. Then, if someone has access to those files, they would need to be authorized to decrypt the files and required to have the right set of keys in order to access that information.

Cloud environment control requisites. Enterprises need smarter controls in their environments to understand where this data is moving. For example, companies like Microsoft or Archer Technologies with their ecosystems, are moving millions of records along with their cloud use, while they perform machine learning with big data in their data lakes on behavior and behavior patterns. Enterprises with these cloud solutions have begun to produce a great number of insights and learnings from their own data. Organizations have enabled the types of controls that deliver robust and comprehensive monitoring capability to identify anomalous activity indicative of compromises or breaches. Employing login monitoring, they bring the login closer to the database, getting the login closer to the machine learning platform, so big data platforms can provide an optimal advantage. It is essential to ensure holistic security across silos to collect all of those events, and specifically tie those to the kind of usage they're supporting.

> *It is essential to ensure holistic security across silos to collect all of those events, and specifically tie those to the kind of usage they're supporting.*

The importance of understanding behavior on a holistic scale. A great deal of consolidation will enable behavioral understanding of the service ID or the application ID. Organizations can enable controls on their database similar to an application login event. With that, organizations will know the typical transactions and queries their database receives. If the SOC analysts see a query trying to select all the customer data, then something is clearly abnormal. Anomalous behavior is in progress, possibly a breach or maybe an attack. The more organizations understand the behavior for their service IDs, the better control they will have on all their data. This is the meaning of 'persistency' within this context. If the data is copied onto a small device, if the data moves elsewhere, SOCs will have the risk-based visibility into who's touching or copying it. They will also know that the data itself is exposed, while at the same time it's rendered useless without the right keys.

Accounting for service and system IDs in hybrid cloud security

Hybrid environment architects must contend with a range of identities in their cloud environments. The identities most people are familiar with are those with a person behind them, personal IDs, or person-to-machine IDs. Add to that the service IDs, or system IDs, which come with different technologies.

> *Hybrid environment architects must contend with a range of identities in their cloud environments... personal IDs... the service IDs, or system IDs, which come with different technologies.*

Threat behavior analytics for system IDs. A MySQL server, or an application for Oracle databases, represents system IDs. These types of machine-to-machine IDs have unique characteristics and require targeted learning to understand their requirements in order to effectively enable controls for them, which tend to be repetitive. Whenever security analysts see a disconnect, which indicates an atypical behavior ID flagged through machine learning security analytics, it indicates further investigation is required.

One response might be for analysts to check against the change management processes. It may be there is an open ticket and the SNEs (system and network engineers) or the developers are troubleshooting an issue. But if not, security analysts will know a compromise has occurred and the SOC must initiate remedial actions. These security solution capabilities are tied to preventative and technical controls.

The role of IAM and identity analytics in a hybrid environment

CISOs and hybrid architects must ensure they own the identities within their environments. To achieve that, organizations need to enable access controls on two different levels. Most companies federate their access with an IAM solution where they issue a set of signatures or keys depending on which service provider the employee will be using. With those access controls in place, the user has an account, and with those keys they can create any authorized access they need within the infrastructure. This would include virtual machines, services, etc.

Federated application access. Organizations need to federate the access to their applications. To implement this within the hybrid cloud, many organizations are adopting an identity as a service (IDaaS) solution. Most cloud service providers now provide the identity as part of the ecosystem, or issue a third party identity. This option offers an open ID architecture that allows users to connect through different service providers within an organization's environment.

Two-layer identity access mapping of the hybrid cloud ecosystem. Organizations need to ensure they reduce the footprint for their identities within the hybrid environment. That's where cloud brokers provide a service that can read identities or involve a third-party solution to map the identity access to the ecosystem across the two layers: the infrastructure and applications. The challenge is to holistically manage identities across silos, across the applications within an organization. This includes detecting access risks, access outliers, excess access, shared high privileged access (HPA) accounts, as well as orphan and dormant accounts. This represents the first stage where identity analytics (IdA), as part of advanced security analytics, comes into play.

Advanced security analytics empowerment of hybrid environment security

Once CISOs and hybrid architects have achieved managing identity and access, the last element of the security model must be brought into operation. This relates to the ability to holistically monitor the activity of all of these identities, within all the separate silos, with a

> ...risk-scored monitoring of an identity's activity must not only address personal identities, but also system and machine-to-machine IDs.

risk-based approach. Employing user and entity behavior analytics (UEBA), as a risk-based component of advanced security analytics, driven by machine learning and drawing context from big data, is key. This risk-scored monitoring of an identity's activity must not only address personal identities, but also system and machine-to-machine IDs. Accounting for this factor is critical for hybrid architects to understand. Assuring that tracking both system and personal IDs are accounted for holistically, with a complete understanding of the requirements behind them, is critical to security success.

Applying IdA within the cloud infrastructure. The infrastructure (which I also refer to as the 'construct layer'), contains the security solutions which include DLP (data loss prevention), SIEM, IAM and PAM (privileged access management). At the construct layer, organizations can use IdA with infrastructure elements to address challenges such as someone trying to send confidential data by email outside the company, attempting to copy data onto a smart device, or even trying to use a common IoT device. CISOs and hybrid environment architects should understand the entire cyber-telemetry across their environment regarding one person or one service. This is crucial to ensure holistic security within the entire hybrid environment.

Hybrid environment elements beyond data, identity and the infrastructure

As a high-level architectural reference, several elements should be considered beyond the fundamental Triad framework of data, identity and infrastructure/construct. Having a deeper, more granular understanding of the elements within this model helps characterize the complexity of critical components for which hybrid architects are responsible. The Cloud Security Alliance's (CSA) website is an important resource: https://research.cloudsecurityalliance.org/tci/. A wide range of informative interactive features are available for the CISO and hybrid architect who need rich reference material to strengthen their security planning and architecture methodology. Located there, as well, readers can refer to the cloud reference architecture diagram I collaborated on with the CSA. It includes the different domains and elements contained within a hybrid environment. This is the big picture, where advanced security analytics, with IdA and UEBA, tie the data, construct and identity together in a risk-based holistic approach to security monitoring.

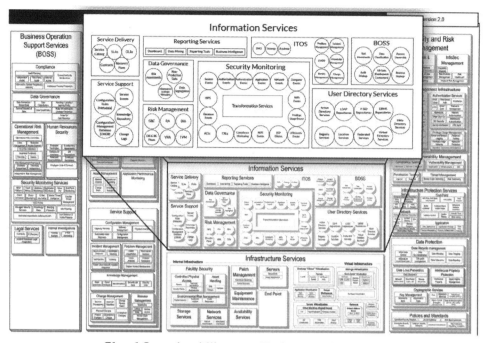

Cloud Security Alliance – Reference Architecture
(Source: https://research.cloudsecurityalliance.org/tci/)
Figure 12.3

Information services domain's central management for security. As indicated with the contextual figure above, and displayed in closer detail in the figure below, all the data an organization has across their entire architecture is accounted for within what the CSA refers to as the Information Services domain. From the monitoring perspective, on the analytical side, that domain can connect to all the critical components within the cloud Triad. SOCs should be able to track data from all these different sources, into behavior analytics. Defining where organizations can have those connectors that collect this information is essential. The other element of prudent central management for security is how organizations integrate a cloud broker. This entails having a solution between an organization's systems and their cloud providers, especially if they have a presence in multiple clouds. (For example, if an enterprise has an ecosystem with a ServiceNow integration.)

Information Services

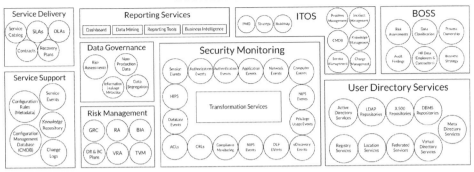

Cloud Security Alliance – Information Services Domain Architecture
(Source: https://research.cloudsecurityalliance.org/tci/)
Figure 12.4

Establishing the right identity access controls. Organizations may have Salesforce, Microsoft Office 365 or Google Apps, Dropbox, etc. This class of services addresses an organization's needs across the broadest range of offerings. Cloud is a reality. CISOs are quickly realizing that with or without them, their business is moving there, to SaaS options. So, the question for CISOs is: "What access do you provide to an identity within an entire ecosystem?" Answering this is at the heart of security and risk management priorities.

> "What access do you provide to an identity within an entire ecosystem?" Answering this is at the heart of security and risk management priorities.

Complexities of privilege management issuance. Within CSA's Privilege Management Infrastructure is the identity management set of services. That shared broker could be a service provided to a company to deliver identity as a service. Hybrid architects can provision infrastructure layer identity, or application layer identities, to the users, but this is the interesting part: to do that, most CISOs will maintain a simplified model to protect the crown jewels. The problem is, the more user repositories you have, the more exposure you have. Imagine you have 100 developers, each creating their own environment for 100 applications. If they create identities for the environment on each one of them, they have 100 user repositories to connect to. Not only that, it will require enabling 100 of everything on the construct layer, such as DLP and DLM (data life cycle management) controls, and more. That's just within the development domain. Then, envision the number of users and entities that will ultimately access those applications from anywhere, at any time with the broadest range of devices.

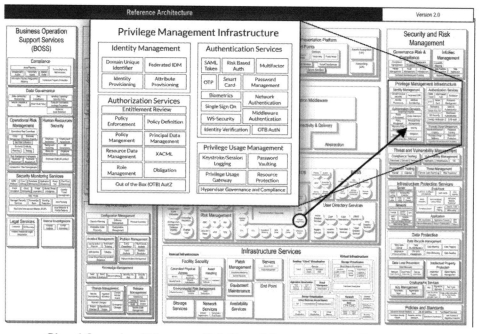

Cloud Security Alliance – Privilege Management Infrastructure
(Source: https://research.cloudsecurityalliance.org/tci/)
Figure 12.5

Evolving array of complexity, risk and unplanned costs. As hybrid architects assess the evolving complexity on each infrastructure that developers create, they must translate that into costs which are too often unplanned for the organization. These costs can manifest themselves and replicate in a number of ways. Developers go into a DevOps model, with an array of applications within the infrastructure where they can create these solution elements with 'one click'. The question is who will manage all that? Those developers are outside the fence, so how will firewalls be configured and managed? Developers must learn how to align with and incorporate established patterns or templates within sanctioned environments.

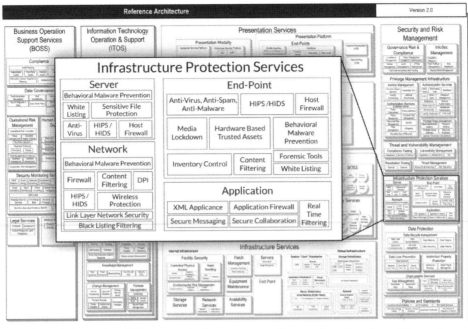

Cloud Security Alliance – Infrastructure Protection Services Domain
(Source: https://research.cloudsecurityalliance.org/tci/)
Figure 12.6

The criticality of internal groups aligning with security patterns. An organization may have a group responsible for infrastructure protection services. They maintain the network controls and application control endpoints. Their objective is to secure these fields. That's the pattern to align with. Therefore, the compromise with the development community should be: "Your team needs to ensure any changes will align with our infrastructure protection process, and any secure input we have." This infrastructure protection services group will always focus on managing the e-mesh (shortest path bridging) and ensure security is up-to-date. This is required because the environment is being refreshed all the time.

Developers' integration of security patterns. This infrastructure protection process policy is a pattern. The pattern may involve the creation of a typical firewall layer supporting a firewall approach with an application presentation for infrastructure or data, for an organization's different services. These have the firewall rules already established between them. So the developers don't need to concern themselves about that. They should just use the infrastructure that is already predefined. They might say, for example: "I want a web application that allows for a server with MySQL (secured query language)." The organization has already created this capability on the front end, and it's preconfigured. The developers just click on it, or use it as code. They have a library to create that infrastructure for them, so they don't have to configure the firewalls. Then, developers just focus on what they're good at, which is creating the services.

Evolving patterns are continuous. Segregation of each one of these capabilities will be required. Along with that, the creation patterns will be required so every developer is translating and combining those patterns into established templates. Developers can just use them and develop what they need to do. There will always be a mix, predefined patterns that organizations establish, and new or emerging patterns that will be incorporated on an ongoing basis, based on evolutionary utility and need.

Innovations in development require new patterns. Traditional cloud adoption requires developers to work through pre-approved patterns, pre-approved services that organizations allow them to use. As they progress, however, there are the developers on the leading edge, using tools like Terraform, the Hashnode technology stack, or similar cutting edge resources. The infrastructure protection services team will work with these developers. They can assign resources to them to help facilitate the development of the emerging patterns that, later, once proven, are moved into the traditional cloud. That's the ninety-five/five percent type of balance organizations will always have. These policy processes should be embedded into what the developers do to encourage new productive patterns. In the architectural planning of the hybrid cloud, all of these issues must be considered.

API's role with cloud security brokers and other hybrid infrastructure elements

Developers tend to want access directly to the APIs. They want a PaaS (platform as a service) framework to facilitate their development projects. This can lead to a direct impact on the hybrid environment infrastructure. The typical cloud provider may offer a variety of application firewall options ranging from their own firewalls, to a selection of third party firewalls. All have their advantages, yet these applications must be compatible within the construct framework of the existing hybrid environment. If developers aren't careful, they may end up adopting a firewall solution that brings benefit to the smaller context of their development project, but which has a deleterious effect on the security and efficiencies of the hybrid environment at large. Developers should develop knowledge on all of them and understand their interrelated impact with each other and their effect within the hybrid environment.

> *If developers aren't careful, they may end up adopting a firewall solution that brings benefit to the smaller context of their development project, but which has a deleterious effect on the security and efficiencies of the hybrid environment at large.*

Managing the utility of the cloud solution inventory. As the developer activates an API, there is a need to enable a governance model with the emerging set of technologies organizations are using to orchestrate their cloud adoptions. A typical concern for a hybrid architect is: "How do I know what is contained in my inventory of cloud adoptions?" This issue is even more pronounced if it is a scenario with multiple cloud

> **A typical concern for a hybrid architect is: "How do I know what is contained in my inventory of cloud adoptions?"**

providers. An organization's private cloud may be spread across an Oracle, Microsoft, AWS (Amazon Web Services), a Google, Rackspace, or whatever cloud solution fits their need. The challenge for hybrid architects is how they can ensure developers use the technologies that are part of the organization's technology portfolio. If the developers want something outside the technology portfolio, and it represents a distinct value for the organization, then collaborating with security or the hybrid architect is applicable. If so, the developers should be responsible for maintaining the currency of the advantages it provides.

The migration of infrastructure and security responsibilities. Developers are continually getting closer to the infrastructure layer. In the future, however, responsibility for infrastructure, and security, along with other types of support or required shared services, will need to transfer into the development environment. They will need to learn Python or Java in order to interact with these APIs and create their services or patterns.

Heightened developer efficiencies with established patterns. As an example of this cloud orchestration potential, developers might have created 100 instances for a particular phase of a project. These patterns, however, make it possible to create just one with those shared services. As a result, organizations save money and streamline efficiencies in process and amplify resource utility. By enabling their cloud orchestration platform, it will allow organizations to contain the 95% of the developers on the traditional cloud. They can go into the API through these platforms, and as they create new instances of access, an inventory is being created.

Consolidating hybrid cloud elements. To pull all of these solution elements together, hybrid architects connect the cloud orchestration broker to the organization's configuration management platform. Whatever platform an organization is using for their CMDB (configuration management database) will facilitate the maintenance of the inventory. It's something like a federated inventory between cloud providers and the organization's own environment. With this, organizations have a proper tie between the application inventory, to the configuration items belonging to their assets on the cloud, as well as the infrastructure constructs. This framework and inventory is of essential importance.

Selection of compatible service components in the Triad. An organization's edge controls can be re-routed to go through the public cloud, through their own perimeter controls, or they can enable them on the hybrid cloud. Hybrid architects must identify which array of cloud solution components works best for their entire hybrid environment. The key architectural element is maintaining the construct controls within the aforementioned Triad. Included in that framework, organizations need reliable and comprehensive governance. The assets must be tracked, and an effective tie-in between the configuration and the application inventories should be in place. These shared services should also be managed by the infrastructure to alleviate the work for developers.

The scale of enterprises and the impact of cloud innovations. There have been cases where developers allowed more unauthorized features than they should have, and where they created issues that directly impacted the hybrid environment's security integrity. Part of developers' responsibility is to learn about firewall management within the hybrid cloud. They must learn about the APIs, about the various managed services options, as well as related cloud solution components. A more ad hoc development model may be fine for startups, however, the complexity that a large organization might have will be more challenging for the developer. The broad range of variables and complexities represent a Pandora's Box of potential risk, if handled incorrectly. To address that, organizations should train or coach their developers, or have centers of excellence where developers are taught to properly create the code for the API access. Their code must be aligned with the existing patterns that the infrastructure group is targeting for use. As the patterns are created, they are integrated into the organization's application frameworks and are the patterns everyone can use.

Additional considerations on the hybrid Triad

Each element on the Triad framework may require a separate broker. This may include an identity broker to manage an organization's applications and infrastructure. A construct broker enables shared services for an organization's ecosystem on the cloud. A data broker controls flow between applications and services and provides visibility into where the structured and unstructured data resides. These brokers all fortify an organization's ability to manage who's touching all components of the hybrid Triad.

Advanced security analytics' central role in hybrid security. At the core, advanced security analytics is the element that ties all the Triad components together. From a traditional solutions standpoint, the scale of framework was much different and very limited. Now, when referring to advanced security analytics, which combines UEBA with IdA, there's an assumption that an organization is leveraging the entire system's collection of data, in all silos, and having the ability to process that information

> *While cloud brings the elasticity of growing at light speed, it also presents the challenge of how to have all these different elements tied together and ensure they are secure.*

meaningfully with risk-based analytics. This bypasses the traditional process of having to scale in a linear fashion, which is what human resources do, and which is what we used to do when assessing how much a SOC analyst can do within the context of security solutions. The challenge hybrid architects face, is how to expand and multiply that capability to make it scale. While cloud brings the elasticity of growing at light speed, it also presents the challenge of how to have all these different elements tied together and ensure they are secure.

The force multiplier of machine learning in big data. While an organization may have three different sets of brokers that might be working independently in their Triad, the glue that holds them together is advanced security analytics. With that capability, organizations have a holistic visibility of users' access and activity with a risk-based approach that draws context through mature machine learning from big data, through horizontal planes across an organization's numerous data silos. Anomalous activity is risk-scored to initiate deeper investigation by analysis if needed, or prompts remedial action where required. With these robust analytic capabilities, SOCs also tie the brokering service between the legacy environment and the cloud. As a result, organizations continually learn from what's okay, and what's not okay. The more organizations know about their users' behaviors, the more they can prevent issues or calibrate their controls.

Evolution of the hybrid cloud environment

In the future, more companies will invest in cloud services, instead of data centers. With that trend, more cloud providers will regionalize their cloud offerings so organizations can comply with local legislation. One example is the European Union General Data Protection Regulation (EU GDPR) which protects the private data of all EU citizens. In Latin America, including countries like Brazil, there are specific conventions for the protection of PII data. Each country has the potential for its own unique requirements, and the emerging cloud solutions should be designed to take that into account, to deliver the same level of service in each region. This cross-regional operational goal will drive the standards for centers of excellence for a cloud provider's solutions and shared services. The more global organizations become, the more they can have shared components that optimize TCO for the companies. Other needs and requirements are emerging as well.

Ubiquitous controls on data. An important requirement observed by a growing number of security leaders is that security controls must be more persistent and ascribe to models prescribed by centers of excellence. Imagine, instead of managing endpoint antivirus and protection tools for an MDM (mobile device management) platform from an organization's network, that they can be managed from anywhere. Today, of course, a company's employees are connected to the network on-site where all their necessary controls at the network layer are in place. However, when they leave their computer, and connect at home and use their WiFi, or connect at their café, Starbucks, or a library, the organization has no control in those environments. As a result, organizations will need to push the controls to the actual asset touching the data. Controls that can detect anomalous activity at these points will be key.

Evolving automated risk response. An expanding collection of use cases in a closed-loop automated risk response cycle continually strengthens the utility of advanced security analytics for the hybrid cloud. As organizations begin to enable these kinds of controls focused on users' access and activity, they see increasingly high value from the behavior analytics these solutions provide, even on the data broker side. As these use cases expand and evolve, security leaders should maintain up-to-date knowledge of how these analytic tools can maximize their efficiencies and strengthen their hybrid environment's security. These solutions' ability to learn the behavior of the applications, with a risk-based approach, indicate if an incident must be responded to with an automated response, or to notify

> An expanding collection of use cases in a closed-loop automated risk response cycle continually strengthens the utility of advanced security analytics for the hybrid cloud.

analysts that a particular activity must be investigated immediately. Instead of being reactive, the controls are more proactive, even blocking certain kinds of high-risk activity without manual intervention.

Database broker with application firewall controls. A new breed of technology growing in popularity relates to innovations from a data broker perspective where solutions sit between the database and the application. This is not an application server; this is a database server, a database broker that enables an application firewall level of controls that provide the necessary telemetry for typical behaviors. These solutions can shift telemetry to migrate to the back end of databases, allowing organizations to maintain the application's agnostic visibility into which generic database they're using, as well as providing monitoring of the actual customized data model schema they have adopted.

Application decoupling and structureless code. Decoupling between the applications and decoupling from an organization's application to the API are emerging trends. This is one reason why governance tools or cloud orchestration tools can help organizations to use the same code regardless if they are with AWS, their own private cloud, on-premises, or hybrid cloud. It doesn't matter, because it's the same code. Trends indicate that more developers are using structureless code. The typical segregation of environments or regions is being phased out, along with testing, development and related processes on the proxy applications and production. New innovations offer superior alternatives to these more standard types of applications.

Disposable environments for substantiating code. Organizations now have just-in-time applications and services that can be substantiated as code. For example, developers want to release a change in the production environment similar to a development environment. Developers take the code, make the change, then substantiate a copy of the code within the just-in-time application instance. If it works, and the users say it's okay, that code gets moved into production with essentially the same code. These self-service clusters, and disposable environments provide an invaluable framework to ensure full operational capability without interruption to the production environment. This capability streamlines processes, maximizes the development team's efforts, and provides redundancy if needed. These kinds of elements will continue to expand in value and be a key to optimized cloud development processes.

Software defining a single security perimeter. On the cloud broker side, which I refer to as the 'construct broker', there is a concerted effort to achieve an evolution for a software-defined perimeter. Imagine an organization with holistic controls in their legacy environment, their private cloud, their public cloud, including several cloud providers, and all of them seen as being one perimeter. When you create firewall rules between all of them, for example with AWS, Google, Archer or Rackspace, and others, you have a complete development environment. Organizations can create their application layer and can also see each element as one layer from the software perspective on the front end. Then you have the presentation layer, the application layer, the database layer, which can go to different providers. The application itself has visibility into elements of those components all integrated with each other.

> *Imagine an organization with holistic controls in their legacy environment, their private cloud, their public cloud, including several cloud providers, and all of them seen as being one perimeter.*

A convergence of development and security. Advancements in software defined perimeters will change how we operate in these constantly evolving environments. Multi-cloud deployments will require solutions to ensure security for those kinds of environments. As a result, the developers are getting closer to infrastructure, which is the traditional domain of security teams. As well, the infrastructure teams are getting continually closer to the development side. A convergence between them is inevitable. Their coordinated focus will be increasingly engaged in DevOps models to achieve and optimize the broader objectives of the hybrid cloud environment.

IT security into the future

Going forward, security professionals should extend their focus beyond the security realm, and become more embedded in understanding the business needs. This means to enable and partner, to work as part of the development communities, or infrastructure communities, to facilitate security becoming a part of their DNA. It's all about *building in* the security as opposed to *bolting on* security at the end. Widespread adoption of that sensibility and engaged process policy will represent a huge evolution. Many terrific

> *Going forward... It's all about* building in *the security as opposed to* bolting on *security at the end.*

companies are already doing it, such as Google. They have a few guys called 'the security dude'. But the reality is that security is everyone's job.

Technology acceleration's impact on security groups' mandate. Ideally, every stakeholder in the organization is checking to ensure they're safe. The developers get savvier, perhaps through their DevOps, or agile initiatives. But will they ever be 100% safe? No. But they will be able accelerate and deepen their security with machine learning and advanced analytics. They can move quickly, they can create service innovations faster, using shared recipes and other best practices. In the end, the patternized approach will enable these developers. Yet hybrid environment architects need to graph their key needs, embed them, and send them to their users, their constituents, to help empower them to perform as rapidly and effectively as they can. As security technologies become more robust, security teams will become leaner. They'll focus more on the cyber aspect of things and layered applications or services. A role migration of security professionals will evolve as well, as they engage with various areas to assist enabling and consulting, versus being perceived as having a 'policing' function.

Possible technology evolution beyond the cloud and hybrid environments

The convergence of technologies into a common framework is the direction for the next generation of hybrid cloud. Applications are being decoupled from database models. The infrastructure is being decoupled from applications, from the API, and the cloud provider. Segregated environments are disappearing because now the components are all code. Patternized solutions are emerging with more regularity. One of the most important innovations is the Software Defined Perimeter (SDP) which will play a critical and expanding role. An increasing number of large companies are developing that approach. The goal of a software defined perimeter is to

> *The convergence of technologies into a common framework is the direction for the next generation of hybrid cloud... the Software Defined Perimeter... will play a critical and expanding role.*

demonstrate security for public and private clouds, for hybrid clouds, and for them to be integrated in a seamless way. No silver bullet exists for them today. Yet when the

SDP is proven as a viable solution approach, it will provide the required elasticity to extend and expand controls into all of an organization's environments.

Cloud evolution delivers greater capabilities and simplicity of use. With SDP achieved, it would almost be as though we wouldn't worry about what's behind the scenes. We're removed from how it's implemented. It could be cloud. It could be anything else, or it could be on-premises, but the orchestration of it would be so seamless that the end user would be much more removed from the implementation and operational details.

Evolution of the security professional

My final thoughts relate to the evolution of the security professional. If they adopt the mentality of us (the organization) versus them (the users), the organization doesn't really learn anything if they win an argument. They lose as a business. Instead, security professionals should take the risk of getting closer to those users. Bring in professional security talent who can speak their language and start the journey into a mutually beneficial partnership. These kinds of evolutionary partnerships are already occurring with a growing number of larger organizations.

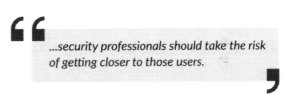

...security professionals should take the risk of getting closer to those users.

CISOs evolving role and career journey. As the role of security leaders is comparatively new to the corporate org chart, with its exact positon not yet standardized, once CISOs reach this level, many wonder: "What's next? What's the next challenge?" A number of them migrate into other roles such as CTOs, or CIOs. Some become infrastructure or development leaders. This is because the forward-looking security leaders recognize their security teams need to become enablers of the business goals. While they must remain risk-averse, they cannot build in security unless they understand what the business objective is. They must prioritize assisting the business to achieve what it needs to do in a secure manner which requires an organizational mindset. The security leaders who move into these other roles understand this key point, and help to expand the awareness and benefit of assuring security concerns have a seat at the table at the top levels of management.

CONCLUSIONS & TAKEAWAYS:
Security in evolving hybrid cloud environments

As security leaders seek to align with the elastic efficiencies of cloud, and plan their strategies for the evolving threats which are continually emerging both inside and outside their environments — from privileged access abuse, 24/7 global access from a myriad of devices, and the exploding scale of data — they must also partner effectively with the hybrid environment architect. With the traditional security perimeter effectively gone, their shared objective is to ensure the systems inside the organization's global environment are properly developed to interact effectively with robust and comprehensive advanced security analytics. A first step is to recognize that identity is the emerging threat plane, and that it should be incorporated into a Triad framework defined by Orea, along with the data and the construct/infrastructure, so they are all integrated holistically and seamlessly.

To achieve that end, Orea stresses the importance of optimizing cloud adoption with proven best practices. These include application containerization, microservices security and the acceleration of services rollout through patternization. Evolving controls and segregation are also fundamental access security requirements in hybrid architecture. As well, management of privileged access requires a two-tiered perspective with insight into the complex realities of cloud tenancy. Forward-looking hybrid security strategies should also involve closer controls on data along with an understanding of structured and unstructured data security requirements and their impact on cloud environment effectiveness.

Orea also observes, with caution, the critical impact of developers as privileged users who have 'one click' empowerment in cloud services development, which can create great solution value, and, possibly, unintended security vulnerabilities. Because of this, Orea then calls out the need for internal groups to educate themselves and align with security patterns with an understanding of how innovations in development require new patterns.

Acknowledging that identity is the new threat plane, Orea observes one element of successful hybrid architecture security planning must account holistically for personal identity, as well as, service and system IDs which can only be achieved effectively through risk-based advanced security analytics. Within the requirements of all-inclusive cloud and on-premises security, Orea stresses the importance of holistically incorporating disparate vertical siloed solutions to ensure comprehensive security. This can only be achieved by employing advanced security analytics, incorporating UEBA and IdA, leveraging the force multiplier of machine learning in big data.

With the critical mass of our experts' insights presented in the first twelve chapters, we next examine the requirements for successful UEBA-IdA and CSA solutions, employing advanced machine learning and drawing from the context of big data.

Following that, Chapter 14 provides a guide to advanced security analytics use cases. The next, and final *Borderless Breach Flashcard*, depicts an episode of a very public, yet avoidable, breach which may have influenced the presidential election of United States of America.

BORDERLESS BREACH FLASHCARD	
Backroom Secrets Spotlighted	
CATEGORY	Political hacktivism, breach of internal communications, or Russian hack.
WHO	**The target:** Democratic National Committee (DNC).
WHAT	First, Julian Assange and WikiLeaks released sensitive internal communications, allegedly from the hacker Guccifer 2.0, of the DNC to the public, which caused widespread embarrassment and a political shakeup. A second release, directly from Guccifer, revealed sensitive information on DNC donors.
WHEN	July and September 2016
WHERE	Washington D.C., or possibly transnational hacking.
WHY	Influence political change.
HOW	The original collection of breached information included over 19,000 emails and 8,000 attachments from the DNC. The exact method of exfiltration has been a matter of heated debate. Some claim it was the product of Russian hacking, while others (including Assange), strongly suggest it was an insider breach. Forbes reported it was from a compromised password and login. Embarrassing disclosures about activities of the DNC were revealed, specifically exposing the DNC's leadership bias for Hillary Clinton over Bernie Sanders, her principal Democratic competitor for the party's presidential nomination. A second release revealed details of DNC donors, their finances, as well as the information technology set up to protect the DNC's sensitive data.
HOW BAD?	The chair of the DNC, Debbie Wasserman, and other top officers, were forced to resign. Allegations of bad faith with the DNC's work against Bernie Sanders, a leading Democratic candidate for President, were revealed. Trust in the DNC's integrity was damaged.
HOW COULD IT BE AVOIDED?	With a political organization of such prominence, both nationally and internationally, it only makes sense to perceive their environment as being a prime target for hackers. Add to that, the intense focus on one leading candidate's relaxed policies on computer security only amplifies the urgency of risk from hackers. If the DNC had an effective UEBA-IdA solution in place, the anomalous activity of accessing sensitive files would alert the security analysts to respond appropriately, and there would have been no mystery about who actually committed the breach.

Requirements for
Borderless Behavior Analytics

Qualifications for predicting risk, now and into the future

Once an organization recognizes the advantages of adopting machine learning with big data for advanced security analytics, and are seriously considering that option, how do they choose the right solution and the right approach?

The other questions security leaders will ask to determine the above will include: What does it take to enable this solution? Is my organization prepared to adopt this class of solution? Do I have all the data in place? What use cases make the most sense? Are all the resources available and is it the right time to adopt?

Part of managing this challenge involves defining the makeup of an organization's infrastructure, its maturity, and what magnitude and phase of change are being considered within their systems. A young organization adopting and integrating new evolving technologies, such as cloud and SaaS, will have quite different concerns and priorities than an established global organization with a pre-existing legacy infrastructure for IAM, SIEM, DLP and in-house applications. One size does not fit all. What are the strong points? Where are the gaps? Included in this assessment is understanding where elements of the infrastructure need to be upgraded, replaced, or supported with new technology solutions, to ensure a system is up-to-date on all the supporting operational required fronts. Proper timing of adoption is another serious consideration given the wisdom and experience reflected in the preceding chapters.

Different environmental states for on-premises and cloud within an organization include:

The big picture

- *Mostly legacy environments* – With an infrastructure heavily based in pre-existing on-premises systems, many system elements are often siloed. Large, well-established banks and some monolithic insurance companies can be examples of this class of environment, including Jerry Archer's environment at his major financial services company. Here SOC teams experience too much signal-to-noise ratio, with a preponderance of false positives from DLP and IDS/IPS. Challenges they face often consist of a preexisting IAM access risk plane with extensive opportunities to reduce access risk. The discovery gap for privileged access is not well known, and much of it is hidden. Many legacy data sources, generating a high volume of digital exhaust, make up this category of environment. The variety of big data compounds security teams' challenges with a complex logging and event environment that is likely struggling with their SIEM deployments.

- *Mostly blank slate environments* – With the ability to choose and adopt the best of new emerging technology solutions, the potential for optimal efficiencies within this environment is high. These organizations did not adopt DLP or SIEM, and have not struggled with IAM projects across an organization. They are, as a result, more flexible. No cumbersome infrastructure of pre-existing IT systems of significance, along with complex logging and events, need to be accounted for. This factor streamlines the prospect for broader environmental efficiencies, something like a developing country adopting wireless communications and skipping legacy wired systems other more developed countries must contend with. Like Joe Sullivan's environment, when he was at Uber, these organizations can bypass a generation of security technologies that have hampered organizations in legacy environments. This factor empowers their potential for streamlined adoption of advanced security analytics with big data and machine learning. The challenge lies in making the right security solution choices at the start. Organizations in this category can leapfrog to big data with machine learning for user and entity behavior analytics to detect unknown threats. In addition, these solutions must address and close the awareness gap for access provided and the associated activity, as well as the discovery gap of hidden privileged access risk, to take a risk-based approach for access governance.

- *Mixed environments, in between* – A common scenario where legacy on-premises systems must be integrated with new cloud solutions. This is the type of setting Gary Harbison is working with at Monsanto and where Gary Eppinger is revamping Carnival Corporation's hyper-hybrid environment. As a result, cloud system frameworks considerably expand the existing complexity of the original legacy environment's makeup. The goal of these cloud solutions is lowering operating costs, increasing productivity and efficiencies, along with gaining flexibility for business enablement that legacy systems cannot provide. The risks include increased digital exhaust and a more complex hybrid environment with growing risk planes. The solution development model also entails moving from a waterfall IT development methodology to an Agile-DevOps one, with continuous iterations of improvement in planned phases, with more frequent releases. For an advanced security analytics solution to be optimized properly within a hybrid environment like this, security leaders should view this adoption not as a specific feature addition offered from a particular cloud solution, for example a CASB-UEBA, but instead from a platform perspective. In a mixed environment, the requirement for machine learning is more crucial for a higher quality of data and broader visibility. Also, in recognition of identity as an access risk and threat plane, UEBA and IdA need to work holistically together in a single platform. The use case of privileged access abuse exemplifies this point.

The technical infrastructure level perspective

Security leaders must decide whether to adopt a UEBA-IdA solution before or after IAM and SIEM projects. The advantages of adopting an IdA component before a major IAM or PAM project provides a decisive reduction of the access risk plane, plus maximizing the effectiveness of the subsequent UEBA integration. Ultimately, the traditional 'red' and 'green' scenarios — the known bads and goods — are generally accounted for with pre-existing declarative security solutions. However the vast and emerging gray zone of unknown unknowns must be managed. This is where risk-scored analytics, powered by machine learning and drawing from big data for context come into play.

Individual technology challenges where UEBA and IdA solutions add value include:

- *New SIEM implementation* – A need exists to reduce dwell time, focus high value 'find-fix' resources, and improve detection response ratios to lower false positives and improve incident response. Manual efforts to threat hunt or find security anomalies, via query, filter and pivot efforts remain unproven. The breadth of data to drive machine learning can be costly due to SIEM indexing fees and expenses must be monitored. When considering a SIEM adoption, security leaders must determine if the SIEM should be deployed to do what it is most proficient at for network operations and compliance, and install an open source big data lake to store data long-term for value to drive security analytics.

- **Upgrading a SIEM solution** – A need exists to expand and optimize existing capabilities. Adding UEBA to a SIEM improves detection and response through machine learning-based risk scoring. However, the more holistic picture should include identity analytics and a future hybrid environment needs to be considered. Like the scenario above, the option of deploying a big data lake to drive security analytics should be considered. This can be a sense of heartburn for security leaders who earlier drove the adoption of a SIEM as an end all answer.

- **A SIEM alternative solution** – Here a UEBA-IdA solution provides a leapfrog opportunity for organizations to bypass a SIEM adoption, as analysts recommend, if enterprises have not purchased a SIEM, they should consider avoiding it. Their advice is to invest in a basic log and event manager (LEM), integrated with UEBA, for security analytics at a lower price. This addresses the challenges noted in the new SIEM solution section above.

- **A new IAM implementation** – Requirement to have an identity access system in place (e.g., OIM, Active Directory) to expand security efficiencies with an assumption that excess access and access outliers will be cleaned up in the process. However a growing awareness gap exists between what access rights have been provided by an IAM solution and how the rights are being utilized by users. This is a serious access risk plane. Therefore, security leaders must justify importing a legacy-defined access plane that was built on manually defined roles and legacy rules, thus putting 'garbage' into the new system. Using the same roles and same definitions makes no sense for addressing the emerging excess access and access outlier problem. Instead, the potential to reduce excess access by 50% or more exists with UEBA-IdA, to start implementations on a fresh footing. IdA provides a risk-based approach for identity and access governance (IGA), and IAM, after years of compliance-driven rubber-stamping and access cloning. Identity analytics closes the IAM awareness gap for access versus activity with risk-based scoring for certifications, requests and approvals.

- **Upgrading an IAM solution** – When moving from a legacy IAM solution to an off-the-shelf version, security leaders must ensure the intelligence inside the solution is accurate, to reduce access risk. Manually defined roles from legacy rules has resulted in excessive group and roles access, access outliers, and over privileging users. A new best-of-breed IAM solution may not provide all the capabilities required to move to a risk-based approach. Integrating identity analytics greatly reduces the access risk plane, and closes the access awareness gap for IAM on what access is provided and how it is being utilized. In addition, the identity analytics need to feed into UEBA to increase its accuracy and value.

- ***A new PAM implementation*** – This is an emerging solution, which 9 out of 10 enterprises have not yet adopted. Common features IT organizations find beneficial with PAM solutions are single sign-on (SSO), multi-factor authentication (MFA), one-time passwords (OTP), and a vault to secure privileged credentials. These components, however, lack the ability to discover privileged access risk at the entitlement level and within applications. For this reason, experts note that 50% of this privileged access lies outside of the existing lists or PAM vaults. Meanwhile, risk officers demand prudent security hygiene to address privileged access risk, inclusive of application privileges, by risk scoring at the entitlement level. Thus, identity analytics, driven by machine learning leveraged from big data, fills the awareness gap for IAM along with the discovery gap for PAM for privileged access risk.

- ***Upgrading a PAM solution*** – While customers may see the need to expand and optimize capabilities of their existing PAM solution adoption, the constraints described directly above remain unresolved. While an existing PAM solution may discover privileged access risk at the account level, the unknown instances of privileged access entitlements which reside outside PAM vaults will remain an open issue. Discovery of this privileged access risk and its associated access risk plane can only be resolved through IdA and risk-based scoring of entitlements, while UEBA provides risk-based visibility into access and activity of all identities across a hybrid environment.

- ***Risk officer governance compliance*** – This entails providing information to support governance and compliance requirements, such as Sarbanes Oxley, and aligning with IT and security mandates from organizational risk management groups. SOCs must deliver accurate and timely entitlement and access risk scores to reduce risk and deliver increased data protection. Requirements include development and support of an effective insider threat program with visibility into access, accounts and activity, with priority visibility into the unknown gray areas of the identity threat plane along with the discovery gap of unaccounted for privileged access entitlements. A self-audit option may be in order for security awareness and deterrence.

The overall approach: A multistep process, to clean up access and then monitor for risk in the gray areas. First assure an identity and access management (IAM) system is in place, and then clean up access with identity analytics (IdA), using a risk-based approach which provides a streamlined access foundation to build upon. On the risk analytics side, harvest data into a data lake or aggregate into a SIEM or LEM (log event manager). From there a UEBA and IdA solution will normalize, correlate and process attributes through machine learning models for advanced security analytics.

The customer challenge perspective

The use case areas below represent a selection of the most common encountered.

- ***Account compromise and highjacking*** – This stands as one of the top risks organizations face today, where attackers compromise access credentials to gain access and bypass existing preventative defenses. Example attacks to compromise credentials include phishing and social engineering. As stated earlier in the book, an identity and credentials can be stolen, however a user's behavior cannot. This scenario also applies more importantly to cloud, as access provides the keys to the kingdom. This use case is frequently included with insider threats, as early detection often appears as an insider until the compromise surfaces.

- ***Privileged access abuse*** – Given experts estimate more than 50% of privileged access risks are outside of known lists and vaults, knowing where privileged access exists is the first step for this use case, a step many UEBA solutions ignore. While account and access data is traditionally ingested from IAM, PAM, and directories, these solutions often lack identity analytics to close the discovery gap. Identity analytics are then ingested by UEBA solutions providing the accuracy for all known privileged access risks for monitoring, baselines, and anomaly detection with risk scoring. Also, with SaaS applications and IaaS (e.g., AWS, MS Azure), the potential for privileged access abuse becomes even more important for cloud as a utility.

- ***Data exfiltration*** – Considered the lifeblood of many organizations, confidential information for customers, patients, employees and partners has become increasingly difficult to protect with the broad range of systems in which it resides. Enterprise-wide insight into access and activity patterns — such as sensitive documents downloaded and copied to USB, large amounts of source code checked out from source code repositories and file uploads to cloud storage, emails to personal accounts, access to competitor and/or job websites — is required. In addition, enhancing DLP solutions with anomaly detection and advanced analytics to reduce the signal-to-noise ratio, plus prioritizing alerts to reduce volume are critical requirements. The adoption of cloud and specific applications such as Office 365 and Box also bring up customer concerns for data exfiltration in hybrid environments.

- ***Insider threat*** – Insider threat trends are solidly consistent for the last four years, and inclusion of account compromise in its definition has increased its visibility. The impact from insiders, malicious, compromised and innocent, represent a challenge that must be addressed to find high-order interactions and patterns in data for complex problems including compromised accounts, network wandering, data collection and data exfiltration. Given insiders have approved access, there is more dependence on context from big data with some solutions including sentiment from user communications.

- **_Identity access management_** – Used to monitor activity against established access rights in IAM, PAM and directories, and to identify access risks via identity analytics (IdA). This use case domain cleans up access, removes excess access, access outliers, dormant accounts, orphan accounts and provides a risk-based approach for identity access governance. Thus risk scores aid in certifications, requests and approvals, plus enable dynamic access provisioning, new intelligent roles and automated risk response such as step-up authentication.

- **_Employee monitoring_** – The combination of endpoint data with directory access and activity are primary data sources for this use case. Inclusion of this use case with a broader UEBA-IdA solution provides more varied context over hybrid environments for anomaly detection. More simplistic employee monitoring solutions with pattern matching and rules are adopting UEBA features, however they remain siloed with limited data and visibility. Employee monitoring has its opponents with privacy concerns over recording employee sessions for playback and review.

- **_Cloud security_** – The emergence of SaaS, IaaS, PaaS and IDaaS presents access risks and unknown threats for the use cases in this category, however for cloud and hybrid environments, not just on-premises. CASB solutions with proxy and API deployments are developing UEBA as a feature, however, within a silo they lack the broader data and visibility of a UEBA platform solution. Mature UEBA solutions ingest CASB data for shadow IT application usage, plus interface into SaaS, IaaS and PaaS with established APIs for visibility into access and activity. In the end, enterprises are likely to own both solutions, a CASB and a UEBA-IdA hybrid platform solution.

- **_Cyber fraud_** – Financial organizations, or departments within larger enterprises, must protect their monetary assets from the risk of cyber fraud. Some organizations deal with transactions to transfer billions of dollars on a daily basis, making human detection of anomalies that much more difficult to detect. Within a scale and setting such as this, the critical signals indicating risky behavior are too fine-grained for analysis by humans. Treasury, accounting, payments and departments responsible for daily fund transfers as part of the standard operation, must have reliable security solutions to uncover the malicious actors. Comprehensive enterprise-wide big data ingestion and monitoring cyber fraud models and risk frameworks in alignment with business context are required.

[NOTE: For a complete overview advanced analytics use cases, refer to Chapter 14.]

Mapping the route through Borderless Behavior Analytics

Through the journey of this book, we have seen a number of accomplished security experts weigh in with their experiences and insights into the challenges of advanced security analytics in the rapidly evolving world of hybrid cloud environments. With the staggering rise of 390,000 *new* malware instances per day (AV-TEST IT-Security Institute's malware statistics report, May 2016), a majority of readers have likely recognized the time for change is at hand. Comprehensive hybrid security visibility and monitoring for on-premises and cloud applications is a requirement for business success and survival. User and entity behavior analytics is a key component of that requirement with its ability to detect account compromise, abuse and unknowns which existing defense frameworks cannot detect. At this juncture of their journey, the path enterprises choose defines their destination. The decision determines a route toward an effective solution, which grows with the company's evolutionary presence in the marketplace with alignment of security defenses, or it brings them to more unknowns.

The requirements are complex and exacting in a new and emerging field, where qualified UEBA and IdA solution quality and delivery experience is at a premium. Proven UEBA solution components, well-established processes and ease of use are the adoption goals. Evidence-based knowledge and actionable intelligence — drawn from rich big data context and empowered by machine learning — can help leaders prepare for unforeseen attacks against IT or information assets. Knowing the direction of future trends, many large enterprises are hiring data scientists to develop custom behavior models and risk-tuning solutions customized precisely to their needs. Other enterprises faced with similar needs, but with fewer resources, must consider a field of UEBA vendors who all represent their solution in the best light, including use cases, data sources and years of experience. However, the prospect of adopting a closed black-box solution, or developing their own homegrown solution, is a non-starter for too many prospective customers.

In the chapter by Monsanto's Gary Harbison, he observed that while cloud adoption is a dynamic business enabler, a game changer, and inevitable for many businesses, "the challenge is in understanding how to consistently have the same baseline security assurance in each of those environments." As Verizon's *Data Breach Investigations Report* cited in 2016, the threat planes are expanding, and continue today at an alarming rate. The risks are not going away. All systems can be compromised. It is no longer enough for companies to merely shore up defenses against generally known threats with manual processes to threat hunt and employ legacy rules and roles for access. And just deploying UEBA to monitor for anomalous behavior is only part of the picture. The need to reduce excess access risks is urgent. Integrating UEBA with identity analytics provides the ability to close the IAM access awareness gap and the PAM discovery gap.

In addition, some organizations have unique requirements for use cases. Government, financial groups, and other organizations with confidential data resources and private use cases, will require the need to develop custom models as vendors cannot analyze the data and are not privy to the use cases. Having a solution with the ability to expand and customize data source attributes for new use cases, along with customer-specific application data sources, is critical. Open choice of big data lake infrastructure, where the solution should compute and store on big data for faster processing and greater data variety, plus store data for long-term value, is also essential. A mature solution delivering cloud security analytics for hybrid environments, providing a combined 360-degree view for identity, and risk-scored behavioral threat monitoring, driven by machine learning, is also part of this newly recognized state-of-the-art UEBA-IdA standard. We are beyond static groups and rules, as well as, threat hunting using the known.

As enterprises must now contend with an increasing number of multiple perimeters and borders in the future, CIO at Large Teri Takai poses three critical questions security leaders must answer for their organizations: "What is the perimeter? What's protecting the perimeter? Is that protection effective?" In essence, Ms. Takai questions the existence of the perimeter itself. Meanwhile, CSO at Large, Joe Sullivan predicts the current trends of activity will ultimately result in total fragmentation, where "increasingly more employees will be accessing sensitive enterprise data and information from more and more fragmented devices, through fragmented paths." The time for intelligent change in advanced security analytics strategies stands before the majority of organizations. Navigating that change is the challenge. In this chapter we draw from the experience of our contributing experts, Gurucul's solution specialists, and insights from leading industry analysts. With this in place, an enterprise will be well-equipped to face the new evolving challenges of BYOD, IoT, mobility and hybrid cloud worlds.

Expert findings identify the path forward for behavioral analytics

While some leaders may still consider numerous elements of the status quo in security sufficient to sustain their strategy requirements for managing risk, others recognize the fast-evolving challenges of the hybrid environment. Drawing from the collective knowledge described above, we have distilled three critical points organizations should consider with the prospect of adopting a UEBA-IdA solution versus maintaining a legacy security approach.

- *Managing rules and threat signatures cannot uncover unknown threats* – Legacy security solutions traditionally consist of comprehensive capacities for managing rules, signatures and patterns to identify known threats. They identify the 'reds' (the bads) and the 'greens' (the goods) and help keep the door closed on the known bads that may resurface. Yet today's business models have changed. Threats have shifted. Identity is the new threat vector. Now a pressing requirement exists to know the unknown unknowns, the vast uncharted grays and their potentially nefarious activities. Behavior analytics uses machine-learning-based behavior and predictive models to detect behavioral anomalies to identify access risk and unknown threats.

- *A single view of users' access and activities is mandatory* – To assure comprehensive advanced security analytics in their environment, security teams need UEBA and IdA solutions to offer actionable intelligence through machine learning. It must be able to create a single and unified view of user and entities' access and activity throughout the network, on-premises, in the cloud and across all mobile devices that interact with them. It must maintain an ability to self-learn and self-train, to assure the exclusion of false positives from feedback and to leverage the rich context provided by big data. Especially essential within hybrid environments, machine learning thrives on context, sourcing from big data in both rich volume and broad variety. Machine learning 'on a siloed diet' is simply counter-productive.

- *Context is critical* – Risk scoring with rich context is a prerequisite for successful advanced security analytics. A self-audit capability delivers risk-scored intelligence for context analysis that is uniquely possessed by employees, teams and project leaders. They have an invaluable contextual perspective that a SOC team can't possess. SOC analysts look for peaks, like someone trying to break a password or multiple logins, not low activity such as a PTO day off for an employee or user. UEBA also has an ability to rank the risk of DLP alerts and send them to project leaders who possess contextual insight into an employee's roles and responsibilities. In cases like these, the SOC team would not normally understand the context of these projects. This context is essential to help understand the gray areas to validate and provide feedback to the behavior analytics machine learning models.

Guidelines for UEBA vendor requirements

Scope the challenge correctly to invest once. Security leaders must plan their solution initiatives to address a collection of existing and emerging challenges, while at the same time, strive to anticipate, as best as possible, the future needs of their environments. Considering the requirement to implement a wide-reaching hybrid cloud solution such as machine learning for advanced security analytics, the goal of any organization considering a UEBA and IdA adoption is to get it right the first time. Within this context, assurance of effectively addressing the issue of privileged access abuse is a crucial consideration that must not be ignored. This involves implementing a set of steps at the front end of a solution adoption to ensure privileged access risks are known first from the access risk plane before machine learning monitoring for abuse.

Proper assessment of all these capabilities to confirm their compatibility effectiveness begins with performing a proof of concept (POC). This irreplaceable step in the solution adoption process ensures the solution performs as the vendor claims it should. Just as importantly, this process also involves choosing the solution capable of performing the exact desired use cases of the organization. This capability often correlates with the maturity of the UEBA and IdA solutions that provide robust machine learning and the ability to process and manage massive sets of big data for both on-premises and in the cloud. This scoping often involves cooperative consulting between the vendor and customer. This entails identifying known popular use cases and project road maps plans with the solution vendor, who traditionally has specialized and qualified insights into the challenges and solutions relating to hybrid environments, based on field delivery experience the customer might not have.

As a prospective organization considers implementing a behavior analytics machine learning solution, it helps to narrow down the field of qualified vendors as efficiently as possible, to assure their solution capabilities align with a customer's challenges and requirements. Knowing where a vendor sits within the arc of UEBA maturity is one filter to apply at this stage. Well before any POC is performed, matching the vendor's strengths and capabilities with an organization's needs and requirements is a critical step in the qualification process. UEBA solution offerings are categorized in four levels of maturity in the market today. They are:

- *First generation UEBA* – *Tools-based analytics.* Vendors in this space first appeared over 10 years ago. Their solutions focus primarily on credit card bust out, account takeover, new account fraud, loan origination, insurance claims, healthcare fraud, tax refund fraud and government benefit programs. The solutions' tool functionality focuses primarily on entity link analysis across structured data. Users drive the analytics, or they are customized by the vendors taking data converted through a comparatively prolonged extraction, transformation and loading (ETL) process, which also involves data cleansing. The objective is to have identities and entities resolved and linked. Many of the vendors in this category have developed network visualization techniques for the user interface.

- *Second generation UEBA* – *Progressive data integration and early canned analytics.* The majority of vendors in this second category offer automatically resolved identities and entities by virtue of their proprietary fuzzy logic and data-matching techniques. These streamline the lengthy data cleansing, resolution and ETL processes, contrasting the experience provided by first generation tools-based vendors. Users must still define underlying data models and are responsible for discovery and linkage of source data. Solution providers in this category of maturity began offering basic packaged intelligence for repeatable use cases targeted on solving cyber fraud in many of the vertical market areas addressed by first generation vendors. The primary use cases offered by both first and second generation UEBA vendors address only detective forensics and the investigation of theft and cyber fraud which have already occurred. This includes threat scenarios that are continuing and spreading. Predictive analytics are generally not features associated with this generation of UEBA. Traditionally, a significant amount of professional services are required to integrate and manage these solutions to assure the solution performs optimally.

- **State-of-the-art UEBA** – *Predictive analytics for cybersecurity and cyber fraud.* This generation of UEBA vendor solutions has been targeted at developing and delivering packaged predictive security analytics, which detect and identify insider and advanced threats. This type of UEBA solution has gained significant success, delivering notable results within challenging parameters, with a number of large corporations. UEBA solutions in this category have significantly exceeded the capabilities of the widely adopted security user monitoring applications like SIEM (security information and event) management and DLP (data loss prevention). These pure-play UEBA vendors continue to innovate in the development of their predictive analytic models. The applications will not be reliant on customer-driven analytics or inquiries of the data.

- **Emerging Next-Generation UEBA** – *Advanced prescriptive cyber defense.* This next generation of UEBA innovation has been achieved only by a very small segment of UEBA vendors beyond the State-of-the-Art category. Gartner considers this the fourth and highest phase of UEBA's evolution. It incorporates comprehensive command of hybrid and siloed security data, using security analytics data and intelligence, along with infrastructure logs, network logs, application audit logs, as well as device attributes and configuration details. Drawing from real-time user and entity risk scoring, prescriptive actions in security analytics are provided to prevent malicious behavior from insiders and sophisticated cybercriminals, as well minimize excess and unnecessary access risks. In security analyses, once the 'what happened' (detective analytics) or 'what is about to happen' (predictive analytics) is determined, 'what should be done in response' (prescriptive analytics) is the next stage of incident resolution. Prescriptive analytics, that either manually, or automatically, orchestrate, implement or recommend next steps help security teams empower their response capabilities that are agnostically integrated with investigative platforms. These solutions also help detect unneeded access and automate access decisions in real time. They bring together siloed context across disparate sources in the enterprise, and the cloud, and provide a unified view of risk that allows an organization to take action. A key driver for this innovation is with the prevalence of constraints associated with detective and predictive security systems, customers need to reduce the total time between detection and impactful response, which is what prescriptive systems address. These mature UEBA vendors continue to innovate in the development of their prescriptive security analytic models. These solutions are the best suited for today's evolving business environments.

The emerging state of Borderless Behavior Analytics resides within the best-of-breed maturity class of UEBA solutions that are part of this category and the requirements described in this chapter address themselves to this evolving class of solutions.

Requirements for state-of-the-art Borderless Behavior Analytics

Note that, even within the state-of-the-art category for UEBA solutions, various gradations of capability exist. Some UEBA vendors claim their solutions are driven by machine learning, yet as CISO at Large Leslie K. Lambert observes, "Let the buyer beware — not all machine learning is created equal." Their definition of machine learning is based on stats, rules and queries, and seeking existing known bads. Advanced machine learning, on the other hand, seeks the unknown extracted from big data via clustering and outlier algorithms, plus dimensionality reduction with risk scoring. An example of machine learning's advanced capabilities is in monitoring millions of entitlements to look for access outliers, and finding privileged access risk. Rules and queries cannot address this challenge in any way. Demonstrating actual use cases in a POC helps confirm a solution's machine learning capabilities. To assure an organization is acquiring the most advanced and comprehensive capabilities from their UEBA-IdA solutions, the following list represents a set of minimum essential requirements.

UEBA and IdA capabilities checklist:
- Hybrid visibility for on-premises and cloud applications
- Open customer choice for big data infrastructure (e.g., Hadoop, Cloudera, Hortonworks, MapR, Elastic/ELK Stack) for architectural scale
- Ability to expand and customize data source attributes for new use cases and customer-specific applications and data sources
- Ability to take any legacy data (mainframe) or new data source (CASB, SaaS application) and map desired fields into attributes without vendor assistance in using the solution

- Custom behavior model development and risk tuning without coding and minimal knowledge of data science, important for confidential data and private use cases outside a vendor's scope

- Identity analytics to reduce excess access, detect access outliers and provide a risk-based approach for IAM and PAM to close the discovery gap between access and activity

- User and entity behavior analytics leveraging peer group analysis including the use of dynamic behavioral-based peer groups to increase accuracy of anomalous outliers and eliminate the issue of bad behavior in baselines

- Cloud security analytics, inclusive of UEBA and IdA, to reduce access risk and detect unknown threats in hybrid environments

- Graphical interface and dashboards, with timelines and drill-down capacities providing a 360-degree view of an identity's accounts, access and activity

- APIs for closed-loop bidirectional deployment with other solutions for data ingestion, risk scores, analytic response codes and analytics, plus automated risk responses

- Dashboards, drill-downs, investigation workbench, open query tool, reporting and data visualizations

- Role-based access control (RBAC), data masking in UI and through workflow, plus tokenization and encryption for privacy to meet large enterprise needs around the globe, including EU privacy regulations

- Self-audits for employees, business partners, and customers providing an individual report of risk-scored access and activity

- Out-of-the-box use cases (UEBA, IdA and CSA) with supporting machine learning models noting required and optional data sources

- Rules and policy engine with step-by-step guidance for ease of use

- Case ticket management with integration for leading solutions (Remedy, ServiceNow, Salesforce) or embedded ticketing and case management feature

UEBA and IdA core components

Delivery on all the requirements above would also include a highly qualified and dedicated professional services team on-site to install the solution, train users and support the solution to assure long-term optimal utility, and future-proof compatibility for the life cycle of the solution. The vendor team's field experience should include knowledge of a broad range of data sources and hybrid environments. These delivery capabilities would include both pre- and post-sales technical support.

Third party integration requirements

To deliver value, a UEBA solution must be integrated with a potentially broad range of data sources, identity management solutions, and more for ingesting into big data infrastructure. This must be for both on-premises and in the cloud. UEBA guidelines for third party interface prerequisites include:

- **Security analytics platforms** – Ready-to-use connectors for popular SIEM platforms are a standard requirement. There should be an open choice for big data infrastructure. UEBA solutions should be built on popular open-source software frameworks, such as Apache Hadoop and support deployments with Cloudera, Hortonworks and MapR.

- **Data loss prevention** – UEBA solutions must provide ready-to-use connectors for leading DLP solutions (e.g., Symantec, McAfee and Forcepoint). These data sources are critical for on-premises data exfiltration analysis use cases. In addition, CASB solutions are increasingly adding DLP features and should also be considered an important data source.

- **Identity access management** – Ready-to-use data connectors for popular identity access management (IAM) solutions must be offered which also facilitate APIs providing risk-scored analysis back to these access solutions, such as automatically detecting access outliers.

- **Privileged access management** – Data connectors for popular privileged access management (PAM) solutions should also integrate seamlessly via APIs to provide risk-scored analysis back to these solutions, such as identifying unknown privileged access risks.

- **Cloud security solutions** – UEBA solutions should provide connectors for cloud access security brokers (CASBs), plus API integration for SaaS applications, identity as a service (IDaaS) and infrastructure or platform as a service (IaaS/PaaS) when possible.

- **Cyber fraud management** – The solution should provide cyber fraud detection within its capabilities, along with the ability to leverage APIs to provide risk scores to fraud and anti-money laundering (AML) solutions.

- **Endpoint solutions** – Endpoint detection and response (EDR) solutions should be available as a data source and provide risk scores and analytic response codes to trigger endpoint recording. This may also include network access control (NAC) solutions as a data source and risk-scoring feedback to enable controls.

- **Governance, risk and compliance** – In a field overwhelmed by the amount of unstructured data analysts must manage, APIs should integrate with governance, risk and compliance (GRC) solutions to provide advanced semantic analysis along with risk scores for assessments.

UEBA feature requirements

More detailed focus on the UEBA component functionality includes:

- ***Diverse data collection*** – Most widely adopted UEBA solutions are built on Hadoop (HDFS) and provide a flexible metadata model for structured and unstructured data sources. Ready to use data connectors that ease data source integration and data ingestion should be included. UEBA solutions should also compute and store on big data infrastructure such as Hadoop, Cloudera, Hortonworks and MapR. Also, to attain the most timely and accurate data context possible to discover access outliers, a UEBA solution providing over 200 attributes — that are both customizable and can be extended for special use cases — bring added benefits. More diverse and deep data provides better analytics while leveraging the scale with machine learning. In addition, providing a flexible data connector for legacy data sources (e.g., mainframe), for new data sources (e.g., SaaS and CASB), is critical.

- ***Single view of identity*** – The ability to link information to single identities is key. A single view of identity of on-premises and cloud applications, made possible by fuzzy logic to map accounts, should be a standard offering. This feature should leverage IAM, PAM, AD, Directories, IDaaS, and HR databases to self-learn and self-train on identities. Within its capabilities, orphan and dormant accounts should be identified, as well as, excess access and access outliers, to reduce access risks. Identities can be users or entities.

- ***Behavior baseline pattern*** – Behavior-based clustering and outlier machine learning algorithms establish behavior baselines for users, entities, static peer groups and dynamic peer groups to detect unusual behavior and access risk. The use of dynamic peer groups delivers a large reduction in false positives over static peer groups, plus eliminating bad behavior baselines. A machine learning model library for a solution should provide hundreds of models for forty to fifty use cases with the ability to optimize in 30 to 60 days. Historical data can be leveraged to reduce self-learning and training to a few days.

- ***Access control and case management*** – Internal case management capability is a standard requirement. A ticketing system, plus integration with other leading solutions such as with Remedy, ServiceNow and Salesforce, should be offered as well. In addition, data masking within the workflow, as well as role-based access control (RBAC), data tokenization and encryption, deliver distinct functional advantages to UEBA solutions.

- ***Dashboards and incident investigation*** – Dashboards with click-through drill-downs for incident investigation have become well-established as integral parts of UEBA solutions for popular use cases, risk groups to watch and color-coding to visualize risk scores. In addition, the ability to create custom reports and open queries and filters are decisively advantageous. Self-audits promote collaboration from users to view their risk-scored profiles for activities and access, to understand the context of their usage and sometimes correct unintentional misuse habits. They also provide the ability to see possible unauthorized use of an individual's identity access.

- *API layer* – While the UI provides dashboards and drill-downs for security analysts to act upon, more than half the value of a UEBA solution is derived via API integration with other solutions for closed-loop response, also called automated risk response. Examples include step-up authentication by risk score, automatic access outlier detection with IAM solutions, dynamic provisioning with IAM and IDaaS solutions to reduce workload, prioritized risk-scored anomalies into SIEM and DLP solutions, and privileged access abuse controls based on risk score with PAM solutions.

UEBA machine learning requirements

'Machine learning' may be one of the more over-used marketing terms currently in vogue. Nonetheless, having an in-depth contextual understanding of its place in user and entity behavior analytics is critical. One perspective to keep in mind is the nature of big data machine learning. This far surpasses what humans and software engineering can detect. It represents a magnitude of processing now coming to a state of wider understanding and adoption within the security technology community. The requirements of advanced and mature machine learning include:

- *No rules, signatures or tuning* – Operational independence from editing rules and signatures is a core benefit of mature UEBA solutions drawing from true machine learning. No preexisting knowledge should be required to iterate models for various use cases where data sources provide attributes for analysis. No rules or signatures are required for deployment. The focus is on data sources, data ingestion and data cleanliness for deployment. Some UEBA providers may optionally provide a rules and policy editor for customers that choose their own unique use cases and may not have a log event manager (LEM) or SIEM.

- *Peer groups creation (users, entities/assets)* – While static peer groups are a standard UEBA feature, their functionality remains limited in comparison to the next generation innovation of dynamic peer groups which can draw from over 200 attributes to create behavior profiles. The most mature UEBA solution vendors should be able to automatically create both dynamic peer groups based on behavior profiles and static peer groups based on one or more attributes for users and entities. They must provide the ability to view analysis by these peer groups in tables, charts and graphs.

- **Peer group behavior baselines** – Leveraging clustering machine learning algorithms to develop behavior baselines, UEBA solutions continuously identify changing behavior with model optimization within 30 to 60 days. In the more advanced UEBA solutions, historical data ingestion can reduce self-learning and self-training to a few days.

- **Outlier detection and scoring** – Using the behavioral baseline of the peer group, the UEBA solution maintains continuous monitoring and scores anomalies. A convention of outlier risk scoring normalized between 0 and 100 using dimensionality reduction provides an advantageous granularity of precision in scoring, and reinforcement against false positives, and should be considered a standard feature. In addition, a vendor providing dynamic peer groups increases outlier accuracy by 8-10x over the use of static peer groups.

- **Investigator feedback and re-scoring** – UEBA solutions provide the ability to send feedback via algorithm study activity or investigator feedback for time-based norms (e.g., an admin on vacation for two-weeks, or a newly accepted process or workflow). Feedback can also include data on false positives and false negatives where models will then re-score historical analysis.

Insights on machine learning: Not all UEBA machine learning is the same

Many UEBA security vendors are currently touting their solutions as being driven by machine learning. However, not all UEBA machine learning delivers the same capabilities. The following list represents criteria to look for in a UEBA solution driven by true machine learning.

- **Hybrid visibility across environments** – A number of solutions are hampered in their effectiveness because they are focused on siloed pools of data. Any machine learning associated with them is hampered as well, since it is limited to processing the data which resides only in the system concerned. This leaves a host of undetected outliers and an unaccounted for threat plane beyond the silos.

- **Big data, big data lake** – True machine learning thrives on large repositories of big data for increased processing and data variety over legacy infrastructure. The richer and more inclusive the source of data, the higher potential for accurate context for risk scores, along with fewer false positives. Solutions not drawn from big data have restricted processing capacity and less data variety. Solutions should provide an open customer choice for big data (Hadoop, Cloudera, Hortonworks, MapR and Elastic/ELK Stack).

- ***No rules or signatures dependence*** – While referenced in the section directly above in a different context, this point bears emphasis and deeper analysis. This issue is the most common complaint of customers and experts in the field who observe that a number of UEBA vendors have simply rebranded their solutions which are heavily dependent on rules and signatures. This is not considered true machine learning. Many of these solutions, for example, only look at limited data sources such as AD and SIEM, or some sort of nomenclature to identify privileged access, such as, tagging and naming prefixes. These solutions do not utilize true machine learning and are severely constrained by the fact that they lack any real context for analytics.

- ***Multi-vector data sourcing*** – Along the lines relating to the limitations and constraints of siloed data, a broader perspective represents the various vectors, or sources of data, that are required for broad context within monitoring. Having complete access to the comprehensive data sets to facilitate all-inclusive monitoring is essential for effective advanced machine learning and to avoid data decay. This includes the complete range of user behavior, in all environments (on-premises and in the cloud, globally, and 24/7), as well as all of the data and applications that the user might interact with, in the hybrid environment, including both company and privately owned devices (BYOD, IoT, etc.).

- ***Human analyst and automated interaction*** – Seamless efficiencies between the machine learning technology aspect and the human analyst is critical to facilitate effective, reliable and evolving (self-learning and self-training) machine learning for advanced security analytics. Many UEBA black box solutions have little to no ability to be customized so the solution might align more closely with customer organizational security goals and data sources. It may also lack the capability to integrate security analyst feedback on false positive and negatives, which is critical for model accuracy. Also, as an open solution, having the capability to customize risk weightings and create custom models for confidential data sources and private use cases, is an essential requirement for some organizations, (e.g., military, financial, federal government). A closed black box solution often lacks this functionality.

- ***Assessing known bads versus learning an environment*** – There are two types of UEBA solutions. Those that are built on rules and signatures, and those that have a foundation in machine learning with the context of big data. Where rules and signatures can show results in a few days, machine learning requires 30 to 60 days to self-learn and self-train and then optimize in the environment to show results. From there machine learning models continue to self-learn and self-train, gaining deeper context and accuracy. Rules and signatures have no growth or evolutionary capabilities as they are not built around self-learning or self-training with a feedback loop.

- ***Integration with identity analytics (IdA)*** – One industry expert recently observed, "How can you protect against insider threats if you don't understand privileged identity access and entitlements?" In today's traditional PAM environments, experts observe that over a half of an organization's privileged access entitlements reside outside of the solution's visibility. This represents a serious unaddressed access risk plane. Having the ability for IdA's machine learning to integrate seamlessly to identify privileged access risk with UEBA to monitor for privileged access abuse is essential for hybrid environments. The same holds true for the awareness gap with IAM solutions benefiting from identity analytics.

Some less forgiving experts in the security field refer to the weak substitutes supporting solutions with siloed UEBA features as 'baby machine learning'. Some solutions still appear to be in these baby step stages, which is a serious concern to any organization thinking that they are possibly protecting their environments with an up-to-date solution. These same experts also recognize that machine learning is best served by a platform or standalone solution with broad visibility, across all data siloes, for the context it provides.

A proven best-of-breed UEBA solution that draws effectively from big data, integrates seamlessly with IdA, draws from a robust set of behavior models and attributes, is a great starting point when considering a vendor for solution adoption. The POC phase is where organizations then see if it all really works for them, which should be longer than 30 days.

UEBA for IAM and PAM requirements

Traditionally IAM business users have employed manual processes and legacy rules with compliance driving rubber-stamping for certifications and access cloning for efficiency. IAM's complexity lends itself an optimal opportunity for machine-aided processes around managing access intelligence corresponding to users' actions and rights. Elements of the UEBA requirements for these identity and access management include:

- ***Risk-based approach for IAM/PAM*** – UEBA solutions provide identity analytics (IdA) via API to IAM and PAM solutions. IAM solutions benefit from risk scores for certifications and to determine access outliers, excess access and a confirmation of orphan and dormant accounts. PAM solutions benefit from unknown privileged access hidden in standard accounts and applications at the entitlement level. More and more CROs (chief risk officers) are requesting increased risk scoring at the entitlement level for these reasons.

- **Risk-based authentication** – Real-time risk scores via API to authentication solutions determine user identity context and requirements for access. The UEBA solution communicates the risk score for the user login attempt and triggers an authentication prompt or prompts based on risk level. For example, a high-risk score may result in multi-factor authentication (MFA) whereas a low-risk score may only require a one-time password.

- **Risk-based IAM governance** – IdA for machine-learning-defined intelligent roles and risk-based access analytics verifies and tracks when and how a given user gets access. This greatly improves IAM governance. It can often replace manual processes and legacy roles. IdA closes the awareness gap for what access has been provided by an IAM solution, and how it is actually being utilized, enabling a risk-based approach for IAM governance.

- **PAM admin risk profiles** – UEBA solutions should provide IdA monitoring down to the level of privileged access analytics to detect unknown privileged access risk including privileged entitlements hidden in standard accounts and within applications. Privileged access abuse starts with knowing the locations of privileged access for users and entities.

UEBA and privileged access abuse

As stated earlier, industry experts have observed that over 50% of privileged access (PA) entitlements within organizations are unknown, and therefore unmanaged. This represents a sobering access risk plane. PA is widely acknowledged as a prime target of hackers, and customers employing traditional security solutions perceive a concerning gap in the discovery of unknown privileged access and privileged access abuse. Gurucul's delivery field experience has uncovered an instance of unknown access risk exceeding 70%.

Due to rapidly evolving conditions in enterprise environments that bear impact outside their original siloed solution design, PAM is currently unable to fully manage all privileged access accounts and entitlements. These solutions lack comprehensive discovery capabilities of hidden or unknown privileged access entitlements. To meet that challenge, a small selection of UEBA vendors employing advanced machine learning, have developed a solution set which integrates IdA and UEBA to create privileged access analytics (PAA). In partnership with PAM and IAM solutions, PAA delivers broad visibility providing the ability to identify and analyze privileged access across all environments, along with the capability to monitor and assess user behavior holistically.

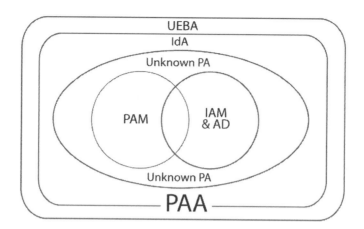

The PAA Solution Domain
Figure 13.1

Phases of privileged access risk reduction. Partnered with IAM and PAM solutions, PAA facilitates comprehensive coverage of all the phases of privileged access management. Understanding the fundamental realities of privileged access management is essential for successful risk reduction. Managing privileged access effectively entails successful implementation of the following solution phases:

- Discovery and analysis
- Life cycle management (IAM/PAM solutions)
- Access control (vaulting solutions)
- Full contextual visibility, monitoring, analysis, risk scoring and remediation

UEBA cloud security requirements

Cloud security gateways (CSGs), also known as CASBs, prevent data exfiltration as UEBA solutions expand that capability with robust comprehensive monitoring of access and activity. Core capabilities include:

- ***Cloud data exfiltration*** – A UEBA solution's integration with a cloud access security broker (CASB) solution strengthens the prevention of data exfiltration for on-premises and cloud workloads. A cloud security analytics (CSA) solution that also deploys via direct API integration, provides transparency for devices on any network by avoiding forward or reverse proxy traffic coordination. The CSA provides both enhanced IdA for access risk reduction and UEBA for detection of insider threats, account compromise and data exfiltration. The CSA also leverages proxy-based CASB solutions as a data source for shadow IT cloud activity, as not all SaaS solutions provide an API.

- ***Risk score behavior for SaaS/IaaS/PaaS*** – A UEBA solution's direct API integration with SaaS, IaaS and PaaS provides risked-scored identity analytics for access risks and user and entity behavior analytics for anomalous behavior and unknown threat detection. Cloud security analytics may also provide hybrid visibility for on-premises and cloud applications in a single solution.

- ***Cloud malware application detection*** – A UEBA solution's role in understanding the behavior of cloud malware applications is critical for identifying normal data movement between cloud applications and detecting anomalies in traffic patterns. In some cases, a UEBA vendor's CSA solution enhanced capabilities are focused on behavior-based anomaly detection to predict, deter and detect cloud-based risks, threats and malware using identity as both as an access risk and threat plane. [NOTE: Industry analysts have observed the limitations of signatures, patterns and rules to detect threats and that behavior analytics provides an important new perspective on these blind spots, even more so for cloud applications.]

Proof of concept – The pre-sale project adoption objectives

As prospective customers approach the final phase of a UEBA solution adoption, the POC is the most crucial. The customer has the opportunity to assess two critical factors in their determination of the solution's suitability for addressing their challenges. The first objective is to confirm the vendor's stated claims for the solution's capabilities as they are represented in marketing collateral and the sales representatives' demonstrations of the solution. Canned demos show a product's features and functionality in their best light and under ideal circumstances created by the vendor. However, working within a live customer environment is a completely different situation, with a range of variables influencing a successful demonstration of the solution's functionality. The second objective is to assure that the solution actually works within a selected targeted challenge, or set of use cases, data sources and requirements, defined by the customer.

Any qualified vendor's field engineering services group should focus on an economical, effective and rapid way to validate key customer use cases and demonstrate specific analytic outputs with genuine metrics tied to risk issues that are meaningful to the customer's core use cases for the project. They should facilitate an understanding of the customer's potential for ROI with the adoption of the solution in consideration.

Only after a demonstration of these customized capabilities, tailored within the customer environment, can a customer be assured that the prospective UEBA solution is appropriate and a cost-effective solution for their needs. Keep in mind that staging a POC is no simple process, and the larger the organization, and the more complex the environment, and data sources to ingest, the more involved the POC. This increases staging time required to deliver the POC properly. A POC is also a trial run, of sorts, for the partnership-like relationship between the customer and the vendor, which is required for the successful delivery of both POC and the life cycle of the solution itself.

UEBA solution adoption process overview

Throughout all phases of an UEBA solution delivery, and especially in the Commitment Phase (see Figure 13.2 below), effective institutionalization of a user and entity behavior analytics initiative within an organization is a two-way process, both from the top down and the bottom up, with the core organizational goal of the solution is to protect their vital information and assets. This is especially the case with a UEBA solution involving a self-audit feature. While some information is at risk due to nefarious behavior, other information is at risk because employee awareness is low as it relates to proper best practices and risky habits that can result in data loss through that condition of unfamiliarity with the importance of and commitment to those best practices.

Part of the successful adoption of a UEBA solution includes training with all levels of users in an organization. This includes the value and utility of user self-audits — to ensure the entire organization is aligned with the best practices that ensure preservation of sensitive IP and protection of access information. The adopting stakeholders' institutionalization role is also to encourage feedback from the bottom up, to ensure the implementation is executed effectively — and does not impact user productivity. Moreover, any challenges to successful implementation are reported up, thereby assuring the smooth, continued, and evolving utility of the solution. Without this engaged and committed two-way institutionalization, a solution's prospects for success may falter.

A perspective of the UEBA solution adoption process is depicted on the S curve configuration below.

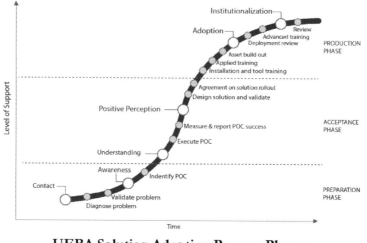

UEBA Solution Adoption Process Phases
Figure 13.2

UEBA Solution future-proofing

CIOs and CISOs, of course, view the evolution of their environments from a number of perspectives, weighing advantages of productivity and increased efficiencies that new technologies and applications offer against maintaining the security requirements to ensure the environment is protected properly. While adopting something like a UEBA-IdA solution, and its suitability for facing the current challenges, they must also take into consideration the evolving hybrid technologies and the innovation trends of future threats. As Carnival's Gary Eppinger's observes, "we maintain the strategy of continuous development and improvement, not adopt some monolithic solution that might be outdated as soon as it is finally implemented." Following on the concept of continuous improvement, CSO at Large, Joe Sullivan shares, "These adjusted solutions must be much more flexible and robust to address the challenge." And on the cautious optimism side, there can be greater benefits in a solution adoption than originally expected. To achieve this kind optimal solution adoption, CIO at Large Teri Takai notes, "the solution must supplement, and perhaps modify the access security strategy, not replace it."

Keeping an eye on the UEBA vendors who possess a proven track record of continuously developing reliable, open and flexible solutions in sync with the market demands is an important qualification to keep in mind when assessing a vendor's prospects of being able to keep pace with future rapid evolving innovations that increasingly fragment our environments.

In addition, a phased or project road map approach of implementing a solution helps customers in two ways:

- The cost of the adoption can be spread across a broader budget cycle and projects, such as privileged access abuse, data exfiltration and insider threat, offering incremental assessment of the solutions suitability and success against organizational objectives and use cases.
- The solution itself is integrated with the evolving factors of an environment taken into account. As the environment is changing from on-premises to cloud, the new phases of the UEBA solution adoption are implemented and integrated with them.

Selecting a UEBA solution partner

The final selection of a qualified UEBA solution partner is a critical decision. This entails an assessment of the solution's capabilities to address the use cases and data sources of the project, but also the people behind the solution as well. Employing a partner providing a team with a deep bench of experts in the field of user and entity behavior analytics is a key factor. This includes the SEs, project leaders, instructors, field teams, and experts in the field delivering the solution along with the support services team.

The solution partner's value is enhanced if UEBA and IdA are core competencies of the company's offerings. The UEBA team should have a holistic understanding of mobility, BYOD, IoT, on-premises, cloud and hybrid cloud environments. They must be able to articulate UEBA benefits and ROI vs. risk. In addition, the UEBA partner should have an established delivery process. Their qualifications are further strengthened if they can provide references of successful implementations that align in some ways with the prospective client's requirements.

Advanced Security Analytics
Use Cases

Introduction

Within the domain of advanced security analytics, the broadening adoption of user and entity behavior analytics (UEBA), and identity analytics (IdA), has been observed by a range of industry analysts. Drawing from big data and driven by mature machine learning to deliver invaluable context, they deliver an effective method to manage and monitor identity-based risks and threats across all of an organization's environments. Both on-premises and in the cloud — in concert, or as standalone solutions — these solutions identify and minimize excess access, establish what normal behavior is and detect what anomalous, possibly malicious, behavior is. The caliber and capabilities a solution vendor delivers within this niche of advanced security analytics is, in part, defined by the use cases they are capable of conducting. While some vendors may offer a limited set of use cases for UEBA, this is only one part of advanced security analytics. More recently, IdA and cloud security analytics (CSA) have expanded the breadth of use cases within advanced security analytics. These categories supported by a vendor should be one of the first factors prospective customers examine when considering adoption of an advanced security analytics solution. Customers must assure the use cases offered by a vendor align with their specific needs and varied requirements, both long term for an initial project and long term as a new defense. This chapter explores a comprehensive and optimal set of use cases across all the solution domains of UEBA, IdA and CSA.

Functional domains of advanced security analytics

The three solution capability categories within advanced security analytics are as follows:

- **Access analytics** – Directly associated with IdA, it involves detecting access risks, access outliers, shared HPA accounts, orphan and dormant accounts. In addition, it reduces the attack surface area for identities with machine-learning-based intelligent roles. Access analytics also reduces identity management manual processes, increases revocations, improves provisioning, and cleanses identity as an access risk plane for compliance and audits with identity analytics.

- **Threat analytics** – Aligned with UEBA, this systematic analysis deters, detects, and prevents insider threats, compromised accounts and data exfiltration with big data machine learning models. Identity is a threat plane that modern defenses miss with signatures, rules and patterns. Machine learning and dynamic peer groups uniquely uncover and monitor these holistically, minimizing false positives and enabling prompt, targeted remedial and automated risk responses.

- **Cloud analytics** – Affiliated with CSA, this category provides access and threat analytics for SaaS, IaaS, PaaS and IDaaS. It is deployed as an API-based CASB (cloud access service broker) to monitor access and activity for identity-based access risks, unknown threats or anomalous behavior. Deployments are also likely to integrate with proxy-based CASBs for shadow IT access and activity data where many SaaS applications do not provide APIs. Cloud-to-cloud connectors for popular software as a service (SaaS) applications including, infrastructure, platform and identity management as a service (IaaS, PaaS and IDaaS), ease installation and deployment to begin analytics.

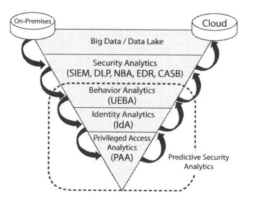

Big Data Security Analytics Funnel
Figure 14.1

Advanced security analytics – Use cases

The depth and range of use cases fundamentally defines the areas of expertise and functionality for advanced security analytics vendors. A number of vendors offer only a limited selection of use cases, while others are more inclusive and comprehensive in their offerings. An optimal list of use cases advanced security analytics is found in the table below. Use cases are organized in three categories: UEBA, IdA and CSA, with PAA (privileged access analytics) use cases overlapping within these groupings. Some of these use cases are correlated and/or parented with use cases in other columns. A good example is the privileged access abuse case, which requires both UEBA and IdA, and has been discussed earlier in this book. Also keep in mind the need and ability to create custom models for private data and confidential use cases common with federal, military and private industry deployments.

Use case summary table

UEBA	IdA	CSA
• Account Compromise, Hijacking and Sharing • High Privileged Access Abuse • Data Exfiltration and IP Protection • Insider Threat Detection and Deterrence • Self-Audit and ID Theft Detection • Cyber Fraud Detection and Deterrence • Trusted Host and Entity Compromise • Stateful Session Tracking • Step-up Authentication (Adaptive Authentication) • Anomalous Behavior and Watchlists • SIEM and DLP Risk Intelligence • Hybrid Infrastructure	• Privileged Access Discovery • Access Outliers and Excess Access • Outlier Access Clean-up (Oracle Identity Manager [OIM]) • Risk-based Access and Certifications • Dynamic Access Provisioning • Role Access Reconciliation • Role Mining and Intelligent Roles • Access Governance and Segregation of Duties (SoD) Monitoring • Dormant and Orphan Account Management	• Cloud Account Compromise, Hijacking and Sharing • Cloud Privileged Access Abuse • Cloud Data Exfiltration and IP Protection • Cloud Insider Threat Detection and Deterrence • Cloud Self-Audit and ID Theft Detection • Cloud Step-up Authentication • Cloud Anomalous Behavior and Watchlists • Cloud to SIEM Integration for Alerts • Cloud to On-Premises DLP Closed-Loop • Cloud Access Outliers and Excess Access • Cloud Risk-based Access Compliance • Cloud Dormant and Orphan Accounts • Cloud Application License Metering (Account Level)

Chapter appendix – Capital Markets Use Cases.

User and entity behavior analytics – Use cases

User and entity behavior analytics use cases are focused on detection of unknown risks and threats beyond the capabilities of rules, signatures and patterns. Using machine learning models to detect anomalous behavior, minimizing false positives, these use cases result in predictive risk scores which drive alerts, actions and case tickets. To assure optimal and comprehensive capabilities, UEBA vendors' use cases should draw from big data utilizing at least 200 plus attributes leveraged in over 150 machine learning models.

This solution model should include data ingestion available via flat file, database, API, message or streaming inputs with ready-to-use data connectors for common enterprise systems and platforms (i.e., HR, IAM, PAM, SIEM, AD, databases, networks, vulnerabilities, DLP, threat intel, cloud applications/SaaS, authentication, physical ID badge systems, file storage and endpoints). This level of advanced solution should support an open choice for big data with Hadoop, Cloudera, Hortonworks and MapR.

Account Compromise, Hijacking and Sharing

One of the Top 10 OWASP (Open Web Application Security Project) vulnerabilities is related to the 'Broken Authentication and Session Management' scenario. Here, attackers exploit vulnerabilities through attacks such as Pass-the-Hash (PtH), Pass-the-Token (PtT), Brute Force and Remote Execution, to gain access to user credentials (passwords and hash). Such attacks can  be detected using the underlying machine learning algorithms tuned to inspect various parameters like timestamp, location, IP, device, transaction patterns, high-risk event codes and network packets, to identify any deviation from the normal behavior of a particular account and the corresponding transactions. This facilitates detection of any potential account compromise or hijacking scenarios based on the anomalous behavior patterns such as: abnormal access to high-risk or sensitive objects, abnormal number of activities, requests in a short timeframe, activity from terminated user accounts or dormant accounts, PtH attacks and session replay attacks. Anomalies identified via clustering machine learning models and outlier analysis inconsistent with a user or peers' normal behaviors are given risk scores based on advanced analytics, to drive alerts, actions and case tickets. Self-audits (reviewed below) may also support this use case.

Benefits

- Detects anomalous behaviors beyond rules, patterns and signatures for account compromise, hijacking and sharing
- Provides 360-degree visibility for user accounts, access and activity for on-premises, cloud and hybrid environments

High Privileged Access Abuse

This use case identifies high privileged access (HPA) abuse by leveraging the combination of accounts, access and activity data. Typically, accounts and access data is ingested from IAM, PAM and/or directory services platforms to identify HPA accounts and discover any non-HPA accounts granted high privileged entitlements. Additionally, the activity data is ingested from the

enterprise level audit or log sources (e.g., SIEM or log aggregators) or obtained directly from the target sources. Once HPA accounts are identified, UEBA can detect suspicious behavior and misuse such as: using HPA to assign special or elevated privileges to the user's own account followed by an activity, transactions outside the window of password value checkout and check-in timeframe. This also includes access to resources and transactions outside normal behavior profiles, abnormal access to classified or sensitive documents, multiple concurrent sessions from the same account, different IPs, devices, locations, etc.

Benefits

- Discovers privileged access and provides visibility on who has the 'keys to the kingdom'
- Reduces high privileged access account abuse and eliminates shared HPA accounts
- Reduces access risks before abuse with risk-scored HPA accounts and entitlements

Data Exfiltration and IP Protection

UEBA identifies data exfiltration and protects intellectual property by ingesting data sources such as DLP and data classification to learn important data locations, access and application activity. Risk scoring DLP alerts are a primary benefit of UEBA machine learning to reduce alert fatigue and prioritize 'find-fix' resources. Analysis by UEBA includes on-premises and cloud applications

for a 360-degree view of data access and activity. This approach helps customers prioritize DLP alerts investigation, as well as identify and monitor even the low severity DLP alerts associated with departing users or high-risk users. UEBA solutions traditionally provide out-of-the-box (OOTB) anomaly models which can identify known patterns such as: sensitive documents downloaded and copied to USB, large amounts of source code checked out from source code repositories and file uploads to cloud storage, emails to personal accounts, access to competitor and/or job websites, etc. Solution customers have also extended UEBA alerts beyond SOC analysts to managers, given their depth of context and relevance regarding employees, data and projects. Self-audits can provide deterrence for data access and unsanctioned activity.

Benefits

- Baselines data access and activity for anomalous events through self-learning and self-training machine learning models
- Supports customized and unique DLP and data classifications, metadata models and big data infrastructure support to each company
- Significantly reduces DLP alerts, time to investigate and false positives through predictive risk scoring

Insider Threat Detection and Deterrence

Advanced UEBA insider threat detection and deterrence leverages research drawing from extensive insider threat databases of real-world incidents to develop, test and refine machine learning (ML) behavior models. Identifying high-risk profiles with abnormal behaviors in conjunction with data risk monitoring, machine learning and statistical analysis, reveals anomalies in data that  humans could not otherwise recognize or detect. A force multiplier, ML far surpasses human capabilities and software engineering for managing large volumes and varieties of data. True machine learning also has the ability to find high-order interactions and patterns in data for complex problems such as insider threats, compromised accounts and data exfiltration. It does this by leveraging useful and predictive cues that are too noisy and highly dimensional for human experts and traditional software to detect. A 360-degree dashboard should provide visibility of an identity's accounts, access and activity for on-premises and cloud hybrid environments. A self-audit feature may support this use case providing deterrence and security awareness. Both access and activity are risk scored for anomalous events with results visible to managers and SOC analysts.

Benefits

- Delivers hybrid visibility for on-premises and cloud across access and activity with machine learning models leveraging big data context to detect anomalies and apply predictive risk scores for insider threat detection
- Highlights insider threats first and in common risk groups, plus watchlists via UEBA dashboard
- Provides unique insider threat deterrence and security awareness to users and managers through self-audits

Self-Audit and ID Theft Detection

A self-audit feature deputizes users into a collaborative relationship with security analysts to provide context and relevance not available to SOC teams. This multiplier of 'eyes on glass' applies to employees, business partners and suppliers, agents in hub-spoke organizations, and in some cases, customers. All of these parties are likely to have one or more accounts with access entitlements to critical applications and data. A frequently issued (usually weekly) self-audit report provides visibility for access, devices, locations and risk-scored anomalous behavior, delivering both detection and deterrence for end users. A case in point: a self-audit was implemented by a company where an employee was out of office on a Wednesday due to a sick child. This employee never logged into her accounts on that day. A self-audit report sent to this individual on the following Friday showed account activity on Wednesday when the employee knew they had not logged in. Further investigation by security analysts discovered the account had been compromised for over three-and-a-half years, where the employee had high privileged access to critical applications and data.

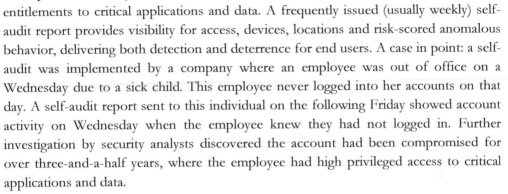

Benefits

- Deputizes end users into a collaborative relationship to quickly identify anomalous behavior and ID compromise
- Leverages end users and managers with unique context and relevance for accounts, applications and data not easily replicated into SOC teams
- Provides an audit and compliance benefit for employees, business partners, suppliers and even customers

Cyber Fraud Detection and Deterrence

UEBA addresses cyber fraud use cases for treasury, accounting, payments and areas concerning funds transactions. Here the UEBA solution provides a flexible data model open to attributes from commercial or homegrown treasury and accounting systems to be quantified for behavior analytics from machine learning models. UEBA solutions have been deployed for merchant environments to monitor for cyber fraud and account compromise. A real-world scenario: in April 2016, SWIFT acknowledged attackers had obtained valid credentials for operators to create and approve SWIFT messages. Over 11,000 financial organizations that use SWIFT daily to transfer billions of dollars were jeopardized by this cyber fraud. SWIFT and supporting vendors issue patches and make recommendations to detect fraudulent use. However, the data volume is overwhelming and signals are too fine-grained for analysis by humans. Ingesting data on access and activity from treasury, accounting and payments areas within organizations, UEBA allows enterprises to integrate their cyber

fraud models and risk frameworks, providing significant benefit of leveraging existing investments and security models in alignment with business context. The use of self-audits may support this use case.

Benefits

- Supports the ingestion of data sources from treasury, accounting and payment systems through an open metadata model
- Detects anomalies for predictive risk scoring with feedback for false positives and negatives powered by machine learning behavior models
- Improves accuracy reflected in risk scores for data quality and relevance through risk weightings that can be customized for attributes

Trusted Host and Entity Compromise

It is well known that one of the widely used tactics to execute cyberattacks is to compromise trusted hosts connected to an organization's network infrastructure. In addition to monitoring anomalous user behavior with UEBA, it is critical for organizations to closely monitor all the endpoints (devices and hosts) connected to the network. UEBA builds an anomaly timeline for an entity  based on the high-risk anomalous events and activities performed from the respective devices and hosts. UEBA correlates a wide range of parameters associated with an entity including: endpoint security alerts, vulnerability scan results (Common Vulnerability Scoring System [CVSS]), risk levels of users and accounts used, targets accessed, packet level inspection of the requested payloads, and more. This correlation facilitates detection of any anomalous activities and events to determine predictive risk scores.

Benefits

- Detects advanced persistent threat (APT) attacks and attack vectors and predicts data exfiltration by performing entity-centric anomaly detection
- Provides risk-based dashboard for closely monitoring high-risk entities and investigation using detailed anomaly timeline based on users, accounts, alerts and activities associated with the entity

Stateful Session Tracking

In this use case, UEBA builds and tracks the user session state, even when a user navigates across heterogeneous resources or applications using different accounts and devices at different times. Leveraging machine learning, UEBA dynamically builds session correlation attributes used to build session context in order to link  any subsequent activities based on a confidence factor. This enables the identification of valid IP switching due to transitions between wired and wireless networks, a workstation and a handheld/mobile device, or accessing enterprise resources from various onsite locations or remotely over VPN. UEBA's ability to track user sessions across these various parameters ensures a significant reduction in false positives while simultaneously delivering greater visibility into the sequence of events. It also provides the capability to drill down to specific activities performed by a user or entity while performing an investigation. This analysis also expedites the detection of session replay and hijacking attacks, highlighting any anomalous activity from a user session or concurrent sessions from the same account.

Benefits

- Provides greater visibility into user activities across multiple resources or applications via with stateful session tracking
- Provides drill-down and raw log views for deep event analysis at the source
- Reduces false positives due to common scenarios like IP, account and device switching while performing day-to-day activities
- Detects session replay and hijacking attacks

Step-up Authentication (or Adaptive Authentication)

The use of passwords to authorize users is core to the problem of identity compromise and misuse. Deploying multi-factor authentication takes time, resources and expenses and can impede high productivity users in low-risk environments. The concept of step-up authentication (also known as adaptive authentication) leverages the UEBA risk score of an identity or entity to determine 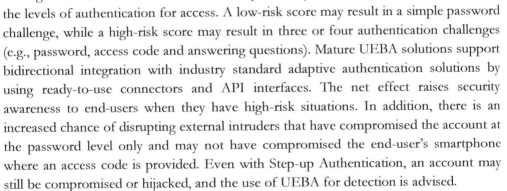 the levels of authentication for access. A low-risk score may result in a simple password challenge, while a high-risk score may result in three or four authentication challenges (e.g., password, access code and answering questions). Mature UEBA solutions support bidirectional integration with industry standard adaptive authentication solutions by using ready-to-use connectors and API interfaces. The net effect raises security awareness to end-users when they have high-risk situations. In addition, there is an increased chance of disrupting external intruders that have compromised the account at the password level only and may not have compromised the end-user's smartphone where an access code is provided. Even with Step-up Authentication, an account may still be compromised or hijacked, and the use of UEBA for detection is advised.

Benefits

- Creates a closed-loop for step-up authentication with API integration between threat analytics and authentication solutions
- Raises security awareness with end users via authentication challenges when their identity shows high-risk behaviors
- Combines Step-up Authentication with self-audit as key parts of an increased security awareness program

Anomalous Behavior and Watchlists

UEBA addresses anomalous behavior with watchlists to quickly profile and maintain an eye on unknowns and apply escalating predictive risk scores. Machine learning behavior models are designed to deliver feedback on false positives and negatives and then update self-learning and self-training models to adapt to time-based norms and conditions unique to each customer deployment.

For example, a database administrator may create a script that runs several commands with security implications at 2 a.m. each evening. This user is an innovator working to improve the enterprise's productivity. However, machine learning models will see these commands during non-business hours as an anomaly and risk score accordingly. Feedback from the models can note the situation is benign. Nonetheless, the database administrator should be put on a watchlist. Watchlists also come pre-defined within UEBA for common high-risk groups like new hires, departing users, terminated users, and high-risk users. These groups should be easily accessed in dashboard drop-down menus to analyze risk scores, anomalies, accounts, access, activity and timelines. UEBA also supports explicitly adding or removing identities within watchlists.

Benefits

- Quickly profiles high-risk user groups from watchlists to monitor their risk scores and anomalies by SOC security analysts
- Facilitates profiling by audit and compliance teams of a specific person or group via a watchlist to analyze their identity, accounts, access and activity
- Controls who has visibility to watchlists and for what data fields through Role-based Access Controls (RBAC) and data masking features

SIEM and DLP Risk Intelligence

UEBA addresses the alert fatigue issue of SIEM (security information and event management) and DLP (data loss prevention) solutions by aggregating the risk scores at the user and entity level, rather than generating a huge number of alerts at the transaction or event level. This allows SOC analysts to focus on the high-risk identities and the associated anomalies detected by UEBA.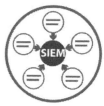

The result is a significant reduction in the number of alerts. This use case employs bidirectional integration via APIs enabling SIEM and DLP data ingestion into UEBA as it provides risk scores back to these systems to allocate 'find-fix' resources. SIEM and DLP solutions provide critical data sources for additional context related to identity profile information and the corresponding access grants (accounts, entitlements), also including the activity and alerts data ingested from on-premises and cloud applications in hybrid environments. While SIEM and DLP solutions work with known variables and identifiers via rules, patterns and signatures, UEBA detects the unknown via robust machine learning behavior models. Leveraging clustering and outlier algorithms, the models identify anomalies for predictive risk scoring. UEBA examines the data from an identity-based perspective analyzing user or entity behavior against itself and peer groups using baselines norms. As companies migrate to the cloud for applications and data, the role of UEBA becomes more essential for security events and data protection.

Benefits

- Provides ready to use data connectors for popular SIEM and DLP solutions to speed connectivity and data ingestion
- Delivers risk-scored SIEM and DLP events and alerts to focus 'find-fix' resources through machine learning behavior models
- Provides bidirectional integration via APIs and enables data ingestion into UEBA as well as the export of risk scores and identities to SIEM and DLP solutions

Hybrid Infrastructure

This use case addresses hybrid infrastructure by providing UEBA platforms for both on-premises and cloud applications, removing the need for any data transfers between environments. These transfers can be expensive and impede the use of big data for traditional security analytics. The threat analytics side would run on-premises and provide ready-to-use data connectors for common  on-premises applications and platforms as data sources. The cloud analytics side is an API-based cloud access security broker (CASB) that integrates with SaaS cloud applications, along with IaaS, PaaS and IDaaS, via APIs. The CASB API architecture enables direct data collection from cloud data sources while providing users a transparent access experience for any location on any network. Proxy-based CASBs are a data source into cloud analytics for shadow IT use, cloud DLP, and more. Threat, access and cloud analytics share combined processes to provide 360-degree visibility for identity accounts, access and activities in hybrid environments.

Benefits

- Enables organizations to avoid data transfer charges between on-premises and cloud (if big data was only in one location)
- Improves the context of data inputs from on-premises and cloud for each identity or entity through user and entity behavior analytics
- Ensures organizations can migrate applications and data from on-premises to cloud with peace of mind

Identity analytics (IdA)

Identity and access management (IAM) is the Achilles heel of organizations. It is quickly becoming a key concern for security leaders understanding the role of identity compromise and misuse as the core of modern threats. Identity analytics (IdA) is the proactive side of advanced security analytics, enabling the reduction of excess access, access outliers, and orphan or dormant accounts, before they are compromised or abused, plus providing risk-based certifications and defining intelligent roles. UEBA is the detection and response side, using machine learning models to detect unknown risks and threats via predictive risk scoring early in the kill chain as a best use case scenario. IdA is the data science that improves IAM and privileged access management (PAM), leveraging machine learning models surpassing human capabilities to define, review and confirm accounts and entitlements for access. If the goal of user and entity behavior analytics is to profile an identity and its accounts, access and activity, then the goal of IdA is to assure this access plane is reduced as much as possible with the removal of any access risks, access outliers, orphan or dormant accounts, etc.

Intelligent roles replace manually defined roles often created from legacy rules. Group and role proliferation, plus the buildup of accounts and entitlements for employees during their career in various roles, create unnecessary access to insiders or attackers. This is an identity access plane ripe for phishing and social attacks. Implementing an intelligent roles policy redefines and minimizes an organization's access risk plane, providing the right person with the right data at the right time and place.

Machine learning models provide 360-degree visibility for an identity, accounts, access and activity with the ability to compare to peer groups, using baselines to determine normal and anomalous access, and nature of activity. The impact of machine learning with IdA can radically reduce accounts and entitlements for an organization. This often represents the first phase in a project plan when adopting UEBA and IdA. The objective is to clean up the access plane with IdA for access only where it should be provided. Analysis with UEBA would follow that step to detect risks and threats beyond rules, patterns and signatures. These two steps work holistically together to address identity as an access risk and threat plane.

Outlier Access and Excess Access

Identity analytics identifies high-risk systems access by consuming access entitlements (rights) data from applications and platforms. This use case identifies access that is considered high-risk including: privileged access, access improperly segregating duties, dissimilar access compared to peers and infrequent access to systems. The average user has more than 100 entitlements making certification a time-consuming process for managers. Organizations realize

managers are too often approving all certification requests without actually validating each one. Certifications are typically a quarterly or yearly process leaving organizations at risk with employees having extended access to which they should not be entitled. Using identity analytics integrated with IAM systems, organizations can detect access outliers leveraging peer groups of users to trigger certifications for outlier access.

Benefits

- Reduces access not associated with job responsibilities and potential account compromise risk
- Reduces the time window of access risk
- Reduces rubber-stamping associated with Sarbanes-Oxley and other compliance related access reviews
- Reduces segregation of duties (SoD) conflicts for access, plus optimizes manager time with high-risk access certifications

Outlier Access Clean-Up

Identity analytics solutions can be configured to automate access clean up. Mature IdA and IAM solutions software should integrate with bidirectional APIs and with each other. The lack of APIs is a red flag of siloed data not open to analytics analysis. Discovered outlier access can be marked for removal. IdA solutions will use API integration to automatically send a de-provisioning request to  the provisioning system, where standard workflows can be applied, to ensure the access is removed appropriately. Removal is validated and user risk scores are adjusted when the identity analytics system receives confirmation back from the provisioning system that access has been removed.

Benefits

- Centralizes access cleanup at the provisioning system, making use of previous integration investments
- Automates access cleanup processes and eliminates the need to go to each endpoint to remove access
- Centralizes auditability; access removal is logged and captured in the provisioning system forgoing the need to consolidate logs to confirm access was removed

Risk-Based Access Certifications

Outlier access capabilities can be extended to automatically send risk-based certifications to the business when outlier access is identified. Identity analytics uses multiple parameters to drive risk-based certification, including a user's overall risk score, entitlement and account level risk score, and outlier scores from a context-rich configurable UI. Configurations may include several context points

such as: access risk rating, peer group metrics, outlier risk scores and status recommendations (*Keep* or *Remove*). Mature identity analytics solutions can send built-in certifications, or use APIs to integrate with other enterprise solutions to send certifications to account owners for review.

Benefits

- Enables the business (managers, data owners, role owners) to make decisions about removing or retaining outlier access to their assets
- Integrates with most enterprise certification systems and eliminates the need for training end users on a new certification platform
- Delivers a configurable context-rich UI for making decisions about access

Dynamic Access Provisioning

Dynamic access provisioning can be used to determine access-control permissions and restrictions based on a user's risk score. Risk scores are defined by machine learning algorithms from identity analytics. They take into account several points of context including: user behavior, resource sensitivity, the job or role of the user, access of the user versus their peers, and the configuration of the device used to access resources. Dynamic access provisioning  reduces IT workload and should also automatically update user permissions independently without additional administrator intervention when the user's job or role changes. *Example 1*: Identity analytics determines user permissions when a user accesses a resource from their office computer versus when they use BYOD over a virtual private network. Access may be reduced if the device is considered high-risk (unknown, not patched, unusual location, etc.). *Example 2*: A user switches jobs, identity analytics software identifies the job change and new peer groups are identified. Dynamic Access Provisioning automatically updates user permissions without administrator intervention for low-risk situations.

Benefits

- Updates access to resources based on risk versus hard-coded rules
- Dynamically manages access for low-risk situations, rather than depending on manual intervention, thus reducing workload for certifications, requests and approvals
- Automatically removes access when unknown devices and locations are in play

Role Access Reconciliation

Identity analytics software reviews role membership and identifies missing access, as well as, access to systems no longer in use by the role members. The solution integrates with provisioning systems to ensure all changes made to access follow the standard provisioning process, and that each transaction is logged accordingly. The system can be configured to automatically inform users and resource owners of access changes. Roles are automatically reviewed for access no longer used or needed by the role members.

Benefits

- Automatically updates users within a role to have all the access that the role provides
- Ensures access additions and removals are centrally logged with integration of provisioning or ticketing systems
- Automatically notifies role owners and business users of access changes due to updates made to role access
- Automatically adds or removes role access based on common use of systems

Role Mining and Intelligent Roles

Identity analytics can be used to review existing roles, or mine and define new roles. Unlike traditional role mining, identity analytics uses machine learning algorithms that take into account access and activity. This ensures unused and unneeded access is removed from roles during the definition process. Roles can be easily exported for consumption by provisioning systems.

Benefits

- Adds or removes role access based on common use of systems
- Analyzes existing roles for unnecessary and unused access
- Removes manual role mining processes based on legacy rules

Access Governance and SoD Monitoring

Segregation of duties (SoD) is an essential control over sensitive transactions. Role-based authorization and access often causes unknown conflicts in securing these transactions. Identity analytics automatically reviews existing roles and entitlements across systems and identifies inter- and intra- application segregation of duty risks. When these risks are identified, the access analytics software can temporarily disable the access and send a notification to the business owner. The business owner can choose to accept the risk and allow the access, or deny the access. In both situations, identity analytics software should support configurations to send updates to the business owner and to the identity access management request system to ensure the central audit log is maintained.

Benefits

- Detects SoD rule violations within applications and between applications
- Automatically removes access from users to enforce SoD rules
- Enables business users to take action with context of what process and transactions are at risk

Dormant and Orphan Account Management

Identity analytics identifies dormant and orphan accounts. These accounts can be sent to system owners or administrators for review. Action can be taken, based on their response, to assign the account to an end user or entity, or remove the account from the system.

Benefits

- Reduces risk of orphan or dormant accounts being compromised or misused
- Automates identification of risky orphan and dormant accounts
- Enables account and system owners to take action by identifying account owners or marking the account for review
- Automatically disables accounts and notifies the owner when there is no decision

Cloud security analytics – Use cases

Cloud security analytics (CSA) utilizes an API-based cloud access security broker (CASB) architecture to deliver advanced security analytics for SaaS cloud applications, including IaaS, PaaS, and IDaaS. The advantage of API cloud integration, versus proxy-based CASB gateways, is that it provides users with a transparent experience in any location or network, with any device. A proxy-based CASB has the advantage of being a chokepoint to monitor shadow IT for unsanctioned cloud applications not providing API visibility, plus cloud DLP monitoring and controls. However, device access control must be in-line for CASB proxy monitoring. CASB proxy gateways are a crucial data source into UEBA and IdA models as part of the solution architecture to deliver predictive risk scores for cloud environments where API visibility is not provided. In addition, web, email, and network cloud gateways are also data sources for machine learning behavior models.

Cloud security analytics should work on its own for cloud-only deployments and also be capable of synchronizing seamlessly with threat analytics and access analytics on-premises for hybrid environments. Having cloud, threat and access analytics holistically integrated and synchronized is essential for comprehensive hybrid environment risk analytics solution success. Cloud environments differ from on-premises, as SaaS cloud applications deliver less data variety via API. They are, however, more consistent in data quality. Whereas on-premises data variety can be much wider, the data quality is lower, and this impacts machine learning behavior models. Using a security model originally developed for on-premises is generally incompatible, and requires adjustments for cloud environments.

Currently the field of UEBA vendors offering an API architecture for cloud security analytics as part of an umbrella platform addressing hybrid environments is quite small as UEBA solutions, for the most part, originated within on-premises. Separate and unintegrated UEBA features from multiple vendors restricts visibility and diminishes the ability to provide comprehensive risk scores from the full context of 360-degree visibility of an identity, accounts, access and activity. CSA, only available within a specific CASB vendor, is limited to cloud environments in the same manner as UEBA features dedicated solely to a SIEM from another vendor with an on-premises focus. Optimally, users' access applications and data in both cloud and on-premises, provides 360-degree visibility and a context, which maximizes machine learning model effectiveness and accuracy. In summary, UEBA, IdA and CSA as an integrated vendor agnostic platform provide the optimal visibility and context for machine learning.

Cloud Account Compromise, Hijacking and Sharing

Cloud security analytics address cloud account compromise, hijacking and cloud account sharing via API integration with SaaS cloud applications, plus IaaS and PaaS. Visibility into Office 365 cloud applications leverages Microsoft Azure visibility for cloud infrastructure and platform information alongside cloud application activity data. The same applies to other popular cloud applications in AWS cloud environments. Identity and access management as a  service (IDaaS) also plays a role for cloud environments. The benefits of big data infrastructure with a flexible data model come into play to develop API data connectors for cloud data ingestion that may mimic on-premises functions in numerous ways. Utilizing advanced machine learning behavior models, cloud security analytics leverages this capability for cloud environments to detect account compromise, hijacking and sharing on-premises. The basic concepts of clustering and outlier algorithms to find anomalies based on normal baselines of the user and peers for predictive risk scores remains consistent with adjustments for data variety and quality. The data sources differ and data ingestion is API-based for cloud environments.

Benefits

- Detects account compromise, hijacking and sharing for cloud application accounts and privileged accounts for IaaS, PaaS and IDaaS
- Detects anomalous behaviors beyond rules, patterns and signatures for cloud account compromise, hijacking and sharing
- Combines cloud security analytics with on-premises security analytics for hybrid environment visibility in one UEBA-IdA platform

Cloud Privileged Access Abuse

Cloud security analytics addresses privileged access abuse via API integration with IaaS, PaaS and IDaaS solutions. This provides visibility to high privileged access (HPA) accounts. This also includes instances where privileged access entitlements are assigned to non-HPA accounts creating a high-risk situation. SaaS cloud applications and other activity data sources, including CASB proxy gateways for shadow IT detection, enable machine learning models to  find anomalous outliers for predictive risk scoring to drive alerts, actions and case tickets. Shared HPA cloud accounts are also included in this analysis. Once HPA cloud accounts are identified, cloud security analytics software can detect suspicious behavior or misuse. This would include: using HPA to assign special or elevated privileges to the user's own account followed by an activity, transactions outside the window of password value checkout and check-in timeframe, access to resources or transactions outside normal behavior profiles, abnormal access to classified or sensitive documents, multiple concurrent sessions for the same account with different IPs, devices, locations, etc.

Benefits

- Discovers cloud privileged access and provides visibility on who has the 'keys to the kingdom'
- Reduces high privileged access cloud account abuse and eliminates shared HPA cloud accounts
- Limits access risks before abuse with risk-scored HPA cloud accounts and entitlements

Cloud Data Exfiltration and IP Protection

Cloud security analytics addresses data exfiltration and intellectual property (IP) protection for cloud environments through API integration with SaaS cloud applications, IaaS, PaaS and CASBs. CASB proxy gateways, email gateways, web gateways and network gateways with DLP features are also key data sources for cloud security analytics software to analyze with machine learning. DLP in the cloud cannot always leverage data  fingerprints from on-premises deployments. This makes UEBA an important platform for data risk monitoring and protection. Identity provides the 'keys to the kingdom' with cloud applications and data access so access compromise and misuse are critical to detect as early as possible. Analysis by a behavior analytics platform includes on-premises and cloud applications for a 360-degree view of data access and activity. This approach helps customers prioritize DLP alert investigation, identify and monitor even the low-severity DLP alerts associated with departing users or high-risk users. In addition, CSA software should provide OOTB anomaly models which can identify known patterns such as: sensitive documents downloaded and copied to USB, large amounts of source code checked out from source code repositories and file uploads to cloud storage, emails to personal accounts, access to competitor and/or job websites, etc. Some solutions also extend risk-scored alerts beyond SOC analysts to managers, given their depth of context and relevance regarding employees, data and projects. Self-audits also provide deterrence and detection for cloud data access and activity.

Benefits

- Baselines cloud data access and activity for anomalous events with self-learning and training machine learning models
- Supports customized and unique DLP and data classifications, metadata models and big data infrastructure support

- Significantly reduces DLP alerts, time to investigate, and false positives, through predictive risk scoring

Cloud Insider Threat Detection and Deterrence

Well-developed cloud insider threat detection and deterrence leverages research, drawing from an extensive insider threat database of real-world incidents, to develop, test and refine machine learning behavior models. Identifying high-risk profiles with abnormal behaviors in conjunction with data risk monitoring, machine learning, and statistical analysis, finds anomalies in data that humans would not otherwise recognize or detect. It also far  surpasses human capability and software engineering for large volumes and variety of data. Machine learning also has the ability to find high-order interactions and patterns in data for complex problems such as insider threats, compromised accounts and data exfiltration by leveraging useful and predictive cues that are too noisy and highly dimensional for human experts and traditional software to detect. A 360-degree dashboard should provide visibility of an identity's accounts, access and activity for on-premises and cloud hybrid environments. A self-audit feature may support this use case where both access and activity are risk-scored for anomalous behavior visible to users and managers.

Benefits

- Utilizes machine learning models with context of big data for machine learning analysis to detect anomalies and apply predictive risk scores
- Highlights insider threats early and organized in common risk groups, along with watchlists, via the predictive risk analytics dashboard
- Provides insider threat deterrence and security awareness to users and managers through customizable self-audit feature

Cloud Self-Audit and ID Theft Detection

A self-audit feature for ID theft detection deputizes users into a collaborative relationship with security teams that leverages context and relevance not available to SOC teams. This multiplier of 'eyes on glass' applies to employees, business partners and suppliers, agents in hub-spoke organizations, and in some cases, customers. All these parties are likely to have one or more cloud accounts with access entitlements to critical cloud applications and  data. A frequent self-audit report provides visibility for access, devices, locations and risk-scored anomalous behavior, providing both detection and deterrence for end users.

Benefits

- Deputizes end users into a collaborative relationship to quickly identify anomalous behavior and ID compromise
- Leverages context and relevance for cloud accounts, applications and data of end users and managers not easily replicated into SOC teams
- Provides an audit and compliance benefit for employees, business partners, suppliers, and even customers

Cloud Step-up Authentication (Adaptive Authentication)

The compromise and misuse of identity lies at the heart of modern threats. The use of passwords to authorize users is core to the problem, even more so for cloud applications. Deploying multi-factor authentication takes time, resources and expenses and can impede high-productivity users in low-risk environments. Step-up authentication (also referred to as adaptive authentication) leverages the UEBA risk score of an identity or entity to  determine the levels of authentication for cloud access. A low-risk score may result in a simple password challenge, while a high-risk score may result in three or four authentication challenges (e.g., password, access code, and answering questions). This use case supports bidirectional integration with industry standard adaptive authentication solutions by employing ready-to-use connectors and API interfaces. The net effect raises security awareness to end-users when they have high-risk situations. It also provides a heightened probability of disrupting external intruders that have compromised the cloud account at the password level only, and may not have compromised the end user's smartphone where an access code is provided. Even with step-up authentication, a cloud account may still be compromised or hijacked, and the use of UEBA for detection is advised.

Benefits

- Creates a closed-loop for step-up authentication via API integration between UEBA/cloud security analytics and cloud IDaaS and IaaS solutions
- Raises security awareness with end users via authentication challenges when their identity shows high-risk behaviors
- Combines step-up authentication with self-audit as key parts of an increased security awareness and deterrence program

Cloud Anomalous Behavior and Watchlists

Cloud analytics addresses cloud anomalous behavior with watchlists to quickly profile and maintain an eye on escalating predictive risk scores. Advanced machine learning behavior models are designed to find unknowns and apply predictive risk scores. Feedback on false positives and negatives update self-learning and self-training models to adapt to time-based norms and conditions unique to each customer deployment. For  example, an IaaS/PaaS administrator may create a script that runs several commands with security implications at 2 a.m. each evening. This user is an innovator working to improve the enterprise's productivity. However, models will see these commands during non-business hours as an anomaly and risk score accordingly. Feedback from the models can note the situation is benign. Nonetheless, the IaaS/PaaS administrator should be put on a watchlist to monitor further innovations. Pre-defined watchlists are also provided within cloud security analytics for common high-risk groups like new hires, departing users, terminated users, and high-risk users. These groups should be easily accessed in dashboard drop-down menus to analyze risk scores, anomalies, accounts, access, activity and timelines. Cloud security analytics also supports explicitly adding or removing identities within watchlists.

Benefits

- Enables quickly profiling high-risk user groups from watchlists to monitor their risk scores and anomalies by SOC security analysts
- Provides profiling for audit and compliance teams of a specific person or group via a watchlist to analyze their identity, accounts, access and activity
- Controls who has visibility to watchlists and for what data fields through role-based access controls (RBAC) and data masking features

Cloud to SIEM integration for Alerts

Cloud security analytics provides a RESTful API infrastructure for integration with other security solutions on-premises and cloud, plus alerts via email or SMS (short message service). Enterprises have built detection and incident response programs around SIEMs to centrally locate SOC alerts. Deploying CSA for cloud provides the ability to send alerts for cloud identities, accounts, access and activity to SIEM solutions. While the SIEM itself may 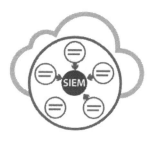 not be analyzing SaaS cloud applications, IaaS, PaaS and IDaaS, the SIEM can be utilized for central alert notifications with predictive risks scores for prioritization. Mature CSA solutions offer a case ticketing management feature. They may also integrate with Remedy, ServiceNow and Salesforce for case ticket management.

Benefits

- Delivers bidirectional API integration with SIEM solutions for alerts, risk scores and event details from cloud security analytics
- Leverages existing SIEM detection and incident response processes for CSA, plus case ticket management
- Maintains a closed-loop for all UEBA-IdA-CSA alerts including SaaS cloud applications and IaaS/PaaS

Cloud to On-Premises DLP Closed-Loop

Cloud security analytics provides alerts via email or SMS, plus a RESTful API infrastructure, for integration with other security solutions such as on-premises DLP. Alerts, risk scores and event details from cloud security analytics software can be provided to DLP solutions to create a closed-loop for data exfiltration detection, IP data protection and data risk mining. The integration of DLP  with CSA and CASB architecture is a requirement to protect data in hybrid environments with existing on-premises DLP solutions and incident response processes. Cloud security analytics provides DLP alert prioritization with predictive risk scores to make security analysts more productive and efficient with investigations and response. CSA integration with SaaS applications, IaaS/PaaS and IDaaS provides monitoring and alerting for cloud environments where legacy DLP may have restricted visibility. Advanced CSA solutions have case management features and integrate with Remedy, ServiceNow and Salesforce for case ticket management.

Benefits

- Sends on-premises DLP solutions alerts, risk scores and event details from cloud security analytics
- Leverages existing DLP detection and incident response processes for cloud security analytics, plus case ticket management
- Maintains a closed-loop for all UEBA-IdA-CSA alerts concerning data exfiltration and protection including SaaS cloud applications and IaaS/PaaS

Cloud Access Outliers and Excess Access

Cloud security analytics identifies cloud access considered high-risk by consuming access entitlements (rights) data and activity from SaaS, IaaS, PaaS and IDaaS. CSA also identifies access that is considered high-risk including: privileged access entitlements, access not properly segregating duties, dissimilar access compared to peers, and infrequent access to cloud accounts. The average user has more than 100 entitlements, making certification a  time-consuming process for managers. Certifications are typically a quarterly or yearly process. Organizations realize managers are too often approving all certification requests without actually validating each one. This leaves organizations at risk with employees having extended access to which they should not be entitled. Using cloud security analytics integrated with cloud IDaaS or IaaS, organizations can detect access outliers leveraging peer groups of users to trigger certifications for outlier access.

Benefits

- Reduces cloud access not associated with job responsibilities and potential cloud account compromise
- Reduces rubber-stamping associated with Sarbanes-Oxley and other compliance related access reviews
- Reduces segregation of duties (SoD) conflicts for cloud access, plus optimizes manager time with high-risk access certifications

Cloud Risk-based Access Compliance

Cloud security analytics outlier access capabilities can be extended to automatically send risk-based certifications to the business when outlier cloud access is identified. The system should be able to be configured to include several context points such as access risk rating, peer group metric,  outlier risk score, and status recommendation (*Keep* or *Remove*). The solution can send built-in certifications, or use APIs to integrate with other enterprise solutions to send certifications to account owners for review.

Benefits

- Enables the business (managers, data owners, role owners) to make decisions about removing or retaining outlier access to their cloud assets and data
- Eliminates the need for training end users on a new certification platform with integration for most enterprise certification systems
- Delivers a configurable context-rich UI for making decisions about access

Cloud Dormant and Orphan Accounts

Cloud security analytics identifies dormant and orphan cloud accounts. These cloud accounts can be sent to system owners or administrators for review. Based on their response, action can be taken to assign the cloud account to an end user, or remove the cloud account from the system.

Benefits

- Reduces risk of orphan or dormant cloud accounts being compromised or misused
- Automates identification of risky orphan and dormant cloud accounts, potentially used for data exfiltration
- Enables cloud account and system owners to take action by identifying cloud account owners or marking the cloud account for review
- Automatically disables cloud accounts and notifies the owner when there is no decision

Cloud Application License Metering (Account Level)

Cloud security analytics can also provide a savings to customers by metering cloud applications at the account level, based on access and activity. Removing orphan and dormant accounts, plus rogue accounts operating under the radar for potential data exfiltration, saves on licensing fees for SaaS cloud applications. Date of last activity or inactive accounts are compared to baselines and peer behaviors to determine abnormal conditions. As

enterprises migrate to cloud applications, the licensing topic becomes more critical to minimize costs. The cloud security analytics API integrates with SaaS cloud applications, IaaS/PaaS and IDaaS to monitor identities, their accounts, access and activity.

Benefits

- Reduces cloud application and infrastructure license fees with metering based on user and entity behavior analytics
- Delivers true step-up licensing in contracts based on normal behaviors, not peak loads or abnormal use
- Provides license metering along with self-audit and step-up authentication provide ROI and raise security awareness

Capital markets – Use cases

Enterprises engaged in trading transactions face a unique challenge to assure the inviolability of trades is assured. To support that objective, a number of advanced security analytics use cases are aligned to address the various challenges these enterprises face.

Trading surveillance

- **Pre-Trade Surveillance** – Pre-Trade Surveillance, prevention of regulatory and compliance violations. Pre-validation to ensure both customer and personal (employee) trades fall within acceptable risk, limit, and price volatility thresholds. Monitor trade order manifests to ensure they are consistent with past requests and identify outliers.

- **At-Trade Surveillance** – Monitoring trade transactions as they occur with near real-time analysis, based on data ingestion. Identifying anomalous patterns in order flow (spoof trading, order entry) to manipulate volumes and security prices.

- **Post-Trade Surveillance** – Comparing trade transactions to historical trading behavior baseline and reviewing order/trade ratios. This process can be run across instruments and/or traders. The process uses supervised learning and rules based on previous abuse and known non-compliant trading patterns. Both customer and in-scope personal (employee) trades are reviewed. Instances of potential illegal insider trading can be identified during this process.

- **Cross-asset Class, Cross-market Surveillance** – Monitoring multiple market classes across geographies for potential abuse. This type of surveillance monitors for events in one class of asset or geography that impacts another class of asset (equities versus bonds, oil, gold, silver, etc.).

Cross-communication trading surveillance

- **Trade Communication Linking** – Monitor voice, chat, and email for market manipulation. Link communications to trading patterns to establish patterns of communications before trades occur.

- **Social Media Monitoring** – Monitor social media feeds to map social media accounts of key employees. Generate an alert when someone posts information that could be considered a compliance violation (market manipulation).

Anti-money laundering (AML)

- ***Misreporting*** – Detect payments to a vendor by unrelated third parties, misclassification or over/under valuation of commodities and double invoicing.
- ***Unusual Trading / Transactions*** – Detection of repeated importation and exportation of the same high-value commodity (carousel transactions) or trades of commodities that do not match the business involved.

Customer accounts – Know your customer (KYC) violations

- ***Consumer Account Breach Deterrence*** – Monitoring of customer accounts for unusual account activities including slow drip attacks, account changes, and link this information with consumer reporting agencies (fraud detection agencies) such as credit freezes, and unusual account activity.
- ***Fraudulent Consumer Account Detection*** – Identity validation and detection of accounts with suspicious combinations of SSN, name, address and phone. Validate information is not the same or similar to an unusually large number of other accounts. Flagged accounts require additional validation prior to allowing transactions.

Personal trading

- ***Personal Trading Checks*** – Pre-validation to ensure personal trades fall within risk, limit, and price volatility thresholds. Ensure trades are consistent with past behavior.
- ***Insider Trading Surveillance*** – Monitoring of personal trading of key employees to identify outlier behavior. Correlate personal trading pattern with available insider information.

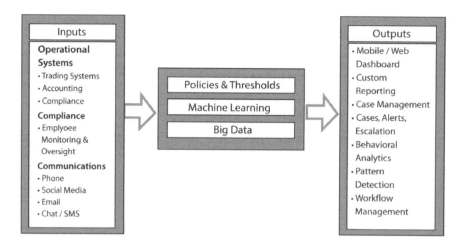

Capital Markets Use Case – Process Flow
Figure 14.2

Custom use cases – Accounting for unique and emerging requirements

At times, IT security teams need the ability to build custom machine learning models that detect identity-based threats and risks. This circumstance may be for a number of reasons including a unique requirement correlating with the individual customer's environment or user and entity profiles. It may also involve the management of very sensitive data with highly restricted access, as is the case in certain government agencies.

Other reasons for the need to develop custom uses exist as well. The fundamental requirement is for organizations to be able to create behavioral models without vendor input or involvement. This requisite would include having a step-by-step graphical interface that requires no coding, a minimal knowledge of data science and supports any big data customer choice. Additional requirements for custom use case development include:

- ***An advanced analytics framework*** – This custom use case capability should deliver a complete behavior-based machine learning model framework where no coding and only minimal knowledge of data science is required. Guidance should be provided at each step for attribute selection, training and baselining parameters, prediction thresholds and scoring, plus providing feedback on detected anomalies in production. Models are self-learning and self-training to optimize over time with the ability to update baselines as desired.

- *Decoupled big data* – Custom use case development should also support models to compute and store data from an open choice of big data infrastructures including: Hadoop, Cloudera, Hortonworks, MapR or the Elastic Stack (previously known as the ELK Stack). Hybrid environments are driving the deployment of data lakes on-premises, and in the cloud, to store data for value, reducing data transfer and indexing fees. Hybrid models, with 360-degree visibility of an identity, accounts, access and activity for anomaly detection and predictive risk scoring should be supported.

- *Flexible data connections* – This aspect of custom use case development enables any custom or unique data with desired attributes to be ingested for custom model development. This capability provides the ability to access data with known methods to map fields to attributes. A flexible meta-model allows the customization or addition of new attributes. Popular scenarios are for mainframe data, new SaaS applications, or CASBs as desired data sources for machine learning model analysis.

- *Analytics response code* – This capability provides a numerical value alongside a predictive security risk score for bidirectional API integration with other security solutions, such as authentication, data loss prevention, security information and event management or identity access management solutions. The numerical value also links to a business-friendly risk and threat description for security analysts to view. This facilitates the growing demand among customers for a closed-loop bidirectional API deployment for automated response when possible. Popular uses are step-up authentication, risk-ranked DLP and SIEM alerts, and access outlier certifications.

- *Model optimization per environment* – This functionality enables the development of custom models for UEBA, IdA or cloud security analytics inclusive of hybrid behavior analytics. Customers can develop multiple model variations in a lab environment to determine which model detected the anomaly, see which models risk score, adjust risk weightings, provide model feedback and review behavior profile comparisons. The most effective models can be moved to a test environment for staging into production. This process also validates data source continuity, as well as cleanliness and quality between environments. Often, special lab projects require privacy in production. Here, this capability provides roles-based access and data masking through workflow, plus tokenization and encryption of data.

Customer use case applications – User profiles

Depending on their roles and responsibilities, different members within an organization have varied use and interaction with advanced security analytics use cases.

- **End users** – With the Self-audit feature, end users have the opportunity to view their activity and behavior for self-analysis. They can view risk-scored access and activity, device inventory, and geolocations, through convenient and regular reporting. This enables them to participate in a collaborative partnership with their organization to protect assets and their identity. End users have the value of context not easily transferred to SOC analysts, making their detection lower for false positives. The self-audit feature is also used with partners and customers, and in some cases it has been monetized.

- **Department leaders** – Taking a risk-based approach to IAM, with identity analytics, department leaders gain the elimination of excess access and access outliers. Security efficiencies are heightened by reducing workloads through dynamic provisioning and using intelligent roles to replace those  defined by legacy rules and processes. The net result is a reduced access risk plane, increased revocations and the elimination of rubber-stamping and access cloning.

- **SOC analysts** – Through UEBA normalized risk scoring, analysts detect insiders, account compromise, data exfiltration and external intruders. Context-aware analysis facilitates Level 1 reviews. Process empowerment is available through canned machine learning models producing risk-scored access and activity in timelines accessed from dashboards for use cases and high-risk groups. Their use also includes as case and ticket management, interfacing with solution applications such as Remedy, ServiceNow, and SFDC, plus email or SMS alerts.

- **Data scientists** – Driven by open architecture, they avoid black box solutions closed to customization. Mature UEBA-IdA-CSA solutions enable these valued resources to create custom machine learning models, without coding or a deep understanding of data science, in a step-by-step guided  process. Also, the ability to adjust risk weightings in pre-packaged analytics and ingest any dataset with desired attributes via an open and flexible metadata model are key uses. Advanced security analytics are a strategic defense that should enable skilled resources to optimize and customize deployments.

Benefits of advanced security analytics use cases

Having a broad selection of advanced security analytics use cases provides customers with the assurance that their behavior security analytics requirements will be addressed. Assuring a vendor can support these use cases across both on-premises and in the cloud, as well as being vendor agnostic, provides the strongest assurance that objectives are achieved. The overall benefits of advanced security analytics use cases include:

- **Empowered security capabilities and quality** – With the mature capabilities of UEBA and IdA integrated together, they provide robust and optimal advanced security analytics across a range of hybrid environments, scoring the gray areas of unknowns and minimizing false positives. The result is improving the focus of 'find fix' resources, and optimizing the time of security analysts, efficiency in the SOC, making operations and people more productive.

- **Extended and optimized, discovery, monitoring and visibility** – This includes the baseline ability to view the full context of a user's access entitlement risks and anomalous activities. In addition, this also includes the prime access risk plane of privileged access with the risk scoring of privileged access entitlements and user activity for any incident in question. A mature solution also includes cloud security analytics for hybrid environments, providing a combined 360-degree view for identity, and risk-scored behavior anomalies, driven by machine learning as part of a newly recognized state-of-the-art UEBA-IdA standard.

- **Improved productivity and cost savings** – By having holistic visibility across all an organization's environments, users and devices, SOC teams' efficiencies are maximized, delivering cost savings. In addition, as enterprises migrate to cloud applications, the licensing topic becomes more critical to minimize costs. Removing orphan and dormant accounts, saves on licensing fees for SaaS cloud applications.

- **Customized and self-audit capabilities** – Through customized model development capability, all conceivable requirements and use cases within advanced security analytics can be addressed. With the self-audit feature, users are part of a collaborative relationship with security teams providing unique context to confirm anomalies with exceptionally low false positive rates, plus providing security awareness and deterrence against identity compromise and insider threats.

Conclusions

The depth and range of use cases fundamentally defines the areas of expertise and functionality for advanced security analytics vendors. This factor represents an important qualification when choosing a solution partner including a UI for analysts and APIs for bidirectional integrations. Having a broad selection of use cases provides customers with the assurance that their behavior security analytics requirements will be addressed comprehensively. Assuring a vendor can support these use cases across both on-premises and in the cloud, as well as being vendor-agnostic, provides the strongest assurance that objectives are achieved. The operative areas of advanced security analytics are: access analytics, threat analytics and cloud analytics. These align directly with UEBA (threat analytics), IdA (access analytics) and CSA (cloud analytics). A wide range of use cases in these categories is key to a vendor's comprehensive capabilities to ensure holistic predictive and prescriptive security assurance. Having the capability of developing custom use cases is a critical advantage for customers seeking the ability to develop confidential use cases outside the vendor's visibility, as is the case with government agencies and organizations dealing with highly sensitive data sources.

Afterword

The journey through ever-changing borderless domains

Where do we go from here? With the second edition of this book, we have continued our comprehensive effort to provide the most up-to-date insights possible on both the emerging security challenges, as well as the value advanced security analytics delivers for facing these challenges. Yet, the future will continue to hold chilling prospects to those who remain unprepared, or worse yet, for those who think they are prepared, but really aren't.

Not long ago, *New York* magazine published an article entitled *Envisioning the Hack That Could Take Down New York City*. In this article, all types of nightmare scenarios are depicted, including SUV's coopted by remote control causing automobile accidents on strategic bridges crossing into the city and paralyzing traffic. Hospitals' computer systems freeze as they become victims of ransomware, making critical information stored in the cloud unavailable and placing patients' lives in danger. Police station computer programs lock up, making any coordinated response to accidents and emergencies impossible. Chlorine valves controlling the amount of chlorine released into public water systems open and close irregularly, seemingly at will. Global anarchists have targeted the city to make a point and demonstrate how easily a major metropolitan area could be crippled by purely digital means.

A chilling portrait, and an exercise in fiction, it is meant to portray to readers modern culture's complacent faith in technology and political authority. So much of it reads like a movie, that it might be easy to dismiss its message as an unsavory fantasy. IT leaders may feel they have that luxury. After all, it's not their job to worry about these things. Well, in actuality, it is. Many IT security leaders have also become responsible for an organization's physical safety.

In his book *Future Crimes*, author, and leading authority on global security, Marc Goodman portrays the innovative and disturbing methods cybercriminals, companies, and even countries, are employing with cutting-edge technologies to compromise our digital worlds. While technological advances benefit us in countless ways, hackers are continually leveraging these advances, and those of their own innovations, to threaten our security in countless ways. Poorly protected WiFi routers, thermostats, cameras and other devices can send spam or cause denial-of-service (DoS) attacks. Smart TVs and game consoles can expose your personal data or take you to malware or phishing sites. iOS and Android tablets, and smartphones, can direct you to bad applications that expose you to malware and websites that phish for your private information and access credentials. Today's cyber criminals steal identities, drain online bank accounts, and wipe out computer servers. As individuals, we're becoming more vulnerable, by the day, as identity is an access risk and threat plane. On the organizational scale, this challenge is the elephant in the room that still remains unacknowledged by far too many IT and security leaders.

On a global scale, when it comes to the prospect of *Future Crimes* threatening enterprises and organizations, including government agencies, the stakes are much higher. The survival of organizations and nations is at risk. With the tidal wave of scientific progress underway, if we equate today's current technology and internet with the size of a pea, in the near future those innovations will deliver a technology boom on a scale the size the largest planet in our solar system, Jupiter, or even larger. That massive lake of big data — *megascale data* — and the accompanying digital exhaust, is rapidly becoming a sprawling and unsettled ocean. Grappling with that reality is a sobering mandate of responsibility for any CISO, CSO, CIO, CEO, board of directors or cyber czar.

On any substantial journey through unknown terrain, especially those with hidden dangers, a map or a guide is always helpful. We've shared with you the experience of a number of eminent cybersecurity experts, many of whom are members of Gurucul's Executive Advisory Board (EAB). They have provided insights into the lessons they have learned while contending with the seismic transformation of their environments. They have dealt with the disappearance of the monolithic security perimeter and the journey to hybrid cloud, along with the infusion of wireless devices, BYOD and the IoT into their environments. As well, we've been fortunate at Gurucul to benefit from their seasoned experience to advise us during different evolutionary phases, through the years, on our path to develop the next generation of solutions we believe are beneficial for emerging technology environments today. What follows is a distilled overview, sharing a selection of our experts' insights.

Gary Eppinger – In Chapter 1, *Impact of Cloud and Mobility for Identity*, a new paradigm is observed. Everyone and everything is globally connected in a 24/7 world.

Consumer IT and data is no longer behind the firewall, resulting in the loss of this critical security control point. The hybrid IT security challenge bears a direct impact on traditional defenses like DLP, SIEM and IAM. Eppinger shares his experience of managing the *hyper-hybrid environment* of Carnival Corporation, drawing from his extensive involvement with generations of security strategy and policy evolution in a range of business verticals. While dealing with the complexities of environments on land, at sea, in the cloud and in constant motion, and in an enterprise that manages a number of enterprise verticals within one umbrella business model, he describes his fundamental strategies for assuring security success. This involves implementation of managed solution integration in phases for bringing unique and separate siloed environments into one centralized management approach. His strategy includes moving security closer to the data itself and with the right controls. Balancing people, process and technology calls out the objective of achieving reliable functionality over perfection with each phase, since technology is perpetually evolving. This phased strategy includes the integration of advanced security analytics and capitalizing on short-term benefits, while refining long-term goals and increasing quality over time, which is best achieved with machine learning driven by the context of big data.

Jerry Archer – In Chapter 2, *The Compromise and Misuse of Identity,* with financial fraud trending more than double in 2015, identity is recognized by a growing number of security leaders as the easiest doorway and path to an organization's most prized assets. Whether leveraged as user, account, entity, entitlement, or through partners, identity is the root cause of most data theft and breaches. Managing identity properly removes excess access and access outliers open to misuse and compromise. The gap between IAM and security teams, however, is a challenge as these groups, in some organizations, are working at cross-purposes. The problem of excess access, privileged access, and orphan or dormant accounts is widespread among enterprises. Archer shares his seasoned perspective on the development of security solutions in the environment since the inception of the internet. Due to the radical and seismic level of infrastructure changes, he observes that 60% of the threat problem resides at the endpoint, an organization's weakest point. But due to the overwhelming number of endpoints, the human ability to monitor them has long passed. Archer recognizes the urgent requirement for solutions detecting anomalous behavior, along with the critical position big data and machine learning hold in today's security strategies, to provide comprehensive and continuous visibility on endpoints. This challenge is complicated by the evolution of hybrid cloud access and the plethora of devices, a majority of them mobile, which malicious actors take advantage of by virtue of stolen credentials. Through addressing these challenges, the prudent security management of privileged access abuse is a core requirement, achieved with solutions leveraging mature identity analytics (IdA) in concert with user and entity behavior analytics (UEBA). Archer also endorses a security strategy of resilient defense, making it as difficult as possible for attackers to exfiltrate the data they seek once they have gained access to the environment. Like Eppinger, he observes the phased approach to implementing complex changes in the environment has proven to be both cost-effective and strengthens the assurance that the new solution is delivered in sync with the existing environment. Metrics behind any solution initiative for executive management review, and having a framework in place for resilient recovery from any breach, are also heightened priorities.

Joe Sullivan – In Chapter 3, *Insider Threats, Account Compromise and Data Exfiltration,* blind spots in the environment are identified — where the unknowns reside. These unknowns translate directly to risk. How do you detect what you do not know? Sullivan's experience with highly sensitive customer accounts, with a broad array of insiders who have access to them, has provided him with insights into solutions and policies that help assure the integrity of the enterprise, while protecting the privacy of customers in a vast and global online environment. In one report by CMU's CERT program, 93% of the insider breaches studied exploited inadequate access controls. This problem is exacerbated as business units strive for more productivity and flexibility, in turn adopt cloud solutions outside IT's purview, and too often as a result place CIO and CISOs at cross purposes. The resulting complex hybrid infrastructures underscore the constraining challenge of traditional threat hunting with known bads, using rules, patterns and signatures. Sullivan observes that these outdated defense models are inadequate. It is a new frontier for security, after decades of declining value with declarative defenses. With limited skilled resources, budgets and time for insider threat detection, allocating more humans to security challenges will not solve the problem. That time has passed. Processing the signal-to-noise ratio and related data volume has grown far beyond human capability. Managing unknowns today is only possible from behavior analytics utilizing advanced machine learning to derive value from big data. The rich context delivered from big data provides lower false positives in identifying the anomalous behavior of insiders. One of Sullivan's strategic approaches to address this challenge is with behavior analytics and includes a three-part security program consisting of securing applications, locking down identity, and having visibility into how authorized identities are using applications. As dwell time for malicious insiders remains over 200 days, new solutions leveraging machine learning no longer need exact attack signatures. Instead of having a significant volume of false positives from IPS and DLP systems, big data is leveraged for context to score access risks and anomalous behaviors. Sullivan also observes that the future holds more and more complexity. Employees accessing data from more devices, applications and paths will eventually result in total fragmentation of the environment.

Devin Bhatt – In the introduction to Chapter 4, *Insider Threat Programs: Lessons Learned and Best Practices,* advanced security analytics applications are correlated with

CMU CERT's Insider Threat Program's best practices. Bhatt goes on to note the emerging influences impacting insider threat, the importance of data-centric security and controls, and the requirement for perpetual due diligence, with IT and in the SOC, to assure that established goals and objectives are being met. Addressing the scale of big data offering valuable insights for discovering blind spots in security is a factor Bhatt considers critical for sound security hygiene. Also, identity's crucial role in security must be acknowledged by security leaders, along with the imperative to move identity closer to data. He also observes the evolving requirements for identity and access management and the consequences of improper identity controls for insider access. Bhatt also outlines the need for establishing uniform access controls and policies for privileged access entitlements. He investigates the core criteria for privileged access entitlement policies, as well as risk targets with malicious privileged access intruders. He then investigates strategies for managing privileged access, as he observes the perils of status quo privileged access management, where new holistic insights into both access and activity are required. With the emerging standards and certification requirements, however, compliance and certification must be seen as a starting point, not an end goal. Incorporating risk-based thinking with compliance adherence is a key to success, Bhatt's insights cover not only the technical elements required for an effective insider threat program, but also include the way the program is staged within the organization. Every element of insider threat programs, from inception to implementation and evolving maintenance, must be approached with the end goal in sight: the long-term success of the program. This includes acceptance and engaged support at all levels.

Teri Takai – In Chapter 5, *Identity, Access Risks and Access Outliers*, two key observations are made. The first is the recognition of a new reality with the borderless perimeter. The second is that identity, as an access risk, has become the primary threat plane for attackers. The mathematics of this challenge is straightforward: *Data + Access = Threat Surface*. While organizations must provide access to whomever needs it, when they need it, and at the level of access required, they must also be able to take it away whenever necessary. This highlights two primary concerns. The first is the separate functional silos numerous organizations maintain between IT and SOCs, and the critical importance to bridge those silos. The second entails the recognition that manual processes and legacy roles driving IAM (identity and access management) solutions (including PAM) are no longer adequate to manage identity effectively or comprehensively. This creates too many open doors. Those gaps in management are a serious access risk plane and privileged access abuse stands at the top of this hierarchy of unaddressed risks, where over 50% of an organization's privileged access entitlements are typically unknown. Included with the insider threat risk, partners, customers, devices, entities and applications must be accounted for in prudent identity management strategies. With the gargantuan data expansion in modern environments, legacy security strategies cannot cope with evolving cloud and mobility technologies. Robust identity management can only be achieved by employing identity analytics, with a risk-based approach, which draws from big data for context, supported by advanced machine learning. As an example drawn from a real-world Gurucul solution delivery, one result and value of adopting this type of solution reduced the identity access surface area by as much as 83%, by removing excess accounts and entitlements.

Robert Rodriguez – In Chapter 6, *We Need a New Approach – Key Drivers*, sobering trends from Verizon's recent *Data Breach Investigations Report* (DBIR) cite a sharp rise in financial motives for malicious activities, while insider threat metrics remain consistent and strong. With IDC Research projecting data growth to expand from 4 zettabytes in 2013 to 44 zettabytes in 2020, Rodriguez voices the urgent need for a new generation of cybersecurity solutions. While research and investments are on the rise for analytics in general, some resistance to adopting this next generation in cybersecurity remains in place. Some of it stems from legacy institutional thinking and bias. Other influences are ingrained business policies that involve adopting a system integrator model of people-intensive responses to security solutions. However, with the sprawling amount of data overload in environments that's overwhelming security teams, this approach simply no longer scales. Rodriguez recommends that for organizations to evolve successfully, they must move from the 80% bodies and 20% technology model, to 80% technology and 20% bodies. While he voices the desire to see leaps in innovation of security technology, Rodriguez recognizes other influences at work, one of which is a reluctance to take costly risks. Incremental solution development is the norm, involving development of solution components that have the ability to integrate and evolve with existing environments. Rodriguez observes how behavior analytics effectively and efficiently minimizes the human touch points, and how behavior defines identity. Recognizing the complexity of a single identity in many systems, Rodriguez observes how identity analytics helps mitigate that challenge. Without proper identity management, excess access is inevitable, as these unmanaged identities and entitlements drastically increase the access risk plane. With the impact of the hybrid cloud, this imperative challenge is amplified by sobering degrees of magnitude. He also observes how numerous forward-looking industry change agents have promoted new insights into the next generation of cybersecurity, along with encouraging productive change. He notes the model in Australia, where organizations are now rapidly adopting cloud by mandate, leveraging established best practices, lessons learned, along with hands-on experience of their peers in North America.

Leslie K. Lambert – In Chapter 7, *Discovering the Unknown – Big Data with Machine Learning,* the age of big data is acknowledged. With its arrival, the only method to successfully leverage that paradigm shift is through advanced machine learning (ML) by extracting meaning from digital exhaust through iterative data reprocessing to discover useful patterns. For advanced security analytics, however, the early path was slower than other disciplines to deliver value, due to the requirement to accurately identify verifiable risk amidst a sea of complex data. Having ultimately met that challenge, Lambert observes how ML is now reshaping security with the support of behavior analytics and notes practical circumstances where its effectiveness applies critical value. As well, Lambert examines numerous scenarios where ML, with UEBA and IdA, deliver crucial security support in cases such as insider spying with 'borrowed' credentials, flaws in privileged access security policy, data exfiltration through remote access malware, and misuse of unmanaged cloud resources. The context of big data and continuous self-learning and self-training that ML delivers are important components of this value. That's because without machine learning, human capacity to handle this volume of data in a timely manner is simply impossible. She also calls out the importance of recognizing the ways big data is essential in gaining a comprehensive sense of visibility through machine learning. Four case studies of machine learning in UEBA provide deeper insight into solution value. Lambert also examines the importance of understanding that not all instances of machine learning are equal in their capabilities, and that some UEBA vendors offer solutions that are fundamentally rules- and signature-based. These solutions only deal with known bads, whereas true advanced machine learning clusters big data to detect the unknown unknowns, which is at the foundational core of value delivered by mature behavior analytics.

Nilesh Dherange – In Chapter 8, *Big Data in Advanced Security Analytics*, Dherange discusses an expansion of the original attributes describing big data — the six 'V's' (*Volume, Velocity, Variety, Veracity, Variability*, and *Value*) to include two more (*Venue* and *Vector*). He notes the ever-evolving nature of big data on all fronts. This highlights the need for advanced security analytics to keep pace with that evolution. This development has a direct bearing on Dherange's observation of how SIEM (security information and event management) solutions, which were originally thought to be a comprehensive answer for organizational security, have now been overshadowed by a paradigm shift in technology and emerging threat patterns. Dherange then focuses on the drivers for next-generation security analytics, which acknowledges identity as the new threat plane. Other factors include the challenges of unintegrated siloed environments and partitioned security data, the accelerating volume of big data, the expanding array of devices and applications accessing from everywhere, hacker innovation, as well as the lack of privileged access oversight and management. The data lake, which holds all this critical siloed data, is the key for holistic and comprehensive advanced security analytics, and Dherange profiles the major data lake providers, along with offering comparisons and historical insights. With advanced security analytics drawing from big data being identified as the most suitable solution set for the emerging challenges CISOs face, Dherange then discusses the range of critical data sources for these analytics. He also explores perspectives on data lake adoption, varieties of data lake models, data lakes from the analytics standpoint, as well as data storage challenges for advanced security analytics. Finally, Dherange coins the term *megascale data*, to replace 'big data' as a term which approaches obsolescence in describing the realities of this class of data.

Jim Routh – In Chapter 9, *Unconventional Controls and Model-Driven Security*, Routh recognizes the sea change in security vulnerabilities. In response, he observes the need to move beyond compliance-based security programs to risk-based ones as an essential requirement to ensure resiliency in today's fast-evolving world of cyber threats. He examines the evolution of the demand for unconventional controls, highlighting the emerging needs to define new requirements in security, noting the fundamental limitations and risks of only using conventional controls which are too often rooted in compliance requirements. He analyzes the various phishing methods, along with providing insight into the unconventional controls that have been developed to contend with them. Routh also focuses on unconventional controls for excess privileged access entitlements and how the absence of a risk focus in conventional controls creates an expanding threat plane in this critical area of growing popularity for hacker intrusion. Incorporating a risk-based approach, and employing machine learning to extract context from big data, constitutes the core effectiveness of privileged access analytics as an unconventional control that is increasing in importance for enterprise-wide security. As well, Routh notes the need for security and audit professionals to become conversant in the new technologies leveraging data science and machine learning. Routh then explores the objectives for next-generation authentication, noting tactics to bypass conventional binary controls, focusing on hacker tactics of credential stuffing. Routh observes the de facto transition away from conventional password controls and the adoption of emerging behavior-based technology for authentication. With that, Routh shares his fundamental perspectives of model-driven security along with the goal of balancing security and facilitating the customer experience by utilizing automation and machine learning. He observes the growing momentum of model-driven security and the advantages of early adoption for enterprises with next-generation security vendors to promote solution development in alignment with enterprise requirements. An underlying goal of model-driven security and the use of unconventional controls is to move at the speed of the customer and to facilitate the effectiveness of that experience.

Gary Harbison – In Chapter 10, *Cloud and Mobility: Unknowns for Identity Risks and Misuse*, new modes of security solution development strategy are explored to facilitate the transition to mobile and cloud adoption. With the waterfall methodology model representing the traditional development approach demonstrated by on-premises environments, Harbison contrasts the Agile-DevOps model of continuous improvement, which more aptly supports today's hybrid environments. Strengthening this strategy is the observation that when adopting UEBA, IdA and cloud security analytics (CSA) security solutions, choosing those which are mature and best-of-breed solutions is a best practice. This means they have demonstrated proven value in an array of complex hybrid terrains and in a range of customer environments. Harbison notes these are critical considerations with emerging multiple cloud security environments, as it's difficult to accomplish with consistency what had been realized with on-premises environments in the past. Achieving this usually requires a retooling of thinking and must incorporate the context of identity, access and trust. This includes new modes of establishing identity. Accounting for all identities in the environment is a critical requirement. Harbison discusses the complicating factors of CASB convergence with traditional environments, API transparency, and the limitations of vendor-specific UEBA features which must be taken into account to ensure seamless hybrid security. Harbison also observes the importance of the partnership between IT and security strategy coordination, through the CIO and the CISO, to achieve optimal results in delivering on their enterprise's business objectives in the market.

William Scandrett – Chapter 11, *Applications Beyond Security – Behavior Analytics and Healthcare*. Once the electronic data standard for healthcare in the U.S. went into full effect, security teams in healthcare struggled to protect their wealth of sensitive data, as cybercriminals capitalized on the industry's systemically weak defenses. While HIPAA compliance requirements have driven assurance of privacy for PII (personally identifiable information) and PHI (personal health information) in healthcare, compliance rarely equals security. Adopting a next generation perspective on security, Scandrett and Allina Healthcare targeted the goal of achieving absolute assurance in security, with UEBA providing advanced capabilities to effectively manage an identity's access to, and activity with, sensitive data. Scandrett underscored the importance of integrating innovation in security controls and balancing risk management with ease of access for legitimate users, while recognizing the growing challenge of insider threat. Supporting their city's hosting of Super Bowl LII, Allina used UEBA to provide specialized controls to manage access to patient information to ensure patient privacy of celebrities and other individuals of special interest. Scandrett also examines the emerging ransomware trend of exploiting medical devices using widely adopted OSs, where UEBA provides risk assessments to help manage this threat. He observes UEBA's capabilities beyond security as UEBA is employed to establish behavior baselines with medical devices to determine medical device malfunctions with operational utilities for medical device maintenance, which deters clinical risk and enhances physician productivity.

Jairo Orea – In Chapter 12, *Hybrid Cloud Environment Architecture*, Orea cites that security leaders must partner with hybrid environment architects to plan and align their strategies for evolving and complex threats, as they seek to leverage the elastic efficiencies of cloud. A first step consists of recognizing that the emerging threat plane is identity, that it should be incorporated into a framework (the Triad), along with the data and the infrastructure, so they are integrated holistically and seamlessly. To facilitate that, Orea highlights the importance of optimizing cloud adoption with proven best practices, as hybrid security strategies should also involve closer controls on both structured and unstructured data. Orea also notes the issue of developers as privileged users with 'one click' empowerment in cloud services development, which can deliver solution value, or possibly, unintended security vulnerabilities. As a result, Orea then calls out the need for internal groups to be educated accordingly. Also, with identity acknowledged as the new threat plane, Orea notes how hybrid architecture security planning must holistically account for personal, service and system IDs. This can only be achieved through a risk-based approach that also stresses the importance of holistically incorporating disparate vertical siloed solutions, to ensure comprehensive advanced security analytics, incorporating UEBA and IdA, leveraging the force multiplier of machine learning in big data.

In summary, our experts agree that maintaining a focus on emerging trends and developing technology is critical. Also, keeping a focus on what threat innovations are emerging is also required to keep in pace with the type of malicious actors depicted in *Future Crime*. This method includes using an incremental approach to add solution components, as needed, within the IT environment, and to maintain a flexible strategy of solution development in sync with the fragmentation of the emerging environments. It's evident as well that IAM will move forward through IdA, and due to the volume of data, detection of unknown threats will come through UEBA. *The Borderless Breach Flashcards* included with each contributor chapter provide insight into the range of threats which are unfolding today, many employing compromised credentials and the misuse of identity to achieve their ends.

In Chapter 13, *Requirements for Borderless Behavior Analytics*, we share the prerequisites for an effective advanced security analytics solution approach that addresses today's hybrid environments. Customer solution requirements also involve a detailed understanding of environmental states within an organization, their individual technology challenges, as well as the problem areas reflected in use cases. With these perspectives, security leaders are better able to leverage the UEBA-IdA-CSA solution components to their best advantage. These requirements also include the need to ensure that any UEBA-IdA-CSA solution's value be demonstrated in a POC (proof of concept) and be delivered by a best-of-breed and vendor-agnostic solution provider, with a level of maturity that assures the solution can grow with an environment into the future. Part of this maturity entails the employment of advanced machine learning, and not relying on rules and signatures. As well, prescriptive security analytics is identified as the emerging phase of UEBA offered by a select few advanced security analytics solution vendors. Another component of this solution maturity is having the ability to employ UEBA, IdA and CSA in a broad range of use cases as are described in Chapter 14.

Today, IT delivery is often in the hands of business units and business leaders where it previously had been the proprietary domain of the IT department. This is where mobility and cloud innovations are being adopted, putting applications on employee's phones without informing IT, leaving IT to be the spectator and sometimes the follower. The playing field has changed completely. Humanity and organizations have crossed the threshold into a brave new borderless world, with a relentless reality of ever-expanding mobility and cloud adoption. The passage into the borderless world was a reactive impulse to leverage the advantages provided from the broad array of technology innovations. While rising risks are part of the reality, we hope that with the right guidance, organizations will be able to remain focused on the rich benefits these innovations offer, all the as the business of cybersecurity maintains a close partnership with those goals and objectives, while also maintaining a critical focus on the priority of safety and any impact on human lives.

The first, and now second, edition of this book has been part of that journey. While the future will continue to deliver more fragmentation and new security challenges, along with empowering opportunities, it will be our goal to be there as well, to maximize the possibilities and minimize the risks. And, as Aetna's Jim Routh aptly observes, we strive to help organizations move at the speed of the customer and to make that experience an optimal one, and, as frictionless as possible.

Craig Cooper
Chief Operating Officer, Gurucul*

* From Sanskrit, 'Guru' = expert and 'Cul' = group: An expert group. As an advanced security analytics company, expertise and learning hold a very special meaning, as it reflects in our name.)